International Relations Theory an Regional Transformation

Regional transformation has emerged as a major topic of research during the past few decades, much of it seeking to understand how a region changes into a zone of conflict or cooperation and how and why some regions remain in perpetual conflict. Although all the leading theoretical paradigms of International Relations have something to say about regional order, a comprehensive treatment of this subject is missing from the literature. This book suggests that cross-paradigmatic engagement on regional orders can be valuable if it can generate theoretically innovative, testable propositions and policy-relevant ideas. The book brings together scholars from the dominant IR perspectives aiming to explain the regional order issue through multidimensional and multicausal pathways, and seeking meeting points between them. Using insights from IR theory, the contributors offer policy-relevant ideas which may benefit conflict-ridden regions of the world.

T. V. Paul is Director of the McGill/University of Montreal Centre for International Peace and Security Studies (CIPSS) and James McGill Professor of International Relations in the Department of Political Science at McGill University. He specializes in International Relations, especially international security, regional security, and South Asia.

International Relations Theory and Regional Transformation

Edited by

T. V. Paul

CAMBRIDGE UNIVERSITY PRESS
Cambridge, New York, Melbourne, Madrid, Cape Town,
Singapore, São Paulo, Delhi, Mexico City

Cambridge University Press
The Edinburgh Building, Cambridge CB2 8RU, UK

Published in the United States of America by Cambridge University Press,
New York

www.cambridge.org
Information on this title: www.cambridge.org/9781107604551

First published 2012

Printed in the United Kingdom at the University Press, Cambridge

A catalogue record for this publication is available from the British Library

Library of Congress Cataloguing in Publication data
Paul, T. V.
    International relations theory and regional transformation / T. V. Paul.
        p.   cm.
    Includes index.
    ISBN 978-1-107-02021-4 (hardback) – ISBN 978-1-107-60455-1 (pbk.)
    1. Regionalism.   2. Regionalism (International organization)
    3. International relations.   I. Title.
    JZ1318.P383   2012
    327.101–dc23
    2011052724

ISBN 978-1-107-02021-4 Hardback
ISBN 978-1-107-60455-1 Paperback

Contents

vi   Contents

Figures and tables

Figures

Tables

About the contributors

Editor

T. V. PAUL is James McGill Professor of International Relations in the Department of Political Science at McGill University and Director of the McGill/Université de Montréal Centre for International Peace and Security Studies (CIPSS). He is the author or editor of thirteen books and nearly fifty journal articles and book chapters. His books include *Globalization and the National Security State* (with Norrin Ripsman; 2010); *The Tradition of Non-use of Nuclear Weapons* (2009); *South Asia's Weak States: Understanding the Regional Insecurity Predicament* (editor; 2010); *Complex Deterrence: Strategy In the Global Age* (with Patrick Morgan and James Wirtz; 2009); *Balance of Power: Theory and Practice in the 21st Century* (with James Wirtz and Michel Fortmann; 2004); and *International Order and the Future of World Politics* (with John A. Hall; Cambridge, 1999, 2000 [twice], 2001, 2002 and 2003).

Contributors

AMITAV ACHARYA is the UNESCO Chair in Transnational Challenges and Governance and Professor of International Relations at the School of International Service, American University, Washington, DC. He is also chair of the American University's ASEAN Studies Center. Previously, he was Professor of Global Governance at the University of Bristol; Professor at York University, Toronto and at Nanyang Technological University, Singapore; and Fellow of the Harvard University Asia Center and Harvard's John F. Kennedy School of Government. He is the author of *Constructing a Security Community in Southeast Asia* (2001, 2009) and *Whose Ideas Matter: Agency and Power in Asian Regionalism* (2009), and is coeditor of *Crafting Cooperation: Regional International Institutions in International Politics* (Cambridge, 2007). His articles have appeared in *International*

Organization, International Security, International Studies Quarterly, Journal of Asian Studies, and *World Politics.*

BARRY BUZAN is the Montague Burton Professor of International Relations at the London School of Economics and honorary professor at Copenhagen and Jilin Universities. His most recent books include *The Evolution of International Security Studies* (with Lene Hansen; Cambridge, 2009) and *Regions and Powers: The Structure of International Security* (with Ole Wæver; Cambridge, 2003). He has published numerous scholarly articles in journals such as *European Journal of International Relations, Millennium, International Affairs,* and *Review of International Studies.*

DALE C. COPELAND is Associate Professor of Political Science at the University of Virginia. He is the author of *The Origins of Major War* (2000). A forthcoming book, *Economic Interdependence and War,* examines the conditions under which interstate trade and commerce will lead to either war or peace. He is the author of numerous articles in such journals as *International Security, Security Studies,* and *Review of International Studies.*

JOHN A. HALL is the James McGill Professor of Sociology at McGill University. His publications include *Coercion and Consent* (1994), *International Orders* (1996), *Is America Breaking Apart?* (with C. Lindholm; 1999), and *Power in the Twenty-first Century* (2011). He has been Honorary Professor of Sociology and Politics at the University of Copenhagen since 2001. He served as Dean of the McGill Faculty of Arts from 2003 to 2005.

STEPHANIE C. HOFMANN is Assistant Professor in Political Science at the Graduate Institute of International and Development Studies in Geneva, and a steering committee member of the Center of Conflict, Development, and Peacebuilding. Previously she has been a Jean Monnet Fellow at the European University Institute, Florence. She has published in journals such as *Perspectives on Politics, Journal of Common Market Studies, Cooperation and Conflict,* and *Politique Étrangère.*

FRÉDÉRIC MÉRAND is Associate Professor of Political Science at Université de Montréal, Professor of European Studies at LUISS University, Rome, and Associate Director of the Centre for International Peace and Security Studies (CIPSS). In 2004–2005 he was a policy advisor with the Canadian Department of Foreign Affairs and International Trade. He is the author of *European Defence Policy:*

Beyond the Nation State (2008), and his articles have been published in *Security Studies, Journal of Common Market Studies, Comparative European Politics,* and *Cooperation and Conflict.*

JOHN R. ONEAL is Professor Emeritus of Political Science at the University of Alabama. He is the author of *Triangulating Peace: Democracy, Interdependence, and International Organizations* (with Bruce Russett; 2001), and was selected as cowinner of Best Book of the Decade by the International Studies Association in 2010. In addition, he has published some fifty scholarly articles in such journals as *American Sociological Review, International Organization, Journal of Peace Research, Journal of Conflict Resolution,* and *International Studies Quarterly.*

JOHN M. OWEN IV is Professor of Politics at the University of Virginia. He is the author of *Liberal Peace, Liberal War: American Politics and International Security* (1997) and *The Clash of Ideas in World Politics: Transnational Networks, States, and Regime Change 1510–2010* (2010). He has published works in numerous journals, including *International Organization, International Security, International Studies Quarterly,* and *Foreign Affairs.*

VINCENT POULIOT is Assistant Professor in the Department of Political Science at McGill University and Associate Director of the Centre for International Peace and Security Studies (CIPSS). He is the author of *International Security in Practice: The Politics of NATO–Russia Diplomacy* (Cambridge, 2010) and *Metaphors of Globalization: Mirrors, Magicians and Mutinies* (2008). He has published articles in *International Organization, International Studies Quarterly, Journal of Peace Research,* and *European Journal of International Relations.*

NORRIN M. RIPSMAN is Professor in the Political Science Department at Concordia University in Montreal, Canada. He is the author of *Peacemaking by Democracies: The Effect of State Autonomy on the Post-World-War Settlements* (2002), a coauthor (with T. V. Paul) of *Globalization and the National Security State* (2010), a coeditor (with Steven E. Lobell and Jeffrey W. Taliaferro) of *Neoclassical Realism, the State, and Foreign Policy* (Cambridge, 2009), and a coeditor (with Jean-Marc F. Blanchard and Edward D. Mansfield) of *Power and the Purse: Economic Statecraft, Interdependence, and International Conflict* (2000). He is author of numerous articles in journals including *International Security, International Studies Quarterly, Security Studies, Millennium, International Interactions,* and *International Studies Review.*

JEFFREY W. TALIAFERRO is Associate Professor of Political Science at Tufts University. He is the author of *Balancing Risks: Great Power Intervention in the Periphery* (2004), for which he received the American Political Science Association's Robert L. Jervis and Paul W. Schroeder Award for the Best Book in International History and Politics. His articles have appeared in the journals *International Security*, *Security Studies*, and *Political Psychology* and he has contributed to two edited volumes. He is coeditor (and a contributor), along with Steven E. Lobell and Norrin M. Ripsman, of *Neoclassical Realism, the State, and Foreign Policy* (Cambridge, 2009).

STÉFANIE VON HLATKY is a senior researcher at the Center for Security Studies, ETH (Swiss Federal Institute of Technology) Zurich. Prior to this position she was a postdoctoral fellow at Georgetown and McGill Universities. In 2010 she was the Canada Institute Junior Scholar at the Woodrow Wilson International Center for Scholars in Washington, DC. In 2011 she was a visiting professor at Dartmouth College. She holds a Ph.D. from Université de Montréal and served as Executive Director of CIPSS. Her research interests focus on alliance politics, Canada–US relations, American foreign policy, and nuclear weapons policy.

Acknowledgments

This volume evolved out of a conference I organized as part of the "Globalization and Regional Security Orders" team project at the McGill/University of Montreal Center for International Peace and Security Studies (CIPSS) in May 2010. The volume is one of several works this project has sponsored that explore the issue of security and peace in an era of deepened globalization, by its core members, John A. Hall, Michel Fortmann, Vincent Pouliot, Norrin Ripsman, and myself. The funding for the conference came from the Fonds Québécois de Recherche sur la Société et la Culture (FQRSC), Social Sciences and Humanities Research Council of Canada (SSHRC), James McGill Chair, and the Security and Defence Forum (SDF) research grants. Two successful panels were held at the March 2011 International Studies Association annual conference, and contributors thoroughly reviewed their papers in view of the comments they received from the discussants and the two anonymous reviewers of Cambridge. I thank the following discussants at the Montreal conference – Zhiming Chen, Peter Jones, Michael Lipson, Vincent Pouliot, Stéfanie von Hlatky, and Norrin Ripsman – and the two discussants at the ISA panels, Patrick Morgan and Steven Lobell. Able research assistance was provided by Steven Loleski and Mahesh Shankar. John Haslam, our editor at Cambridge University Press, showed much interest in this book project.

T. V. Paul

Part 1

Introduction

1 Regional transformation in international relations

T. V. Paul

Regional transformation has emerged as a major topic of research during the past few decades. The transition of Western Europe into a pluralistic security community and the limited but meaningful efforts at security-community-building in Southeast Asia and the Southern Cone of Latin America have contributed to this upsurge in scholarly interest. With the end of the Cold War, the proper understanding of regional conflict and cooperation patterns assumed wider significance. Today, conflicts and the spillovers they produce in regions such as the Middle East and South Asia are acknowledged as being of paramount concern to international security. International Relations (IR) theory has made much progress in explaining change in regions. Yet, these often remain as "islands of theories" and it is time to take stock in order to see if connections can be made among them to obtain a comprehensive understanding of regional transformation.

From a practical standpoint what is significant here is the failure of many regions and subregions to transform into peaceful communities after the end of the Cold War. Moreover, in some regions the earlier trend toward greater cooperation and peaceful order has not been progressing all that well, following the initial enthusiasm of the post-Cold War years. Knowing when and how a region transforms into sustained peaceful order or the opposite – a conflictual order – is of utmost importance for crafting appropriate policy initiatives. This is all the more crucial given the intensity of conflicts in the regions of enduring rivalries, some of which are nuclearized, and their significance to the larger international order. Is regional transformation a linear process or is it possible to achieve a semblance of order only to return to disorder at different points in time? It is also significant to understand how and why some regions remain characterized by perpetual conflict or enduring rivalries despite efforts at resolution from within and outside.

What are regions?

Defining "region" has been a challenging exercise in the IR literature, with differences between perspectives which focus on geographic proximity as central to identifying regions on the one hand, and those that contend that some form of cultural uniformity is the crucial variable on the other.[1] Others have focused on ideational variables to argue that regions are "socially constructed"[2] and they are not simply geographical constants, but expressions of changing "political practices" with "distinctive institutional forms."[3] Taking into account these considerations, I define a region as a *cluster of states that are proximate to each other and are interconnected in spatial, cultural and ideational terms in a significant and distinguishable manner.* The justification for this definition is that in order to make the concept of regions less woolly one may need to focus on a specific yet limited number of variables rather than a host of them. This definition will also allow us to incorporate perceptions held within and outside on what constitutes a specific region. In other words, people and states in a region ought to perceive themselves as belonging to this entity, although they need some level of physical and cultural proximity to do so. Interconnectedness also implies sustained interaction among the states and societies comprising a region. Going by the above definition, it is also possible to think in terms of sub-regions such as the Caribbean and the central or Southern Cone of Latin America within a larger region as useful conceptual units of analysis.

From a systemic perspective, regions develop into subsystems because of the regularized interactions and interconnectedness among states that comprise them. The regularity and intensity of the interactions are such that a change at one point in the subsystem can affect other points, although some changes may have more effect than others.[4] While the

---

[1] Amitav Acharya has brought forth the value of "regional worlds," a concept originally used by the now defunct regional worlds project at the University of Chicago. Here regions are defined as those that "not only self-organize their economic, political and cultural interactions and identity, but also produce their own mental image of other regions and the global space in general." Amitav Acharya, "Regional Worlds in a Post-hegemonic Era," SPIRIT Working Papers, June 2009. Others have spoken in terms of "regional identity," which implies the mixing of cultural-historical and political-economic contexts. Anssi Paasi, "Region and Place: Regional Identity in Question," *Progress in Human Geography* 27, no. 4 (2003), 478.

[2] Barry Buzan and Ole Wæver, *Regions and Powers: The Structure of International Security* (Cambridge University Press, 2003), 48.

[3] Peter J. Katzenstein, *A World of Regions: Asia and Europe in the American Imperium* (Ithaca, NY: Cornell University Press, 2005), 12.

[4] William R. Thompson, "The Regional Subsystem Subsystem: A Conceptual Explication and a Propositional Inventory," *International Studies Quarterly* 17, no. 1 (1973), 89–117.

larger international system is defined in terms of the interactions among major powers, a regional subsystem can similarly be defined in terms of the interactions among the key states of that region and the major power actors heavily involved in regional affairs.[5] Security concerns link the states to the extent that "national securities cannot realistically be considered apart from one another."[6] A great power active in a region may be part of the regional security complex by imposing or receiving negative and positive security externalities.[7] This characterization of a regional subsystem takes us away from geographical and cultural proximities and may suffer from measurement problems beyond the strategic arena. I am not fully convinced that the great powers should be part of the definition of a region (unless they are spatially and culturally linked) other than when we talk of a "regional subsystem" or "regional security complex," wherein a distant power may have powerful influences over the course of interactions in a region in the security arena.

Of importance for our purposes are the conflict and cooperation patterns in a given region. Are these conflicts enduring or episodic? Is war, defined as organized violence, a real possibility in a given region? Or is war unimaginable for the members of the region whose disputes rarely escalate to military conflicts? However, there may well be in-between categories, that is regions with no war yet, with periodic crises, and weak levels of cooperation patterns. This may well be a function of deterrence or some normative factors. The question is what critical variable or variables determine the transition from one state to the other for a given region?

Change in this context is viewed not as episodic but as longer-term with meaningful consequences to war and peace in a region. Change means serious alterations have occurred in relations among states, and in terms of their core national interests, strategies, behavioral patterns, perceptions, and institutional structures. Meaningful change is similar to the fundamental or transformational change that Kal Holsti has identified. Among the types of change he posits are: "change as replacement," "change as addition," "dialectical change," and

---

[5] David A. Lake, "Regional Security Complexes: A Systems Approach," in *Regional Orders: Building Security in a New World*, ed. David A. Lake and Patrick M. Morgan (University Park: Pennsylvania State University Press, 1997), 45–67; Barry Buzan, "A Framework for Regional Security Analysis," in *South Asian Insecurity and the Great Powers*, ed. Barry Buzan and Gowher Rizvi (Houndmills: Macmillan, 1986), 8; Buzan and Wæver, *Regions and Powers*.

[6] Barry Buzan, *People, States and Fear: The National Security Problem in International Relations* (Chapel Hill: University of North Carolina Press, 1983), 106.

[7] Lake, "Regional Security Complexes," 64.

"transformation." These have different markers and consequences.[8] For instance, "change as replacement" may occur when the status of dominant power(s) in a region changes, whereas "change as addition" may reflect a new source of internal or external disorder in the region. "Transformational change" may happen when the existing power structures and interstate relationships are uprooted and an order based on deep peace or deep conflict emerges. Limited changes can occur when a region mired in conflict changes to somewhat less conflictual order or vice versa – that is, a region somewhat peaceful would transform to episodic conflict and crises.

Transformational change in a region could occur through the introduction of democratic order, robust economic interdependence, or an institutional framework among the core countries that constitute a region. Similar to social change, "identifying significant change" in regions "involves showing how far there are alterations in the underlying structure of an object or situation over a period of time," or to "what degree there is any modification of basic institutions during a specific period."[9] Understanding why regions change into different modes and possibilities or under what conditions such changes take place from the vantage points of different IR theoretical lenses is the focus of much of this volume.

International Relations theory and regional order

IR theory has much to offer us in understanding regional transformations. All the leading theoretical paradigms of IR have something to say about regional order, although they may differ on what order means – be it a simple state of affairs of strategic stability, or something more normatively oriented whereby in addition to strategic stability, some level of justice and predictability in relations among states is needed to characterize the prevalence of order.[10] In other words, does order imply

---

[8] See K. J. Holsti, "The Problem of Change in International Relations Theory," Institute of International Relations, University of British Columbia, Working Paper no. 26, December 1998.

[9] Anthony Giddens, *Sociology*, 6th edn. (Cambridge: Polity Press, 2009), 121–22.

[10] Bull's definition of international order as a "pattern of activity that sustains the elementary or primary goals of the society of states, or international society," is widely used as a starting point in discussing order. But it suffers from problems like conflating international society with international order. Andrew Hurrell's conception of pluralist and liberal-solidarist notions of order appears to give more clarity to the concept. See Hedley Bull, *The Anarchical Society: A Study of Order in World Politics* (New York: Columbia University Press, 1995); Andrew Hurrell, *On Global Order* (Oxford University Press, 2007). Muthiah Alagappa defines order as "a formal or informal arrangement that sustains rule-governed interaction among sovereign states in their

a minimum condition of coexistence of nation-states by avoiding warfare, or a broader conception in which they can "live together relatively well" and "prosper simultaneously."[11]

The specific logic of each paradigm on regional order is based on several assumptions and core premises. Yet a comprehensive treatment of this subject is missing from the literature, as scholarship remains atomized among different theoretical perspectives. Cross-paradigmatic engagement on regional order has much virtue if it can generate theoretically innovative and testable propositions and policy-relevant ideas.

Let us consider each of the leading IR perspectives and how they view regional order and regional change.

Realism

Realism and its different manifestations – classical, structural, offensive, and neoclassical – all have relevance to understanding regional order. Given the anarchic nature of the international system, and by extension regional subsystems, the fundamental source of regional order in Realism is balance of power.[12] For realists, if a proper balance or equilibrium in power distribution is achieved and maintained among the major powers and the leading states of a region, no aggressive state is likely to emerge. This is especially true of Neorealism, which posits that regional order is very much a function of the structure of the larger international system, as well as of the balance of power among the great powers. Bipolarity at the international level preserves regional peace while multipolarity promotes disorder.[13] In this perspective, the great powers are the main keepers of regional order.

This logic of balance-of-power theory is based on the premise that two states or coalitions of states are unlikely to go to war if there exists an approximate parity or equilibrium in their power capabilities. Since it is usually the stronger state that goes to war in order to dominate

pursuit of individual and collective goals." For a discussion of the different definitions of order, see his "The Study of International Order: An Analytical Framework," in *Asian Security Order: Instrumental and Normative Features*, ed. Muthiah Alagappa (Stanford University Press, 2003), 39.

[11] Stanley Hoffmann, ed., *Conditions of World Order* (New York: Simon & Schuster, 1970), 2.

[12] Joseph M. Greico, *Cooperation among Nations: Europe, America, and Non-Tariff Barriers to Trade* (Ithaca, NY: Cornell University Press, 1990); Michael Mastanduno, "A Realist View: Three Images of the Coming International Order," in *International Order and the Future of World Politics*, ed. T. V. Paul and John A. Hall (Cambridge University Press, 1999), 19–40.

[13] Kenneth N. Waltz, *Theory of International Politics* (Reading, MA: Addison-Wesley, 1979).

its weaker opponents, hegemony of a single actor is the most dangerous condition, because the hegemon will be encouraged to impose its will on others. When a hegemonic state emerges, weaker states, fearing domination or extinction, tend to flock together in order to prevent conquest or domination by the stronger side.[14]

Another variant of Realism (opposite to balance-of-power theory) is presented in hegemonic stability theory, which posits that order is the function of the presence of a powerful state with the capacity to impose peace, and which commands both respect and power.[15] The logic here, as Gilpin states, is: "a group or state will attempt to change the system only if the expected benefits exceed the expected costs; that is there must be an expected net gain."[16] This is also the basis of theories that suggest that a peaceful regional order can be achieved only if a powerful state – be it at the global or regional level – achieves overwhelming preponderance as it would deter lesser powers from engaging in violent conflictual behavior. This is why power-transition theorists, in contrast to their balance-of-power counterparts, argue that the overwhelming preponderance of a status quo power is a necessary condition for peace. The logic here is that if there is rough equality in power, both the status quo power and its challenger could foresee possible victory in a conflict, whereas if one side, especially the status quo power, has a clear military advantage, the weaker party has little incentive to use war as a means to obtain its goals.[17] As Blainey argues, "wars usually end when the fighting nations agree on their relative strength, and wars usually begin when fighting nations disagree on their relative strength."[18]

One example of such a transformation is the Americas, where the United States managed to establish its preponderance since the mid nineteenth century. Such relationships in international politics show that hierarchies can exist in international politics (despite the realist

---

[14] Ibid., 127. See also Inis L. Claude, *Power and International Relations* (New York: Random House, 1964), 56. For the theory and its various dimensions, see T. V. Paul, James Wirtz and Michel Fortmann, eds., *Balance of Power Theory and Practice in the 21st Century* (Stanford University Press, 2004). On the role of power capabilities, see Jacek Kugler and Douglas Lemke, eds., *Parity and War: Evaluations and Extensions of The War Ledger* (Ann Arbor: University of Michigan Press, 1996); Randolph M. Siverson and Michael P. Sullivan, "The Distribution of Power and the Onset of War," *Journal of Conflict Resolution* 27, no. 3 (September 1983), 473–94.
[15] Robert Gilpin, *War and Change in World Politics* (Cambridge University Press, 1981).
[16] Ibid., 50.
[17] A. F. K. Organiski, *World Politics*, 2nd edn. (New York: Alfred A. Knopf, 1968), 364–66; See also Kugler and Lemke, eds., *Parity and War*.
[18] Geoffrey Blainey, *The Causes of War* (New York: Free Press, 1973), 114. For a more nuanced realist view of conflict and cooperation, see Charles L. Glaser, *Rational Theory of International Politics* (Princeton University Press, 2010).

insistence on anarchy) and that dominant states can develop authority relationships with subordinate states on a durable basis.[19] Moreover, even when major powers do not obtain preponderance, they may still intervene episodically or regularly in the affairs of a region.

More clarity to realist conceptions of regional order is offered by Gil Merom. According to Merom, a "regional void" due to inattention toward the understanding of regions exists in Realism. He attempts to fill this by arguing that a leading power or systemic actor could dominate a region and make it "captive," or it could engage in a "contested" relationship with other dominant actors. Dominant actors intervene in a region for the "intrinsic, extrinsic, and negative value" that its serves for the great power competition.[20] Great power involvement in a region may take the shape of competition, cooperation, dominance, and disengagement and all these have implications for regional order and peace.[21] This characterization implies that regions can attract much major power interest, and the security order in a given region would depend heavily on how the major power politics plays out in it over a period of time.

Although realists do not accord much prominence to international or regional institutions, they do consider them as possible as an epiphenomenon of power politics among leading states.[22] In this perspective, it is the Cold War competition, and within it the presence of the US and its security umbrella, that helped to create the European Union and its institutions. Without this background structural condition, the Union would not have occurred. Similarly, in Southeast Asia, the Association of Southeast Asian Nations (ASEAN) developed in the context of Cold War rivalry and the relative stability offered by the American military presence in the Asian waters.

[19] David A Lake, *Hierarchy in International Relations* (Ithaca, NY: Cornell University Press, 2009).

[20] "The intrinsic value of a region is primarily a function of it being a 'significant element in the world balance of power,'" while the extrinsic value "is a function of its auxiliary potential as a site for the defense of a region of intrinsic value (including the homeland), or a site for an offensive deployment against competitors." "A region acquires a high negative value in the eyes of one systemic actor only in so far as it seems important for its competitors." Gil Merom, "Realist Hypotheses on Regional Peace," *Journal of Strategic Studies* 26, no. 1 (March 2001), 112.

[21] Benjamin Miller and Korina Kagan, "The Great Powers and Regional Conflicts: Eastern Europe and the Balkans from the Post – Napoleonic Era to the Post – Cold War Era," *International Studies Quarterly* 41, no. 1 (March 1997), 51–85.

[22] This notion is articulated most strongly by Susan Strange in the context of international regimes. See, her "Cave! Hic Dragones: A Critique of Regime Analysis," *International Organization* 36, no. 2 (1982), 479–96; see also John J. Mearsheimer, "The False Promise of International Institutions," *International Security* 19, no. 3 (winter 1994/95), 5–49.

One challenge to this argument is whether the initial condition for the rise of regional institutions inevitably means that the same structural conditions need to be present for their continued survival and progression. It is not clear whether the US decline or its unwillingness to provide security would inevitably lead to the collapse of regional institutions.[23] One may postulate that in the absence of US hegemony, the states in Europe may seek greater institutionalization even if they spend more resources on military capabilities. Moreover, in some other regions, like Southeast Asia, it was not the US but the states within the region that took the initiative to establish and institutionalize ASEAN as the core regional umbrella institution for cooperation.[24] Similarly, the Asia–Pacific Economic Cooperation (APEC)was first proposed and promoted by smaller regional powers like Australia.

Realist insights can be translated to power politics among dominant regional states within regions. Accordingly, the dominant states of a region and the balance of power dynamics among them could be the source of security and order. The alternative also is possible, that is the preponderance of a dominant regional state could bring peace and order on a somewhat durable basis.[25] However, this is rarely achieved as balances of power often tend to recur, especially given the involvement of great powers in a region as supporters or opponents of the dominant regional actor or actors. These great powers rarely allow one regional power to dominate by siding with the relatively weaker power. The occasional alignment of the US and the regular alliance of China with Pakistan are examples of major powers indirectly balancing regionally dominant states such as India.

In sum, Realism's main concern is interstate interactions and not conflict or cooperation generated by forces within states. A key problem for Realism is its overemphasis on structure and the distribution of power while giving less importance to agency, although the newer version of Realism, neoclassical Realism, attempts to rectify that

---

[23] For a perspective on these lines in international political economy, see Robert Keohane, *After Hegemony: Cooperation and Discord in the World Political Economy* (Princeton University Press, 1984).

[24] There is indeed some difference of opinion on this. For instance, Micheal Leifer has argued that the ASEAN Regional Forum (ARF) would not have come about without "a stable, supporting balance or distribution of power that would allow the multilateral venture to proceed in circumstances of some predictability." Michael Leifer, "The ASEAN Regional Forum: Extending ASEAN's Model of Regional Security," *Adelphi Papers* no. 302 (1996), 53–54.

[25] Douglas Lemke, applying power transition theory to regions, argues that multiple hierarchies exist in the world's regional subsystems, similar to the overall international power hierarchy. For this, see Douglas Lemke, *Regions of War and Peace* (Cambridge University Press, 2002).

problem.[26] I believe neoclassical realists are yet to develop a coherent theoretical approach to regional order, unless we consider works of Benjamin Miller that link systemic variables with state capacity and state to nation balance as in line with the neoclassical orientation, although he does not seem to make such a claim. Moreover, when we take into account the regional distribution of power, what is noticeable is the absence of peace in a region like South Asia where a form of regional dominance on the part of India exists.[27] A key weakness of realist theories is the relative inattention to change in regional orders and how one can achieve transformation, beyond order or stability, to enduring peace. This may be a general problem with much of social science theories relying on structural variables, as deeply embedded structures tend to change very infrequently.

Emphasis on structural/systemic forces can impart some value to an analysis on regional order, but often scholars of this vein neglect the subsystemic and internal sources of order. A good example is the end of the Cold War and its differing impact on various key regions of the world. For instance, South Asia and the Middle East saw less impact of the demise of the Cold War for regional peace, while Latin America, Africa, and Southeast Asia witnessed the resolution of some conflicts and strengthening of regional institutions. This is because the main sources of regional conflict in South Asia and the Middle East may have little to do with systemic rivalry, although superpower activism aggravated or affected the dynamics of conflict and cooperation in these regions. In fact the processes occurring within these regions themselves seem to affect the larger international system, often disproportionately. The regional powers such as Israel or Pakistan are not simple bystanders of great power politics in their regions; they attempt to asymmetrically influence the major power system often in their own distinct ways.[28] In regions such as Southeast Asia, regional states have actively pursued (and

---

[26] Steven E. Lobell, Norrin M. Ripsman, and Jeffrey W. Taliaferro, eds., *Neoclassical Realism, the State, and Foreign Policy* (Cambridge University Press, 2009).

[27] I have argued elsewhere that the regional power balance in South Asia is "truncated," i.e., although India is seven times larger than Pakistan in many parameters of power capabilities, this asymmetry is constrained by Pakistan's alignments with major powers, clever strategies, possession of weapons systems including nuclear arms, and a terrain that offers some advantages especially in waging asymmetric warfare. See T. V. Paul, "Why has the India–Pakistan Rivalry Been so Enduring? Power Asymmetry and an Intractable Conflict," *Security Studies* 15, no. 4 (October–December 2006), 600–30.

[28] Robert O. Keohane, "The Big Influence of Small Allies," *Foreign Policy*, no. 2 (spring 1971), 161–82.

somewhat successfully) strategies of enmeshing great powers and achieving a "complex balance of influence."[29]

Additionally, a regional order can be generated by processes within regional states themselves and their spilling over to other states, especially in the case of relatively weak states that have an ethnic affinity with populations living across their boundaries. Great powers, therefore, may contribute to regional conflict or peace,[30] but they need not be the key determining actors in a region. In the era of transnational terrorism, the notion of regional order as dependent on great power distribution of power has become less of a salient perspective. The ability of nonstate actors to engage in asymmetric, pinching operations has gained wider significance. Moreover, much of the security threat to regional order is coming from failed states that are also the targets of nonstate actors. However, earlier great power conduct in a region may have something to do with how it evolved over the years. The Afghanistan/Pakistan area typifies this form of a regional pattern.

Realist explanations for regional order and regional transformation appear to be incomplete, as they cannot offer nuances to specific regional contexts, especially the creation of, challenges to, as well as transformation of regional orders. In this sense, a fuller understanding of regional order may require insights from other perspectives, especially Liberalism.

Liberalism

Liberalism, the significant alternative perspective to Realism, offers perhaps the most dynamic theories of regional change with high policy relevance. Here the emphasis for change is on agency and the ability of nations and leaders to ameliorate their regional insecurities through pursuing concrete policies built around liberal principles. There are at least three core liberal ideas or mechanisms for regional peace and order. They are inherent in the Kantian tripod: democracy, economic interdependence, and institutions.[31] The processes inherent in these

---

[29] Evelyn Goh, "Great Powers and Hierarchical Orders in Southeast Asia: Analyzing Regional Security Strategies," *International Security* 32, no. 3 (winter 2007/08), 113–57. See also, David C. Kang, "Getting Asia Wrong: The Need for New Analytical Frameworks," *International Security* 27, no. 4 (spring 2003), 57–85; Amitav Acharya, *Constructing a Security Community in Southeast Asia: ASEAN and the Problem of Regional Order* (London: Routledge, 2001).

[30] Benjamin Miller, *States, Nations, and the Great Powers: The Sources of Regional War and Peace* (Cambridge University Press, 2007).

[31] Bruce Russett and John R. Oneal, *Triangulating Peace: Democracy, Interdependence and International Organizations* (New York: W. W. Norton, 2001); John M. Owen IV,

mechanisms are also pivotal for proper regional integration to take place, as in the case of Europe.[32] If these three mechanisms are fully developed in a region, the emergence of a pluralistic security community is possible. If regional states are all truly democratic, they would not engage in armed conflicts vis-à-vis one another. Economic interdependence would generate high levels of mutual vulnerabilities for states to engage in conflict with one another. Proper regional institutions would cap this process by offering a vehicle for cooperation, engagement, and dispute settlement along expected peaceful pathways.

While there is much merit in these three sources of order, the transition to a peaceful regional order could be characterized by a number of ups and downs. The meddling of external powers could upset the three processes.[33] Internally, the norms inherent in the Kantian tripod need not be observed, especially if a state is in the early stages of political and economic development or has societal actors who do not believe in liberal principles.[34] Looking at peace-building challenges in postconflict societies, Michael Barnett argues that many such societies do not have necessary institutions or civic culture for absorbing "pressures associated with political and market competition" espoused by Liberalism, and more attention may be needed in creating republican principles of deliberation, constitutionalism, and representation in order to generate legitimate power and address the myriad of challenges created by arbitrary power and factional conflict.[35]

A key source of regional transformation in this literature is economic interdependence and more recently the onset of increased globalization since the early 1990s. Globalization, specifically in the economic arena, can have both integrative and disintegrative effects. Countries tied by the desire for economic growth could reduce their conflictual behavior. The key disintegrative effect of globalization is the onset of transnational terrorism and weak states that arise from the pernicious aspects of globalization.[36] The question for us, though, is whether states

---

Liberal Peace, Liberal War: American Politics and International Security (Ithaca, NY: Cornell University Press, 1997).

[32] Walter Mattli, *The Logic of Regional Integration: Europe and Beyond* (Cambridge University Press, 1999).

[33] Miller, *States, Nations, and the Great Powers.*

[34] Edward D. Mansfield and Jack L Snyder, "Democratic Transitions, Institutional Strength, and War," *International Organization* 56, no. 2 (spring 2002), 297–337.

[35] Michael Barnett, "Building a Republican Peace: Stabilizing States after War," *International Security* 30, no. 4 (spring 2006), 87–112. See also, Daniel H. Deudney, *Bounding Power: Republican Security Theory from the Polis to the Global Village* (Princeton University Press, 2008).

[36] Norrin M. Ripsman and T. V. Paul, *Globalization and the National Security State* (Oxford University Press, 2010). See also, Stephen G. Brooks, *Producing Security:*

in regions increasingly adopt and observe the core liberal principles of democracy, institutional engagement, and economic interdependence. Can we have states observing one or two of these mechanisms while disregarding the others (e.g., note the national policies of China, Vietnam, and Singapore)? Does the adoption of these mechanisms inevitably lead to order and stability without the attendant or preceding realist mechanisms of balance of power or hegemonic stability being present? Can a region emerge as peaceful even when liberal mechanisms are absent there?

Do the liberal mechanisms by themselves generate a peaceful security community, or do we need to look at the intersubjective and ideational processes as well as the diplomatic practices among elites and the public that lead to the creation of such communities? Here the constructivist logic may have much to offer in unraveling the sources of regional transformation in a fundamental sense.

Constructivism

Constructivism, the youngest of the three mainstream IR paradigms, posits that order is fundamentally a function of the intersubjective ideas about peace or conflict that regional elites hold, rather than a consequence of particular material/structural conditions or distribution of power.[37] If proper norms, ideas, and practices are developed, war can be prevented and peaceful order can be developed. A region can transform into a pluralistic security community, that is, "a transnational region composed of sovereign states whose people maintain dependable expectations of peaceful change," where organized violence is no longer the means to settle disputes.[38]

Some in this perspective also give much value to diplomatic practices.[39] Here the agency, by way of ideas, norms, and practices, is given considerable significance in the formation and persistence of a given regional order. These norms can be created and diffused internationally

---

Multinational Corporations, Globalization, and the Changing Calculus of Conflict (Princeton University Press, 2005); Jonathan Kirshner, ed., *Globalization and National Security* (New York: Routledge, 2006).

[37] Alexander Wendt, *Social Theory of International Politics* (Cambridge University Press, 1999); Acharya, *Constructing a Security Community in Southeast Asia*; Amitav Acharya, *Whose Ideas Matter? Agency and Power in Asian Regionalism* (Ithaca, NY: Cornell University Press, 2009); Craig Parsons, *A Certain Idea of Europe* (Ithaca, NY: Cornell University Press, 2003).

[38] Emanuel Adler and Michael Barnett, eds., *Security Communities* (Cambridge University Press, 1998), 29.

[39] For example, see Vincent Pouliot, *International Security in Practice: The Politics of NATO–Russia Diplomacy* (Cambridge University Press, 2010).

with the help of norm entrepreneurs.[40] According to Acharya, norm diffusion need not be a one-way process where a region is always the taker of international norms. Regions such as Asia-Pacific have created powerful norms on their own and have influenced international normative discourse and diffusion.[41] The internalization of a powerful norm of territorial integrity can be attributed to the variance in regional orders. However, do these ideas develop without material preconditions? Do we need realist or liberal conditions to emerge prior to ideas taking effect? Or do ideas have a life of their own and even if material conditions are not present, can they arise and shape the behavior of states? Do we need proper structural conditions to emerge before agents develop ideas and practices toward creating a peaceful security community? It is indeed a chicken-or-egg question as to what comes first. What if the ideas are embedded in realpolitik notions or conditions, and if so, how do we get peace under such circumstances? More fundamentally, can Constructivism only explain the rise of peaceful communities? What about regions that are mired in enduring rivalries and protracted conflicts? Aren't these rivalries also based on ideational factors and intersubjective notions of amity and enmity? Much progress is needed in this area of constructivist literature. Norms can be both positive and negative, and often constructivist scholars (similar to liberals) focus on the positive aspects of norm creation and diffusion.

Table 1.1 offers a summary of the main variables and expectations each of the three core perspectives and their subsets offers on regional order. The absence or opposite configuration of these main variables will lead to nonbenign outcomes such as instability/conflict, war (for realists) or lack of regional cooperation and integration, as well as development of a security community (for liberals and constructivists). These opposite outcomes are rarely discussed in liberal and constructivist perspectives, while realist views do not accord much role to agency such as institutions, or to positive norms as drivers of change in world politics. From Table 1.1 it is clear that each IR paradigm or perspective can offer explanation most prominently for one type of outcome. For instance, realists can explain stability but not permanent peace or pluralistic security community development. Can we go beyond these core IR paradigms and examine the specific linkages through which order is created, sustained, and evolved in a given region? Each stage in the evolution of regional order may be driven by a variable crucial to a

---

[40] Martha Finnemore, *National Interests and International Society* (Ithaca, NY: Cornell University Press, 1996).
[41] Acharya, *Whose Ideas Matter?*

Table 1.1 *Sources of regional change*

Paradigm	Main variable	Outcome
Classical Realism	Balance of power; hegemonic preponderance	Stability; stability
Neorealism	Distribution of power among major powers	Bipolarity – stability; other structures – instability
Neoclassical Realism	Balance of power + domestic-level factors	Stability/peace or conflict
Liberalism	Institutions; democracy; economic interdependence	Peace
Constructivism	Proper ideas, identity, practices	Security community

given paradigm. If so, can we combine them without losing rigor and parsimony?

Eclectic perspectives

Several *eclectic* perspectives on regions have been developed over the years by individual scholars who do not claim allegiance to any single IR paradigm.[42] They include Buzan and Wæver's securitization and regional security complex models.[43] Yet others try to combine material and ideational variables, thereby bringing Constructivism closer to material/structural interpretations.[44] A recent work argues that diplomatic engagement is the key to peace among rivals although similar

---

[42] "Analytical eclecticism" means borrowing explanatory variables and causal logic from two or more distinct traditions or approaches in order to gain greater purchase on the cases or issue areas that scholars want to analyze. For this approach, see Rudra Sil and Peter Katzenstein, *Beyond Paradigms: Analytic Eclecticism in the Study of World Politics* (Basingstoke: Palgrave Macmillan, 2010); T. V. Paul, *The Tradition of Non-use of Nuclear Weapons* (Stanford University Press, 2009).

[43] Buzan and Wæver, *Regions and Powers*. For other eclectic approaches, see John A. Hall and T. V. Paul, "Preconditions for Prudence: A Sociological Synthesis of Realism and Liberalism," in *International Order and the Future of World Politics*, ed. Paul and Hall, 67–77; Dale C. Copeland, "Economic Interdependence and War: A Theory of Trade Expectations," *International Security* 20, no. 4 (spring 1996), 5–41. See also two articles by Peter Jones: "Structuring Middle East Security," *Survival* 51, no. 6 (2009), 105 22; and "South Asia: Is a Regional Security Community Possible?," *South Asian Survey* 15, no. 2 (2008), 183–93.

[44] Jeffrey T. Checkel, "International Norms and Domestic Politics: Bridging the Rationalist–Constructivist Divide," *European Journal of International Relations* 3, no. 4 (December 1997), 473–95; Thomas Risse, "Constructivism and International Institutions: Towards Conversations across Paradigms," in *Political Science: The State*

social order and ethnicities can also be a factor in promoting stable peace.[45]

The domestic–international interaction is well captured in Benjamin Miller's analysis of state to nation balance or imbalance as the source for regional order and disorder. To Miller, "the specific balance between states and nations in a given region determines the more intense, or hot and warm, outcomes (i.e., whether the region will experience hot wars or a warm peace). The international system – more specifically, the type of engagement in the region by the great powers – "affects the cold outcomes, that is whether the region will be the scene of a cold war or a cold peace."[46] According to Miller's argument, transformation toward a peaceful regional order can take place only when the state to nation imbalance diminishes considerably or ends and the great powers show a supportive approach toward regional peace. While this argument sounds plausible, the implication is that many regions where such imbalances already exist are unlikely to achieve peace anytime soon, given that the state to nation imbalance is seemingly perpetual.

Norrin Ripsman has provided another compelling eclectic perspective. He argues that none of the three dominant IR paradigms – Realism, Liberalism, and Constructivism – can adequately explain the process of Franco-German reconciliation after seventy-five years of bitter conflict. Accordingly, peace in Europe required the original precondition of geopolitical imperative. The Cold War competition, coupled with active American hegemonic presence, was necessary for the creation of regional institutions. Over time these institutions emerged as liberal mechanisms for sustaining and deepening regional peace, and the development of a security community was due to this stage-by-stage transition. This condition, according to Ripsman, is absent in many other regions, and as a result there is no similar security community emerging.[47]

---

of the Discipline, ed. Ira Katzenelson and Helen Milner (New York: W. W. Norton, 2002), 597–629. See also Jeffrey T. Checkel, *Ideas and International Political Change* (New Haven, CT: Yale University Press, 1997), for an effort to link domestic and international level sources of change using an ideational framework.

[45] Charles A. Kupchan, *How Enemies Become Friends: The Sources of Stable Peace* (Princeton University Press, 2010).

[46] Miller, *States, Nations, and the Great Powers*, 2. For another attempt at understanding domestic–international relationships in the creation of regional orders, see Imad Mansour, "The Domestic Sources of Regional Orders: Explaining Instability in the Middle East," Ph.D. Thesis, McGill University, 2009.

[47] Norrin M. Ripsman, "Two Stages of Transition from a Region of War to a Region of Peace: Realist Transition and Liberal Endurance," *International Studies Quarterly* 49, no. 4 (December 2005), 669–93.

Table 1.2 *Selected regions – sources/outcomes of regional order*

Region	Initial	Subsequent	Current outcome
Western Europe	Cold War/US umbrella	Institutions, economic interdependence, collective identity	Pluralistic security community
Middle East	Regional rivalry/ Cold War	Regional rivalry	Enduring rivalry
South Asia	Regional rivalry/ Cold War	Regional rivalry	Enduring rivalry
East Asia	Regional rivalry/ Cold War	Regional preponderance; economic interdependence	Stability/limited conflict
Southeast Asia	Regional rivalry/ Cold War	Regional institutions; economic interdependence	Partial security community
Latin America	Preponderance/ Cold War	Preponderance/limited economic interdependence, institutions	Partial security community

Other broader approaches, such as the English School, also offer eclectic conceptions on regional order by applying the neo-Grotian ideas of international society to the regional level. This way, the "English school is able to provide answers to issues regarding the legitimacy, stability and durability of international order" and "a bridge" "between structural Realism and regime theory."[48] Perhaps we can look at regional order as a continuum and see the initial and subsequent sources of change and the specific outcomes they produce.

Based on the analysis of each paradigm selected, a group of regions is created. What led to the particular order that we see in a given region? A reader might note that Africa is missing in this discussion. This is because Africa comprises several regional subsystems similar to Asia. For instance, Southern Africa may be considered as somewhat a distinct region and can be studied with the help of IR paradigms. With its dominant power South Africa, Southern Africa resembles a hegemonic order or an institutionalized order based on the South African Development Community (SADC), depending on the IR perspective applied. Northern, Central, and Western Africa are other regions that may be studied in the same way. However, prominent IR paradigms

---

[48] Mohammed Ayoob, "From Regional System to Regional Society: Exploring Key Variables in the Construction of Regional Order," *Australian Journal of International Affairs* 53, no. 3 (1999), 247. See also Barry Buzan, "From International System to International Society: Structural Realism and Regime Theory Meet the English School," *International Organization* 47, no. 3 (1993), 327–52.

may not be the most suitable when exploring a region comprising very weak states. Many African states do not have the capacity to engage in realist-type state behavior or lack liberal mechanisms to generate a peaceful order.[49] It must, however, be noted that African states have intermittently attempted to create regional institutions, the African Union being the most prominent one, with limited success.

Eastern Europe could also be included as a nascent security community with the incorporation of several of its states into the European Union. The post-Soviet space comprising the ex-Soviet republics is another area where there is some amount of stability due to a mixture of Russian hegemony and norms of cohabitation, which appear to be in existence. Dominant IR paradigms are yet to come up with powerful explanations for the kind of regional order present in these regions partly because of the limited time span for explorations, since they came into being as somewhat autonomous regions. They do indeed offer fertile grounds for eclectic perspectives to be developed even beyond what we accomplish in this volume.

Significance of this volume

This volume brings together a group of IR theorists from all the key perspectives discussed above with the intent of exploring the regional order issue through multidimensional and multicausal pathways. The effort is to see if there are meeting points in these perspectives. Positioning research on the singular dimension of a particular paradigm has generated considerable difficulties in explaining variations

---

[49] On this, see Norrin Ripsman and T. V. Paul, *Globalization and the National Security State* (Oxford University Press, 2010), ch. 6; Robert H. Jackson and Carl G. Rosberg "Why Africa's Weak States Persist: The Empirical and the Juridical in Statehood," *World Politics* 35, no. 1 (1982): 1–24; Jeffrey Herbst, *States and Power in Africa* (Princeton University Press, 2000). Other approaches that could be useful are post-colonial and post-structural perspectives. This volume does not cover these perspectives due to space constraints. Moreover, they are yet to make substantial and rigorous contributions to regional order, although they may be valuable in understanding the conditions of specific states that are constituent members of a region. For examples of such writings, see Richard Ashley, "The Achievements of Post-Structuralism," in Steve Smith, Ken Booth and Marysia Zalewski, eds., *International Theory: Positivism and Beyond* (Cambridge University Press, 1996), 240–53; Partha Chatterjee, *Nationalist Thought and the Colonial World: A Derivative Discourse* (London: Zed Books, 1986); Gregory Castle, ed., *Postcolonial Discourses: An Anthology* (Oxford: Blackwell, 2001); A. K. Ramakrishnan, "The Gaze of Orientalism: Reflections on Linking Postcolonialism and International Relations," in *International Relations in India: Bringing Theory Back Home*, ed. Kanti Bajpai and Siddharth Mallavarapu (New Delhi: Orient-Longman, 2005), ch. 6; Sankaran Krishna, *Globalization and Postcolonialism: Hegemony and Resistance in the Twenty-first Century* (Lanham, MD: Rowman & Littlefield, 2009).

in different regions and may well have come to a dead-end. We are interested in crafting future research trajectories using the insights of IR theory and in developing policy-relevant ideas so that some of the conflict-ridden regions of the world, such as the Middle East and South Asia, could benefit from scholarly works. However, our attention is heavily focused on the European model, which has something to offer for all the perspectives stated above. The European model emerged out of a material condition of Cold War rivalry and the alliance system, yet institutions, democracy, and interdependence helped shape the model. Certain ideas of cooperation and integration were developed prior to and during the progression of the European project. In some sense, all the core IR theories could claim some significant share in explaining the rise and persistence of the European model. Can we then synthesize their core premises? A fundamental challenge to the European model is the curvilinear progression that it has been making. Why hasn't it achieved greater salience in the five decades of its existence and what explains this? Is the absence of certain critical variables identified as realist, liberal, or constructivist causing this outcome?

Research questions

Since none of the paradigms can singularly account for regional peace and conflict that we witness in the world today, it is useful to examine when and where we find realist, liberal, or constructivist explanations most salient. Why do some regions fail to move away from an intense security dilemma (realist emphasis) while others manage to reduce or mitigate anarchy (through variables presented in liberal or constructivist accounts)? Why do institutions and interdependence fail to develop or stick in some regions while they do so in others? What lessons have been learned from the five decades of institution-building in regions such as Western Europe? Can we transfer these ideas to other regions? If so, how? Or do we need tailored and region-specific ideas taking into account their particular situations and contexts?

Can we visualize positive regional transformation, as described by Mohammed Ayoob, as a continuum? In this perspective, change can take place along the continuum of regional system to regional community, with regional security and regional society in between. While order and stability in the regional system without a society or sense of community is characterized by balance of power politics (very close to the realist world), regional society "requires a conscious recognition on the part of regional states that they have certain common interest which they need to preserve despite the existence of differences, even disputes

among them." Regional society could be a halfway house toward the
building of a genuine "regional community," in which the security of
a state is heavily intertwined with the other and in which there is an
unwillingness to even consider the use of force among the members.
States in this case would be deeply interconnected through a web of
security and economic institutions.[50] The important question for this
project is: what are the mechanisms through which a region transforms
from one stage to the other? If a region is mired in enduring rivalries –
over territory, identity, and power – can it ever hope to achieve a society let alone move on to a security community? Do we need powerful
triggers – external and internal – in order for such a transformation to
take place? If so, what are they? Are they purely structural factors or do
agents and their ideas make a difference in regional change?

The chapters

Following the introductory chapters on thematic and conceptual issues
by T. V. Paul and Barry Buzan, Part 2 addresses the realist positions on
regions. Dale Copeland brings in the classical and neorealist perspectives on regional order, while Jeffrey Taliaferro presents the neoclassical
realist viewpoint. The liberal notions, especially economic, institutionalist, and democratic sources of regional order and peace, are presented in the next section by John Owen, Frédéric Mérand, Stephanie
Hoffmann, and John Oneal. The constructivist perspectives, especially in terms of the power of ideas and security communities, are presented by Amitav Acharya and Vincent Pouliot. Part 5 offers eclectic
perspectives by John Hall and Norrin Ripsman, with the examples of
the European Union and the Middle East. The concluding chapter, by
Stéfanie von Hlatky, discusses the central themes in this volume while
offering new theoretical guidelines for the study of regional order, for a
greater understanding of regional conflict and peace. The aim here is
to engage the differing IR approaches and develop cross-paradigmatic
perspectives that may provide greater value for the analysis of regional
order and transformation. This cross-fertilization of ideas is essential to
understanding the differing regional orders as well as the mechanisms
of transitions to peace or conflict.

[50] Ayoob, "From Regional System to Regional Society," 247–48.

2   How regions were made, and the legacies for world politics: an English School reconnaissance

Barry Buzan

Introduction

This chapter focuses on the formation of modern regions as a precursor to the discussion of their transformation in later chapters. For those unable to think outside of positivist vocabulary, its dependent variable is the degree and character of differentiation among contemporary regional interstate societies. In line with mainstream approaches to International Relations (IR), by "region" I understand a geographically clustered subsystem of states that is sufficiently distinctive in terms of its internal structure and process to be meaningfully differentiated from a wider international system or society of which it is part. Region is a level of analysis located between the international system (global) level, and the unit (state) level. Like the state itself, region privileges a territorial mode of differentiation as a way of understanding world politics. The geographical element in the concept of region is crucial. Regions are not just any subsystem of states in an international system, but a specific type of subsystem defined by geographical clustering. The significance of geographical clustering rests on the idea that most types of interactions amongst units will travel more easily over short distances than over long ones. In historical terms, it is easy to see how invasions, migrations, pollutions, cultural penetrations, and suchlike have all worked more easily and quickly over short distances than over long ones. This means that, other things being equal, it is reasonable to expect that interactions amongst a regional cluster of states will be more intense than between those states and more distant ones. In a world historical context, this means that states and peoples who share a region are, again other things being equal, more likely to share a history and culture than are states and peoples further away from each

For helpful comments on an earlier draft I would like to thank particularly Hyun Seung Cho, Lene Hansen, T. V. Paul, Karen Lund Petersen, Norrin Ripsman and Ole Wæver, and the other authors, and the participants in the Copenhagen seminar generally.

other. By this definition, it is clear that the Commonwealth is not a region even though its members share some culture, and neither is the Alliance of Small Island States even though its members share some geographical features. Neither is the so-called "Third World". APEC (Asia–Pacific Economic Cooperation) is sometimes referred to as a region, and so is the ASEAN Regional Forum, but both of these have memberships that are too large and too scattered to count as regions. A "region" that spans oceans and contains half the world stretches the concept beyond breaking point. Also worth noting is that regions would not exist if the political units comprising the international system were themselves mobile, as some, most notably the "barbarian" tribes of the premodern world, were. Regions presuppose that states are more or less fixed into geographic positions, and have to reach out from an anchored position.

The existence and significance of regions thus depends on the historically contingent factor of logistics, which I call *interaction capacity*.[1] Regions will only exist when there is a significant difference between the capability to move people, things, and ideas over short distances than over long ones. This has been the normal condition in human history. In a fully globalized world, where interaction capacity was high and distance made no, or little, difference to the ability to move people, things, and ideas, regions would weaken and perhaps disappear. Given the stupendous and ongoing achievements of the past two centuries in both the physical technologies of transportation and communication, and the social technologies of intergovernmental and transnational organization, we seem to be moving rapidly towards such a world. In that sense the logic that generates regions should be weakening, though it is certainly not gone yet.

The other side of this equation is that there has to be enough interaction capacity to form a system that regions can be a part of. If we look back before the rise of Europe, the concept of region as just defined is quite tricky to apply. Before the late fifteenth century there was no global-scale international or social system in any sense. The main centers of civilization in the Americas were barely in touch with each other and had no regular interaction with the rest of the world. Australia was likewise isolated. There was a long-standing economic and cultural system across Eurasia and North Africa, but this was very thin and slow-moving by contemporary standards, and would not qualify as an international system in the politico-military terms understood by

[1] Barry Buzan and Richard Little, *International Systems in World History: Remaking the Study of International Relations* (Oxford University Press, 2000), 80–84.

Waltz and other realists.[2] What we might today think of as regions were in the classical era better understood as international systems in their own right. There could not really be a modern regional level until the making of a global-scale international system, and that did not happen until quite recently. Circumnavigation of the world was not achieved until early in the sixteenth century, and only towards the end of that century could one begin to speak of a global economy, as the Europeans connected the resources of the Americas to the long-standing trading system of Eurasia. A global-scale international system in the Waltzian sense was really only achieved during the nineteenth century, by which time Europeans had both the transport and the fire power to take on and defeat the last remaining bastions of the classical world in China and Japan. A global-level international society in the sense understood by the English School did not happen until the post-Second World War decolonizations allowed most nonwestern states to join on terms of sovereign equality.[3] Before that, international society was only global in the sense that the Europeans and their offshoots controlled most of the planet and spoke for the colonized peoples. It was a globalized European international society rather than a global international society in its own right.

But interaction capacity is not the only variable in play, and modern regions are even more recent than logistical factors alone would suggest. The reason is that modern regions require independent states as their members, and in many parts of the world independent states have not been available because of extensive colonization by a small number of empires. The exceptions are Europe, which has, excepting the Balkans and parts of Spain, been uncolonized for more than a millennium, and Northeast Asia, which was heavily penetrated by the West from the nineteenth century, but never fully colonized. From the sixteenth century onwards European states became both the principal makers of a global-scale international system/society and the principal colonizers whose presence prevented the formation of modern regions of independent states. For most modern regions, existence begins with decolonization. The Americas achieved independence two centuries ago, but for most of Africa, the Middle East, and South and Southeast Asia the process of decolonization followed the Second World War. The disintegration of the Soviet Empire at the end of the Cold War also unleashed a new region of independent states.

[2] Kenneth N. Waltz, *Theory of International Politics* (Reading, MA: Addison-Wesley, 1979).
[3] Hedley Bull and Adam Watson, eds., *The Expansion of International Society* (Oxford University Press, 1984).

The dominant story in the English School about all of this is the rise of a distinctive, Westphalian form of international society in Europe, and the expansion of that society to global scale by the process of colonization and decolonization sketched above.[4] The idea of a global-level international society rests on the fact that decolonization produced a set of states that were homogenous in the sense of all being sovereign equals. Looked at another way, the price of independence, or for those not colonized, the price of being accepted as equals by the West, was the adoption of western political forms and acceptance of the basic primary institutions of Westphalian international society: sovereignty, nonintervention, diplomacy, international law, great power management, nationalism, and suchlike. Although the English School concentrates on the global level of international society, there is nothing in its theory to say that such social structures cannot form distinctively at the regional level. Although the English School has not looked much at the EU, it is obvious that the EU represents a distinctive and very highly developed form of regional international society. One could also tell a less West-centric story about the making of contemporary international society in which the outcome is not so much a homogenous, if thin, social structure at the global level, but more a core–periphery structure with a still dominant western core surrounded by postcolonial regional international societies that are in varying degrees of differentiation from, and subordination to, that core. In this perspective, there is still a thin global international society that is partly based on genuinely shared primary institutions (most obviously sovereignty, diplomacy, international law, nationalism, human equality) and partly a reflection of ongoing western hegemony. But the continued projection of contested western values (human rights, democracy, the market) on to the rest of the world creates considerable scope for differentiation between the West and the rest. This view of international society is partly global and partly hegemonic, and it leaves more room for regional social structures within it. I will refer to it as *western/global international society*.

Colonization and decolonization has thus been the birth process for most modern regions, and that process has had an enormous impact both on the character of regions and on how they relate both to the western core and to each other. Most colonization was perpetrated by European powers and their offshoots (mainly the US) and imitators (mainly Japan). This process has left behind a set of regions that is both homogenous and very uneven. Modern regions are homogenous because they all take the

[4] Ibid.; Barry Buzan, "Culture and International Society," *International Affairs* 86, no. 1 (2010), 1–25.

political form of sovereign states imposed by the West, and mainly play by the rules of the game (international society) that go with that political form. They are uneven in two senses. First, they still fall into a core–periphery pattern reflecting the extreme inequalities that gave birth to them. And second, they underwent very different formative processes, which means that while some regions connect firmly to deep historical roots, others have few or no such roots, or if they do, only connect to them in broken and fragmented ways. The superficial homogeneity of modern regions is thus subverted by the deep differences in their formative processes and the cultural and political consequences of those differences.

Regions are thus recent, and to the extent that globalization is taken seriously, might not have a very long future as rising interaction capacity erodes one of their necessary conditions. But for more than half a century regions have been an important feature of the contemporary international system/society, and I argue that they will remain a central feature for at least some decades to come. Indeed, I argue that a regional perspective may tell us more about the current transformation in the structure of the international system/society than the currently fashionable focus on whether the US can remain the sole superpower or will be challenged by others rising to superpower status.

The next section looks at these formative processes in more detail, indentifying four different routes by which today's regions came to be formed along the broadly Westphalian lines pioneered by Europe. The third section combines two theoretical perspectives: regional security complex theory (RSCT) from the Copenhagen School, and international society from the English School. RSCT focuses on how security dynamics have shaped modern regions since their formation. International society focuses on the extent to which these security dynamics, plus underlying cultural and political patterns given more scope by decolonization, have generated constructions of international society at the regional level that are significantly distinctive from the western norms and institutions that define the global level of international society. These perspectives enable one to take a nuanced view of the differentiation among contemporary regions. The final section concludes by looking at how this differentiation is likely to play out in relations between the regional and global levels of the international system/society over the coming decades.

The formative processes of modern regions

At some risk of oversimplifying, it can be said that contemporary regions are the result of a monocentric vanguardist process in which, especially during the nineteenth century, one of the civilizational cores of the premodern world, Europe, became sufficiently more powerful than all the others both to make a global system and to impose its own model of political economy on the rest of the world.[5] The alternative process would have been a polycentric one in which the major civilizational cores of the classical world expanded into encounters with each other. These encounters would mostly have been on fairly even terms, such as that between Christendom and Islam from the seventh century, though others might have been very uneven, like that between Europeans and the peoples of the Americas. Overall, a polycentric process of encounters would have created a more pluralist international society in which most regions would have a strong and unbroken connection with their own history. The monocentric, vanguardist process suggests an immediate distinction between Europe, whose formation was the most independent and unbroken, and all the others, whose formation was shaped in varying degrees by the intrusion of the dominant vanguard. Within this latter group the historical record differentiates three distinct formative processes: repopulation, colonization/decolonization, and encounter/reform.

Unbroken creation

Because Europe was the vanguard that remade the rest of the world, only it can claim an unbroken formative process. Other regions, most conspicuously in Asia, certainly had long histories as international societies before their encounter with the Europeans. But all of these societies were in one way or another broken by that encounter, sometimes leaving little legacy to the modern regions that emerged with decolonization.

To say that Europe's formative process was unbroken is not to say that it was pristine and self-contained. Some accounts of Europe's rise from medieval to modern easily give the impression that it was pristine, but this is misleading. There is no historical case of pristine unbroken creation. Europe's formation was independent in the sense that Europe was never occupied or subordinated by outside powers. But it was far from being pristine in the sense of wholly self-contained. To make only the most obvious points, many technological and social ideas filtered into medieval and early modern Europe from what were then the considerably more advanced civilizations elsewhere in Eurasia:

---

[5] For a more nuanced view see Buzan, "Culture and International Society."

China, South Asia, and the Middle East.[6] In addition, as the buffer of a declining Byzantine Empire slowly decayed, developing Europe was in continuous economic, military, and political encounter with the Islamic world to its south and southeast. From the long Moorish occupation of Spain from the seventh century, through the Crusades, to Europe's rivalry with the Ottoman Empire from the fifteenth century, Europe was deeply challenged, but not overwhelmed, by what was until the seventeenth century a more advanced and powerful neighboring civilization. That encounter played powerfully into the formative process of Europe in terms of transfers of knowledge, the development of "Westphalian" international society, and the creation of a hostile Other.[7]

Thus while Europe's development as a region was unbroken, it was also syncretic, being influenced by encounters with other Eurasian civilizations from an early stage. As fifteenth-century Europe began the expansion that peaked with its global domination in the nineteenth century, this process of encounter became more lopsided in Europe's favor, though this lopsidedness was much more marked in some parts of the world than in others. During these centuries Europe steadily became, and by the nineteenth century certainly was, the core region of a global-scale political economy and imperial international society. By the late nineteenth century the European vanguard was well advanced in remaking the world in its own political image, whether by repopulation, as in the Americas and Australia; colonization, as in much of Africa, South and Southeast Asia; or coercive encounter, as with China, Japan and the Ottoman Empire.

Europe's unbroken creation was driven by a mixture of war and its commanding position in the world economy. As writers such as Tilly and Howard have shown, the intra-European dynamic of war played a pivotal role in the evolution of the modern state.[8] This state was both the perpetrator of, and the model for, the imposition of European practices on the rest of the world. Yet from the late eighteenth century

---

[6] Jerry H. Bentley, *Old World Encounters: Cross-Cultural Contacts and Exchanges in Pre-Modern Times* (Oxford University Press, 1993); Donald F. Lach, *Asia in the Making of Europe*, vols. I–III (University of Chicago Press, 1965, 1970, 1993); John M. Hobson, *The Eastern Origins of Western Civilisation* (Cambridge University Press, 2004).

[7] Martin Wight, *International Theory: The Three Traditions*, ed. Gabriele Wight and Brian Porter (Leicester University Press, 1991), 52; Nuri Yurdusev, "The Middle East Encounter with the Expansion of European International Society," in *International Society and the Middle East*, ed. Barry Buzan and Ana Gonzalez-Pelaez (Basingstoke: Palgrave Macmillan, 2009), 70–79.

[8] Charles Tilly, *Coercion, Capital and European States AD 990–1990* (Oxford: Basil Blackwell, 1990); Michael Howard, *War in European History* (Oxford University Press, 1976).

onwards Europe, and by this time also the US, Canada, and Australia/
New Zealand, also underwent a profound transformation in the nature
of its society. This transformation was deep, complex, and ongoing. It
can be labeled modernity, the industrial revolution, functional differentiation, capitalism, "the great transformation," "the empire of civil
society," or "open access orders." However labeled, it signified a change
not just in the dominant mode of production, but also in the whole
political, social, and economic structuring of western societies.[9] This
new type of open access social order, with its distinctive separation of
economics and politics and its unleashing of civil society into both the
economy and politics, was then projected outward by the West during the nineteenth century. It created a still ongoing encounter with
more traditionally structured "natural" states in which economics and
politics remained fused, control over the means of violence dispersed,
patron–client relations dominant, and most access to rents restricted
to elites.

In this perspective the nineteenth century becomes a period of major
world-historical transformation. The leading western states radically
remade their internal social structures, and in so doing remade how
they related to the rest of the world. Open-access orders rapidly became
substantially richer and more powerful than the rest of the world, and
at the same time opened an ongoing social and political gap between
themselves and natural states. As open-access orders took deeper root in
the leading states, their relationship with the periphery shifted from the
imperialism of direct territorial control typical of natural state empires,
to the demand for access typical of "the empire of civil society." Open-
access orders make permeable the boundaries of territorial states and
generate a transnational economic, social, and political space in which
private nonstate actors can operate alongside, within, and through the
formal political sphere of states.[10] Since the leading colonial powers were
also the most developed open-access orders, their evolving domestic
structures became incompatible with old-style imperialism, a process
helped by the weakening of Britain and France by World Wars I and
II. These two wars also undermined European pretensions to "civilization" as Europeans applied to each other the racist attitudes, colonial
practices, and violent brutalities that they had previously reserved for

[9] See for example Justin Rosenberg, *The Empire of Civil Society* (London: Verso, 1994);
and Douglass C. North, John Joseph Wallis and Barry R. Weingast, *Violence and Social
Orders: A Conceptual Framework for Interpreting Recorded Human History* (Cambridge
University Press, 2009). I take the term "empire of civil society" from the former, and
"natural state" and "open access order" from the latter.
[10] Buzan and Little, *International Systems*, 362–67.

their relations with non-Europeans.[11] The transformation beginning in the nineteenth century to open-access orders among the leading powers thus pushed toward the decolonization that took place after 1945. Decolonization exposed and exacerbated the tensions between the open-access orders of the western core (First World), and the mainly natural states of the Third World, many of which felt more comfortable in the company of the Soviet bloc states. By the second half of the nineteenth century open-access orders dominated the core, and China's late 1970s reform and opening up, plus the end of the Cold War in 1989, marked the final victory of economic liberalism over its major totalitarian, natural state, ideological challengers. But while the core increasingly organized itself as a transnational open-access order ("the zone of peace"), much of the periphery remained in natural-state form, unable to avoid either local conflicts or deep structural tensions with the open-access order.

Repopulation

By far the most extreme form of disjuncture between modern regions and preencounter history occurred in those places, mainly the Americas and Australia, but up to a point also in New Zealand and South Africa, where the native populations and cultures were largely displaced by European settler populations and in some places also by slaves imported from Africa. In the Americas,the main work of reducing the indigenous populations to a small fraction of their preencounter size was done by Eurasian diseases. The destruction of indigenous peoples and cultures marginalized those that remained in the social and political development of these "new worlds," whose subsequent social and political development was dominated by transplanted Europeans.[12] Relatively little of the historical indigenous pattern of politics or culture survived to influence the emergent regions, which meant that the disconnection from history was extreme. But since the people of these repopulated lands were mostly of European stock, they had a cultural compatibility with the vanguard that had created them, with the consequence that it was easier to fit these new countries into European international society, transforming it from European to western.[13] The settler colonies were founded early in the process of European expansion, and

---

[11] Wight, *International Theory*, 61.
[12] Paul Keal, *European Conquest and the Rights of Indigenous Peoples: The Moral Backwardness of International Society* (Cambridge University Press, 2003).
[13] Gerritt W. Gong, *The Standard of 'Civilization' in International Society* (Oxford: Clarendon Press, 1984), 4–6.

they also constituted the first round of the decolonization process in the late eighteenth and early nineteenth centuries. Yet although there was cultural and racial affinity, many of these countries (with the notable exceptions of Canada, Australia, and New Zealand) had to rebel against their Europe metropoles in order to win independence, and therefore brought some revolutionist attitudes into international society.

In terms of the formation of modern regions, the settler colonies split into three distinct stories: North American, Latin American, and Antipodean. The North American story quite quickly became dominated by an expanding United States. After its civil war, the US was clearly on a trajectory to becoming a great power and then a superpower. North America largely disappeared from view under US hegemony, being seen more as part of the West. It is seldom thought of as a region, though its history as a postcolonial regional security complex can certainly be told in terms comparable to other postcolonial regions.[14] The US went on to become a player at the global level, transcending its region, and becoming interestingly, along with Japan, a non-European great power participating in international society. During the twentieth century the US became in its own right a principal shaper of both international society and regions.

The South American story is one where a distinctive region forms after decolonization but is increasingly penetrated by the US. Interestingly, this region does not so obviously become seen as part of the West, and therefore carries a much stronger sense of being a region than does North America. Indeed, with the second round of decolonization following the Second World War, Latin America came to be seen mainly as part of the Third World of "developing countries." One explanation for this is that the Latin American states, unlike the US and Canada, failed to follow the revolution in the West from natural states to open-access orders, as described above, and thereby became differentiated from an increasingly modernist western core. A key difference here lies in the particularity of the colonizing metropole. North America was dominated by Britain, which carried its own open-access order into its settler colonies early on. Latin America was colonized by Spain and Portugal, countries that not only arrived well before modernity took hold, but also were very much laggards in the nineteenth-century transformation to open-access orders. Latin America therefore received a very different European heritage from that transmitted to North America.

---

[14] Barry Buzan and Ole Wæver, *Regions and Powers: The Structure of International Security* (Cambridge University Press, 2003), 268–303.

In the Antipodean story, Australia and New Zealand are generally thought of as a separate region. Like North America, they are seen as part of the West on ethnic and cultural grounds, and also because under British influence they also became open-access orders. These two are more often defined, not as being part of East Asia but as being a region in their own right.

Colonization/decolonization

A less extreme, but still sometimes large, disjuncture with the past is the story of those peoples who lost their political and economic independence to Europeans, but not their existence as peoples occupying their ancestral lands. This is the main story for most of Africa, South and Southeast Asia, the Pacific Islands, and briefly for much of the Middle East. These peoples underwent a process of colonization and decolonization by Europeans (and in a few cases Americans and Japanese) in which their political structures, and often their boundaries, were remade along western lines and reflecting western interests. The price of decolonization was acceptance of both the western form of state, and its associated international society, and for the most part of the boundaries created by the colonial powers. The colonizing process often took a regional scale (most obviously the British domination of South Asia), which helped to shape the postcolonial regional structures. Many colonized peoples made effective use of nationalism and sovereignty, two of the key institutions of western international society, as conceptual weapons to combat colonialism. While the outcome of the colonization/ decolonization process was to create a set of states superficially compatible with western forms, the degree of disjuncture from the local history was extremely varied. At one end of the spectrum were postcolonial states whose boundaries and people retained clear lineage to precolonial formations. This was true for most of the states in mainland Southeast Asia, for several in the Middle East (e.g., Oman, Iran, Egypt, Morocco), and for a few in sub-Saharan Africa (e.g., Swaziland, Lesotho). At the other end of the spectrum were postcolonial states that were little more than arbitrary assemblages of people finding themselves corralled by boundaries drawn with little or no reference to local history, culture, or geography. There were many of these in sub-Saharan Africa, and some in the Middle East and the offshore archipelagos of Southeast Asia. Many ethnic groups found themselves divided by the new borders, and most states contained anything from several, through dozens, to hundreds of such groups. For these postcolonial states, nationalism often turned into a two-edged sword. One edge was useful for mobilizing opposition to colonialism, and therefore had integrating potential. But the other edge tended either to fragment countries internally, or lead them into conflict with neighbors, by legitimizing ethnic claims for self-government against rootless new "national" identities such as Nigerian or Congolese or Indonesian. In the middle of the spectrum one finds states like most of those in the Indian subcontinent, where there was a mix of arbitrary boundaries and links to precolonial forms.

Regardless of their degree of continuity or discontinuity with earlier history, all of these postcolonial states were recast in the modernist mould of the sovereign, territorial, "nation-state," and so integrated into international society. As independent states, they were able to express once again their cultural distinctiveness from the West, and this allowed patterns of cultural identity to play both into the formation of regions and into how the new regions related to, and differentiated themselves from, both each other and western/global international society. These relationships were also affected by the political differentiation of most postcolonial regions from the western core. Most postcolonial states were natural states, often weak ones, making them very ill at ease with, and threatened by, the still rapidly evolving open-access orders of the core. All of these regions faced what was in effect a new "standard of civilization" projected from the West in terms of demands about human rights, democracy, property rights, financial practices, and suchlike, all cast in terms of the practices prevailing in the western core of open-access orders. Since the transition from natural state to open-access order is fraught with difficulties, acceptance of these standards and practices had as much chance of collapsing a natural state into a failed one as it had of transforming it into an open-access order. The formative process for these states has thus left a very mixed legacy of internal instability and an awkward combination of tension with and dependence on western/global international society.

Encounter/reform

The least disjuncture with their own history was mainly reserved for those states that were not colonized, but underwent a coercive encounter with the West and a process of reform towards the western "standard of civilization" needed to retain independence and gain diplomatic recognition as members of international society. This story is quite well told in the English School literature on China and Japan,[15] and

---

[15] Gong, *Standard of 'Civilization'*; Gerritt W. Gong, "China's Entry into International Society," in Bull and Watson, eds., *Expansion of International Society*, 171–83; Hidemi

also covers the Ottoman Empire/Turkey, Iran, Siam, and Ethiopia. For Northeast Asia and the Middle East (Ottoman Empire), these encounters took place on a regional scale and involved great powers that had succeeded in keeping the West largely at bay from the first contacts until the West broke down their doors in the nineteenth century. At that point the Middle East story becomes one of colonization, whereas Northeast Asia is one of encounter/reform. China and Japan correctly saw international society as based on a double standard, with recognition as equals given to those deemed "civilized" and those not so deemed treated as less than equal, as barbarian or savage, and open to varying degrees of subordination. Japan responded to the challenge by adopting a rapid and extensive modernization program aimed not just at enabling it to match western military strength, but also to get it accepted by the West as a "civilized" power. It accomplished this with astonishing speed, and between the Sino-Japanese war of 1894–5 and the Russo-Japanese war of 1904–5 was accepted by the West as the first nonwestern great power, although still denied racial equality, in 1919. China took the opposite view, seeking to adapt only inasmuch as was necessary to increase its power to hold out against the West and defend its own identity and system. It failed at this, and after being unexpectedly and easily defeated by Japan in the war of 1894–5,[16] it spiralled into decades of fragmentation and civil war, albeit achieving courtesy recognition by the West as "civilized" and as a great power during the Second World War.

Both countries retained something close to their original boundaries and population, and in that sense a high connectivity with their own history. Yet, the depth of disjuncture caused by their remaking into modern nation-states, and the ongoing tension between modernization and westernization, should not be underestimated. The classical social order in East Asia was overthrown both within and between states, and traditional patterns of culture, power, and identity were transformed. Yet because they retain significant historical and cultural continuity, both China and Japan can differentiate themselves culturally from the West. Japan, partly through its own reforms and partly because of its

---

Suganami, "Japan's Entry into International Society," in Bull and Watson, eds., *Expansion of International Society*, 185–99; Shogo Suzuki, *Civilization and Empire: China and Japan's Encounter with European International Society* (London: Routledge, 2009); Yongjin Zhang, "China's Entry into International Society: Beyond the Standard of 'Civilization,'" *Review of International Studies* 17, no. 1 (1991), 3–16; Yongjin Zhang, *China in International Society since 1949* (Basingstoke: Macmillan, 1998).
[16] S. C. M. Paine, *The Sino-Japanese War of 1894–5: Perceptions, Power and Primacy* (Cambridge University Press, 2003).

occupation by the US after the Second World War, is a rare case of a nonwestern state making the transformation to being an open-access order. It remains an interesting question whether Japan wants to think of itself as part of Asia or part of the West. China is perhaps best understood as being in the difficult transition process from natural state to a more open-access order. While pursuing economic modernization, it retains strong opposition to both political and cultural westernization.

In sum, these formative processes, and the particular nature of encounters with the West, have massively shaped modern regions and their place in the contemporary international system/society. Yet the most extreme historical disjuncture – repopulation – ironically underpins the least tension with contemporary international society, while, arguably, the least extreme historical disjuncture – encounter/reform – triggered huge transformations and left a legacy of major tensions with western/global international society.

Although these four models of formation are ideal types, they do in fact fit quite nicely with most actual histories. One case in which they don't is Russia, which is probably a history best told as distinct from Europe's. Russia's story has elements of all four models. It has a bit of unbroken development; quite a lot of repopulation as Russia (and Russians) expanded east and south; some encounter (with Europe), and some colonization and partial decolonization (for non-Russians).

The postcolonial development and differentiation of modern regions

Once modern postcolonial regions formed along Westphalian lines, their operation became more independent, at least politically and culturally, and they embarked on their own developmental processes. They did so, however, in the context of a powerfully emergent global political economy that was still very much controlled by the former metropolitan powers now led by the US. These postcolonial regions also emerged into and were much influenced by the system-spanning superpower rivalry of the Cold War. This section blends two theoretical perspectives to survey how postcolonial regions developed: regional security complex theory (RSCT) highlighting the strategic aspects of region formation, and the international society perspective applied at the regional level highlighting the social and political aspects. There is a prima facie case for thinking that these two perspectives should relate, and not just because they depend on similar political conditions and share a close historical link to decolonization. Hedley Bull's whole approach to international society was about the concern of states to create a degree of social order amongst themselves. His giving of priority to order (over justice) suggests that the incentive to form international societies arises either from fear of unrestrained conflict, or if not from fear (where the warrior ethic is strong) then from the desire to pursue other activities, such as trade, that require a degree of international social order. The classical coexistence/Westphalian model of international society, with its emphasis on institutions of war, balance of power, diplomacy, great power management and international law, therefore suggests rather strongly that international societies arise in response to the costs and difficulties of living in a modern conflict formation.[17] On this logic one might expect regional security complexes (RSCs) and regional international societies to be geopolitically coterminous. Yet while the boundaries of RSCs have been mapped with some precision, those for regional international societies have not been much studied, and where they have, they seem to be vaguer or more contested than those for the RSCs. The EU has its concentric circles; the Middle East has a clear differentiation between Arab and non-Arab states; and the very definition of East Asia is still contested between natural states and open-access orders. The question of how and to what extent the strategic and societal processes of modern regions play into each other despite the seeming differences in their origins is one that needs to be part of the ongoing research agenda of how regions transform.

Regional security complex theory (RSCT) and the history of how contemporary RSCs formed after decolonization has been laid out elsewhere and covers the whole international system in some depth and detail.[18] The underlying supposition is that distance matters in strategic interaction, and that there will be a natural tendency for security interdependence to cluster regionally. This assumption can be, and as is clear from the previous section, was, overridden where outside great powers exercise imperial control over regions ("overlay" in RSCT jargon), removing the condition of independence from the local states and imposing their own security priorities. By *international society* I mean the institutionalization of shared interests and identity amongst states and the creation and maintenance of shared norms, rules, and institutions among them. There is only just beginning to be a literature on regional international society. The possibility for regional international society depends on a similar set of conditions to that for RSCs:

---

[17] The qualification "modern" is necessary because it is not clear from earlier history, when empire (and therefore inequality) was more the model than sovereign equality, that the inconveniences of conflict led so strongly to a desire for international order (rather than imperial order).

[18] Buzan and Wæver, *Regions and Powers*.

independent states, geographical scale, and diversity, and the existence of a global-level social structure strong enough to justify seeing regional subsystems. The emergence of regional international society is therefore similarly linked to decolonization. Another pointer to the regional level is the strong strand of thinking within the English School that follows Wight's idea that "We must assume that a states-system will not come into being without a degree of cultural unity among its members."[19] Cultural unity is more likely to be found regionally than globally.

Few studies of the regional level of international society have been done, though as suggested above, one can infer the existence of distinct regional social structures from looking at the EU and other regional institutions. To distinguish between western/global international society and regional ones, two kinds of possible difference can be tracked. The first is in their primary institutions, and here there are three possible types of variance:

1. The regional international society contains primary institutions not present at the western/global level.
2. The regional international society lacks primary institutions present at the western/global level.
3. The regional international society has the same nominal primary institutions as at the western global level, but interprets them differently and so has significantly different practices associated with them.

The second difference is what kind of state dominates in any given international society. Many schemes are available here, and two useful ones are Cooper's differentiation among *premodern, modern,* and *postmodern* states, and North and colleagues' distinction between *natural states* and *open access orders*.[20] There is also Wight's question of whether international societies shape themselves around civilizational groupings.

Combining the English School and RSCT perspectives creates a lens through which the differentiation of postcolonial regions can be viewed as a set of ideal types for comparing regional international societies both with each other and with the western/global core. My preferred English School scheme has four general types of international society:

---

[19] Martin Wight, *Systems of States* (Leicester University Press, 1977), 33.
[20] Robert Cooper, *The Postmodern State and the World Order* (London: Demos, 1996), paper no. 19; North et al., *Violence and Social Orders.*

Power-Political represents much the same as the traditional English School's "international system" pillar, namely an international society based largely on enmity and the possibility of war, but where there is also some diplomacy, alliance-making and trade. Survival is the main motive for the states, and no values are necessarily shared. Institutions will be minimal, mostly confined to rules of war, recognition, and diplomacy. There are no contemporary cases of this type, although the Middle East comes closest.

Coexistence focuses on the exemplar of pre-1945 Europe, meaning a pluralist, Westphalian system in which the core institutions of interstate society are the balance of power, sovereignty, territoriality, diplomacy, great power management, war, and international law. South Asia and the Russian sphere are of this type. East Asia is mainly coexistence with significant elements of cooperative.

Cooperative requires developments that go significantly beyond coexistence. It incorporates the more solidarist side of the English School and might come in many guises, depending on what types of values are shared and how/why they are shared. Examples of interstate cooperative projects might include the creation of a shared market economy, the pursuit of human rights, joint pursuit of big science, collective environmental management, and suchlike. The western/global core is in this category, and probably also South America.

Convergence means the development of a substantial enough range of shared values within a set of states to make them adopt similar political, legal, and economic forms. The main empirical case is the EU. The range of shared values has to be wide enough and substantial enough to generate similar forms of government (liberal democracies, Islamic theocracies, communist totalitarianisms, etc.) and legal systems based on similar values in respect of such basic issues as property rights, human rights, and the relationship between government and citizens.

These four types overlap quite comfortably with the well-established set of three ideal types from RSCT,[21] which depends on whether security interdependence is defined more by amity or more by enmity:

[21] Barry Buzan, Ole Wæver and Jaap de Wilde, *Security: A New Framework for Analysis* (Boulder, CO: Lynne Rienner, 1998), 12.

conflict formations, in which the main drivers of security interdependence are fear, rivalry, and mutual securitizations
(mainly power-political and some coexistence)[22]

security regimes, in which states have made arrangements to
reduce the security dilemma among them, and therefore to
constrain processes of mutual securitization (bridging across
coexistence and cooperative)[23]

security communities, in which states have desecuritized their relationships and no longer expect or prepare to use force against
each other (bridging across cooperative and convergence)[24]

In what follows I will use both terminologies as appropriate.

In terms of the four formative stories set out in the previous section, the regions of the contemporary set came into being at different
times. As the only unbroken formative story, Europe's regional history
stretches back many centuries. In the Americas, two regions formed
as the US and the Latin American countries broke away from colonial
control in the late eighteenth and early nineteenth centuries. In East
Asia, a long-standing Sinocentric regional international society, which
had some elements of both hierarchy and convergence, broke down
under western impact, and with the rise of Japan in the later nineteenth
century emerged as a modern region. The rest of the regions – in South
Asia, the Middle East, Africa, and Southeast Asia – were formed by the
decolonizations that followed the Second World War and stretched into
the 1970s. One more round followed in the early 1990s when the Soviet
Union broke up into fourteen new states.

What is striking is that, with the possible exception of the post-
Soviet space, all of these regions came into being as conflict formations
combining elements of power-political and coexistence international
society. Charles Tilly famously summarized the European story thus:
the state makes war and war makes the state.[25] In North and South
America, war both accompanied and followed decolonization. Japan
and China fell into conflict in the late nineteenth century. The South
Asian and Middle Eastern and Southern African regions were all born
with their states fighting among themselves, and in a lesser way so too
was Southeast Asia. This pattern suggests that the mode of formation,

---

[22] Raimo Väyrynen, "Regional Conflict Formations: An Intractable Problem of
International Relations," *Journal of Peace Research* 21, no. 4 (1984), 337–59.

[23] Robert Jervis, "Security Regimes," *International Organization* 36, no. 2 (1982),
357–78.

[24] Emanuel Adler and Michael Barnett, eds., *Security Communities* (Cambridge
University Press, 1998).

[25] Tilly, *Coercion, Capital and European States.*

whether relatively unbroken and independent, or being born into a pre-existing western/global international society, has no influence on the type of region that initially forms. Nor do differences in culture, nor the timing (whether decolonization is all in one go or stretched out), nor the type of state (whether natural state or open access order). In the historical record, the odds are strongly stacked in favor of the initial regional development being a conflict formation, where war is a defining feature, and the institutions of international society are relatively thin and minimal (power-political and/or coexistence). This history therefore also suggests that the development of regions, at least initially, is more driven by geography and politico-military factors than by cultural patterns. Cultural patterns too are importantly shaped by considerations of distance, so there may be some overlap between these and the shape of regions, but it does not seem to be determining in any big way. Europe and South America, and more arguably North America, might each be thought of as single cultures, but few other regions have this type of cultural homogeneity. The Middle East, South Asia, East Asia, and the post-Soviet space are all divided by both religion and ethnicity. Martin Wight notwithstanding, there seems to be no necessary line-up at the regional level between the cultural sphere and the military-political one.

How things begin, however, does not determine how they end up, and in this postformation story of regional differentiation, the formative process and cultural and political variables play more of a role. Although all modern regions started life as conflict formations with thin power-political or coexistence regional international societies, it is clear that much differentiation among them has taken place in their subsequent developments. Some postcolonial regions have remained as conflict formations, containing mainly modern natural states in a power-political/coexistence international society, most obviously the Middle East and South Asia. The EU contains a mix of modern and postmodern states, all open-access orders, and is evolving from a cooperation to a convergence international society. East Asia and South America contain mainly modern states, but a mix of natural states and open-access orders, in coexistence/cooperation international societies that have moved towards becoming security regimes. As yet, insufficient research on modern regions along these lines has been done to enable the setting out of a full and detailed typology, though some work along these lines is beginning.

A recent study of the Middle East concluded that there was sufficient differentiation from the global level to see a distinct regional international society there.[26] Part of this differentiation was to do with the radically different form of state that predominates in the Middle East. Compared to the dominant type of state in the EU (postmodern/ open-access orders), these postcolonial states (mainly modern, "natural" states) have deep divisions between rulers and ruled, no clear separation between economics and politics, a much higher degree of elite dependence on outside support to stay in power, and a much higher degree of mass alienation from both domestic and international political structures. This difference highlights the consequences of the formation stories (in this case colonization/decolonization) set out in the previous section. And although the region shares many institutions with the western/global international society, it does not share all (most obviously democracy), has some distinctive ones of its own (most obviously patrimonial ruling elites and the Israel–Palestine conflict), and often varies substantially in its interpretations and practices within "shared" institutions (most obviously regarding sovereignty [weaker], war [stronger], and nationalism [Arab nationalism as a transnational structure]). The Middle East has made no progress beyond its starting point as a conflict formation.

Preparatory work for a similar study of East Asia again suggests that the formation process matters, and that there is a distinctive set of East Asian states and institutions defining a regional international society different from both the one in the Middle East and from the western global core.[27] In terms of type of state, East Asia is divided between modern/natural states (China, North Korea, most of Southeast Asia) and mainly modern/open-access orders (Japan, South Korea, Taiwan). Distinctive institutions and/or practices in East Asia, especially among the modern/natural states, include strong sovereignty (and sovereign equality); traditional Westphalian views on nonintervention; anti-imperialism and antihegemonism (and a preference for multipolarity at the global level); resistance to human rights and democracy; a desire to preserve distinctive cultural values; strong support for regime security; economic liberalism as shared regional development; and peace through economic interdependence (i.e., liberal economic values, not political or social ones). Despite East Asia's political and cultural differences, it has evolved from its modern start as a conflict formation/ power-political international society to being a mix of coexistence and

[26] Barry Buzan and Ana Gonzalez-Pelaez, "Conclusions," in Buzan and Gonzalez-Pelaez, eds., *International Society and the Middle East*, 226–50.
[27] Barry Buzan and Yongjin Zhang, "International Society and East Asia: English School Theory at the Regional Level," unpublished paper, 2009.

cooperation international society and conflict formation and security regime RSC.

In both of these cases the question of the link to shared culture is surprisingly complicated and indeterminate. One can see elements of it in play in both regions: Arabism and Islam in the Middle East; Confucianism in East Asia. But in neither case is the region anything like culturally coherent, and elements such as Islam are much broader than any region.

Similar exercises could, and should, be done for other regional/peripheral international societies. They would doubtless show the same general pattern in which the particular formation story generates a type of state significantly different from those in the western core (e.g., a concentration of premodern natural states in Africa, and the general difficulty of making the transition from natural states to open-access orders in Latin America), plus local variations in institutions, securitizations, practices, and cultures sufficient to differentiate them from both the western/global core and other regions. This logic of regional differentiation is also supported by Acharya's argument that regions only absorb norms from outside if they can be interpreted in such a way as to be compatible with existing norms within the region.[28] As with culture, and related to it, what goes into the making of different types of states within regions is quite complicated. One aspect is the formative process, and the interplay between local culture and the imposition of the European state form, often including a fairly arbitrary territorial definition. Another is the broader interplay between cultural patterns and types of state. That the two cases just reviewed contain both elements suggests that the general term "sovereign equality" hides a very considerable, deep-rooted, and significant diversity of state types. The two cases also suggest that the type of state dominant within a region tells us a lot about what the dynamics of the region will be like. Perhaps the maximum that one can say about this, in line with the "two worlds" theory,[29] is that postmodern open-access orders are associated with zones of peace and thicker forms of international society; premodern and modern natural states with zones of conflict and thinner forms of international society. Open-access orders are a necessary but not sufficient condition for security communities,

---

[28] In this volume, and Amitav Acharya, *Whose Ideas Matter? Agency and Power in Asian Regionalism* (Ithaca, NY: Cornell University Press, 2009).

[29] James M. Goldgeier and Michael McFaul, "A Tale of Two Worlds: Core and Periphery in the Post-Cold War Era," *International Organization* 46, no. 2 (1992), 467–91; Max Singer and Aaron Wildavsky, *The Real World Order: Zones of Peace/Zones of Turmoil* (Chatham: Chatham House Publishers, 1993).

while natural states are more likely to generate conflict formations. It is a big and difficult question as to whether culture is a major independent variable in this equation. The historical record suggests that it might be. The story of how the modern state developed in the specific European Christian culture is well known, and one can readily find other strong state traditions as well, most obviously in China and Japan, that could be associated with particular cultures. Elsewhere, the dominant culture seems to work against the formation of strong states. One version of this is where the culture independently supports some functions that elsewhere are taken by the state, as in Islamic umma and the Hindu caste system, and thereby creates powerful transnational identities, resulting in a history in which the state tradition has never been deeply rooted. Another version is where the culture is too fragmented to easily support modern state structures, as most obviously in Africa. If this kind of argument has any force, it too supports regional differentiation.

One last issue regarding the development process of modern regions is what impact outside powers have had. In *Regions and Powers*, Wæver and I argued that outside global-level powers impinge on RSCs in various ways, but seldom, short of overlay, determine the regional security dynamics. During the Cold War the rival superpowers influenced regional development in various ways ranging from arms supplies (e.g., the Middle East, South Asia) through alliances (most regions) to direct interventions (e.g., Southeast Asia). Local states may well seek help from outside powers in relation to their local enemies (e.g., Pakistan, Israel, Egypt, Japan). Great powers may also have security concerns that transcend the regional level, such as nuclear proliferation, but that play specifically into regions as well (e.g., North Korea, Iraq, Iran). But these regions represented security dynamics that were independent of great power influence even though they were amplified or muted by great power involvement. For all of its many engagements in the Middle East, both successful and unsuccessful, the US, for example, has not changed that region's basic conflict formation or power-political character. The international society story gives much more influence to great powers both through the various encounters that shaped the formative processes of modern regions and because the great powers provided the general western/global framing of international society that others were forced to adopt in order to gain recognition. It could be argued, for example, that the US was instrumental in facilitating the development of the EU as a cooperation/convergence international society, and that its interventions in East Asia are at least partly responsible for the weak institutions and differentiated structure of state types in that region. *Dependencia* theorists would argue that the US bears considerable responsibility for weak state structures in Latin America and the Middle East, and there can be no doubt that the Soviet Union left its peculiar stamp on its successor states.

In sum, it is clear that the varied formative and development processes of modern regions have generated a substantially differentiated set of regions. These differences are not fixed because the development process is ongoing. But they are deep and durable. The question therefore remains, what are the implications of this fact, and of the formative and developmental stories behind it, for the future transformation of regions?

Conclusions

This story is important to the overall theme of *International Relations Theory and Regional Transformation* because we need to understand not only where regions came from and what they actually are within world politics, but also what the outlook for them is, whether they are intensifying or dissolving, and what their evolutionary prospects are. On the face of it, globalization suggests that as the significance of distance decreases in the world, regions should increasingly dissolve. But the historical record suggests that despite rising interaction capacity, regions have if anything been getting stronger. It might be argued that at least some of their apparent dynamism comes from the fact of globalization, where regions become economic and political bastions within which local states can better defend themselves from, and operate within, an increasingly dense and pervasive international economy and society. It might also be argued that regions are on the rise because some key drivers of globalization are now ebbing. The Washington consensus has been exposed as unsustainable, and for that and other reasons the US in particular and the West in general, though still strong, are in relative decline. One way of understanding this is to see that the era that began in the late eighteenth century, in which the great transformations of industry, economy, and society gave the West an extraordinary and unprecedented predominance of power in the world, is now coming to an end. It is doing so because the many mechanisms behind that transformation, and the power it generated, are being steadily, if still unevenly, diffused throughout the world. This diffusion might well end not only the singular concentration of power that the West has enjoyed for the last two centuries, but also the possibility of any such concentration occurring again. The US may well be the last superpower, as well as the last gasp of western hegemony, because no state will ever again be capable of dominating the planet. The end of superpowers makes the regional structure and its differentiation a much more important feature of world politics. The story of regions as told above is in many ways an expression of the uneven diffusion of modernity, and is likely to remain so for a considerable time to come. Contemporary regions reflect divergent strands of this central story, and the differentiation amongst them is deep enough that it is not going to disappear any time soon.

Where the story points is that what once might have been seen as a western core hegemonic over a variety of Third World regional peripheries, and likely to succeed in homogenizing them in its own image, now seems fated to drift toward a more polycentric structure where the West is but one region (or possibly two!) in a more decentered international system/society containing several regional cores. The outcome would be a layered international society in which regional differentiations and dynamics would become more important, and the global dynamics of hegemony and western/global international society less important. The strength and type of international society at the regional level would vary, depending not only on the degree of cultural unity but also on the types and mixtures of states to be found there. Given a declining western core, what goes forward is the diversity or regional stories and their outcomes. There will be no one-size-fits-all solution for achieving regional stability because each region needs to find its own way of reconciling its particular cultural and political legacy with modernity. Some have succeeded at this already, most obviously in the West and some parts of East Asia. Other countries seem close to finding possibly stable ways forward (perhaps China, India, Brazil, Turkey), but as yet with unclear implications for their regions. Some regions have hardly progressed at all (most obviously those in Africa and the Middle East) and seem to face mountainous difficulties in finding any way forward.

The world will divide on whether this is a good thing or not. Liberals both in the West and elsewhere will lament the failure of their universalist project, and fear the rise of various nondemocratic parochialisms, some possibly quite nasty. Some in the West will be relieved to end an increasingly unsuccessful and unpopular and costly hegemony, and many in other parts of the world will be equally glad to get the West off their backs. A consensus might emerge that a period of regional-scale experiments in organizing a capitalist political economy is desirable before any return to globalization is attempted. Against that will be those who fear that the hegemonic dynamics of their local region will be more threatening than western hegemony. As the western vanguard declines relative to the rise of nonwestern powers, the global level of international society will weaken. Antihegemonism will add to this weakening and reinforce a relative strengthening of regional international societies as nonwestern cultures seek to reassert their own values and resist (at least some of) those coming from the western core. On current evidence there seems to be little danger of a new Cold War type of scenario, where the global level becomes a power-political contest for control. All the major players are capitalist now. Regions seem more concerned to be left alone to pursue their own versions of capitalist development. The result would be a decentred, but still antihegemonic, coexistence international society with some cooperative elements, in which different regions, including the West, mainly pursue their own cultural values and regional international orders.[30]

A global-level international society would still exist, based partly on the successful diffusion and naturalisation of some western values and partly on syncretic values emerging between cultures, partly on an unprecedented degree of ideological convergence at least on economic issues and partly on the pragmatic necessities for all cultures of cultivating a degree of social order at the global level. The big question would be whether a world regionalized in this way could still come up with the level of management necessary to deal with collective problems such as climate change, crime, trade, migration, and arms control. Grounds for some confidence here can be found in the degree to which a number of key institutions have been naturalized across nearly all of international society. These include sovereignty, territoriality, diplomacy, nationalism, international law, progress, human equality, science, and up to a point the market, which provide an important foundation for a second-order pluralism among the regional international societies. To some extent the reduced management capacity caused by weaker leadership and the removal of hegemony at the global level would be balanced by a reduced agenda of things to be managed. All of this suggests that what regions represent is not just subsets of some universal story, but the main theme of how world politics might transform itself at the end of the western era.

---

[30] Charles A. Kupchan, "After Pax Americana: Benign Power, Regional Integration and the Sources of a Stable Multipolarity," *International Security* 23, no. 2 (1998), 40–79; Charles A. Kupchan, *The End of the American Era: US Foreign Policy and the Geopolitics of the Twenty-first Century* (New York: Alfred A. Knopf, 2002).

Part 2

Realist perspectives

3 Realism and Neorealism in the study of regional conflict

Dale C. Copeland

When it comes to the study of regional conflicts, realists as a group have been loath to put forward a clear and generalizable theory. This is not to say that realists have not offered insights into the probability of militarized conflict in particular regions. In the early 1990s, for example, John Mearsheimer and Aaron Friedberg offered well-known and controversial arguments for the likelihood of war in Europe and the Far East based largely on the insights of realist logic.[1] Yet there are few realist scholars who have attempted to derive a theory of conflict that would predict the relative stability of different regions based on an understanding of the power dynamics *within* these regions, as opposed to simply examining how external great powers might exploit regional politics for their own purposes.[2]

This chapter will sketch the initial outlines of a realist theory that does seek to explain and predict the relative levels of stability across regions, both in historical terms and within the contemporary global system. Drawing on my previous work on major war between great powers, I will attempt to show that the logic of dynamic differentials theory (DDT), a structural realist theory designed to explain major wars at the level of the global great power system, can also be used effectively, with some qualifications, at the level of regional subsystems. Dynamic differentials theory argues that crises and wars are most likely when the most dominant military states in a system begin to anticipate steep and largely inevitable decline and thus start to fear the future

I am grateful to T. V. Paul, Stéfanie von Hlatky, and the other participants of the Montreal workshop for their helpful comments on previous drafts of this chapter.

[1] John J. Mearsheimer, "Back to the Future: Instability in Europe after the Cold War," *International Security* 15, no. 1 (summer 1990), 5–56; Aaron L. Friedberg, "Ripe for Rivalry: Prospects for Peace in a Multipolar Asia," *International Security* 18, no. 3 (winter 1993/94), 5–33.

[2] For two notable exceptions see: Douglas Lemke, *Regions of War and Peace* (Cambridge University Press, 2002); and Gil Meron, "Realist Hypotheses on Regional Peace," *Journal of Strategic Studies* 26, no. 1 (March 2003), 109–35.

intentions of rising actors.[3] As I will discuss, whether these dominant states will initiate preventive attacks or destabilizing crises that might avert their decline will depend on a host of important structural variables, including the polarity of the system (in a regional subsystem, the number of important actors), the offense–defense balance, and the levels of relative economic and potential power. For now, it is important to grasp the essence of the approach: wars and militarized conflicts are driven by the dynamics of the power balance, and profound decline by the leading military state or its nearest rival can destabilize a system to the point of bilateral or subsystem-wide war.

I will set this argument against the "big three" realist theories of war: classical (and neoclassical) realism, hegemonic stability theory, and neorealism in both its offensive and defensive variants. Classical realism focuses on the stabilizing role of balances of power. Hegemonic stability theory argues that such balances can be dangerous, since rising and near equal states will attack to gain the status and rewards denied by the established order. Neorealism emphasizes the impact of polarity and uncertainty about leader intentions. Although each of these arguments was originally designed to explain war in the core great power system, I will show how their logics can be taken down to the level of regional subsystems. I will then try to show how dynamic differentials theory provides a deductive argument that integrates the best elements of the big three realisms but resolves most of their logical problems.

The question of regional stability and transformation is an imminently practical one. If American leaders can understand what leads regions away from conflict and toward peace, or from relative stability back into war, they can adopt policies that give regional players fewer incentives for aggression. Realist theories of war cannot answer all the relevant questions of war and peace, of course. But they can offer officials an overview "map" to guide them through the complexities of regional geopolitics. Moreover, because the conditions that led to peace in Europe after 1945 were so unique and difficult to replicate,[4] external great powers, such as the United States, that are seeking to maintain peace around the world must look first to the power dynamics of regions. It

---

[3] Dale C. Copeland, *The Origins of Major War* (Ithaca, NY: Cornell University Press, 2000).

[4] See Norrin M. Ripsman, "Two Stages of Transition from a Region of War to a Region of Peace: Realist Transition and Liberal Endurance," *International Studies Quarterly* 49, no. 4 (December 2005), 669–93, and Chapter 11 in this volume. Western Europe was occupied by the United States, underwent massive domestic restructuring, faced a massive Soviet threat that required close cooperation, and had the continued US presence to moderate security dilemmas between constituent actors.

is difficult in the short term to change the domestic characteristics of regional actors. Power issues, however, can be addressed fairly quickly through great power action, including arms transfers, economic aid, and the commitment of forces. This makes realism the necessary foundation and starting point for all policy-making debates on regional questions, whether in Washington, DC or in Beijing, Moscow, and Brussels.

Yet the most difficult theoretical task in applying realism at the regional level is figuring out, through a stand-alone deductive logic, what impact the external great powers should likely have on the interactions of the important states within the subsystem. Any realist theory designed to work at the systemic level cannot be applied lock, stock, and barrel at the regional level. This is for one simple reason: realist theories have been formulated for situations of pure anarchy where no larger actors exist to enforce agreements and protect them from attack.[5] In regional subsystems, however, there are indeed "higher" actors with significant power – namely, the great powers external to the subsystem. Such actors can at times play the role of the central authority in domestic or imperial orders, thus moderating the chance of conflict between regional actors. An obvious example of this has been the role of the United States in the relative peace of the Latin American subsystem over the last 120 years. While civil unrest has been pervasive, interstate wars have been exceedingly rare for more than a century. The unwillingness of the United States to permit such wars within its "backyard" provides a straightforward and powerful example of external actors shaping regional dynamics.

Most regions, however, lack a powerful outsider willing to act as a central enforcer of interstate relations. And this is precisely what makes the central question of this book so interesting, since it means that war can indeed occur in regions even when powerful external actors exist and are opposed to conflict. But how does one deal with the confounding influence of extra-systemic powers on the application of realist theories to regions that, by their very nature, lack the "pure" anarchy lying at the foundation of all realist arguments?

Before we plunge into a discussion of the realist theories of war, we need to deal upfront with this important theoretical question. To help resolve it, I would argue that all realist theories, when descending to the regional level, must be founded on a two-step approach to theory development. The critical first step is to assume, for theory-building

---

[5] The seminal work here is Kenneth N. Waltz, *Theory of International Politics* (Reading, MA: Addison-Wesley, 1979).

purposes, that external great powers have no interest in the affairs of a region. Through this assumption, we can deductively establish a regional situation that is close to the pure anarchical starting point of most IR theories. When dominant regional states have to accept that they cannot rely on extra-systemic actors, they can be expected, from a realist point of view, to formulate their policies according to the power dynamics of the subsystem seen in isolation. As long as geography and the limits on power projection keep other smaller actors from neighboring regions from having much influence on events, the subsystem can then be viewed with the tools of our competing realist theories without significant theoretical modifications.[6]

Needless to say, this starting assumption is an abstract ideal designed to get the theory-building process going. It is unlikely to play out in practice, mainly because global great powers usually have good strategic reasons – both military and economic – to be "interested" in the diplomatic relations and stability of particular regions. Thus dominant states within regions cannot typically count on the extra-systemic powers' noninvolvement in their affairs. This is where the second step comes in. We need to modify the pure logic of any particular realist theory to show how great power interventionism and regional power dynamics interact to shape the likely policies of dominant regional states and thus the overall stability of the subsystem. In essence, the power concerns of two sets of geopolitical actors – regionally dominant states and extra-systemic great powers – have to be considered simultaneously, a difficult and complicating task from the point of view of IR theory.

The second step attempts to crack this theoretical nut in the following way. To build a workable realist theory of regional conflicts that can apply across time and space, we must assume that regional actors look only to the impact of extra-systemic great powers on their local power levels and trends, and not to commitments by such powers to insert their own forces into the region from the outside. In terms of building strong theory, this assumption allows us to predict when and under what conditions dominant regional states will initiate war or crises that risk an escalation to war independent of the desires and goals

---

[6] See David A. Lake, "Regional Security Complexes: A Systems Approach," in *Regional Orders: Building Security in a New World*, ed. David A. Lake and Patrick M. Morgan (University Park: Pennsylvania State University Press, 1997) for a definition of regional subsystems based on major regional powers and the limits on power projection imposed by geography. Lake muddies the waters by automatically including external great powers with an interest in a region's affairs as part of the subsystem itself. Step one is designed to avoid this problem. (For more on the conceptualization of regions and for additional references, see Chapters 1, 2 and 12 in this volume.)

of external great powers. Extra-systemic material support for the power of regional players can be brought within a theory's purview, but the direct extending of an outsider's military forces is excluded. The power dynamics of a region and their likely effects on state behavior can then be studied without having the immediate action or threat of action by external great powers driving the process.

In a subsequent third step, we can then ask how extended deterrence commitments by external actors moderate (or perhaps accentuate) the incentives for war by dominant regional states, given what we know about the power dynamics of the subsystem. But to bring in issues of extended deterrence too early in the process only muddies the theoretical waters, obscuring the causal role of these power dynamics on the probability of war in any subsystem. The projection of an outside great power's navy and troops into a region provides a form of "central authority" that essentially eliminates the very thing that makes regional subsystems interesting to the realist scholar, namely, their quasi-anarchical character. It is this character that allows regions to fall into war for reasons similar to great powers systems of pure anarchy.

My theoretical argument – and my reworking of the big three realist theories of war – will thus rely on the propelling force of regional power dynamics in situations where extra-systemic actors are not expected to intervene directly but where they may send military and economic aid to regional actors. This theoretical stipulation of the second step keeps the application of realist logic to a regional subsystem "clean": it allows us to understand how power differentials and trends shape regional state behavior when the subsystem remains largely anarchic and states still worry about the present and future intentions of possible adversaries. Self-help at the regional level is still therefore a necessary fact of life, and states can be expected to act according to realist predictions. Only by starting with steps one and two can a rational understanding of step three – the circumstances for the extending of great power deterrence to a region – be properly understood. External powers seeking to maintain the peace must understand when that peace is likely to break down and which states are mostly likely to initiate conflict, and why. So it is only when these powers can anticipate in what way regional power dynamics are producing incentives for conflicts that they can intervene with the timely and effective use of their own military forces. Any theory of regional stability and war, realist or otherwise, must therefore begin at a point prior to direct great power intervention if it is to prove useful to extra-systemic actors considering the extension of formal commitments to regional allies.

The rest of this chapter will proceed as follows. I will start with a short overview of the competing realist theories for war in a great power system, suggesting how they can be reworked to apply to questions of regional politics. I will then lay out the alternative argument derived from dynamic differentials theory, but including the possible complicating impact of extra-systemic aid and support on the contending regional actors. Given space considerations, I will only briefly touch upon some of the actual historical evidence, interspersing it throughout the chapter to illustrate deductive points and to suggest areas for future research. My larger purpose here is not to confirm the superiority of any one approach, but rather to lay out an agenda for future realist work on regional war and peace.

Regional subsystems and realist theories of war

All realist theories start with the assumption that relative military power is one of the principal, and often predominant, determining factors in international politics. Within the broader realist camp there are three well-known theories of war that, while designed to work at the level of the global system, could be applied to the question of war and peace in regional subsystems.[7] The first is classical realism. It argues that systems are stable when a balance of power exists between the main actors. They only become unstable and prone to war when one actor builds a preponderant level of military power. A balance of power keeps the peace by convincing potential aggressors that war will have both high costs and a low probability of victory. When an imbalance of power arises, however, the preponderant state is more likely to expand in the belief that war can pay, that its net benefits will be greater than its costs.[8] As for why this superior state might decide to attack its neighbors, most classical realists would agree with Hans Morgenthau that it initiates war for unit-level reasons, that is, because of pathologies arising from within the initiator itself. Such pathologies include greed, glory, ideological motives, and what Morgenthau saw as a "lust for power" often manifested in extreme nationalism.[9] This logic has recently been reworked by so-called neoclassical realists, who contend that wars are almost

---

[7] These three are not the only realist theories of war, just the most discussed. For summaries of other important realist arguments, including power cycle theory and long cycle theory, see Greg Cashman, *What Causes War? An Introduction to Theories of International Conflict* (New York: Lexington Books, 1993).

[8] Hans J. Morgenthau, *Politics Among Nations: The Struggle for Power and Peace*, rev. 5th edn. (New York: Alfred A. Knopf, 1978); Edward V. Gulick, *Europe's Classical Balance of Power* (New York: W. W. Norton, 1962); Michael Sheehan, *The Balance of Power: History and Theory* (London: Routledge, 1996).

[9] See especially Morgenthau, *Politics Among Nations*, chapters 3–5 and 16; and Hans J. Morgenthau, *Scientific Man versus Power Politics* (University of Chicago Press, 1946).

always the result of predatory actors that use their superior power to prey on weaker states. In the absence of such actors and their unit-level pathologies, systems should be peaceful. Any latent security dilemmas fostered by the need to build power as a hedge against possible threats will tend to dissolve away in such circumstances. As actors learn of the security-seeking intentions of others, they will become more moderate in their behaviors, creating a virtuous cycle of reassurance and trust.[10]

When it comes to pure power politics, classical realists note that it is usually difficult in practice to maintain perfect equality in military power between all major states. For this reason, they prefer multipolarity (systems of many large powers) to bipolarity (systems of only two big states). Multipolar systems allow actors that have become unequal to restore a balance of power through alliance restructuring. That is, when the key states in a system can shift alliances in response to the growth of one state, a preponderant state can often be deterred by the net power of the coalition set against it. Conversely, bipolar systems are likely to be unstable because any inequality that opens up between the two key actors cannot be offset by alliances. The other states in the system are simply too small to create the requisite balance of power needed to deter the now dominant state.[11]

Applied to a regional subsystem, classical realism would make a straightforward argument: war will be likely when a single state achieves a degree of military preponderance and when it possesses clear unit-level reasons for aggression. Any degree of regional multipolarity would reduce this likelihood somewhat because of the opportunity for balancing through alliances. The inclusion of domestic-level factors as causes of war does make classical realism and neoclassical realism less parsimonious than their neorealist competitors. But it also permits a clear test of their theories' relative predictive value. If we see most wars in regional systems driven primarily by dominant states that take advantage of the imbalance of power to realize their predatory nonsecurity ends, then the classical/neoclassical approach is clearly

---

[10] See especially: Randall L. Schweller, "Neorealism's Status Quo Bias: What Security Dilemma?," *Security Studies* 5, no. 3 (spring 1996), 90–121; Randall L. Schweller, "Bandwagoning for Profit: Bringing the Revisionist State Back In," *International Security* 19, no. 1 (summer 1994), 72–107; Andrew Kydd, "Sheep in Sheep's Clothing: Why Security Seekers do not Fight each Other," *Security Studies* 7, no. 1 (autumn 1997), 114–55; Andrew Kydd, *Trust and Mistrust in International Relations* (Princeton University Press, 2005). On neoclassical realism's use of domestic characteristics as intervening variables, see Steven Lobell, Norrin Ripsman, and Jeffrey Taliaferro, eds., *Neoclassical Realism, the State, and Foreign Policy* (Cambridge University Press, 2009) and Chapter 4 in this volume.

[11] See Morgenthau, *Politics Among Nations*; Gulick, *Europe's Classical Balance of Power*.

on to something. Utilizing our two-step technique, we should expect that extra-systemic actors will try to provide arms and economic aid to weaker states within a regional subsystem and that this should be able to moderate the overall likelihood of war. Even without direct military action or the extending of alliance guarantees, such material support should help to right the balance of power and reduce any preponderant actors incentive for expansion.

Classical realism has many strengths, most importantly its emphasis on power differentials, which provides a fine-grained sense of the relative weights that go on to the scales of the balance of power. It also corrects a flaw in theories such as neorealism that argue for the stability of bipolar systems by showing that multipolar systems have another mechanism – alliances – that can help deter states even when near equality cannot be maintained. In bipolarity, if a gap in military power opens up, the weaker actor has no viable alliance option to fall back on when arms racing alone cannot close the gap.

The main logical problem with classical realism, however, lies in its static nature. By focusing on snapshots of the balance of power, it cannot explain how war might break out in systems where a military equality has indeed been established between either the top two states or between their alliance blocs. For example, Sparta attacked a near equal Athens in 431 BC in the bipolar world of ancient Greece, and Germany/Austria took on the near equal Triple Entente in the multipolar world of 1914 Europe.[12] Taken to the regional level, classical realism has trouble with wars such as the 1980 Iran–Iraq war, Israel's attack on Egypt in 1956 and the US Civil War of 1861. In such cases, both sides in the conflict were again about equal in overall military power.

The possibility of war between near equals has been the focal point of research for a second realist school, hegemonic stability theory (or what is often labeled power transition theory). This theory turns the classical realist argument on its head, contending that systems will be most stable when there is a single preponderant state that has a natural self-interest in maintaining the political-military order. It is when a second-ranked state rises to near equality with the now former hegemon that system stability is undermined. At this point of power transition, the rising and now equal state has an incentive to initiate war because it now has enough power to make war pay, or at least to reduce the costs from what they were previously. Why the rising state initiates war is

---

[12] For more on this, see Copeland, *Origins of Major War*, chapters 3–4 and 8.

straightforward: it wants to gain the status and rewards that have been denied to it by the existing system.[13]

Note that hegemonic stability theory (HST) has some commonalities with the first theory. It agrees with classical realism's belief that the aggressor states are driven by nonsecurity predatory motives. The ascending state is not after security when it attacks, but rather the territorial goodies and prestige that the former hegemon has kept from it. Overall, however, the theory constitutes a fundamental challenge to classical realism on the most critical realist question of all: that of power. Classical realists believe that equalities of power deter by raising the costs and risks of aggression. Hegemonic stability theorists believe that equalities of power encourage aggression because they allow formerly inferior states to believe they now stand a chance of achieving their long-desired domestic objectives.

The implications of HST for regional subsystems are straightforward. We should expect regions that are dominated by single predominant states to be more peaceful relative to regions that have many "near equal" states. If war does occur, it will likely be started by a rising near equal state that has strong unit-level reasons for changing the status quo.[14] Following the two-step logic, extra-systemic actors that help prop up the region's traditional hegemonic state through material aid should be able to keep the peace or at least delay the onset of war, as long as the regional hegemon is able to maintain military superiority and thus dissuade the rising actor from starting a war. In essence, this aid is serving to avert an impending power transition that would have otherwise destabilized the system. Notice again how different this implication is from the arguments of classical realism. Whereas classical realists assert that outside powers should aid the weaker states in a region to create a balance of power, hegemonic stability theorists would argue that this is exactly the wrong thing to do. Material support for

---

[13] A. F. K. Organski, *World Politics* (New York: Alfred A. Knopf, 1968); A. F. K. Organski and Jacek Kugler, *The War Ledger* (University of Chicago Press, 1980); Jacek Kugler and A. F. K. Organski, "The Power Transition," in *Handbook of War Studies*, ed. Manus Midlarsky (London: Unwin Hyman, 1989); Robert Gilpin, *War and Change in World Politics* (Cambridge University Press, 1981); Jacek Kugler and Douglas Lemke, *Parity and War: Evaluations and Extensions of the War Ledger* (Ann Arbor: University of Michigan Press, 1996); Lemke, *Regions of War and Peace*; Douglas Lemke, "War and Rivalry Among Great Powers," *American Journal of Political Science* 45, no. 2 (2001), 457–69.

[14] For a large-N correlational study supporting these hypotheses, see Lemke, *Regions of War and Peace*. Lemke provides no documentary evidence showing that initiating states acted for the reasons hypothesized by hegemonic stability theory, nor that the initiating states were rising in power at the time they attacked.

the inferior states will only help them catch up to the dominant actor, encouraging them to initiate war.

Hegemonic stability theory's main advantage over classical realism and most forms of neorealism is the incorporation of dynamic power trends into its analysis. This helps overcome the static nature of much of classical and neorealist thinking. As we will see below, however, the theory does a very poor job at explaining the driving forces behind any of the key cases of regional war that one can identify. The reason for this has to do with a logical flaw at the theory's core. It argues that rising states are the ones that initiate most of the wars in world history. Yet states that are still growing in relative power have a very large incentive to be moderate in their policies in the short and medium terms in order to buy time for their own growth. So even if a state had grown in power and now has the resources to defend its interests more vigorously, there is simply no logical reason why it should initiate a large-scale war at the "transition point" if it is still rising. If it has waited this long to catch up, why not wait a bit longer? After all, even if it is motivated by unit-level desires of greed and prestige, it will be even more able to achieve the realization of these ends by attacking when it is preponderant rather than risking war when only equal to the declining actor. In a study of thirteen major wars between great powers across ten major historical periods, I could not find one war that was initiated for HST reasons, even though the theory was precisely designed to explain such cases.[15] Thus it is not surprising that there is little or no documentary evidence supporting its logic for cases of regional war, notwithstanding large-N correlations between power equality and war in some historical regions.[16] Because of its fundamental deductive problems, I will largely ignore hegemonic stability theory's hypotheses in the discussion that follows.

Neorealism in its two main forms – offensive realism and defensive realism – challenges the unit-level assumptions and systemic logics of both classical realism and hegemonic stability theory. Neorealists start from the common realist presumption of anarchic systems that force states to worry about attack and therefore about their relative power positions. Like classical realists, they also argue that relative equality between major states facilitates deterrence and thus peace by increasing the costs and risks of aggression. In this sense, neorealism is most at odds with hegemonic stability theory, since for neorealists significant inequalities in power will encourage superior states to expand against their neighbors. As with classical realism, this basic point should apply to regional subsystems as well as great power global systems: inequality

---

[15] Copeland, *Origins of Major War.*   [16] Lemke, *Regions of War and Peace.*

undermines the ability of states to practice effective deterrence against potential aggressors.

The reason why states engage in expansionism differs, however, across offensive realism and defensive realism. Offensive realists contend that major states are always worried about the future intentions of other actors, and therefore need to expand as a hedge against problems down the road. Maximizing power is the best means to increase one's security. Superior states will thus constantly look for opportunities to use their preponderance over small parties to realize even more dominant positions in the system, a competitive process that is likely to end only when one state has achieved regional hegemony. This logic is founded on the crucial assumption that states in anarchy are forced to make worst-case assessments of their adversaries' present and especially future intentions, given the absence of any higher authority to protect them.[17] To the extent that regionally important states feel they lack extra-systemic bodyguards – that the subsystem is essentially anarchic – these states will act like their great power counterparts at the systemic level.[18]

Defensive realists reject the worst-case assumption as unrealistic and downright dangerous. At any point in historical time, states do indeed vary considerably in terms of inherent aggressiveness. Thus instead of simply assuming that other states are bad, rational security-maximizing states will make choices based on how likely it is that the other is currently hostile.[19] To expand based on the assumption that others are aggressive can lead a state into unnecessary wars against other security-driven actors, wars that the initiator may end up losing. Defensive realists will therefore still expect inequalities of power to make war more likely. But they believe that states overall have an incentive to act cautiously even when superior in power, at least when they are security-maximizing actors (as defensive realists, like offensive realists, assume). This logic should apply to regionally important actors and not just the global great powers.[20]

---

[17] John J. Mearsheimer, *The Tragedy of Great Power Politics* (New York: W. W. Norton, 2001); Eric J. Labs, "Beyond Victory: Offensive Realism and the Expansion of War Aims," *Security Studies* 6, no. 4 (summer 1997), 10–12.

[18] Mearsheimer in "Back to the Future," for example, starts with the fundamental assumption that both America and Russia have pulled out of Europe and have left it to its own devices. The fact that the United States has not departed and that NATO is still a viable alliance can help Mearsheimer explain why Europe did not fall into arms racing and conflict over the last twenty years.

[19] Stephen Brooks, "Dueling Realisms," *International Organization* 51, no. 3 (summer 1997), 445–77.

[20] Jack L. Snyder, *Myths of Empire: Domestic Politics and International Ambition* (Ithaca, NY: Cornell University Press, 1991), 10–12; Charles L. Glaser, "Realists

How, then, do wars at the systemic or subsystemic level occur in a defensive realist world? Surprisingly, self-proclaimed defensive realists offer no coherent answer to this question. Most will argue that when systems are clearly offense dominant and when balancing alliances are weak or nonexistent, strong powers will aggress against small and undefended states, especially if they see threats to their economic and frontier interests. They can thus account for imperialist wars such as British and American expansion in the nineteenth century using solely a systemic causal logic. But for costly wars between strong actors, such as the great power wars within Europe in the nineteenth and twentieth centuries, defensive realists have a problem. Since they believe that technology and geography usually favors the defense and that alliance balancing is usually an efficient mechanism to counter threats, they assert that states have an incentive to avoid big wars against near equal neighbors. Initiating such wars will leave a state bogged down in costly bilateral wars or defeated by superior coalitions. And even if the state is victorious, it will gain a reputation as an "aggressive" actor, forcing it to pay a high cost after the war via heightened arms racing and the formation of counteralliances against it.[21] Given that major states have an incentive for moderation, they should, if they are rational unitary actors, refrain from starting costly wars with other major powers.

This means that the important wars of modern history, either globally or within regions, are not well explained by the strictly systemic side of defensive realism. As a result, we often see defensive realists "turn classical" to cover the key wars of the last two centuries. They fall back on unit-level pathologies within the initiating states to explain such costly wars of expansion: the distorting effects of cartelized politics, cults of the offensive, hypernationalism, irrational misperceptions of power and resolve, and so forth.[22] Interestingly, offensive realists can

as Optimists," *International Security* 19, no. 3 (winter 1994/95), 50–90; Charles L. Glaser, *Rational Theory of International Politics* (Princeton University Press, 2010); Stephen M. Walt, "The Enduring Relevance of Political Realism," in *Political Science: State of the Discipline,* ed. Ira Katznelson and Helen V. Milner (New York: W. W. Norton, 2002), 204–09; Shiping Tang, *A Theory of Security and Strategy for Our Time: Defensive Realism* (Basingstoke: Palgrave Macmillan, 2010).

21 Snyder, *Myths of Empire,* 11–13; Stephen Van Evera, *Causes of War* (Ithaca, NY: Cornell University Press, 1999), chapter 1; Stephen M. Walt, *The Origins of Alliances* (Ithaca, NY: Cornell University Press, 1987); Walt, "Enduring Relevance of Political Realism."

22 See especially: Snyder, *Myths of Empire*; Edward Mansfield and Jack L. Snyder, *Electing to Fight: Why Emerging Democracies go to War* (Cambridge, MA: MIT Press, 2005); and Van Evera's *Causes of War* and manuscript, *Causes of War,* volume two. This fallback on unit-level factors was first identified by Fareed Zakaria in "Realism and Domestic Politics: A Review Essay," *International Security,* 17, no. 1 (summer 1992), 177–98.

also have trouble explaining large, costly wars. The preeminent offensive realist, John Mearsheimer, argues that states are rational to initiate war only when the benefits of war outweigh the costs. When costs are higher than benefits, states should be cautious in their policies.[23] The arising of an "unbalanced" system can lead the superior state to believe that the costs of war have fallen, and unbalanced systems are particularly likely to arise in multipolar systems because of incentives to buck-pass (to let others counter ascending actors). This, for Mearsheimer, means that multipolar systems are more likely to fall into large-scale wars than bipolar ones.[24] Yet Mearsheimer is well aware that general wars in multipolarity are likely to be very costly. Like defensive realism, he tends to fall back on unit-level variables to explain them. He evokes Nazi "hypernationalism" to cover World War II and he acknowledges that "nonstructural factors" are often needed to explain why dominant powers which have existed in peace for decades suddenly decide to initiate devastating conflicts such as World War I.[25] Needless to say, such invoking of unit-level factors to account for particular cases significantly undermines the systemic explanatory power of neorealism, and, when done in an ad hoc manner, leads to charges that neorealism has become a degenerative research program.[26]

There is a critical problem with most forms of offensive realism and defensive realism. Their core theoretical logics typically focus on snap-shots of the power balance. Fears of long-term decline as motivating drives for war, if they are discussed at all, are usually given secondary roles in their causal logics next to the factors discussed above.[27] Fortunately, many systemic realists have realized that neorealism can be improved by making the theory more dynamic, that is, by incorporating the trends in the power balance that can give states strong incentives to launch preventive wars or risky crises in order to shore up their declining security situations.[28] Fears of decline provide a simple and

---

[23] Mearsheimer, *Tragedy*, 37; Labs, "Beyond Victory," 13–14.

[24] Mearsheimer, *Tragedy*.

[25] Mearsheimer, "Back to the Future"; Mearsheimer, *Tragedy*, 335. The tendency of offensive and defensive realists to dip down to the unit level to explain war is shown by John Mearsheimer and Stephen Walt's explanation of the Iraq War in *The Israeli Lobby and US Foreign Policy* (New York: Farrar, Straus, & Giroux, 2007).

[26] See Jeffrey Legro and Andrew Moravcsik, "Is Anyone Still a Realist?," *International Security*, 24, no. 2 (fall 1999), 5–55.

[27] See in particular Mearsheimer and Labs for offensive realism, and Glaser and Snyder for defensive realism. A defensive realist that does discuss preventive war arguments, at least in the context of modern US foreign policy, is Robert Jervis, *American Foreign Policy in a New Era* (New York: Routledge, 2005), 84–86, 115–16.

[28] From the now voluminous literature on preventive war, see especially: Jack S. Levy, "Declining Power and the Preventive Motivation for War," *World Politics* 40, no. 1

powerful answer to the puzzle of why states will enter into large-scale wars where the costs are likely to be much greater than any benefits. In many circumstances, security-seeking states in steep decline will initiate war as the rational lesser-of-two-evils choice. War is known to have a negative expected value, but allowing the adversary to rise to predominance, given the risks of having to attack later, has an even more negative value. Uncertainties about the future intentions of rising actors and their inability to commit to being peaceful later can thus lead declining powers to initiate war now out of a rational fear of the future. There is no need to invoke unit-level pathologies in the initiator to explain large-scale war in a system or subsystem. In the next section I will briefly outline the essence of dynamic differentials theory as my particular take on the question of decline and the preventive motivations for war.

Dynamic differentials theory and regional stability

Dynamic differentials theory is a systemic realist theory that combines elements of offensive and defensive realism but frames the larger logic within a dynamic conception of the interstate power balance. From offensive realism it takes the notion that security-driven states are primarily worried about the future intentions of potential adversaries. Even if other actors are currently also moderate security seekers, they may not be so in the future, either because of a change of leadership/regime type or simply a change of heart. Thus rational security maximizers (RSMs) must consider actions now that will consolidate their power positions into the long-term future. I make a key departure from offensive realism, however. In Mearsheimer's set-up, offensive realism starts with a static snapshot of the power balance at any time t and then argues that all major states will be forced to grab opportunities to maximize their power bases or at least not fall behind.[29] I argue that at any time t, RSMs will look to the immediate differentials of power but also at the trend lines of power. When state Y is rising in power relative to

---

(October 1987), 82–107; Jack S. Levy and Joseph R. Gochal, "Democracy and Preventive War: Israel and the 1956 Sinai Campaign," *Security Studies* 11, no. 2 (winter 2001/02), 1–49; Marc Trachtenberg, "Preventive War and US Foreign Policy," *Security Studies* 16, no. 1 (January–March 2007), 1–31; Randall L. Schweller, "Domestic Politics and Preventive War: Are Democracies More Pacific?," *World Politics* 44, no. 2 (January 1992), 235–69; Woosang Kim and James D. Morrow, "When Do Power Shifts Lead to Wars?," *American Journal of Political Science* 36, no. 4 (November 1992), 892–922; Norrin M. Ripsman and Jack S. Levy, "The Preventive War that Never Happened: Britain, France, and the Rise of Germany in the 1930s," *Security Studies* 16, no. 1 (January–March 2007), 32–67.

[29] Mearsheimer, *Tragedy*, chapters 1–2.

state X, Y will have an incentive to be moderate in its policy in order to buy time for its future growth. But if Y starts to decline relative to X, it will have to consider whether more hard-line policies, including war, should be chosen in order to safeguard its long-term position. If Y is not declining too steeply, hard-line policies short of war, including increased arms spending and economic containment, are generally safer bets: they can avert the Y's relative decline without all the costs and risks of war. But if decline for Y is seen as deep and inevitable, then preventive war will start to be seen as the rational lesser-of-two-evils choice.[30]

Whether state Y will initiate preventive war depends on three important system-level conditions and one (potentially) unit-level parameter. The first system-level condition is the polarity of the system or subsystem. Dynamic differentials theory argues that bipolarity is a more unstable system type than multipolarity, once we bring in the dynamics of power. Decline in a system of only two major powers is very frightening for state Y, since it knows that after X overtakes it, it has no real alliance partners to rely on. But Y also knows that it can take on X now without having to worry about third parties either joining X's side or sitting on the sidelines to "take the peace" should the Y–X war prove long and costly. State Y will therefore be more likely to see preventive war both as the solution to its security problem – it can win the war if it only has to take on one other big power – and as a critical necessity, given that rising state X, once preponderant, will not be terribly restrained by any alliances Y can form. State Y will certainly consider preventive war a viable option if it is superior to X in the short term. But because of the lack of concern about sideline-sitting third parties, Y will also consider taking a chance on war even if only roughly equal with X.[31] Thus deterrence is very difficult for state X in a bipolar system, which would explain why in the three bipolar great power systems before the nuclear age – Sparta–Athens 431 BC, Carthage–Rome 218 BC, and France–Habsburgs 1521 – each fell into preventive war despite the near equality of the two great powers.[32]

In multipolar systems declining states do have strong allies to rely on and are thus less worried about decline, all things being equal. But they should also be more worried about starting a big war if they do not possess marked superiority in military power. A bilateral war against a rising and near equal X will likely be protracted and costly, reducing Y's subsequent relative strength versus sideline-sitters W and Z. And of

---

[30] Copeland, *Origins of Major War*, chapters 1–2.
[31] Ibid., chapter 1.   [32] Ibid., chapter 8.

course if W and Z decide to join X in a coalition against Y's attack, then Y is in an even more problematic position. For these reasons, declining states are likely to be more cautious about initiating preventive war in a system of many major powers. They will tend to require a high level of military superiority before contemplating it – both to end bilateral Y–X wars quickly and as a hedge against the possible intervention of other important states.

Preventive war in both bipolarity and multipolarity will be more probable when two other key system-level conditions are met. First, a system that is offense dominant because of technology or geography will encourage state Y to believe that it can win quickly, and will also make it worry more about rising state X overtaking it and having an incentive to attack later. Second, if state Y is strong in military power but is inferior in economic power and potential power – the latter including anything such as territory, population, human capital, and resources that could be translated into future GNP – then preventive war is more likely. In this circumstance Y will believe that it will not be able to keep up with X's growth by simple arms racing: state X has a larger economic and potential base from which to build its long-term military strength, and it will therefore be hard for Y to stop X from overtaking it. Decline is more likely to be deep and inevitable in this situation.[33]

The potentially unit-level parameter that declining state Y must also consider is the likelihood that rising state X will attack it later if X is allowed to become preponderant in military power – that is, if Y allows itself to decline "gracefully" and does not initiate preventive war when it has the chance. This parameter allows a declining state to determine whether preventive war is really "necessary" for security relative to the alternative options, including alliance restructuring and even appeasement of rising state X. Preventive war, after all, is a risky and uncertain option, mainly because state Y might lose any war that it starts, but also because even victorious war against X can so alienate other powers that Y will find itself boxed in after the war ends. But if rising state X is very likely to attack later once it overtakes Y, then preventive war now makes a great deal of sense. Domestic factors inside X will be important to Y's assessment of this parameter. An ascending fascist state, for example, is more likely to be feared than a democratic one, as is an X that is led by leaders obsessed with glory, the spread of their religion, or the internal stability of their state.[34]

[33] Ibid., chapters 1–2.
[34] Ibid., ch. 2, 38–39 and ch. 9, 238–40. One might think that the argument here is smuggling in unit-level variables at odds with its larger systemic orientation. My purpose, however, is simply to recognize how domestic parameters might interact with

As the theory has been laid out so far, it could apply either to the global great power system that, by definition, lacks a central authority, or to a regional subsystem that is close to the "pure" anarchy of the larger super-system. But for the latter to hold, regional actors must believe that extra-systemic great powers have absolutely no interest in the region and will neither provide material aid nor intervene, regardless of what happens within it. In practice, this is an unrealistic condition for almost all regions. Thus we must turn to step two in the theory-building process: the specification of the expected impact of great power material support on the dynamics of power within the region, keeping to the side any questions of extended deterrence commitments by extra-systemic actors.

A fully developed regional version of dynamic differentials theory requires that we see how outside powers are able to shape the power differentials and trends of the major regional actors to either moderate the likelihood of conflict or increase it. Similar to the implications of hegemonic stability theory, my argument would suggest that great powers that act to support the power position of the dominant state in a region may indeed help that subsystem to avoid war. But the reasons why this might work to secure the peace are fundamentally different from the HST logic. From the HST perspective, the outside powers are trying to keep the rising state from catching up to the declining regional hegemon because these powers believe rising states will attack if they reach a point of power transition. But for DDT the material support is designed to reassure declining state Y about its future and thus to be less inclined to start a preventive war. This logic, for example, has been an integral part of US strategy toward Israel since 1977: provide ongoing economic and material aid so that Israeli leaders believe that Israel will never lose its qualitative superiority vis-à-vis its neighbors.

Because DDT also draws from neorealism, it also recognizes the importance of balances of power in a rising actor's effort to dissuade a declining state from starting a preventive war. Especially in subsystems of many major players (regional multipolarity), we would expect outside actors to worry that it might be hard to prop up declining states. In such situations support for other actors will be seen as necessary to forge

---

systemic variables to drive behavior (more on this in the Conclusion). Note also that the state whose behavior we are interested in explaining, declining state Y, is still driven solely by the rational maximization of its security. Moreover, because Y might be uncertain about X's future character, it may make estimates based solely or primarily on how far X will rise (an X that rises to 70–30 relative power balance might be anticipated to attack with a 70 percent probability, for example). So while unit-level variables may be important to Y's final calculation, they are not necessarily so.

a credible deterrence posture for the rising regional actors. Against a declining Iraq in the late 1980s, for example, Washington continued to supply advanced planes and weaponry to Saudi Arabia and other Gulf states, hoping that this would signal to Saddam Hussein that war against the Gulf region would be a losing venture. Needless to say, outside powers have to be careful, since the very act of supplying weaker but rising states can only exacerbate the declining state's fears of the future, making it believe that preventive action is indeed necessary. This seems to have been the inadvertent downside of US policy when, by 1990, Saddam attacked Kuwait.

Dynamic differentials theory would also point to the importance of regional polarity when one is looking at the power trends of the major actors. Situations with two major regional players will be inherently fragile, especially if these actors believe that neighboring states are too far away to project power effectively into the subsystem. Any sense of deep decline on the part of one of the players is likely to push that state into a preventive war posture. This was the situation of Lincoln in March–April 1861 when he faced an industrializing and independent Confederacy with strong economic ties to Britain and the ability to choke off western trade down the Mississippi River. It has also been a critical part of the story of India and Pakistan in the region of South Asia for more than half a century. With neighboring states and the great powers disinclined to intervene, both India and Pakistan have been highly aware of any perceived shift in the military balance of power and have been inclined to use issues such as Kashmir and cross-border terrorism as rallying points for war.[35] Multipolar regional subsystems are less prone to instability in the face of changing power differentials. But they can also fall into war when dominant military states perceive deep and inevitable decline and believe that they have clear but temporary military superiority, superiority that is waning with each passing day. This in a nutshell was Israel's situation in 1956 when it saw Egypt acquiring arms from the Soviet bloc.[36]

Dynamic differentials theory would predict that extra-systemic powers will vary their strategies of material support depending on the polarity of the regional subsystem. In situations of bipolarity, given the fragility of deterrence, they will likely focus on trying to reassure both sides that they are not in deep decline and that preventive war

[35] In bipolar situations, the weaker of the two powers may initiate conflict if it perceives steep decline (Copeland, *Origins of Major War*, 17) or it has limited aims that it believes it can achieve at low cost (T. V. Paul, *Asymmetric Conflicts: War Initiation by Weaker Powers* [Cambridge University Press, 1994], chapter 1).

[36] Levy and Gochal, "Democracy and Preventive War."

is therefore too risky to attempt. This, of course, will be very tricky, since large-scale material aid for either side will likely be seen to kick in decline for the party receiving fewer goodies. The United States has faced this dilemma for many decades in trying to navigate the shoals of India–Pakistan relations. In more multipolar regions, given the importance of alliances and strong third-party sideline sitters to overall deterrence, outside powers will likely adopt a two-track policy. They will try to reassure the most powerful state that it is not declining while simultaneously keeping its inferior neighbors strong enough to maintain a credible deterrent posture.

The US policy after 1977 of helping Israel, Egypt, Jordan, and Saudi Arabia simultaneously can be seen in this light. By almost all accounts, Israel is the dominant military power in the region, primarily because of its qualitative superiority (as it has demonstrated effectively in previous wars). Washington has thus been smart to help Israel maintain its top-dog position; any major decline from this position could destabilize the whole subsystem, as the preventive war of 1956 showed. But US policy has also been oriented to helping Israel's Arab neighbors maintain their military and economic power. From the perspective of dynamic differentials theory, this is not simply a policy to "buy" these states' goodwill or to help them to deter third parties such as Iran or Iraq (although these other aspects are clearly part of the logic). By keeping Israel's neighbors relatively strong – but still weaker than Israel on a bilateral basis – the United States is making it harder for Israel to contemplate another war against many Arab states. It also serves to reassure the Arab states that while they cannot beat Israel should they start a war, they also are not likely to be attacked by Israel in the future.

Even when an outside power tries to maintain the stability of trend lines through material aid, it may not be enough. Another aspect of DDT may kick in, namely, a state's feeling of inferiority on economic and potential power. One of the most dangerous situations in all of history is where a state believes itself to have military superiority but is weak in relative GNP and in the territory, resources, and population that go into potential power. Germany twice took on the system (1914 and 1939) because of fears of the industrial growth of Russia, a state with three times Germany's population and forty times its landmass.[37] The same problem can bedevil regional subsystems. Through most of the 1970s Iraq and Iran were mortal enemies, but the rough military balance ensured prudence on both sides. The Iranian Revolution of 1979, however, temporarily reduced Iran's military strength. Yet its new

[37] See Copeland, *Origins of Major War*, chapters 3–6.

ideology posed a huge future threat to Iraq.[38] With three times Iraq's population and four times its landmass, Iran had the potential power to overwhelm Iraq in the long term. Saddam Hussein thus had a strong preventive reason for grabbing some of its oil-rich territory to keep Iran down economically.

The Korean War of 1950 showed aspects of this problem. By January 1950 North Korea had to admit to Stalin that the Communist insurgency in the south had failed. In the short term, given Soviet funding and the withdrawal of US forces, the north had marked military superiority. As I show elsewhere, however, both the North Koreans and the Soviets had good reason to worry about the south's long-term economic growth after July 1950. In February 1950, with Truman's encouragement, Congress passed legislation authorizing $60 million in economic aid to South Korea, starting 1 July 1950, with another $60 million to follow six months later (the equivalent of more than $1.2 billion in current dollars). The south also had richer agricultural land and twice the population of the north. Thus over the long term, with US material support, the south would likely overwhelm the north in economic power. The need to fight a war now was self-evident, especially given South Korea's proclamations of its intention to unify the peninsula under the southern banner.[39]

Up to now I have assumed that both regional actors and outside powers understand the logic of dynamic differentials theory and act accordingly. But what if outside powers are operating on the basis of another realist logic? What we can predict is that these extra-systemic powers will act in ways that may encourage regional actors to go on the attack, even when all states prefer regional stability.[40] The most obvious case of this is the Israel–Egypt War of 1956. Washington had refused repeated Israeli requests for military aid after Egypt's announcement in September 1955 of a large purchase of Soviet bloc arms. This purchase of top-of-the-line Soviet weaponry meant that Israel's qualitative advantage over Egypt would soon be negated, and it was forced to launch a preventive war. Note how this case undermines the arguments of both classical realism and hegemonic stability theory. Israel launched the war for security reasons, not for greed, status, or a "lust for power." Moreover, if Israel had been given *more* power – enough to sustain its qualitative superiority – it would very likely not

---

[38] Stephen M. Walt, *Revolution and War* (Ithaca, NY: Cornell University Press, 1996).

[39] Dale C. Copeland, *Economic Interdependence and War*, forthcoming, chapter 9.

[40] The outside powers are, within my framework, "irrational" in such situations. Dynamic differentials theory cannot explain their behavior, but it can explain the actions of prudent regional states and why war due to decline may break out.

have launched the war. The initiator of war was not the rising state but the declining one. And Israel went to war not because of an imbalance of power per se, but because of the downward power trends.[41]

Dynamic differentials theory also helps to explain something that is highly problematic for offensive realism, namely, war in essentially bipolar regional subsystems. Two critical cases come to mind here: the US Civil War of 1861 and the Japanese attack on the United States in 1941. The first case was not a true civil war, since the southern states had already formed an independent nation by the time Lincoln took office in March 1861. If bipolarity is stable because actors know the true costs of war, as offensive realism claims, then North America by 1860–61 should have settled down into decades of peace. Yet the sudden emergence of regional bipolarity was anything but stable, with major war occurring within months of its realization. The southern states hoped that Lincoln would allow the south to secede without a fight. But Lincoln understood that the north could not remain a viable entity in the face of an industrializing Confederacy that could lure western territories into its sphere.

The US–Japan case of 1941, when we treat the Far East as a region distinct from the European great power core, also constitutes a critical case against bipolar stability. When Japan faced four main regional adversaries from 1937 to 1940 – the British in Malaysia, the French in Indochina, the Soviets in Siberia, and the Americans in the Philippines – the Japanese leadership remained cautious. Everything changed, however, when Hitler attacked Britain and France in May 1940 and the Soviet Union in June 1941. By forcing these nations to pull their forces out of the Far East, the European war converted a multipolar subsystem into essential bipolarity. This allowed Japan to consider war against the one remaining rising power, the United States. In the face of the massive American naval build-up and economic restrictions on oil and raw materials, the Japanese realized they could not maintain regional military superiority for long against a state with a much larger base of economic and potential power. They thus struck preventively to acquire the resources needed to preserve their long-term position in the regional system.[42] Because it does not bring in the dynamics of power, offensive realism cannot explain why the shift to a two-power subsystem in the Far East did not improve stability but actually undermined it.

[41] Levy and Gochal, "Democracy and Preventive War."
[42] See Dale C. Copeland, "A Tragic Choice: Japanese Preventive Motivations and the Origins of the Pacific War," *International Interactions* 37, no. 1 (January–March 2011), 116–26.

Great powers within regions

Up to now I have ignored a key issue, namely, the implication for theory-building of states that are both great powers at the global level and major players within regions. Great powers often find themselves straddling both the systemic and subsystemic levels by their simple geopolitical placement. China today, for example, is a rising player on the world stage but also a major actor within both the East Asian and Central Asian subsystems. Russia plays a role in the European, Central Asian, and East Asian subsystems simultaneously.

When and under what conditions will regional subsystems containing one or more great powers fall into war? Dynamic differentials theory would suggest that regions that possess one major great power and a bunch of small neighbors will likely be peaceful, as long as that great power sees no regional state consolidating enough power to pose a long-term threat. To be sure, the regional hegemon may decide to launch short small-scale military operations to tidy up the domestic politics of the region, as the United States did on a number of occasions in Central America from 1885 to 1930. But barring the growth of a true regional challenger, the preponderant great power should refrain from large-scale war against the region, while the smaller states will be very cautious about fighting each other for fear of bringing down the wrath of the great power. This is a simple but powerful explanation for the lack of interstate warfare in the western hemisphere since 1900. Note again, however, that such examples do not confirm hegemonic stability theory, since the reason for peace is the secure situation of the regional hegemon, not any absence of a domestically driven rising challenger. And the subsystem would quickly become unstable should a challenger arise. Regional unipolarity would start to look like emergent bipolarity, and the declining regional hegemon would have good reason to contemplate preventive action (as the US case of 1861 indicates in dramatic fashion).

More dangerous than a subsystem of one great power is a situation where two great powers have strong footprints in a region. Here, all the problems of bipolarity at the systemic level get translated down to the local level. Both great powers fear the potential growth of the other within the region and its ability to draw smaller states into a secure and possibly restrictive economic empire. Today we see China and Russia competing for influence and control in the resource-rich Central Asian region. This amounts to a replaying of the Great Game between Britain and Russia throughout the nineteenth century. Going back even further, the Ottomans and Persia struggled for centuries over dominance of Iraq, a struggle that paralleled the Near East conflict between the Roman Empire and the Parthian Empire at the turn of the first millennium. Finally, we should not forget that the bipolar struggle of Austria and Russia over control of the Balkans led to innumerable conflicts after 1825, including crises and wars that on at least five occasions (1833, 1839, 1853, 1878, 1914) forced outside powers to intervene.

Regional subsystems that contain many powerful states that are also great powers at the global level should be more peaceful than the bipolar scenarios just described. The great powers will have a checking influence on each other within the region, just as they do in the core system, making any decline less worrisome, all things being equal. If, for example, we broaden our view and consider "Eurasia" today as a single region, we can see how the moderating influence of multipolarity could have its effect. Russia, China, India, and the European Union would all be major players within this broader region, each with interests to uphold. It would be more difficult for Russia and China to fight over Central Asia in this context without bringing in the restraining influence of India and the EU. Classical balancing against the state identified as the "initiator" would probably be enough to pull either the Chinese government or the Russian government back from the brink. Moreover, US material support for the weaker states would likely keep either Beijing or Moscow from believing it could exert its military power in the region without high costs.

Here dynamic differentials theory draws heavily upon classical realist thinking about multipolarity. But because the theory is dynamic, we can see that conflict might still occur in Eurasia should either Russia or China believe that it was declining deeply and inevitably. China, for example, might come to believe that the other powers were trying to contain its growth through economic restrictions. Its optimism and moderation might quickly turn into the pessimism and aggressiveness of a declining state with much to lose if it does not act. Such pessimism could push Beijing to project its military power into Central Asia or Southeast Asia to ensure the flow of oil and raw materials, notwithstanding the reaction of Russia, India, and of course the United States. And as the German and Japanese wars of the twentieth century show, declining powers can be pushed into the most costly of conflicts when they believe that war has become the tragic lesser of two evils.

Conclusion

This chapter had two main goals: to show how existing realist theories can be applied to the question of regional war and peace, and to

outline the advantages of dynamic differentials theory as an alternative systemic realist approach. Classical realism, hegemonic stability
theory, and neorealism all have their strengths. Overall, however, they
either are too static in their understandings of relative power or are too
quick to blame domestic pathologies for the costly wars of world history.
Dynamic differentials theory improves on these theories by showing
how differentials of power and polarity interact with declining power
trends to push security-seeking states into hard-line behavior and war.
There is not the space for a proper empirical test of the various theories. But glimpses into some prominent cases of regional war indicate the
potential value of the alternative argument while suggesting an agenda
for future research.

Critics might argue that, like many realist studies, the chapter suffers
from omitted variable bias: it fails to consider cases where unit-level
factors were predominant while downplaying the importance of such
factors in the cases that it does discuss. There is indeed good reason
to believe that domestic variables have more significance than I have
granted them. Two recent books by Benjamin Miller and by Edward
Mansfield and Jack Snyder, for example, offer powerful arguments for
the role of unit-level factors in regional affairs. Miller contends that an
imbalance between the number of states in a region and the number
of national groups seeking autonomy plays havoc with regional stability: too few states, and independence movements arise that encourage
outside intervention; too many states, and wars will occur to bring
compatriots abroad back into the fold.[43] Mansfield and Snyder contend
that states going through a transition from autocracy to democracy
will become aggressive as elites scrambling for legitimacy use interstate
conflict to rally support behind their causes.[44]

Miller and Mansfield/Snyder provide numerous examples of unit-
level forces pushing actors into regional war: the Balkan wars of
1912–13; the Egyptian attack on Israel in 1973; the Iran–Iraq war of
1980; and so forth. I do not contest the possible causal roles played by
these forces across a variety of historical cases. What is of interest for
future research, however, is how unit-level and systemic variables might
work together to destabilize a region.

This chapter has suggested one such way that declining power and
domestic factors interact to create an incentive for war, namely, when

---

[43] Benjamin Miller, *States, Nations, and the Great Powers: The Sources of Regional War and Peace* (Cambridge University Press, 2007).

[44] Mansfield and Snyder, *Electing to Fight*. For more on the domestic and ideational forces behind regional conflict and cooperation, see Chapters 4, 5, 6, 7, 8, 9, and 11 in this volume.

a declining security seeker has good reason to fear the unit-level character of the rising actor. This is where the 1956 Sinai war and the 1980 Iran–Iraq war show a strong similarity. In both cases the initiating state attacked for fear of deep decline. Yet it also had reason to believe the other would be aggressive later if allowed to rise, given its domestic characteristics (Egypt's pan-Arab nationalism and Iran's Shi'a fundamentalism). By allowing for a parameter that takes the nature of the ascending state into account, dynamic differentials theory can predict an increased incentive for preventive action over what one might expect by looking at power alone. But note how different its logic for war is from the theories of Miller and Mansfield/Snyder. It is not unit-level factors within initiators that are pushing them to start wars, but rather the characteristics of the Other that makes them believe that war now is better than likely destruction later.

The task for future scholarship is clear. It must carefully specify the interactive effects of systemic and unit-level variables while providing more substantive empirical studies of the key cases of regional peace and war. The conditions that created peace in Europe after 1945 are too hard to replicate. For all other regions, then, we must focus on the combination of power conditions and domestic conditions that can keep the peace even when external great powers are unable to intervene directly in regional affairs. Through our second step, dynamic differentials theory provides a number of insights into the kind of material support outside states can provide to moderate the chances of war.

Yet sometimes material aid alone is not enough. In such circumstances global great powers such as the United States must vigorously extend their deterrents to particular hot spots to maintain order through the threat of active intervention. The theory of this chapter indicates that when economic and material aid cannot keep dominant regional states from fearing deep and inevitable decline, then the "third step" of extended deterrence will probably be required. But by keeping the question of extended deterrence separate from our core logic, we can determine the conditions that tend to increase the incentives for regional war. This will help to inform external powers as to when a more active projection and commitment of their own power into a region is necessary. The first and second steps of theory-building, by providing us with a "clean" understanding of regional conflict dynamics, can thus tell us how and when to use extended deterrence to maintain regional order. From a practical perspective, this is what good theory is supposed to do.

4 Neoclassical realism and the study of regional order

Jeffrey W. Taliaferro

Introduction

T. V. Paul observes in this volume's introduction that regional transformation – the conditions under which some geographically delimited regions are more likely to evolve toward greater cooperation and
peaceful relations among their constituent states, while other regions
remain trapped or degenerate into enduring rivalries and endemic
interstate and intrastate war – is "of the utmost importance for crafting appropriate policy initiatives."[1] He defines a region as "a cluster of
states that are proximate to each other and are interconnected in spatial, cultural, and ideational terms in a significant and distinguishable
manner." Regions, therefore, are a defined subsystem within a broader
international (or interstate) system.[2] According to Robert Jervis, we
are dealing with a system when there are (a) a set of units or elements
interconnected so that changes in some elements or their relationships
produce changes in other parts of the system, and (b) the entire system
exhibits properties and behaviors that are different from those of the
constituent parts.[3] Further, as Barry Buzan points out, "regions" are
recent historical phenomena. The existence of a single international
system of a sufficient geographic scope and interaction capacity to

---

[1] See Chapter 1 in this volume, 3 and 4.
[2] Different definitions of regions include: Barry Buzan and Richard Little, *International
Systems in World History: Remaking the Study of International Relations* (Oxford University
Press, 2000), 48; Barry Buzan, *People, States, and Fear: An Agenda for International
Security Studies in the Post-Cold War Era*, 2nd edn. (Boulder, CO: Lynne Rienner,
1991), 190; Peter J. Katzenstein, *A World of Regions: Asia and Europe in the American
Imperium* (Ithaca, NY: Cornell University Press, 2005), 12.
[3] Robert Jervis, *System Effects: Complexity in Political and Social Life* (Princeton University
Press, 1997), 6. Other definitions include Kenneth N. Waltz, *Theory of International
Politics* (Reading, MA: Addison-Wesley, 1979), 79; Robert Gilpin, *War and Change in
World Politics* (Cambridge University Press, 1981), 25–29; Hedley Bull, *The Anarchical
Society: A Study of Order in World Politics*, 3rd edn. (New York: Columbia University
Press, 2002), 8–16.

comprise multiple regions only dates to the eighteenth and the nineteenth centuries.[4]

Between 1848 and 1945 Prussia and its successor state Germany initiated six interstate wars, the Schleswig–Holstein wars of 1848–49 and 1862, the 1866 Austro-Prussian (or Seven Weeks') War, the 1870–71 Franco-Prussian War, World War I, and World War II. During approximately the same period Japan initiated five wars: the First Sino-Japanese War of 1894–95, the Russo-Japanese War of 1905, the Manchurian (or Mukden) Incident of 1931, the Second Sino-Japanese War of 1937–41, and the Pacific theater of World War II. Yet since their respective defeats in 1945, neither Germany nor Japan has threatened to use force, let alone actually gone to war, against its neighbors.[5] Western Europe has not experienced an interstate war, let alone a major (or hegemonic) war, in almost seventy years.[6] Similarly, since the Korean War armistice in 1953, there have been no full-fledged great power wars in East Asia, although there have been a number of crises that risked escalation to war, most recently the 1995–96 Taiwan Strait Crisis. There have been four instances since 1945 where China has gone to war, albeit against adversaries outside of Northeast Asia or against great powers that intervened in existing conflicts in the region. These include China's intervention in the Korean War in 1950–53, the Sino-Indian War in 1962, Sino-Vietnamese War in 1979, and the Sino-Soviet border clashes in 1969. For a variety of reasons – nuclear deterrence, the bipolar distribution of power in the global system, and power asymmetries between combatants – none of those conflicts escalated to a regional level. Nonetheless, compared to the respective dynamics in the pre-1945 (or pre-1953) era and compared to other regions of the globe today, both Western Europe and East Asia have been remarkably stable.

Consider, on the other hand, the Middle East and South Asia during the same period. Israel and its neighboring Arab states went to war in 1948, 1956, 1967, and 1973. There have been numerous crises that risked escalation to full-scale war, as well as limited uses of force short of war against both state and nonstate actors, most recently the Israeli operations against Hamas in Gaza and Hezbollah in Lebanon. Iran and

---

[4] Buzan and Little, *International Systems*, 80–84 and 276–99.
[5] The Federal Republic of Germany (FRG) and the German Democratic Republic (GDR) were separate states from their establishment in 1949 until the former's absorption of the latter in 1990. When I speak of post-World War II Germany in this chapter, I refer mainly to the FRG, unless otherwise noted.
[6] On the attributes of major wars see Dale C. Copeland, *The Origins of Major War* (Ithaca, NY: Cornell University Press, 2000), 3.

Iraq fought a bitter and inclusive war between 1980 and 1988. Iran's quest to develop a nuclear weapon may yet provoke Israel to launch preventive air strikes. In the past twenty years the United States has fought two wars against Iraq, the first in 1991 to reverse the Iraqi invasion of neighboring Kuwait and the second in 2003 to bring about regime change in Baghdad. Likewise, South Asia has been particularly conflict-prone. India and Pakistan fought wars in 1948, 1965, 1971, and 1999, and have come to the brink of war on several other occasions, most recently in 2001.

What might explain variation in the likelihood of interstate and intrastate war over time and across different regions in the present international system? For example, what factor or factors may account for the transition of Western Europe and East Asia from zones of intermittent warfare to ones of relative stability since 1945, in the case of the former, and since the Korean War armistice in 1953, in the case of the latter? Conversely, why have South Asia and the Middle East remained zones of recurrent interstate and intrastate conflict for most of the past sixty years?

This chapter outlines a neoclassical realist theory of regional transition.[7] I contend that the relative distribution of power and the clarity of emerging threats at both the systemic and the regional levels provide incentives for extra-regional hegemons and pivotal states within particular regions to coordinate their respective foreign and security policies. Unit-level variables, specifically state power or the ability of the great power and the pivotal state to extract and mobilize human and material resources, channels those systemic incentives into the types of coordinated strategies that decrease the near-term likelihood of interstate conflict and make regional transformation over the long term more likely. Since World War II the most common form such coordinated strategies take are so-called *pacta de contrahendo* or alliances of restraint contracted between the extra-regional hegemon, on the one hand, and the pivotal state, on the other.[8]

---

[7] Overviews of neoclassical realism and its relationship with neorealism and classical realism include: Jeffrey W. Taliaferro, Steven E. Lobell, and Norrin M. Ripsman, "Introduction: Neoclassical Realism, the State, and Foreign Policy," in *Neoclassical Realism, the State, and Foreign Policy*, ed. Steven E. Lobell, Norrin M. Ripsman, and Jeffrey W. Taliaferro (Cambridge University Press, 2009), 1–41; Gideon Rose, "Neoclassical Realism and Theories of Foreign Policy," *World Politics* 51, no. 1 (October 1998), 144–77; Brian D. Rathbun, "A Rose by Any Other Name: Neoclassical Realism as the Logical and Necessary Extension of Structural Realism," *Security Studies* 17, no. 2 (April 2008), 294–321.

[8] Paul W. Schroeder, "Alliances, 1815–1945: Weapons of Power and Tools of Management," in *Historical Dimensions of National Security Problems*, ed. Klaus Knorr

Neoclassical realism asserts the primacy of power. It builds upon the three core assumptions that underlie the realist tradition: that individuals can only survive as members of a larger collectivity or group (such as tribes, city-states, empires, or sovereign states) that commands their loyalty and offers some level of protection from external enemies; that politics is a perpetual struggle among such groups for power and security in a world of scarce resources; and that the relative distribution of power is the currency of politics. Like Dale Copeland's dynamic differentials theory and the power-transition (or hegemonic) variants of realism, neoclassical realism recognizes the importance of anticipated power trends in the strategic calculations of states.[9] It presents quintessentially "top-down" hypotheses about the phenomenon under study: a causal explanation of regional order must first proceed from an analysis of the global distribution of power. In order for the systemic power distribution to affect regional order, at least two conditions must obtain: the capabilities of systemic actors (namely the great powers) must be superior to that of regional ones, and the former must have a strategic interest in the latter.[10]

That said, neoclassical realism departs from the neorealism of Kenneth Waltz, Robert Gilpin, John Mearsheimer, and others and shares greater affinity with the twentieth-century classical realism of Hans Morgenthau, Nicholas Spykman, Arnold Wolfers, and E. H. Carr in positing an important intervening role for unit-level variables, specifically leaders' subjective assessments of the international balance of power and the ability of the "state" or central government institutions to extract and mobilize human and material resources for national security.

Neoclassical realism proceeds from a "top-down" conception of the state. Systemic forces can only shape patterns of grand strategic adjustment through the medium of a national security or foreign policy executive comprised of the head of state and/or head of government and

(Lawrence: University of Kansas Press, 1976), 227–62; Jeremy Pressman, *Warring Friends: Alliance Restraint in International Politics* (Ithaca, NY: Cornell University Press, 2008), 6–7; Balkan Develen and Özdamar Özgür, "Neoclassical Realism and Foreign Policy Crises," in *Rethinking Realism in International Relations: Between Tradition and Innovation*, ed. Annette Freyberg-Inan, Ewan Harrison, and Patrick James (Baltimore, MD: Johns Hopkins University Press, 2009), 158–96.

[9] Copeland, *Origins of Major War*; Dale C. Copeland, "Neorealism and the Myth of Bipolar Stability: Toward a New Dynamic Realist Theory of Major War," *Security Studies* 5, no. 3 (spring 1996), 29–89; Jonathan M. DiCicco and Jack S. Levy, "Power Shifts and Problem Shifts: The Evolution of the Power Transition Research Program," *Journal of Conflict Resolution* 43, no. 6 (December 1999), 675–704.

[10] Gil Merom, "Realist Hypotheses on Regional Peace," *Journal of Strategic Studies* 26, no. 1 (March 2003), 109–35, at 112.

the senior officials charged with formulating and implementing grand strategy. This executive, sitting at the juncture of the state and the international system, with privileged information from the state's politico-military and intelligence apparatus, is in a position to perceive systemic constraints and opportunities. Thus, leaders define the "national interests" based upon their subjective assessments and perceptions of the international distribution of power and other states' intentions, but always subject to domestic constraints.[11] The process of threat assessment is inherently difficult. Even in the very rare situations where an international or regional subsystem provides unambiguous information about threats and "optimal" policy responses, a foreign policy executive still faces the daunting task of making subjective probability assessments, prioritizing among various threats and opportunities and discerning future intentions and shifts in the distribution of power.[12]

Contrary to the claims of some critics, I submit that neoclassical realism incorporates systemic-level explanatory variables and unit-level intervening variables in a deductive and consistent manner.[13] Rather than simply explaining anomalies for various neorealist theories, especially balance-of-power theory, neoclassical realism elucidates and predicts the circumstances under which unit-level variables are more likely to impede an "objectively efficient" response to international or systemic imperatives.[14] In situations where the international system provides clarity about the nature and magnitude of external threats but little clarity about the appropriate strategy to redress threats, neoclassical realism would expect unit-level factors such as state power and elite perceptions and calculations to shape the style, timing, and nature of a state's foreign and defense policies.[15] Neoclassical realism's comparative advantage lies in its willingness to integrate unit-level and

[11] Taliaferro, Lobell, and Ripsman, "Introduction: Neoclassical Realism, the State, and Foreign Policy," 25.
[12] See Norrin M. Ripsman, Jeffrey W. Taliaferro, and Steven E. Lobell, "Conclusion: The State of Neoclassical Realism," in Lobell, Ripsman, and Taliaferro, eds., *Neoclassical Realism, the State, and Foreign Policy*, 283–84.
[13] For criticisms of neoclassical realism on this point, see Stephen M. Walt, "The Enduring Relevance of the Realist Tradition," in *Political Science: The State of the Discipline*, ed. Ira Katznelson and Helen V. Milner (New York: W. W. Norton, 2002), 211; Jeffrey W. Legro and Andrew Moravcsik, "Is Anybody Still a Realist?," *International Security* 24, no. 2 (fall 1999), 5–55, especially 28–33.
[14] Not all neoclassical realists are proponents of balance-of-power theories, theories of power balances, or theories of balancing. For the distinction see Daniel H. Nexon, "The Balance of Power in the Balance," *World Politics* 61, no. 2 (April 2009), 330–59. The theory developed herein explicitly builds upon the hegemonic or power preponderance strand of neoclassical realism.
[15] Ripsman, Taliaferro, and Lobell, "Conclusion," 284–85.

systemic-level, as well as ideational and material, variables into a coherent explanatory framework. As Nicholas Kitchen writes, it "places the impact of ideas alongside the imperatives of material power in the making of foreign policy, rejecting the notion that either ideas or material factors are somehow 'most fundamental' and therefore deserving of analytic focus to the exclusion of the other."[16]

At the same time, one might question whether neoclassical realism, or the specific neoclassical realist theory I present, is particularly useful in explaining the transition from mere regional stability – defined as a low likelihood of war among states in a region – to regional transformation – defined as amicable relations among regional states that are so deep and institutionalized as to make armed conflict unthinkable or at the very least, prohibitively expensive. I agree with Norrin Ripsman about the sequential nature of such transformations and the comparative advantages of different theories in explaining those stages. While causal mechanisms generally associated with realism – such as regional balances of power, alliances of restraint, or great power concerts – are initially required to bring peace to warring regions, Ripsman contends that causal mechanisms generally associated with liberalism, constructivism, and the English School – such as high levels of economic interdependence, the consolidation of liberal democracy, international institutions, identities and conceptions of international society – are ultimately useful to strengthen and deepen that peace.[17]

Likewise, Benjamin Miller explicitly draws upon structural realism, as well as elements of liberalism and constructivism, in developing a theory that purports to explain not only variation in the incidence of interstate and intrastate warfare across different regions, but also the intensity and character of relations among the states within that region. Miller contends that great power involvement in the region is responsible for "cold war" or "cold peace," the latter being the existence of a formal peace treaty or armistice between regional adversaries without deep reconciliation or economic interdependence. The causes of what he terms "hot war," that is actual interstate or intrastate warfare, and "hot peace," meaning a deep and sustained rapprochement between former adversaries, lie in the regional balance of power and in the "state-to-nation balance." This last term refers to the extent to which

---

[16] Nicholas Kitchen, "Systemic Pressures and Domestic Ideas: A Neoclassical Realist Model of Grand Strategy Formation," *Review of International Studies* 36, no. 1 (January 2010), 127.

[17] Norrin M. Ripsman, "Two Stages of Transition from a Region of War to a Region of Peace: Realist Transition and Liberal Endurance," *International Studies Quarterly* 49, no. 4 (December 2005), 669–93.

state borders are or are not reflective of the demographic patterns of the various national, ethnic, linguistic, or sectarian groups within the region.[18] Again, explaining variation about the likelihood of cold war, cold peace, hot war, or hot peace among states in a particular region is outside the purview of the neoclassical realist theory I present here.

The dependent variable in this chapter is the likelihood that the extra-regional hegemon and the pivotal state (or states) will pursue strategies that increase or decrease the likelihood of warfare among the states in that region. Unlike some of the other theories represented in this volume, neoclassical realism does not purport to explain international systemic outcomes per se. Systemic outcomes, such as the historical prevalence of hegemonic orders versus balancing dynamics among great powers or the likelihood of major war across different types of interstate systems, are inexplicable by simply looking at the separate behavior of individual states or pairs of states (dyads). Each state's strategic adjustment is contingent upon the strategies of other states. States' behavior can and often does change the environment.[19] Neoclassical realism may not directly address some of the questions about systemic outcomes posed in the introduction. Nonetheless, it can explain covariation in the external strategies of pairs of states, which in conjunction with systemic feedback might contribute to regional stability.[20]

The remainder of this chapter proceeds as follows. The next section defines the terms extra-regional hegemon and pivotal state. A consideration of the systemic constraints on the extra-regional hegemons and on the pivotal states within particular regions follows. I show how the relative distribution of power and the degree of clarity about emerging threats and opportunities create incentives for great powers to redefine their strategic interests outside their home region. Likewise, relative power distributions and clarity about threats within particular subsystems and the international system as a whole create incentives for pivotal states to seek the involvement of a potential extra-regional hegemon as a route to security. Systemic forces, whether operating at the global or the regional level, however, can only set parameters for the likely external

---

[18] Benjamin Miller, *States, Nations, and the Great Powers: The Sources of Regional War and Peace* (Cambridge University Press, 2007).

[19] See Jervis, *System Effects*, chapter 2; Waltz, *Theory of International Politics*, chapter 4.

[20] Examples of neoclassical works that do this include: Hans Mouritzen, "Past Versus Present Geopolitics: Cautiously Opening the Realist Door to the Past," in *Rethinking Realism in International Relations: Between Tradition and Innovation*, ed. Annette Freyberg-Inan, Ewan Harrison, and Patrick James (Baltimore, MD: Johns Hopkins University Press, 2009), 261–91; Thomas J. Christensen, *Useful Adversaries: Grand Strategy, Domestic Mobilization, and Sino-American Conflict, 1947–1958* (Princeton University Press, 1996); Pressman, *Warring Friends*.

behavior of states. Therefore, a brief consideration of state power follows in the chapter's fourth section. The conclusion briefly discusses the broader implications of the argument. If the logic of the neoclassical realist theory I develop is correct, there is very little room for optimism about the near-term stability of South Asia and the Middle East.

Given space considerations, I can only provide illustrative examples from Western Europe and East Asia, two regions that transitioned from intermittent warfare to relative stability in part because of the restraining alliances the United States contracted with the Federal Republic of Germany (FRG) through its inclusion in the North Atlantic Treaty Organization (NATO) and Japan through the US–Japan Security Treaty. In the conclusion, I reference other regions, such as South Asia and the Middle East, that remain zones of intermittent warfare and intense security competition.[21] Subsequent research will have to subject these hypotheses to more systematic empirical scrutiny.

Identifying extra-regional hegemons and pivotal states

The likelihood of regions making a transition from zones of intermittent interstate warfare to relative stability is at least partly a function of the grand strategic choices of an extra-regional hegemon and the pivotal state (or states) within that region.

By "extra-regional hegemon," I am referring to one of the poles or great powers within an international system as a whole that has the capabilities and the interest to project its influence into often geographically distant regions. In order to be a pole within the system a state must (1) command an especially large share of resources, which they can use to achieve their ends, and (2) excel in all component elements of material capabilities, generally defined as size of population and territory, resource endowment, economic capacity, military strength, political stability, and competence.[22] In order to be an extra-regional hegemon, however, a state must not only excel in material capabilities

---

[21] Miller attributes part of this cross-regional variation to the state-to-nation balance in Western Europe, as opposed to the state-to-nation imbalance in the Middle East and South Asia. See Miller, *States, Nations, and the Great Powers*, 372–73.

[22] Waltz, *Theory of International Politics*, 131. For other discussions of measuring power and determining the number of poles in an international system, see William C. Wohlforth, "The Stability of a Unipolar World," *International Security* 24, no. 1 (summer 1999), 5–41; Randall L. Schweller, *Deadly Imbalances: Tripolarity and Hitler's Strategy for World Conquest* (New York: Columbia University Press, 1997), 17–26; Copeland, *Origins of Major War*, 247–54; Stephen G. Brooks and William C. Wohlforth, *World out of Balance: International Relations and the Challenge of American Primacy* (Princeton University Press, 2008), 12–13.

relative to most other states but must also define the geographic scope of its strategic interests broadly. It is the wherewithal to project military power and diplomatic influence over some distances *and* a strategic interest in doing so, therefore, that set extra-regional hegemons apart from all other great powers and lesser powers within a system. For example, the United States from the 1940s onward has played the role of an extra-regional hegemon with respect to Western Europe, East Asia, and the Middle East.[23] The Soviet Union undertook a similar function with respect to Eastern and Central Europe during the Cold War. Great Britain was an extra-regional hegemon with respect to the Mediterranean basin, South Asia, the Middle East, and parts of Central Asia at various points from the late eighteenth century until the demise of the British Empire in the decades following World War II.[24]

A "pivotal state" is one which, by virtue of its geography, relative capabilities, and/or revisionist aspirations, could become the principal source of interstate or intrastate conflict within a region.[25] Generally, this means the state in question has the ability to align with either of the two great power antagonists who lack that flexibility or is at risk of being captured by either great power antagonist. In either scenario, the loss or the addition of the pivotal state to either great power's camp would shift the balance of power within the regional subsystem and possibly the system as a whole.[26] A pivotal state need not always be the most powerful state in the region. In many instances a state may be pivotal precisely because its collapse – whether resulting from a large-scale revolution, a civil war, an economic collapse, or a natural disaster – would have adverse and immediate consequences for neighboring states and possibly the great powers. Physical size is a necessary but not a sufficient condition for a state to play a pivotal role in its region. A pivotal state need not always have revisionist aspirations, let alone act up such aspirations.[27]

---

[23] See Christopher Layne, *The Peace of Illusions: American Grand Strategy from 1940 to the Present* (Ithaca, NY: Cornell University Press, 2006).

[24] Extraregional hegemony and empire are not synonymous, although both terms connote power asymmetries and formal hierarchic relationships between actors. To a certain extent, they exist along a continuum of idealized political systems, with "pure" anarchy at one extreme and formal empire at the other. For a discussion see David A. Lake, *Hierarchy in International Relations* (Ithaca, NY: Cornell University Press, 2009).

[25] For a similar definition see Robert S. Chase, Emily B. Hill, and Paul Kennedy, "Pivotal States and US Strategy," *Foreign Affairs* 75, no. 1 (January 1996), 37–38.

[26] Jervis, *System Effects*, 181–88.

[27] On revisionist states in neoclassical realism see Jason W. Davidson, "The Roots of Revisionism: Fascist Italy, 1922–39," *Security Studies* 11, no. 4 (summer 2002), 125–59; Sten Rynning and Jens Ringsmose, "Why are Revisionist States Revisionist?

Just as the number of great powers and the identities of those powers within an international system change over time due to the so-called "law of uneven growth," so too do the number and the identities of the pivotal states within particular regions.[28] Based upon the above criteria, China, Indonesia, South Africa, Egypt, Iraq, Iran, Turkey, Mexico, and Brazil are the current pivotal states within their respective regions.[29] Some of these regions, such as the greater Middle East and South America, contain two or more pivotal states. Contemporary South Asia, however, is unusual because the distribution of power between its two pivotal states is so lopsided. Even though India has an overwhelming advantage over Pakistan in terms of potential, economic, and military capabilities, the latter is arguably also a pivotal state because of its geographic locale, its revisionist aspirations in neighboring Afghanistan, its conventional force advantage in the disputed province of Kashmir, and its nuclear arsenal.[30] As I explain below, Germany was the pivotal state in Western Europe during the Cold War, while Japan played a similar role in East Asia. Despite their devastating defeats in 1945 and subsequent occupations, both retained enough potential capabilities to shift the balance of power in their respective regions and the international system as a whole.[31]

Systemic constraints on extra-regional hegemons

All great powers across history and indeed all actors within an international system or a regional subsystem face systemic constraints.[32] By

---

Reviving Classical Realism as an Approach to Understanding International Change," *International Politics* 45, no. 1 (January 2008), 19–39; Schweller, *Deadly Imbalances*, 24–25.

[28] On the "law of uneven growth" see Gilpin, *War and Change in World Politics*, 94.

[29] Chase, Hill, and Kennedy argue the following should be considered pivotal states: Mexico and Brazil, Algeria, Egypt and South Africa; Turkey, India and Pakistan; and Indonesia. See Chase, Hill, and Kennedy, "Pivotal States and US Strategy," 37–38.

[30] See T. V. Paul, ed., *The India–Pakistan Conflict: An Enduring Rivalry* (Cambridge University Press, 2005); Sumit Ganguly and S. Paul Kapur, *India, Pakistan, and the Bomb: Debating Nuclear Stability in South Asia* (New York: Columbia University Press, 2010).

[31] See James McAllister, *No Exit: America and the German Problem, 1943–1954* (Ithaca, NY: Cornell University Press, 2002); Marc Trachtenberg, *A Constructed Peace: The Making of the European Settlement, 1945–1963* (Princeton University Press, 1999).

[32] Elsewhere I have cited the metaphor of coworkers in an office building to illustrate this point. See Jeffrey W. Taliaferro, "State Building for Future Wars: Neoclassical Realism and the Resource Extractive State," *Security Studies* 15, no. 3 (July–September 2006), 464–95. The original metaphor appears in David Dessler, "What's at Stake in the Agent–Structure Debate?," *International Organization* 43, no. 3 (summer 1989), 441–73.

systemic constraints, I refer to strong conditional constraints, which Stephen Brooks and William Wohlforth define as those that "power-fully affect the ability to use [material] resources in pursuit of security goals," but which "are triggered only if the United States adopts certain policies."[33] The concept of strong conditional and weak conditional constraints, however, is not solely applicable to the United States, other great powers, or the present unipolar system. The relative strength and conditionality of the constraints on any state are a function of relative power, anticipated power trends, and leaders' subjective time horizons for identifying and redressing external threats, and geopolitics – defined as "the influence of geography on the political character of states, their history, and especially their relations with other states."[34]

Permissive international environments impose constraints that are both conditional and relatively weak. In other words, a state may face only minor impediments in using material capabilities to advance its interests. Such an environment may exist when a state enjoys a pre-ponderance of military, economic, and other capabilities because of its victory in a major war or an enduring rivalry. Here a state enjoys a temporary windfall of power because of the destruction or the relative weakness of its former adversaries, as well as its allies. Leaders may be aware of possible future threats, but those threats are often ambiguous or latent and there are multiple avenues for dealing with (or not dealing with) them in the present.[35]

A restrictive environment imposes constraints on states that are both conditional and relatively strong. Under these conditions, as Waltz puts it, "the game of power politics [is] played really hard."[36] That statement could also apply to non-great powers as well. Any restrict-ive environment, whether at the level of the system or within a region, provides states with relative clarity as to the identity and the magnitude of the threats to a state's interests. Furthermore, the time horizon for redressing those threats has narrowed considerably.[37] In a restrictive

[33] Brooks and Wohlforth, *World out of Balance*, 14–15.
[34] See William Anthony Hay, "Geopolitics of Europe," *Orbis* 47, no. 2 (spring 2003), 296. On the evolution of "geopolitics" and its influence on twentieth-century clas-sical realism in the US (especially the writings of Nicholas Spykman), see Jonathan Haslam, *No Virtue Like Necessity: Realist Thought in International Relations since Machiavelli* (New Haven, CT: Yale University Press, 2002), 162–82.
[35] Ripsman, Taliaferro, and Lobell, "State of Neoclassical Realism," 282–87; Mark Brawley, *Political Economy and Grand Strategy: A Neoclassical Realist View* (New York: Routledge, 2009), 5–7.
[36] See Waltz, *Theory of International Politics*, 168.
[37] On time horizons and threat assessment in neoclassical realism, see David M. Edelstein, "Managing Uncertainty: Beliefs About Intentions and the Rise of Great Powers," *Security Studies* 12, no. 1 (autumn 2002), 1–40; Mark Brawley, "Neoclassical

international environment a state may find itself at a relative power disadvantage. Present power distributions and longer-term power trends are very difficult for states to measure and anticipate. The difficulties that states encounter in assessing relative power trends and systemic feedback are persistent themes in the neoclassical realist literature; a point to which I return later.[38]

How does the permissiveness or restrictiveness of an international environment shape the likely strategies of great powers and regional states? All other things being equal, a great power facing a restrictive international environment would be likely to adopt a more expansive geographic conception of its security interests. Specifically, great powers are more likely to include areas beyond their homeland and the homelands of immediate neighbors as among regions of intrinsic, extrinsic, or negative interest. However, a great power facing a permissive international environment – wherein there is more clarity about threats to survival and interests but less clarity on the appropriate range of strategies in response to them – might be less likely to adopt a more expansive geographic conception of its security interests. Why might this be the case? In any restrictive international environment great powers have an incentive to hedge their bets against their adversaries, since systemic constraints are both conditional and relatively strong. Yet the range of possible strategies for redressing threats varies depending upon the polarity of the system and the geopolitical circumstances of the state in question.[39]

A unipolar power is unlikely to confront a restrictive environment simply because the relative distribution of material capabilities skews so heavily in its favor. Indeed, one definition of a unipolar system would be a structure in which one state's capabilities are too great to be counterbalanced.[40] Other states conclude that the costs and risks of actively opposing the system leader – whether through arms racing and alliance formation ("hard balancing") or the initiation of a major war – is

Realism and Strategic Calculations: Explaining Divergent British, French, and Soviet Strategies toward Germany between the World Wars (1919–1939)," in Lobell, Ripsman, and Taliaferro, eds., *Neoclassical Realism, the State, and Foreign Policy*, 78–81.

[38] For discussion see Randall L. Schweller and William C. Wohlforth, "Power Test: Evaluating Realism in Response to the End of the Cold War," *Security Studies* 9, no. 3 (spring 2000), 60–107, at 186–89; William Curti Wohlforth, *The Elusive Balance: Power and Perceptions During the Cold War* (Ithaca, NY: Cornell University Press, 1993), 306–307; Aaron L. Friedberg, *The Weary Titan: Britain and the Experience of Relative Decline, 1895–1905* (Princeton University Press, 1988), 285–88.

[39] For a discussion of how explicit considerations of geopolitics might inform neoclassical realism, see Mouritzen, "Past Versus Present Geopolitics," 164–90.

[40] Wohlforth, "Stability of a Unipolar World," 14.

prohibitively expensive and will likely remain so for some time. Systemic constraints on the United States since the end of the Cold War have been largely inoperative, for better or ill depending upon one's vantage point.[41] That does not mean, however, that Washington always gets its way on the international stage; or that its resources are inexhaustible; or that use of economic and military power in the pursuit of various security goals might not produce some negative consequences or entail real opportunity costs. Rather, it does mean that systemic incentives or disincentives for the United States to intervene or not intervene in particular regions are slight. Unit-level forces may play a larger role in shaping when, where, and how the United States employs force abroad or pursues diplomatic initiatives in particular regions than would otherwise be the case in a more restrictive international environment.[42]

In a bipolar system where by definition the principal threat to each great power's physical survival and security interests comes from the other great power, restrictive environments create additional incentives for both sides to view their relationship in zero-sum terms. Anything that might constitute an increase in relative power or influence for one side constitutes a loss of power and influence of equal magnitude for the other side. As Waltz famously put it, "In a bipolar world, there are no peripheries ... Bipolarity extends the geographic scope of both powers' concern."[43] Such zero-sum calculations become more likely when the initial gap in relative capabilities between the two great powers is narrow. It also becomes more likely when one or both sides confront a "window of vulnerability" or a "power oscillation," that is, an anticipated near-term shift in the balance of military capabilities caused by the perceived success of the other side's armament programs or alliance formation.[44] In practical terms, however, a range of possible strategies

---

[41] Brooks and Wohlforth, *World out of Balance*, 21–50; Robert Jervis, "Unipolarity: A Structural Perspective," *World Politics* 61, no. 1 (January 2009), 188–213.

[42] On this point see Colin Dueck, *Reluctant Crusaders: Power, Culture, and Change in American Grand Strategy* (Princeton University Press, 2006), chapter 5; Layne, *Peace of Illusions*, chapter 6. See also Benjamin Miller, "Democracy Promotion: Offensive Liberalism Versus the Rest (of IR Theory)," *Millennium: Journal of International Studies* 38, no. 3 (May 2010), 561–91.

[43] Waltz, *Theory of International Politics*, 171. Of course, Waltz's theory contradicts itself by also holding that bipolar systems are stable because the superpowers rely on internal balancing (i.e., arms racing and emulation) and can avoid allied quarrels that could drag them into war. For a discussion of the tension between the normative and descriptive aspects of neorealist balance-of-power theory with respect to the Cold War, see Jervis, *System Effects*, 118–20.

[44] See Dale C. Copeland, *The Origins of Major War* (Ithaca, NY: Cornell University Press, 2000), 47–48. See also Stephen Van Evera, *Causes of War: Power and the Roots of Conflict* (Ithaca, NY: Cornell University Press, 1999), 73–75; Marc Trachtenberg, "A 'Wasting Asset': American Strategy and the Shifting Nuclear Balance, 1949-1954,"

to avert such anticipated power shifts depends upon each superpower's relative capabilities, existing factor endowments, time horizons, and geopolitics.

For example, during the Cold War the two superpowers expanded the geographic scope of their strategic commitments in response to perceived impending shifts in military capabilities. However, the venues where the two sides sought to expand their interests and the types of strategies available to them were often quite different. The Soviet Union was a continental-sized land power that enjoyed an advantage in conventional force numbers and geographic proximity to the main centers of industrial capacity in Eurasia. It was always at a disadvantage relative to the United States in terms of economic and potential capabilities, as well in naval and aerial power projection capabilities. Despite its geographic size and strategic depth, the USSR was in close proximity to the two pivotal states (and former great powers) in Western Europe and East Asia. Its western and eastern borders were vulnerable to conventional attack, as the German invasion in June 1941 illustrated.[45] The United States, on the other hand, was a continental-sized maritime power that enjoyed an advantage over its superpower rival in terms of economic and potential capabilities. Despite the advent of transoceanic aviation and later nuclear weapons and ballistic missiles, the Atlantic and the Pacific oceans still protected North America from a ground invasion. Unlike the Soviet Union in Eurasia, it was the only current or even potential great power in the western hemisphere.[46]

Geopolitical and relative power considerations delimited the manner and the venues in which the two superpowers reacted to power oscillations. The United States would dramatically increase defense spending and investments in military or dual-use technologies; expand the geographic scope of its military commitments in regions of extrinsic and sometimes negative value; and periodically fight limited wars ostensibly on behalf of weaker allies threatened by Soviet aggression or

---

International Security 13, no. 3 (winter 1988/89), 5–49; Marc Trachtenberg, "Preventive War and US Foreign Policy," *Security Studies* 16, no. 1 (January 2007), 1–31. Copeland uses the term "power oscillation," whereas Trachtenberg and Van Evera use the term "window of vulnerability." I treat the two as synonymous.

[45] Wohlforth, *Elusive Balance*, 51–58.

[46] See John J. Mearsheimer, *Tragedy of Great Power Politics* (New York: W. W. Norton, 2001), 234–52; Colin Elman, "Extending Offensive Realism: The Louisiana Purchase and America's Rise to Regional Hegemony," *American Political Science Review* 98, no. 4 (November 2004), 563–76. Mearsheimer argues that the US is only a regional hegemon, not a global hegemon. I disagree. For an extended discussion of regional hegemony versus global hegemony and why the US has actually exercised the latter, see Christopher Layne, "The 'Poster Child for Offensive Realism': America as a Global Hegemon," *Security Studies* 12, no. 2 (winter 2002/03), 120–63.

subversion.[47] The Soviet Union, in contrast, would provoke crises (such as the 1948 and 1958–61 Berlin crises, and the 1962 Cuban Missile Crisis) or exploit armed conflicts between its proxies and those of the US (such as the 1973 Middle East War and the Angolan Civil War) in an effort to win concessions from the western camp even at a heightened risk of inadvertent escalation to war.[48] The pattern broke down in the mid 1980s, as the Soviet economy went into steep relative decline and the range of options available to Yuri Andropov and later Mikhail Gorbachev and other Soviet leaders for redressing the growing power gap with the United States became ever more circumscribed.[49]

In a multipolar system each great power must not only be concerned about its power relative to several other states but also about the likely trajectory of those different power distributions over time. Each great power coexists with at least two other states with the wherewithal to threaten its interests, independence, and possibly even its physical survival. This is especially the case in a multipolar system, such as Europe in the early 1910s or the late 1930s, where four of the six great powers (Britain, France, Germany, and Russia/USSR) were in close proximity to one another and the differentials in economic and military capabilities among them often fluctuated. Simply put, in a restrictive multipolar environment proximate great powers will be more concerned with relative power balances and trends in their home region. For example, the rapid expansion of German military and economic power after 1894 created incentives for Whitehall to reorient British grand strategy away from the defense of the empire and toward a more active role on the European continent.[50]

Under multipolarity, restrictive environments may create incentives for distant great powers to expand the geographic scope of their interests, again as a hedge against other great powers. For example, as the threat of another war in Europe increased in 1938–39 so the United States began to adopt a broader geographic conception of the country's

[47] See Aaron L. Friedberg, *In the Shadow of the Garrison State: America's Anti-Statism and Its Cold War Grand Strategy* (Princeton University Press, 2000), 63–75.
[48] Benjamin Miller, *When Opponents Cooperate: Great Power Conflict and Collaboration in World Politics*, 1st pbk. edn. (Ann Arbor: University of Michigan Press, 2002), 148–50; Trachtenberg, *Constructed Peace*, 251–82; Wohlforth, *Elusive Balance*, 157–66.
[49] Schweller and Wohlforth, "Power Test: Evaluating Realism in Response to the End of the Cold War," 86–91. See also Stephen G. Brooks and William C. Wohlforth, "Power, Globalization, and the End of the Cold War: Re-Evaluating a Landmark Case for Ideas," *International Security* 25, no. 3 (winter 2000/01), 5–53.
[50] Friedberg, *Weary Titan*; Steven E. Lobell, *The Challenge of Hegemony: Grand Strategy, Trade, and Domestic Politics* (Ann Arbor: University of Michigan Press, 2003), chapter 3.

security and economic interests. Simply preventing a hostile great power from gaining a foothold in the western hemisphere and maintaining freedom of navigation in the Atlantic and the Pacific would no longer suffice. That growing recognition among elites did not result in an immediate grand strategic adjustment away from hemispheric defense and toward a strategy of preponderance or extra-regional hegemony, albeit for the unit-level reasons (namely high domestic mobilization hurdles and the limited extractive capacity of the federal government). Nonetheless, elite perceptions of relative power shifts and a more threatening international environment were a necessary condition for the extensive mobilization campaign the Roosevelt administration undertook in 1940–41 to bring the United States into World War II.[51]

Systemic and regional constraints on pivotal states: Western Europe and East Asia

The preceding pages have discussed how the relative permissiveness or restrictiveness of three ideal types of international systems might delimit the interests and likely strategic behavior of the great powers. Nevertheless, how might systemic forces shape the likely strategic behavior of a pivotal state? Neoclassical realism and various structural realist theories would agree that pivotal states and all other states within a geographic region encounter two types of structural constraints: those originating from the global international system, on the one hand, and those originating within the regional subsystem, on the other.[52]

The more serious threats to states within a region generally come from either domestic actors or proximate states, and not from geographically distant great powers.[53] While regional subsystems possess their own power dynamics, they are also rarely completely independent

[51] See John A. Thompson, "Conceptions of National Security and American Entry into World War II," *Diplomacy & Statecraft* 16, no. 4 (December 2005), 671–97; Mark A. Stoler, *Allies and Adversaries: The Joint Chiefs of Staff, the Grand Alliance, and US Strategy in World War II* (Chapel Hill: University of North Carolina Press, 2000).

[52] See for example: Miller, *When Opponents Cooperate*; Stephen M. Walt, *The Origins of Alliances* (Ithaca, NY: Cornell University Press, 1987); Timothy W. Crawford, *Pivotal Deterrence: Third-Party Statecraft and the Pursuit of Peace* (Ithaca, NY: Cornell University Press, 2003); and Pressman, *Warring Friends*.

[53] Steven R. David, "Explaining Third World Alignment," *World Politics* 43, no. 2 (1991), 233–56; Michael N. Barnett and Jack S. Levy, "Domestic Sources of Alliances and Alignments: The Case of Egypt, 1962–73," *International Organization* 45, no. 3 (1991), 369–95; Malik Mufti, *Sovereign Creations: Pan-Arabism and Political Order in Syria and Iraq* (Ithaca, NY: Cornell University Press, 1996).

of the broader international system.[54] Regional states, therefore, have an incentive to be attuned to shifts in the distribution of capabilities in their respective region, as well as to shifts in the distribution of capabilities among the great powers to the extent that the latter would likely influence the former. This is especially the case for regional states in proximity to an expansionist great power.[55]

To return to the example of postwar Western Europe, strong conditional constraints on the extra-regional hegemon, the pivotal state, and other regional states created incentives for them to coordinate strategies aimed at regional stabilization. Specifically, the threat to the United States and Western Europe posed by the Soviet Union, amplified by both the vulnerability of Germany in the wake of World War II and mutual fears of a revived German military machine, facilitated this process. Britain, France, and other war-ravaged states lacked the indigenous economic and military capabilities to readdress the immediate Soviet threat or the latent German threat. Therefore, they actively sought economic assistance and later security guarantees from Washington.[56] The Truman administration, like the Roosevelt administration before it, perceived Europe to be of intrinsic importance for long-term US military and economic security.[57] Finally, one should not discount the mutual fear and loathing between the Soviets and the Germans. By late 1944 most German leaders and average citizens recognized they faced several years of military occupation after the war, and if the choice fell between being occupied by the US, Britain, and even France or, alternatively, the Soviet Union, then most Germans preferred the former.[58] Soviet territorial ambitions in Eastern and Central Europe, the brutality of its occupation regime in eastern Germany, and intransigence over the implementation of wartime agreements created both a shared sense of threat among the Americans and Europeans and provided an opportunity for the United States to assert itself as an extra-regional hegemon.

---

[54] The two possible exceptions would be what Gil Merom calls "autonomous drifting regions" and "autonomous intractable regions." In both cases, the absence of sustained great power involvement renders the particular subsystem a "pure" anarchic environment in which interstate war is an ever-present possibility. See Merom, "Realist Hypotheses on Regional Peace," 116–17.

[55] Ibid., 118.

[56] Melvyn P. Leffler, *A Preponderance of Power: National Security, the Truman Administration, and the Cold War* (Stanford University Press, 1992), 182–219.

[57] John Lewis Gaddis, *Strategies of Containment: A Critical Appraisal of American National Security Policy During the Cold War*, rev. and expanded edn. (Oxford University Press, 2005), 56–59.

[58] David M. Edelstein, *Occupational Hazards: Success and Failure in Military Occupation* (Ithaca, NY: Cornell University Press, 2008), 28–29.

President Franklin D. Roosevelt, British Prime Minister Winston S. Churchill, and Soviet General Secretary Josef Stalin agreed in principle to a unified postwar Germany at the February 1945 Yalta Conference, but they also agreed on the division of the country into four occupation zones – American, British, Soviet, and French – to be administered as a single economic unit under the direction of an Allied Control Council (ACC) comprised of representatives of the four occupying powers.[59] However, neither the United States nor the Soviet Union would countenance a unified Germany that might fall into the other side's sphere of influence or that might again become the source of instability in Europe. The inability of former allies to agree on terms for an "amicable" divorce – that is, to disengage from each other and run affairs in their respective occupation zones in Germany and implicitly in the other parts of Europe their armies occupied as they saw fit – set the stage for the subsequent efforts by the Americans, the British, and eventually the French to merge the economies of their occupation zones in 1948.[60] The Soviets responded by imposing a blockade of Berlin, which had the effect of solidifying perceptions of a Soviet threat among the Germans and their western occupiers. Since the goal of creating a peaceful, unified, and secure Germany now seemed infeasible to both the occupiers and the occupied, the US, Britain, and France took steps toward the creation of an independent federal West German state. The Federal Republic of Germany came into existence the following year and Konrad Adenauer of the Christian Democratic Union (CDU) was elected its first chancellor.[61] A month after Adenauer's government took office the Soviets responded by creating the German Democratic Republic (GDR), or East Germany, with Walter Ulbricht, the general secretary of the Socialist Unity (or Communist) Party, as its paramount leader.

The Truman administration concluded that a disunited Western Europe with a disarmed, devastated, and diplomatically isolated West Germany could not be an effective bulwark against Soviet expansion. Consequently, US occupation strategy switched from demilitarization and aggressive de-Nazification to the economic rehabilitation and the integration of FRG into Western Europe.[62] The origins and the significance of the Marshall Plan, the North Atlantic Treaty, the European Coal and Steel Community, and the abortive European Defense

---

[59] McAllister, *No Exit*, 56–73; Trachtenberg, *Constructed Peace*, 15–33.

[60] Trachtenberg, *Constructed Peace*, 66–78.

[61] Ibid., 60–65; Leffler, *Preponderance of Power*, 182–98; McAllister, *No Exit*, 117–20.

[62] McAllister, *No Exit*, 135–41; Edelstein, *Occupational Hazards*, 32–33.

Community (EDC) are analyzed at great length elsewhere (including other chapters in this volume) and do not need repetition here.[63] For the purposes of this chapter, however, the following points are pertinent.

The leaders of the US and West Germany, as well as the leaders of other Western European states, perceived a common and immediate threat from the Soviet Union. A combination of German vulnerability, mutual fear of German revanchism, and preponderant American power enabled the US to fill the power vacuum created by the military defeat of Nazi Germany and the relative decline of Britain and France. This does not imply that the United States simply rearmed and economically rehabilitated Western Germany against the wishes of Britain and France. On the contrary, in July 1947 French Foreign Minister Georges Bidault admitted privately to the US ambassador in Paris that his government recognized that "the reconstruction of Germany is an element of any European reconstruction," with the proviso that it did not take precedence over French recovery.[64] His successor, Robert Schuman, saw German economic recovery as a means of avoiding a resurgence of German nationalism. Likewise British Foreign Secretary Ernest Bevin privately viewed a German military contribution to western defense as both necessary and inevitable, although other members of Prime Minister Clement Attlee's cabinet disagreed.[65] However, until the outbreak of the Korean War in June 1950 the depth of popular and legislative opposition to German rearmament in Britain, France, and the US led the Truman administration, the Attlee government, and the French cabinets under Schuman and André Marie to avoid public discussion of the issue, despite privately agreeing that Western Europe's defense would founder without a German military contribution.[66] While officials in the Truman administration quickly concluded that the Korean hostilities were not a precursor for a near-term Soviet attack on Western

---

[63] For recent debates see Michael Cox and Caroline Kennedy-Pipe, "The Tragedy of American Diplomacy? Rethinking the Marshall Plan," *Journal of Cold War Studies* 7, no. 1 (winter 2005/06), 97–134. See the rejoinders by Trachtenberg, Lázló Borhi, Günter Bischof, and Charles S. Maier in the same issue of the *Journal of Cold War Studies*. On the EDC see Trachtenberg, *Constructed Peace*, 120–25; Mark S. Sheetz, "Exit Stratgies: American Grand Designs for Postwar European Security," *Security Studies* 8, no. 4 (summer 1999), 1–43; Ronald R. Krebs, "A Debate Miscast – or What Can We Learn from the Case of the EDC?," *Security Studies* 11, no. 3 (spring 2002), 188–99; McAllister, *No Exit*, 200–44.

[64] See "Ambassador in France (Jefferson Caffery) to the Secretary of State," July 11, 1947, in *Foreign Relations of the United States, 1947*, vol. II, *Council of Foreign Ministers; Germany and Austria* (Washington, DC: GPO, 1947), 984–86.

[65] Norrin M. Ripsman, "The Curious Case of German Rearmament: Democracy, Structural Autonomy, and Foreign Security Policy," *Security Studies* 10, no. 2 (winter 2000/01), 1–48.

[66] Leffler, *Preponderance of Power*, 388–89.

Europe, the crisis did underscore the critical need for West German rearmament.

In early July 1950 Truman ordered the Defense Department and the State Department to begin preparations for German rearmament.[67] Secretary of State Dean Acheson argued that the overall need to rearm Europe justified the risks inherent in rearming Germany, but that pursuing rearmament as part of a broader West European security framework would mitigate those risks. As US High Commissioner for Germany John McCloy wrote, and Acheson concurred, "At one step it would fully integrate Germany into Western Europe and be the best possible insurance against further German aggression."[68] While the Attlee government remained officially opposed to a German military force, it admitted privately that German rearmament was essential and began to take a number of incremental steps in that direction. Schuman and French Premier René Pleven, however, were not willing to defy public opposition to German rearmament, unless they could escape responsibility through deception. At the risk of gross oversimplification, many of the disagreements among Washington, London, and Paris over the next four years were not over the broader issue of whether the FRG ought to be rearmed. Rather, the Western Allies disagreed over specific mechanisms to control the pace and scope of German rearmament in order to ensure the integration of the reconstituted German armed forces into a broader West European security framework, the extent of US and British security guarantees to France, and the need to package these issues so as not to destabilize the succession of weak coalition governments of the French Fourth Republic.[69]

Adenauer and other leaders in the governing CDU understood that the Western Allies did not trust Germany. Therefore, in order to end the four-power occupation and to gain military protection from the Soviets, Adenauer was willing to bind the FRG to its neighbors, in effect to accept semi-sovereign status, by entering into a series of bilateral and multilateral agreements that restricted the unilateral use of West German economic (and later) military power. In order to assuage European (especially French) concerns about West Germany, as well to solidify its own hegemonic role on the continent, by 1955 the United

---

[67] Ibid., 386–87.
[68] "US High Commissioner for Germany (McCloy) to the Secretary of State," August 3, 1950, *Foreign Relations of the United States, 1950*, vol. III, *Western Europe* (Washington, DC: GPO, 1950), 181–82.
[69] For a detailed examination see Norrin M. Ripsman, *Peacemaking by Democracies: The Effect of State Autonomy on the Post-World War Settlements* (University Park: Pennsylvania State University Press, 2002), 194–219.

States had undertaken a series of expensive and unprecedented peace-time commitments. These included (1) championing West Germany's accession to NATO, (2) the placement of the reconstituted German armed forces under the direct control of a Supreme Allied Commander in Europe (SACEUR) who would always be an American flag or general officer, and (3) a pledge by the US and Britain to station their troops on German territory indefinitely.[70]

In post-World War II East Asia, as in Western Europe, strong conditional constraints on extra-regional hegemons and the pivotal state created incentives for them to coordinate strategies aimed at regional stabilization. However, unlike Europe where the United States constructed a single multilateral defense pact that bound West Germany to its neighbors, in East Asia the US adopted a "hubs-and-spokes" model by forging bilateral alliances with Japan (the pivotal state), the Republic of China (ROC or Taiwan), and the Republic of Korea (ROK or South Korea) between 1951 and 1954.

In East Asia the administrations of Presidents Harry S. Truman and Dwight D. Eisenhower faced the tasks of simultaneously (1) deterring possible expansion by the Soviet Union, and after 1949, the People's Republic of China; (2) avoiding entrapment in unwanted East Asian wars launched by rogue leaders of allied states, namely ROK president Syngman Rhee and ROC president Chiang Kai-shek from his base of exile on Taiwan; and (3) hedging against the possibility of a resurgence of Japanese militarism.[71]

In entering into an alliance with Japan in September 1951, the United States sought to both defend East Asia against Soviet or Chinese Communist expansion and to control the future development of Japanese foreign policy.[72] The transformation of the US–Japan relationship from one of bitter enmity to one of close (albeit asymmetrical) security cooperation in the span of six years illustrates how strong conditional constraints on the extra-regional hegemon and the pivotal state can facilitate grand strategic adjustment, and by extension, regional stabilization.

---

[70] On French governments' efforts to secure a permanent American military presence in Europe and French public opposition to (West) German rearmament in the early 1950s, see Trachtenberg, *Constructed Peace*, 118–19; Ripsman, *Peacemaking by Democracies*, 190–205; Michael Creswell and Marc Trachtenberg, "France and the German Question, 1945–1955," *Journal of Cold War Studies* 5, no. 3 (summer 2003), 5–28.

[71] Victor D. Cha, "Powerplay: Origins of the US Alliance System in Asia," *International Security* 34, no. 3 (winter 2010/11), 167–68.

[72] Richard J. Samuels, *Securing Japan: Tokyo's Grand Strategy and the Future of East Asia* (Ithaca, NY: Cornell University Press, 2007), 39.

The stated goals of the US occupation of Japan after World War II were to prevent the latter from ever again becoming a threat to the United States or the security of the world and to bring about the establishment of a "peaceful and responsible government" in Tokyo.[73] Among the top priorities of General Douglas MacArthur, the supreme commander of the Allied Powers, were the rapid demobilization and abolition of the Imperial Army and Navy; the dismantlement of the arms industry; the purge of nationalists and military officers from the postwar government; the prosecution of war criminals; and the enactment of comprehensive economic, social, and political reforms. Those reforms culminated in the May 1947 enactment of a new Japanese constitution, originally drafted by the Government Section of MacArthur's General Headquarters (GHQ) and modified in subsequent negotiations with the cabinets of Prime Ministers Shidehara Kijūrō and Yoshida Shigeru. The constitution's Article 9 "forever renounced war as the sovereign right of the nation" and pledged toward that end "land, sea, and air forces, as well as other war potential, will never be maintained."[74]

By 1948, however, the onset of the Cold War led the Truman administration and MacArthur's GHQ to shift occupation strategy from democratization and demilitarization and toward bolstering Japan as a front-line ally.[75] As State Department Policy Planning Director George F. Kennan observed, Japan was the key to East Asian stability, just as Germany was the key to European stability. "Our primary goal," he argued in January 1948, must be to ensure that the US would "never again be threatened by the mobilization against us of the complete industrial area [in the Far East] as it was during the Second World War."[76] The US objective had to be "to win Japan as an ally," and doing so would require not only guaranteeing the physical security of the Japanese islands, but also providing markets and raw materials for

---

[73] Supreme Commander for the Allied Powers. Government Section, *Political Reorientation of Japan, September 1945–September 1948*, 2 vols., vol. I (Washington, DC: US Government Printing Office, 1949), 423–26. For a detailed analysis of the wartime planning for the occupation of Japan, unconditional surrender, and the Potsdam Declaration, see Dale M. Hellegers, *We, the Japanese People: World War II and the Origins of the Japanese Constitution*, 2 vols. (Stanford University Press, 2001), vol. I, 159–223; Takemae Eiji, *Inside GHQ: The Allied Occupation of Japan and Its Legacy*, trans. Robert Ricketts and Sebastian Swann (New York: Continuum, 2002), 3–52.

[74] On the origins of Article 9, see Hellegers, *We, the Japanese People*, vol. II, 576–78; John W. Dower, *Embracing Defeat: Japan in the Wake of World War II* (New York: W. W. Norton and New Press, 2000), 365–73.

[75] For an analysis of the "reverse course" in US occupation policy, see Richard B. Finn, *Winners in Peace: Macarthur, Yoshida, and Postwar Japan* (Berkeley: University of California Press, 1992), 195–209; and Eiji, *Inside GHQ*, chapter 10.

[76] Quoted in Leffler, *Preponderance of Power*, 253.

the Japanese economy.[77] Kennan's analysis won widespread support among senior officials in the State Department, including Secretary of State George C. Marshall, Undersecretary of State Robert Lovett, and Marshall's successor Dean Acheson, as well as Secretary of Defense James V. Forrestal and the Joint Chiefs of Staff, and was subsequently accepted by the National Security Council and approved by Truman.[78]

The Truman administration considered three options to bring the occupation of Japan to a close. The alpha option called for a harsh peace treaty that would limit Japan to its four main islands and allow it only minimal defense capabilities. However, while this option initially had the support of MacArthur and the British and Chinese Nationalist governments and was consistent with a strict interpretation of Article 9, it would have precluded Japan serving as a front-line ally.[79] The gamma option envisioned a lenient peace treaty and a militarily autonomous Japan capable of defending its territory against possible Soviet or Chinese attack and projecting force on to the Asian mainland. While this second option may have minimized the long-term US military burden in East Asia, it also ran the risk that Japan might again become a source of regional instability. The beta option, which the Truman administration ultimately pursued, aimed to create a postwar Japan strong enough to serve as a front-line ally, but also firmly tied to the United States in a bilateral (and asymmetric) alliance.[80] The CCP victory in the Chinese civil war in October 1949, followed by the Sino-Soviet alliance in February 1950 and then the outbreak of the Korean War, led the Truman administration to accelerate plans to end the occupation and conclude a US–Japan security pact.[81]

Prime Minister Yoshida saw the Soviet Union and communist subversion as threats, but recognized that postwar Japan lacked the military forces-in-being and economic capabilities to redress either one. Therefore, he encouraged the United States to keep its military bases in Japan as a way to accelerate the end of the occupation, and even granted considerable extra-territorial privileges as an inducement. Allowing US

[77] George F. Kennan, *Memoirs, 1925–1950* (London: Hutchinson, 1968), 41.
[78] "NSC 48/2 the Position of the United States with Respect to Asia, 30 December 1949," in *Foreign Relations of the United States, 1949*, vol. VII, *Far East and Australasia, Part 2* (Washington, DC: GPO, 1949), 1215–220; Leffler, *Preponderance of Power*, 257–60; Kenneth B. Pyle, *Japan Rising: The Resurgence of Japanese Power and Purpose*, 1st edn. (New York: PublicAffairs, 2007), 221–23.
[79] Samuels, *Securing Japan*, 39.
[80] Cha, "Powerplay," 184–85; Leffler, *Preponderance of Power*, 333–37.
[81] Leffler, *Preponderance of Power*, 391–92; Edelstein, *Occupational Hazards*, 129–30.

forces effective control of the air and sea lanes around Japan would obviate the need to reconstitute a large Japanese military. In return for basing rights, Japan would receive access to US markets and technology. In effect, Yoshida would accept a semi-sovereign Japan, if doing so would allow his government to focus on economic reconstruction and to pursue what Richard Samuels terms a mercantile realist grand strategy.[82]

The Truman administration saw the US–Japan Security Treaty as serving two purposes.[83] First, it would establish Japan as a bulwark against the USSR and China. Second, the treaty allowed the US to manage the pace and scope of Japan's rearmament, as well as its reintegration into the East Asian region. As John Foster Dulles, Truman's special envoy to East Asia, assured the foreign ministers of Australia and New Zealand in February 1951, "if Japan is basically committed to the free world and accepts US troops in and about its territories, we [the US] would have complete control over any rearmament that Japan might adopt." A US–Japan alliance, Dulles argued, would shield former Japanese colonies in East Asia, as well as Australia and New Zealand, from a resurgent Japan. [84]

For Yoshida and his supporters within the ruling Liberal Party, however, the danger in any US–Japan alliance was entrapment, not abandonment. They feared that Japan might be drawn into a conflict with the USSR or China, rather than the US reneging on its security guarantee. The two most contentious issues in the security treaty negotiations involved the future of Japan's economic and diplomatic relations with China and Taiwan and the scope of Japanese rearmament. In order to secure the Diet's ratification of the security treaty, Yoshida had to simultaneously marginalize fellow conservatives, industrialists, and former military officers who wanted to rebuild an autonomous Japanese military; deflect US demands for greater Japanese contributions to common defense; and silence leftist politicians who opposed any alliance.[85]

---

[82] Samuels, *Securing Japan*, 39–42; Finn, *Winners in Peace*, 245–57; Christopher W. Hughes, "Japan's Postwar Security Trajectory and Policy System," *Adelphi Papers* 44, no. 368 (November 2004), 21–40. See also Eric Heginbotham and Richard J. Samuels, "Mercantile Realism and Japanese Foreign Policy," *International Security* 22, no. 4 (spring 1998), 171–202.

[83] Samuels, *Securing Japan*, 40; Pyle, *Japan Rising*, 228–29; Cha, "Powerplay," 185–86.

[84] "Memorandum on Conversation among Ambassador Dulles, Australian and New Zealand Ministers of External Affairs and Staffs, Secret, 26 February 1951," in *Foreign Relations of the United States, 1951*, vol. VI, *Asia and Pacific, Part 1, Foreign Relations of the United States* (Washington, DC: GPO, 1951), 160.

[85] Eiji, *Inside GHQ*, 502–03; Samuels, *Securing Japan*, 40–41.

For their part, the Truman and later the Eisenhower administrations tacitly agreed to what became known as the Yoshida Doctrine: Japan would maintain a relatively low-profile military (the National Safety Force from 1952 and then the Self-Defense Forces after 1955) without power projection capabilities. The United States would agree to defend Japan against a possible third-party attack, but Japan would have no obligation to participate in any joint military operations beyond the immediate defense of its territory.

Linking the levels: a few words on external threats and state power

The formation of a *pactum de contrahendo* between an extra-regional hegemon and a pivotal state requires that both parties be relatively "strong states" from the outset, that their respective foreign policy executives have a certain degree of autonomy from other domestic actors in the conduct of foreign and security policy, and that domestic mobilization hurdles are not prohibitively high.[86] Below, I briefly discuss why this is the case, drawing upon the previous examples of US alliances with the pivotal states in Western Europe and East Asia during the Cold War.

Pacts of restraint involve more than a simple aggregation of capabilities to deter or defeat a common adversary. An extra-regional hegemon has to make credible security guarantees to its would-be pivotal state ally. Those commitments often entail forward military deployments, large foreign military assistance programs, and sometimes favorable technology transfer and trade agreements. For example, in contracting the North Atlantic and the Japan alliances, the United States not only broke with its 150-year policy of avoiding entangling alignments but it also agreed to the deployment of American troops abroad in peacetime and to provide its pivotal state ally with a host of economic benefits.

It would simply not have been possible for the Truman and the Eisenhower administrations to undertake these types of expensive strategic commitments absent the tremendous growth of the federal government's extraction and mobilization capacity during World War II, followed shortly thereafter by the creation of the institutions of the

---

[86] On the distinction between "strong states" and "weak states" see Michael C. Desch, "War and Strong States, Peace and Weak States?," *International Organization* 50, no. 2 (spring 1996), 237–68. On variations in the degree of the foreign policy executive's autonomy see Ripsman, *Peacemaking by Democracies*, chapter 1; Norrin M. Ripsman, "Neoclassical Realism and Domestic Interest Groups," in Lobell, Ripsman, and Taliaferro, eds., *Neoclassical Realism, the State, and Foreign Policy*, especially 179–88.

"national security state" in the early years of the Cold War.[87] Even then, in order to generate and maintain support among the electorate and the Congress for these overseas commitments both administrations had to engage in threat inflation and frame containment as an ideological crusade.[88] To be sure, in the late 1940s and early 1950s Truman, Acheson, Kennan, Marshall, Dulles, and Eisenhower, among others, did not envision the "permanent" deployment of US conventional (and later nuclear) forces in Western Europe and East Asia. They fully expected that, in time, the NATO allies, as well as Japan, would bear a more proportionate share of the burden of their own defense. However, it was precisely the large US military presence and the extensive foreign military assistance Washington provided to these pivotal states that made the NATO system and the US–Japan alliance "work" in facilitating regional stabilization. Over time, officials in Washington came to realize that both alliances solidified the US preponderant position in the international system. Senior officials in the Kennedy administration concluded that a withdrawal of US forces from Europe or East Asia was undesirable.[89] Since the end of the Cold War and the collapse of the USSR two decades ago the United States has continued to pursue a strategy of extra-regional hegemony in Europe and East Asia and has gone to extraordinary lengths to preserve the NATO and US–Japan alliances.[90]

For the pivotal state, on the other hand, a *pactum de contrahendo* may entail accepting "semi-sovereign" status in terms of granting an extra-regional hegemon permanent or at least long-term basing rights on its territory and effectively surrendering the ability to use its own military forces unilaterally or to enter into agreements with third states (particularly those that the hegemon views as an adversary).[91] Both the FRG and Japan were willing to accept a "semi-sovereign" status in return for US security guarantees.

In order for a pivotal state to enter into such an arrangement, four conditions are necessary. First, and most importantly, a pivotal state and the extra-regional hegemon must perceive a common external

---

[87] See Friedberg, *In the Shadow of the Garrison State*, chapter 2; Douglas T. Stuart, *Creating the National Security State: A History of the Law that Transformed America* (Princeton University Press, 2008), chapter 6.

[88] See Christensen, *Useful Adversaries*, chapter 3; Dueck, *Reluctant Crusaders*, chapter 3.

[89] Trachtenberg, *Constructed Peace*, especially chapters 4 and 5.

[90] See Mary Elise Sarotte, "Perpetuating US Preeminence: The 1990 Deals to 'Bribe the Soviets out' and Move NATO in," *International Security* 35, no. 1 (summer 2010), 110–37; Christopher Layne, "US Hegemony and the Perpetuation of NATO," *Journal of Strategic Studies* 23, no. 3 (September 2000), 59–91; Layne, *Peace of Illusions*.

[91] On this last point see Jervis, *System Effects*, 213–17.

threat that would be very difficult for either party to redress without the material assistance of the other. Indeed, in the absence of a common threat pivotal states would have no incentive to accept (nor would extra-regional hegemons have an incentive to extend in the first place) a *pactum de contrahendo*.[92]

Second, old grand strategies have to be thoroughly discredited in the minds of pivotal states' leaders, or at least the range of grand strategic alternatives has to be narrowly circumscribed. Restraining alliances with the US were not only attractive to West German and Japanese leaders because of the perceived magnitude and the imminence of the Soviet or Chinese Communist threat, but also because the grand strategies pursued by their immediate predecessors had disastrous consequences and the range of options to redress them was limited.[93] Germany and Japan were exceptional in this respect: the grand strategies pursued by their prewar leaderships resulted in catastrophic military defeats, the loss of territory, large civilian and military casualties, the loss of great power status, and several years of foreign military occupation. Few other pivotal states, both during the Cold War or since, have experienced the magnitude of negative systemic feedback that Germany and Japan experienced in 1945.[94]

Third, the pivotal state or states have to be capable of mobilizing and extracting human and material resources for purposes of national security. Again, here postwar Germany and Japan stand apart. Allied bombing destroyed most major German and Japanese cities and industrial plants, but even in defeat both states retained sufficient potential capabilities to shift the balance of power in their respective regions and possibly the international system as whole. Both had industrial economies, strong technological bases, highly educated and relatively homogenous populations. They also had a civil bureaucracy which, if not wholly intact at war's end (as was the case in Japan), could be reconstituted in a short period of time (as was the case in the British, French, and American occupation zones in Germany).

Fourth, the foreign policy executives of the pivotal states need a certain degree of autonomy from domestic interest groups in order to

---

[92] On common threats as a necessary condition for alliance formation in general see Walt, *Origins of Alliances*, chapter 2. More recently see Sebastian Rosato, "Europe's Troubles: Power Politics and the State of the European Project," *International Security* 35, no. 4 (spring 2011), 45–86.

[93] On the importance of exogenous shocks in prompting grand strategic adjustment see Dueck, *Reluctant Crusaders*, 39–40. See also Kitchen, "Systemic Pressure and Domestic Ideas," 130–32.

[94] On negative feedback in international politics see Jervis, *System Effects*, 139–46.

conclude alliances. In general, the foreign policy executives in multi-party parliamentary democracies tend to have less autonomy in the conduct of foreign policy than do their counterparts in strong two-party parliamentary systems or in presidential systems.[95] The FRG and Japan both had multiparty parliamentary systems, but their respective parliamentary institutions and political parties were still in flux in the late 1940s and early 1950s. Furthermore, Germany and Japan were still effectively occupied by the Western Allies and the US, respectively, during the negotiations over postwar security arrangements. The fact that both Yoshida and Adenauer were operating from positions of relative weakness on the world stage created a window of opportunity to shape the menu of strategic alternatives and to then build the domestic coalitions needed to support them.

Conclusions: implications for other regions

This chapter has sought to address one part of the broader phenomenon of regional transformation from the perspective of neoclassical realism. At the outset I drew a distinction between regional stabilization – defined as a low likelihood of war among states in a region – to regional transformation – defined as amicable relations among regional states that are so deep and institutionalized as to make armed conflict unthinkable or at the very least, prohibitively expensive. Different schools of international relations theories may have a comparative advantage in explaining different aspects or different stages of that transition. I argued the likelihood of regions making a transition from zones of intermittent interstate warfare to relative stability is at least partly a function of the grand strategic choices of an extra-regional hegemon and the pivotal state (or states) within that region.

The relative distribution of power and the clarity of emerging threats at both the systemic and the regional levels provide incentives for extra-regional hegemons and pivotal states within particular regions to coordinate their respective foreign and security policies. State power or the ability of the great power and the pivotal state to extract and mobilize human and material resources channels those systemic incentives into the types of coordinated strategies that decrease the near-term likelihood of interstate conflict. For the past half-century such coordinated grand strategic adjustments by extra-regional hegemons and pivotal states have taken the form of *pacta de contrahendo* or alliances of restraint. Case studies of the United States' formation of restraining

---

[95] Ripsman, *Peacemaking by Democracies*, 43–59.

alliances with West Germany (through NATO) and Japan (through the US–Japan Security Treaty) in the early years of the Cold War illustrate the plausibility of this argument.

The transitions of Western Europe and from East Asia zones of recurrent instate warfare to zones of relative stability (or in the former case, regional transformation) in the decades after World War II constitute "most likely" cases for many of the theories represented in this volume. Arguably, the relative stability of East Asia in the decades following the Korean War also constitutes a "most likely case" for neoclassical realism and the modified version of dynamic differentials theory Copeland outlines in Chapter 3 in this volume.[96] One might ask how well neoclassical realism (or at least the theory I outlined here) might fare in predicting the likelihood of mutual grand-strategic adjustment by extra-regional hegemons and pivotal states in other geographic regions that might facilitate regional stability.

As noted earlier, neoclassical realism does not suggest much room for optimism for regions such as the Middle East, North Africa, or South Asia. The United States is currently the only country with the wherewithal to project military power and diplomatic influence to geographically distant regions *and* a strategic interest in doing so. Yet the regional and systemic constraints on pivotal states in various regions today are quite different from those faced by the FRG and Japan sixty years ago. For example, in South Asia while the US may be fixated with countering the threat of Islamist terrorism and a resurgence of the Taliban in Afghanistan, the region's two pivotal states – India and Pakistan – continue to view each other as an existential threat. The wave of popular uprisings against long-time autocratic regimes across the Middle East and North Africa – the so-called Arab Spring of 2011 – may bring to power new elites in several capitals, especially Cairo, whose strategic calculations may differ from their predecessors.

There are also internal constraints on the ability or willingness of the extra-regional hegemon and pivotal states to coordinate their strategies. After spending a decade fighting wars in Iraq and Afghanistan as part of the George W. Bush administration's "global war on terrorism," there is little support among the American public, and especially top officials in the Obama administration and the military, for undertaking yet another set of expensive strategic commitments. Entering into

---

[96] On "most likely" and "least likely" cases see: Harry Eckstein, "Case Studies in Political Science," in *Handbook of Political Science*, ed. Fred I. Greenstein and Nelson W. Polsby (Reading, MA: Addison-Wesley, 1975), 94–137; and Alexander L. George and Andrew Bennett, *Case Studies and Theory Development in the Social Sciences* (Cambridge, MA: MIT Press, 2005), 120–21.

a *pactum de contrahendo* with the US is simply not a viable (let alone attractive) option for pivotal states such as Iran, for obvious reasons. The pivotal states that do have such security arrangements with the US, such as Egypt and Pakistan, also lack extractive and mobilization capacity or face a host of internal security problems.

Part 3

Liberal perspectives

5   Economic interdependence
       and regional peace

John M. Owen, IV

Any serious treatment of how regions become more cooperative and peaceful must consider the commercial-liberal thesis. The thesis asserts that economic links among states alter those states' incentives and hence their actions and interactions.[1] National economies may be linked in various ways, including trade in goods and services, investment, borrowing and lending, and guest workers. The welfare of one state may come to depend to some extent upon links with another; when two states depend on each other – when bilateral trade, for example is so high that its disruption would harm both states – the relationship is one of *interdependence*. The commercial-liberal claim is that economic interdependence pacifies relations among states. With some refinement, discussed below, the claim should be applicable not just to pairs of states but also to regions as T. V. Paul defines them in this volume – that is, as "clusters of states that are proximate to each other and are interconnected in spatial, cultural, and ideational terms in a significant and distinguishable manner."[2]

The interdependence thesis is widely held, intuitive (to some), and empirically supported. It also is relevant as never before, as economic barriers among states around the world are so low that we speak of an era of "globalization."[3] Surely, many say, at least one cause of the extraordinary peace in Europe since 1945 is the tight economic ties between the economies of member states: the ongoing free movement of goods, capital, and labor, and more recently the single currency

The author wishes to thank Peter Jones, Dale Copeland, T. V. Paul, Norrin Ripsman, John Oneal, Steven Lobell, Peter Furia, Stephen Brooks, and the participants in the Dartmouth College International Relations Seminar for comments on previous drafts. Any errors remain the author's sole responsibility.

[1] Andrew Moravcsik, "Taking Preferences Seriously: A Liberal Theory of International Politics," *International Organization* 51, no.4 (autumn 1997), 513–53.

[2] T. V. Paul, Chapter 1 in this volume, 4.

[3] On globalization's effects on international security, see Norrin M. Ripsman and T. V. Paul, *Globalization and the National Security State* (Oxford University Press, 2010), 124–35.

most members use, the harmonization of product regulation and labor standards, and so on. Surely, at least most of these would add, this sort of economic integration is one of the keys to a peaceful future in East Asia. Surely the Middle East would be more peaceful and cooperative if its national economies likewise became more integrated – if Israel, Saudi Arabia, Iran, and so forth, traded and invested extensively in one another.[4]

A long tradition of skepticism about interdependence and peace runs through International Relations (IR) scholarship, however. For centuries, realists have argued that interdependence does not suppress international conflict, and might even aggravate it by rendering states more vulnerable to exploitation. Marxists have held that deep commercial links among societies can increase conflict because the true nature of economic relations among capitalist states is asymmetric and exploitative. If skeptics are right, then the impressive European peace endures irrespective of, even in spite of, interdependence, and the quest for peace in South Asia or the Middle East must look to other solutions.

The past decade has seen a rejuvenated research program on commercial peace, involving impressive advances in data measurement and analysis. These advances have by no means eliminated disagreements over the effects of interdependence, but a very general convergence seems to be emerging among scholars that interdependence does work as advertised at least under some conditions. What those conditions are remains contested, as do the exact mechanisms by which interdependence pacifies international relations. In this chapter I rehearse briefly the modern history of the commercial-liberal or interdependence thesis. I summarize recent empirical findings, attending to methodological controversies that have hampered scholarly consensus. I lay out the chief theoretical explanations for the alleged commercial peace that are predominant today: the familiar opportunity-cost mechanism, which says that interdependence makes war too expensive; a signaling mechanism, which says that interdependence gives states an extra way to demonstrate resolve and thereby avoid unnecessary conflict; and social ties among peoples. I discuss explanations of how states come to trade more and current scholarly attention to the capitalist underpinnings of commercial peace. Finally, I discuss some difficulties in applying this literature to *regions*, or sets of geographically proximate states. It is not enough for dyads or pairs of countries to liberalize trade: to avoid bloc formation and possible intraregional conflict, entire regions

---

[4] See the now poignant Shimon Peres with Arye Naor, *The New Middle East* (New York: Henry Holt, 1993).

must become interdependent. But regional integration, while enjoying a superficial vogue globally, is difficult to achieve in substance. It seems to require either hegemony – an unacceptable price to many – or democracy. I discuss the case of South Asia to illustrate some of these problems and prospects.

Following most of the empirical literature, I consider mainly international trade rather than finance, foreign direct investment, or other modes of interdependence. This emphasis comes at a cost, for many scholars consider these other modes more important.[5] But trade data are much more plentiful and reliable.

An old thesis

Claims that international commerce is somehow linked to peace have their origins at least as far back as the seventeenth-century French monk Émeric Crucé. Arguing in 1623 against the absolute monarchical sovereignty of his contemporary Jean Bodin, Crucé maintained that war did not pay the monarchs who waged it, and that it was caused by the warrior class that stubbornly adhered to destructive notions of honor and had too little else to do but fight. Princes should encourage commerce, even practice free international trade, to maximize employment in peaceful productive pursuits. Crucé, then, offered a sociological explanation for why commerce causes peace; foreshadowing a current scholarly debate, he also argued that the causation runs the other way, that universal peace encourages international commerce.[6]

In the eighteenth century, when Enlightenment thinkers began to apply to political economy the notions about mechanics and equilibria that were proving so fruitful in physics, commerce became a more prominent topic in discourse about international affairs. In arguing against the colonial-mercantilist system then predominant, Adam Smith was chiefly concerned with prosperity rather than peace, but did argue that free markets reduced the incentives for war. Other writers argued that, in addition, economic openness and the interdependence that would follow would likewise bring international harmony. It is worth noting

---

[5] On finance, see Jonathan Kirshner, *Appeasing Bankers: Financial Caution on the Road to War* (Princeton University Press, 2007); on direct investment and multinational production chains, see Stephen G. Brooks, *Producing Security: Multinational Corporations, Globalization, and the Changing Calculus of Conflict* (Princeton University Press, 2007).

[6] Émeric Crucé (1623), *The New Cineas*, trans. C. Frederick Farrell, Jr. and Edith R. Farrell (New York: Garland, 1972). Crucé even called for an international standardization of money and weights to ensure that trade was fair; ibid., 130–35.

at the outset that the argument was not about capitalism per se, for the English and Dutch were capitalist. But they were also mercantilist, insisting on exclusive trading rights with their colonies. The Anglo-Dutch wars of the seventeenth century showed that capitalism could produce trade wars insofar as it was mercantilist.

The Lumières argued instead for *free-market* capitalism, including free trade.[7] They developed what is now called the opportunity-cost argument for a commercial peace. Just as a division of labor within a village makes violence among its inhabitants too costly, interdependent countries will find war too expensive (I elaborate this argument below). Montesquieu argued that trading states will not make war on one another; French physiocrats, the Prussian Kant, and various American founders built on the claim. In the nineteenth century the Manchester School elaborated the claim further. With Anglo-American writing in the early twentieth century, the thesis reaches its high point. For Norman Angell, war for the industrial powers of the world was now a "Great Illusion."[8]

Through the decades the commercial-liberal thesis has attracted skepticism and rejection. Some anti-Enlightenment thinkers rejected the thesis on normative grounds. For Adam Müller, liberal political economy might indeed lower the incidence of war, but that was precisely the problem: war was good because it could restore the unified, organic society that the economists were destroying.[9] Second-generation Marxists took things in the opposite direction, arguing that the commercial-liberal thesis got things exactly backwards: capitalist states were more prone to war owing to their inexorable competition for new targets for investment and exports.[10] The death blow to commercial liberalism, however, appeared to be dealt by realists following the two world wars of the twentieth century. The First World War took place among countries more interdependent, on some measures, than the states of Europe are even today; the Second World War took place among capitalist states and, argued realists, might have been prevented

---

[7] Hence recent attempts to recast the commercial peace as a "capitalist peace" (see below) should be understood in historical context. It seems to be free-market rather than state capitalism that is at work.

[8] Michael Howard, *War and the Liberal Conscience* (New Brunswick, NJ: Rutgers University Press, 1977); Michael W. Doyle, *Ways of War and Peace: Realism, Liberalism, Socialism* (New York: W. W. Norton, 1997).

[9] R. T. Gray, "Hypersign, Hypermoney, Hypermarket: Adam Müller's Theory of Money and Romantic Semiotics," *New Literary History* 31 (2000), 295–314. I thank Mark Henrie for directing me toward Müller.

[10] V. I. Lenin, *Imperialism, the Highest Stage of Capitalism* (London: Pluto Press, 1996).

had statesmen not clung to liberal Enlightenment dogmas about a natural harmony of interests among societies.[11]

But the commercial-liberal thesis revived in the 1970s and 1980s, owing perhaps to the peaceful and prosperous relations within the US-led Western bloc. The thesis began to branch into various versions, with some emphasizing the role of transnational actors rather than states,[12] some the preferences of 'trading states,'[13] some the importance of industrialization.[14] Notwithstanding the increasing sophistication of realist arguments that economic ties among states are inconsequential,[15] literature on commercial liberalism multiplied in the 1990s, to the point where it is again a full member of the liberal research program in IR.[16] It must therefore be taken seriously as one potential route to peace within regions.

In the remainder of this chapter I survey recent literature on three sets of questions. (1) Does economic openness or interdependence correlate to international cooperation? Is the correlation conditional? If so, upon what? (2) What is the causal relationship between interdependence and cooperation? Does interdependence produce peace? How? Or might peace produce interdependence? Or both? (3) What happens when we consider interdependence within *regions*, as opposed to pairs of states? What happens when interdependence is uneven across a region? What conditions make regional interdependence more likely? How we answer these questions and complications, in turn, affects how we think about the prospects for intraregional cooperation.

Does interdependence correlate to cooperation and peace?

Most empirical research on the commercial-liberal thesis is quantitative, and it seems that most of the findings are affirmative: states that have more economic ties tend to have fewer violent conflicts, even when

---

[11] Hans J. Morgenthau, *Scientific Man vs. Power Politics* (University of Chicago Press, 1946); E. H. Carr, *The Twenty Years' Crisis* (London: Macmillan, 1946).
[12] Robert O. Keohane and Joseph S. Nye, Jr., *Power and Interdependence: World Politics in Transition* (Boston: Little, Brown, 1977).
[13] Richard N. Rosecrance, *The Rise of the Trading State: Commerce and Conquest in the Modern World* (New York: Basic Books, 1986).
[14] John E. Mueller, *Retreat from Doomsday: The Obsolescence of Major War* (New York: Basic Books, 1989).
[15] Kenneth N. Waltz, *Theory of International Politics* (Reading, MA: Addison-Wesley, 1979); Joseph Grieco, *Cooperation among Nations* (Ithaca, NY: Cornell University Press, 1990).
[16] Moravcsik, "Taking Preferences Seriously."

other variables such as alliances, hegemony, democracy, and geographical proximity are controlled for.[17] But a number of studies yield more cautious or skeptical conclusions. Ripsman and Blanchard,[18] Beck and colleagues,[19] Green and colleagues,[20] and Goenner[21] all find no relationship between interdependence and peace, and Ward, Siverson, and Cao are skeptical as well.[22] Who is right? The differences among the quantitative studies turn in part on technical differences: how to measure interdependence or conflict, and which statistical techniques to use on the data. Behind those technical questions lie disagreements over what is actually meant by these words – interdependence and conflict – and, in a sense, how the world works.

Scholars have differed on whether trade or foreign direct investment (FDI) is a better measure of interdependence.[23] One large difficulty in using FDI is that bilateral data are scarce. Empirical studies have also employed different measures of the dependent variable, international conflict itself. Most studies use not outright war but militarized interstate disputes (MIDs), which are threats, displays, or uses of force by one state against another.[24] Using MIDs allows scholars to test if interdependence is associated with lower-level threats to use force. Some scholars argue, however, that MIDs are still not adequate to test for the putative effects of economic ties. These scholars prefer "events

[17] Bruce M. Russett and John R. Oneal, *Triangulating Peace: Democracy, Interdependence, and International Organizations* (New York: W. W. Norton, 2001); John R. Oneal, "Empirical Support for the Liberal Peace," in *Economic Interdependence and International Conflict*, ed. Edward Mansfield and Brian Pollins (Ann Arbor: University of Michigan Press, 2003), 189–206; Christopher Gelpi and Joseph Grieco, "Democracy, Interdependence, and the Sources of the Liberal Peace," *Journal of Peace Research* 45, no.1 (2008), 17–36; Erik Gartzke, "The Capitalist Peace," *American Journal of Political Science* 51, no.1 (2007), 166–91; Zeev Maoz, "The Effects of Strategic and Economic Interdependence on International Conflict across Levels of Analysis," *American Journal of Political Science* 53, no.1 (2009), 223–40.

[18] Norrin M. Ripsman and Jean-Marc F. Blanchard, "Commercial Liberalism under Fire: Evidence from 1914 and 1936," *Security Studies* 6, no.2 (1996), 4–50.

[19] Nathaniel Beck, Jonathan N. Katz, and Richard Tucker, "Taking Time Seriously: Time-Series – Cross-Section Analysis with a Binary Dependent Variable," *American Journal of Political Science* 42, no.4 (1998), 1260–288.

[20] Donald P. Green, Soo Yeon H. Kim, and David Yoon, "Dirty Pool," *International Organization* 55, no.2 (2001), 441–68.

[21] C. F. Goenner, "Uncertainty of the Liberal Peace," *Journal of Peace Research* 41, no 5. (2004), 589–605.

[22] Michael D. Ward, Randolph M. Siverson, and Xun Cao, "Disputes, Democracies, and Dependencies: A Reexamination of the Kantian Peace," *American Journal of Political Science* 51, no.3 (July 2007), 583–601.

[23] Richard Rosecrance and Peter Thompson, "Trade, Foreign Investment, and Security," *Annual Review of Political Science* 6, no.1 (2003), 377–98.

[24] Available at http://psfaculty.ucdavis.edu/zmaoz/dyadmid.html.

data," data sets that include all interactions among states, cooperative as well as conflictual. Two such sets, the Conflict and Peace Databank (COPDAB)[25] and the World Event Interaction Survey (WEIS),[26] have their advocates.[27] Thus far, the commercial-liberal thesis has weathered these tests fairly well.[28]

More complex are the disagreements over which statistical models are appropriate. Through the late 1990s researchers used models that do not take history into account. If Canada and Mexico traded at the same rate in 1990 and 1991, then, it was assumed, that is because the same conditions – factor endowments, transportation costs, and so on – must have obtained in both years; each event year may be treated as a random observation.[29] But is it not likely the case that 1991 Mexican–Canadian trade was partly caused by 1990 Mexican–Canadian trade, in the sense that relationships among firms in 1990 were maintained in 1991 because of contracts and efficiency?[30] In that case event years are not random and a statistical model that assumes they are will yield biased results.[31] Early in this controversy it appeared that modeling

[25] Principal investigator Edward P. Azar; available at www.icpsr.umich.edu/icpsrweb/ICPSR/studies/07767.

[26] Principal investigator Charles McClelland; available at www.icpsr.umich.edu/icpsrweb/ICPSR/studies/05211.

[27] Jon C. Pevehouse, "Trade and Conflict: Does Measurement Make a Difference?," in Mansfield and Pollins, eds., *Economic Interdependence and International Conflict*, 239–53; and Rafael Reuveny, "Measuring Conflict and Cooperation: An Assessment," in Mansfield and Pollins, eds., *Economic Interdependence and International Conflict*, 254–72.

[28] Regarding how to measure interdependence, see Katherine Barbieri, "Models and Measures in Trade-Conflict Research," in Mansfield and Pollins, eds., *Economic Interdependence and International Conflict*, 207–21; Erik Gartzke and Quan Li, "War, Peace, and the Invisible Hand: Positive Political Externalities of Economic Globalization," *International Studies Quarterly* 47, no.4 (2003), 561–86; Håvard Hegre, "Identifying How Trade Matters in Empirical Studies of Interstate Conflict," *Conflict Management and Peace Science* 22, no.3 (2005), 217–24; Erik Gartzke and Quan Li, "Mistaken Identity: A Reply to Hegre," *Conflict Management and Peace Science* 22, no.3 (2005), 225–33. On FDI and peace, see Mark Souva and Brandon Prins, "The Liberal Peace Revisited: The Role of Democracy, Dependence, and Development in Militarized Interstate Dispute Initiation, 1950–1999," *International Interactions* 32, no.2 (2006), 183–200.

[29] Bruce M. Russett, "Violence and Disease: Trade as a Suppressor of Conflict when Suppressors Matter," in Mansfield and Pollins, eds., *Economic Interdependence and International Conflict*, 159–74.

[30] See Paul Pierson, *Politics in Time: History, Institutions, and Social Analysis* (Princeton University Press, 2004), on "path-dependency" in social phenomena.

[31] Janet M. Box-Steffensmeier, Dan Reiter, and Christopher J. Zorn, "Temporal Dynamics and Heterogeneity in the Quantitative Study of International Conflict," in Mansfield and Pollins, eds., *Economic Interdependence and International Conflict*, 273–88.

time erased the effects of interdependence on peace,[32] but here again more recent studies have restored the original finding.[33]

It depends?

Some advocates of the commercial-liberal thesis qualify their support by claiming that the relationship is contingent. Under what conditions does interdependence correlate with peace? Gelpi and Grieco find that the relationship holds only among democracies; interdependent authoritarian states are no less likely to fall into conflict than any random set of states.[34] Dorussen distinguishes types of interdependence according to what sorts of goods are traded; he reports that interdependence is associated more strongly with peace when the goods traded are manufactured, and less strongly when the goods can easily be appropriated by force.[35] In a finding with clear implications for regions, Robst and colleagues find that the effects of trade vary with geographical distance: the closer the states, the more trade is associated with decreased conflict.[36] Some scholars argue that the relationship depends on the presence of international institutions such as preferential trade areas (PTAs, about which more below).[37]

Some scholars note that inasmuch as interdependence renders states vulnerable to the decisions of foreigners, it might sometimes heighten the chances of conflict. Copeland argues that interdependence only causes peace when states expect high levels of trade to continue; when they expect trade to diminish, violence is more likely to result.[38] Crescenzi reports that the costs of exiting an economic relationship matter – that

---

[32] Beck et al., "Taking Time Seriously." See also the debate over whether fixed-effect models should be used: Green et al., "Dirty Pool" and replies from John R. Oneal and Bruce M. Russett, "Clear and Clean: The Fixed Effects of the Liberal Peace," *International Organization* 55, no.2 (2001), 469–85 and Gary King, "Proper Nouns and Methodological Propriety: Pooling Dyads in International Relations Dyads," *International Organization* 55, no. 2 (2001), 497–507, which both conclude that fixed-effect models are inappropriate in this case.
[33] E.g., Håvard Hegre, John Oneal, and Bruce Russett, "Trade Does Promote Peace: New Simultaneous Estimates of the Reciprocal Effects of Trade and Conflict," *Journal of Peace Research*, 47, no. 6 (2010), 763–74.
[34] Gelpi and Grieco, "Democracy, Interdependence."
[35] Han Dorussen, "Heterogeneous Trade Interests and Conflict," *Journal of Conflict Resolution* 50, no.1 (2006), 87–107.
[36] John Robst, Solomon Polachek, and Yuan-Ching Chang, "Geographic Proximity, Trade, and International Conflict/Cooperation," *Conflict Management and Peace Science* 24, no.1 (2007), 1–24.
[37] Edward D. Mansfield and Jon C. Pevehouse, "Trade Blocs, Trade Flows, and International Conflict," *International Organization* 54, no.4 (2000), 775–808.
[38] Dale C. Copeland, "Economic Interdependence and War: A Theory of Trade Expectations," *International Security* 20, no.4 (1996), 5–41; Dale C. Copeland,

is, the availability of alternative trading partners: if those costs for one state exceed a particular threshold, low-level conflict increases, as states use the threat as a bargaining tool, but high-level conflict decreases (see the discussion of costly signaling in the next section).[39]

In sum, a preponderance of studies – although by no means all – agrees that interdependence is indeed associated with peace, and some scholars insist that the relationship is conditional. The disagreement over which conditions matter may be taken as a weakness of the thesis. But let us set that aside and assume that there is a significant relationship. The next question must be: is the relationship *causal*? If so, what causes what and how?

Does interdependence cause cooperation and peace?

Among those who accept at least a conditional relationship between interdependence and peace, the most common explanation is that interdependence does indeed cause cooperation and peace, and does so because states with extensive economic ties find it too costly to fight or threaten violence for fear of severing those ties.[40] Interdependence, that is, raises the opportunity costs of war.[41] The intuition is straightforward, and is stated by Norman Angell in his famous 1911 book *The Great Illusion*:

[W]ealth in the economically civilized world is founded upon credit and commercial contract (these being the outgrowth of an economic interdependence due to the increasing division of labor and greatly developed communication). If credit and commercial contract are tampered with in an attempt at confiscation, the credit-dependent wealth is undermined, and its collapse involves that of the conqueror; so that if conquest is not to be self-injurious it must respect the enemy's property, in which case it becomes economically futile. Thus the wealth of conquered territory remains in the hands of the population of such territory. When Germany annexed Alsatia, no individual German secured a single mark's worth of Alsatian property as the spoils of war. Conquest in the modern world is a process of multiplying by x, and then obtaining the original figure by dividing by x. For a modern nation to add to its territory no more adds to the wealth of the people of such nation than it would add to the wealth of Londoners if the City of London were to annex the County of Hertford.[42]

"Trade Expectations and the Outbreak of Peace: Détente 1970–74 and the End of the Cold War 1985–91," *Security Studies* 9, nos.1 and 2 (1999), 15–58.

[39] Mark J. C. Crescenzi, "Economic Exit, Interdependence, and Conflict," *Journal of Politics* 65, no.3 (2003), 809–32.

[40] Rosecrance, *Rise of the Trading State*.

[41] Jack S. Levy, "Economic Interdependence, Opportunity Costs, and Peace," in Mansfield and Pollins, eds., *Economic Interdependence and International Conflict*, 127–47.

[42] Norman Angell, *The Great Illusion: A Study of the Relation of Military Power in Nations to their Economic and Social Advantage* (New York: G. P. Putnam's Sons, 1911), x–xi.

In other words, conquest does not pay for modern interdependent states: they already make money from one another's assets via commerce and investment, and conquest would destroy those assets and impoverish them.

Angell does not argue here that interdependent states will never fight one another, only that it would be irrational for them to do so. Schumpeter makes similar arguments at roughly the same time. Commercial societies have no interest in aggression, imperialism, or war. Their citizens do best when they have equal access to foreign commerce. Only atavistic warrior castes and export monopolists have an interest in war, and their influence is bound to wane under modern conditions.[43] But, as Simmons notes more recently, a complete opportunity-cost explanation requires more fleshing out. In particular, we need to know what happens within states that allow those opportunity costs to affect foreign policy. A state whose institutions allow the median voter's preferences to win would calculate costs differently from a pluralist state in which coalitions of factions win, as would the autonomous, unitary-rational state depicted by realism.[44] Thus the opportunity costs of military conflict would only induce more international cooperation among states with particular institutions – say, liberal democracies – another point to which I will return below.

Some scholars regard the opportunity-cost mechanism as misspecified[45] or even internally inconsistent[46] because it ignores the problems that emerge when states, even those with common interests, bargain with one another. The increasingly prominent rationalist approach to conflict conceives of international relations as bargaining among unitary rational states with fixed, coherent preferences. Like any parties negotiating a settlement, bargaining states have incentives to bluff and exploit one another.[47] Interdependence does not alter these incentives. If Iran and Israel are interdependent and in some serious dispute, each

---

[43] Doyle, *Ways of War and Peace*, 244–45.

[44] Beth Simmons, "Pax Mercatoria and the Theory of the State," in Mansfield and Pollins, eds., *Economic Interdependence and International Conflict*, 31–43.

[45] James D. Morrow, "Assessing the Role of Trade as a Source of Costly Signals," in Mansfield and Pollins, eds., *Economic Interdependence and International Conflict*, 89–95; Arthur A. Stein, "Trade and Conflict: Uncertainty, Strategic Signaling, and Interstate Disputes," in Mansfield and Pollins, eds., *Economic Interdependence and International Conflict*, 111–26.

[46] Erik Gartzke, "The Classical Liberals were Just Lucky: A Few Thoughts about Interdependence and Peace," in Mansfield and Pollins, eds., *Economic Interdependence and International Conflict*, 96–110.

[47] James D. Fearon, "Rationalist Explanations for War," *International Organization* 49, no.3 (1995), 379–414; Dan Reiter, "Exploring the Bargaining Model of War," *Perspectives on Politics* 1, no.1 (2003), 27–43.

state will tend to drive a harder bargain with the other, downplaying how much it values its trade with the other in the hope that the other will capitulate. For the state-centric rationalist approach, raising the opportunity costs of war does not bring peace.

Instead, interdependence brings peace by a different mechanism: namely, by increasing the supply of costly signals among states.[48] Costly signals are moves that entail clear risks or costs; a state issuing such signals demonstrates resolve, which in turn helps the other state to know how to calibrate its response so as to minimize the prospects for war.[49] Interdependence can augment the supply of costly signals in various ways. If Iran and Israel are interdependent and have a serious dispute, Israel can impose economic sanctions on Iran at some cost to itself; Iran will then have reason to believe that Israel is determined; Iran is thus less likely to miscalculate by pushing Israel too far, and the crisis is more likely to be resolved short of war. Another way in which interdependence might increase the available costly signals is via the threat of capital flight.[50] Insofar as autonomous foreign capital responds to threats of conflict by exiting a state, Israel will be deterred from "cheap talk" or idle threats to Iran; when Israel does make a threat and risk capital flight, Iran will credit the threat and come to terms.

Yet, the charge is false that the opportunity-cost mechanism is incoherent. It is perfectly coherent as long as we assume that states are not unitary rational actors but rather arenas of political competition in which leaders want to remain in power.[51] Solingen,[52] Papayoanou,[53] Lobell,[54] and Press-Barnathan[55] all make this type of argument, disaggregating

---

[48] Erik Gartzke, Quan Li, and Charles Boehmer, "Investing in the Peace: Economic Interdependence and International Conflict," *International Organization* 55, no.2 (2001), 391–438; Morrow, "Assessing"; Stein, "Trade and Conflict"; Levy, "Economic Interdependence."

[49] Thomas C. Schelling, *The Strategy of Conflict* (Cambridge, MA: Harvard University Press, 1960); James D. Fearon, "Signaling Foreign Policy Interests: Tying Hands *versus* Sinking Costs," *Journal of Conflict Resolution* 41, no.1 (1997), 68–90.

[50] Gartzke and Li, "War, Peace, and the Invisible Hand."

[51] Giacomo Chiozza and H. E. Goemans, "International Conflict and the Tenure of Leaders: Is War Still *Ex Post* Inefficient?," *American Journal of Political Science* 48, no.3 (2004), 604–19; Moravcsik, "Taking Preferences Seriously"; John M. Owen IV, "Liberalism and Security," in *The International Studies Encyclopedia*, vol. VIII, ed. Robert A. Denemark (New York: Wiley-Blackwell, 2010), 4920–939.

[52] Etel Solingen, *Regional Orders at Century's Dawn: Global and Domestic Influences on Grand Strategy* (Princeton University Press, 1998).

[53] Paul A. Papayoanou, *Power Ties: Economic Interdependence, Balancing, and War* (Ann Arbor: University of Michigan Press, 1999).

[54] Steven E. Lobell, *The Challenge of Hegemony: Grand Strategy, Trade, and Domestic Politics* (Ann Arbor: University of Michigan Press, 2003).

[55] Galia Press-Barnathan, *The Political Economy of Transitions to Peace: A Comparative Perspective* (University of Pittsburgh Press, 2009).

the state into factions that differ according to their interests in foreign economic ties. Suppose that Israel and Iran are interdependent and transparent democracies, each domestically divided between an internationalist coalition that favors free trade and a nationalist coalition that does not. Suppose too that the first priority of leaders in both states is to remain in power. Because economic openness is more lucrative in each country if the other is open, internationalists in each have a better chance to govern if internationalists govern the other. Now suppose internationalists do govern both Iran and Israel, and the two countries fall into a serious dispute. The opportunity costs of war for the governments of each country are not only lost national wealth but also lost political power. The game is not a noncooperative one between unitary states seeking to exploit new information, but a cooperative one between two governing factions in similar domestic straits. Neither government will exploit the other's keen desire to avoid war by driving a harder bargain, because each knows that in the event of war nationalists could win the next election. Kastner argues along these lines when he points out that China and Taiwan – which have avoided war notwithstanding serious conflicts of interest – have extensive economic ties and that those ties are due to the prominence within each country of economic internationalists.[56]

A third type of mechanism is suggested by constructivism, a prominent approach to IR that emphasizes norms and culture as shapers of identity and preferences. Kant suggests a constructivist mechanism in 1795: "The spirit of commerce ... is incompatible with war."[57] Angell recognizes that it is not enough that economies be interdependent: their citizens must understand the opportunity costs of war. "It is not things which matter so much, but people's opinions about things," Angell quotes a leading statesman of his time as saying. In Angell's time, he writes, they were in the grip of the "great illusion" that aggression paid. Angell toiled so in publicizing what he regarded as the plain facts of political economy so as to demolish that illusion; until that time, England must remain fully armed against Germany.[58] In other words, in 1911 Europeans remain in the grip of false ideas, and those ideas make war possible notwithstanding its irrationality.[59] At roughly the same time, Schumpeter argues that over time capitalism makes people unwarlike. Doyle's paraphrase is apposite: "The disciplines of industry

---

[56] Scott L. Kastner, "When do Conflicting Political Relations Affect International Trade?," *Journal of Conflict Resolution* 51, no.4 (2007), 664–88.

[57] Kant, *Perpetual Peace*, First Supplement (1795).

[58] Angell, *Great Illusion*, 364–75.

[59] See also John Mueller, "Capitalism, Peace, and the Historical Movement of Ideas," *International Interactions* 36, no.2 (2010), 169–84.

and the market train people in 'economic rationalism'; the instability of industrial life necessitates calculation. Capitalist pluralism also 'individualizes' as 'subject opportunities' replace the 'immutable factors' of traditional, hierarchical society."[60] Constructivism also allows for transnational networks – in this case, of merchants, bankers, and so forth – to form and build trust across national borders.[61]

Schumpeter's emphasis on capitalism points to a recent recasting of the commercial-liberal thesis by a number of scholars: it is better to refer to a *capitalist peace*, because private property and free commerce within states are the more fundamental causes. These scholars employ various measures of capitalism – and they all have in mind free-market capitalism rather than the mercantilist capitalism of early modern England or the Netherlands – but agree that capitalism is causally prior to interdependence. No doubt challenges are forthcoming, but to date the empirical findings are robust. Proponents of a capitalist peace do differ on causal mechanisms. Mousseau looks to strong norms of contract within societies.[62] Gartzke argues that free markets and high economic development allow states better to signal resolve.[63] For McDonald, high private ownership of assets and liberal foreign economic policies tend states toward peace.[64] The future may lie with studies of a capitalist peace, but for now there is some question over whether it can be distinguished empirically from the more traditional commercial peace.[65]

Notwithstanding all of these plausible accounts about the causal mechanisms linking free commerce with peace, it might be that the causation runs the opposite way, with peace and cooperation producing international interdependence. Of course, that conflict inhibits trade is perfectly consistent with the commercial-peace thesis,[66] and indeed this causal direction is envisaged by Crucé, who writes in 1623 of free trade emerging when universal peace is established. But if the causation runs *solely* from peace to trade, and not vice versa, then the

---

[60] Doyle, *Ways of War and Peace*, 245.
[61] Hans Dorussen and Hugh Ward, "Trade Networks and the Kantian Peace," *Journal of Conflict Resolution* 47, no.1 (2010), 29–42.
[62] Michael Mousseau, "Market Prosperity, Democratic Consolidation, and Democratic Peace," *Journal of Conflict Resolution* 44, no.4 (2000), 472–507.
[63] Gartzke, "Capitalist Peace."
[64] Patrick J. McDonald, *The Invisible Hand of Peace: Capitalism, the War Machine, and International Relations Theory* (Cambridge University Press, 2009).
[65] Gerald Schneider and Nils Petter Gleditsch, "The Capitalist Peace: The Origins and Prospects of a Liberal Idea," *International Interactions* 36, no.2 (2010), 107–14. This entire issue of this journal is devoted to the capitalist peace and contains articles by some of the authors cited.
[66] Hegre, Oneal, and Russett, "Trade Does Promote Peace."

commercial-liberal thesis falls to the ground. For realism itself can allow that, when peace is assured, actors are free to become interdependent and divide labor among themselves. Indeed, for realists it is precisely the threat of war that inhibits them from interdependence. The problem, they say, is that universal peace can never be assured.

Timpone argues that the causality probably runs in both directions – interdependence causing and caused by cooperation – and that treating endogenous variables as if they were exogenous leads to biased inferences.[67] More sophisticated statistical techniques can be used to untangle causality in a relationship of this sort, but are not without their own problems. For example, if researchers can find a so-called instrumental variable that correlates with interdependence but cannot plausibly be caused by international cooperation, then that new variable may be used as a substitute for interdependence. The difficulty is in finding suitable instrumental variables for interdependence and for conflict. A number of studies have attempted to address this endogeneity question. Polachek uses simultaneous equations to find that trade decreases international conflict.[68] Polachek and Seiglie report similar results using time series data.[69] Keshk and colleagues use simultaneous equations on MID data and find that conflict inhibits trade but trade does not inhibit conflict.[70] Kim and Rousseau publish similar findings using different data and statistical techniques.[71] Hegre, Oneal, and Russett rebut these findings with their own study that affirms that the causality runs in both directions.[72]

Can commerce pacify dangerous regions?

Let us stipulate, with a preponderance of the literature, that increasing trade between two countries can help dampen violent conflict and

[67] Richard J. Timpone, "Concerns with Endogeneity in Statistical Analysis: Modeling the Interdependence *Between* Economic Ties and Conflict," in Mansfield and Pollins, eds., *Economic Interdependence and International Conflict*, 289–309.

[68] Simon W. Polachek, "Conflict and Trade," *Journal of Conflict Resolution* 24, no.1 (1980), 55–78.

[69] Simon W. Polachek and Carlos Seiglie, "Trade, Peace, and Democracy: An Analysis of Dyadic Dispute," in *Handbook of Defense Economics: Defense in a Globalized World*, vol. II, ed. Todd Sandler and Keith Hartley (Amsterdam: Elsevier, 2007), 1018–65.

[70] Omar M. G. Keshk, Brian M. Pollins, and Rafael Reuveny, "Trade Still Follows the Flag: The Primacy of Politics in a Simultaneous Model of Interdependence and International Conflict," *Journal of Politics* 66, no.4 (2004), 1155–179.

[71] Hyung Min Kim and David L. Rousseau, "The Classical Liberals were Half Right (or Half Wrong): New Tests of the 'Liberal Peace,' 1960–88," *Journal of Peace Research* 42, no.5 (2005), 523–43.

[72] Hegre, Oneal, and Russett, "Trade Does Promote Peace."

induce cooperation between them, at least under certain conditions. What causes regions to become more economically integrated? The first step to answering the question is to ask why states open themselves to economic penetration in general. The answer offered by Economics 101 – that trade raises the welfare of all states that participate in it owing to the efficiency gains from specialization – is obviously insufficient, else all (rational) states would practice free trade. Thus many scholars take politics into account in one way or another. The most common approach has been a domestic political-economy approach, sometimes called endogenous protection theory because it endogenizes the domestic effects of trade and feeds them back into trade policy. Liberalizing trade creates winners and losers within a society: the winners are those firms – owners and workers – at a comparative advantage, which export more and gain revenue when barriers to trade are lowered; the losers are those firms at a comparative disadvantage, which lose exports and revenue. Both winners and losers have a stake in foreign trade policy and will pull the government in their direction. Should the losers have enough relative political clout, they may successfully push the government into protecting them from foreign competition by raising trade barriers. Thus a political economy explanation for free trade looks to conditions under which the winners from liberalization have more sway than the losers over foreign economic policy. A great deal of literature on endogenous protection exists, with many subtleties and conditional statements.[73]

Another way to incorporate politics into international trade is to look to the international system, specifically the power environment in which states operate. Hegemonic stability theory asserts that free trade is more likely in general when a leading state, with a disproportionately large economy and (perhaps) military, makes it so. Snidal notes that there are two versions of this theory.[74] Benign hegemony obtains when the hegemon simply pays for the public goods necessary to keep free trade going by, for example, providing liquidity to the international economy, maintaining an open market for distress goods, and so on.[75]

---

[73] E.g., Mancur Olson, *The Rise and Decline of Nations: Economic Growth, Stagflation, and Social Rigidities* (New Haven, CT: Yale University Press, 1982); Helen V. Milner, *Resisting Protectionism: Global Industries and the Politics of International Trade* (Princeton University Press, 1988); Daniel Trefler, "Trade Liberalization and the Theory of Endogenous Protection: An Econometric Study of US Import Policy," *Journal of Political Economy* 101, no.1 (1993), 138–60.
[74] Duncan Snidal, "The Limits of Hegemonic Stability Theory," *International Organization* 39, no.4 (1985), 579–614.
[75] Charles Kindleberger, *The World in Depression, 1929–39* (Berkeley: University of California Press, 1986); Robert O. Keohane, "The Theory of Hegemonic Stability

Coercive hegemony obtains when the hegemon threatens, bribes, or otherwise uses its leverage to change the incentives facing smaller states so that they continue to trade freely. A coercive hegemon, for example, may threaten to withdraw access to its large market, or even security protection.[76]

An alternative international-systemic explanation for free trade derives from Waltz's neorealism. States, argue neorealists, will resist interdependence because the condition of international anarchy causes them perpetually to fear one another's relative gains.[77] They will tend to trade only with allies, states with whom they share an enemy, which is to say states whose relative gains they fear less at least in the short term.[78]

From dyads to regions

So much for pairs of states. How do *regions* – geographically proximate sets of states – become more interdependent? In this volume Amitav Acharya, Barry Buzan, John Hall, and Vincent Pouliot all discuss how regions are constructed. It is important to note that my discussion below treats regions as exogenous – that is, not constituted by interdependence. If regions are constituted by interdependence then we cannot gain an analytical foothold on the question of how interdependence might cause regional peace. Thus, following T. V. Paul's introductory chapter, I shall take regions to be functions of space, culture, and ideas rather than of interdependence.

Elsewhere in this volume Dale Copeland discusses how structural realism must be modified when we move from the international system down to regions. Just so, commercial liberalism must be refined when we aggregate *up* from dyads, or pairs of states, to regions. Interactions among three or more states are more complex than those between two states. To illustrate some of the complexities, let us consider South Asia, one of the more dangerous regions of the world owing chiefly to persistent tensions between India and Pakistan, both nuclear-armed

and Changes in the International Economic Regimes, 1967–1977," in *Change in the International System*, ed. Ole R. Holsti, Randolph M. Siverson, and Alexander L. George (Boulder, CO: Westview Press, 1980), 131–62.

[76] Stephen D. Krasner, "State Power and the Structure of International Trade," *World Politics* 28, no.3 (1976), 317–47; Robert Gilpin, *War and Change in World Politics* (Cambridge University Press, 1981).

[77] Waltz, *Theory*; Grieco, *Cooperation among Nations*.

[78] Joanne Gowa, *Allies, Adversaries, and International Trade* (Princeton University Press, 1994).

states.[79] South Asia seems to satisfy Paul's criteria for a region: its states are geographically proximate; its diversity notwithstanding, it has a common culture at least on the elite level owing in part to its history in the British Empire; and it clearly exists intersubjectively. But South Asia is not well integrated; many of the economies trade and invest hardly at all in each other. Whereas intraregional trade is 58 percent in NAFTA, 54 percent in the European Union, 25 percent in ASEAN, and 22 percent in Comesa (Eastern and Southern Africa), in South Asia it is only around 5 percent.[80] As Taneja writes, "Intraregional trade in South Asia is only 0.8 percent of GDP, one-eighth of Latin America's level and only a fraction of East Asia's nearly 27 percent of GDP."[81]

The low level of integration is not due to the absence of any regional institutions. The South Asian Association for Regional Cooperation (SAARC), comprising Pakistan, India, Sri Lanka, Bangladesh, Nepal, Bhutan, and the Maldives has existed since 1985 (and in 2007 it admitted Afghanistan). Notwithstanding a rhetorical commitment to a common identity – and real historical kinship among some of the societies stemming from British colonialism – South Asia is little more than what Italy was for Metternich: a "geographical expression."

Key to an increase in intraregional trade would be India, by far the region's largest economy. But consider just how far short of its potential trade is India's actual trade in its own region. Batra uses an augmented gravity model on data from 2000 to generate a table (Table 5.1) depicting the ratio of India's potential trade with several other SAARC countries to its actual trade. Measured according to the purchasing power parity (PPP), Indian bilateral trade with Nepal, the Maldives, and Sri Lanka is in line with gravity model predictions. But Indo-Pakistani trade should have been 52 times greater than it is. The extra trade would be worth US$6.6 billion annually.[82] India and Pakistan do trade semi-legally and illegally through third countries – mostly, it seems, through

---

[79] For evidence that globalization, or global increases in economic and social transactions, have not lessened Indo-Pakistani security tensions, see Ripsman and Paul, *Globalization and the National Security State*, 124–35.

[80] Ashok B. Sharma, "India to Play a Proactive Role in SAARC," *Financial Express* (India), November 20, 2009, www.bilaterals.org/article.php3?id_article=16333 (accessed April 3, 2010).

[81] Nisha Taneja, "India–Pakistan Trade," Indian Council for Research on International Economic Relations (ICRIER) Working Paper no. 182, June 2006. Taneja cites figures from the World Bank (2004).

[82] Amita Batra, "India's Global Trade Potential: A Gravity Model Approach," *Global Economic Review* 35 (2006), 327–61.

Table 5.1 *India's trade with SAARC countries*

Country	(P/A) PPP	(P/A) C
Pakistan	52.2	26.7
Nepal	1.3	0.8
Maldives	1.0	0.7
Sri Lanka	1.0	0.5
Bangladesh	—	—
Bhutan	—	—

Dubai – but a World Bank study in 2005 found that such informal Indo-Pakistani trade is not as high as many experts had believed.[83]

In 2000 India and Sri Lanka formally ratified a bilateral free-trade agreement, and in the ensuing decade Indo-Lankan trade has increased dramatically: "The average annual exports to India between 1995 and 1999 amounted to US$39 million. Imports from India amounted to US$509 million. In 2008, eight years after the FTA was signed, exports to India reached US$418.3 million. Imports amounted to US$3,443 million."[84]

It is now likely that growth in Indo-Lankan trade has increased total South Asian regional trade. But the Indo-Lankan agreement poses two potential problems for economic regional integration. First is the trade-diverting effect of any free-trade agreement: to some extent – how much is an empirical question – a free-trade area, by increasing the benefits of trade within itself, increases the relative costs of trade between its members and outsiders, hence lowering such trade. In other words, Indo-Lankan trade has increased but probably at some cost to both countries' trade with the rest of the world, including other South Asian countries.[85] Thus while overall South Asian trade might increase, overall Indo-Pakistani trade might decrease. Second is a possible political

[83] Shaheen Rafi Khan, Moeed Yusuf, Shahbaz Bokhari, and Shoaib Aziz, "Quantifying Informal Trade between Pakistan and India," Sustainable Development Policy Institute for the World Bank (June 28, 2005), www.sdpi.org/tkn/Quantifying%20 Informal%20Trade%20Between%20Pakistan%20and%20India.pdf (accessed April 3, 2010).

[84] Devan Daniel, "Indo–Lanka FTA is 10 Years Old," *The Island* (Sri Lanka), March 14, 2010, www.bilaterals.org/article.php3?id_article=16941 (accessed April 3, 2010).

[85] The classic explanation of the trade-diverting effects of free-trade areas is Jacob Viner, *The Customs Union Issue* (New York: Carnegie Endowment for International Peace, 1950). Viner had in mind customs unions, which are free-trade areas with a uniform tariff against imports from outside the area. The literature on trade diversion is huge; for synopses of the issues by the WTO itself see www.wto.org/english/

effect. More Indo-Lankan trade could increase India's material and social power: its material power by raising its national income, and its social power by affording it greater influence over Sri Lanka.[86] Indeed, in 2007 New Delhi urged Colombo not to buy weapons from Pakistan – that is, to increase its trade in a particular sector – leading to Pakistani charges that India was using trade to increase its hegemony over South Asia.[87]

Thus statistics on intraregional trade do not tell us much about trade over a region as a whole; such statistics might mask the existence of trading blocs or hegemony and resistance within a region. A region is more than the sum of its dyads. If we were to treat Europe as a region in 1960, we might find a high level of intraregional trade; but that aggregate figure would obscure that the "region" was divided into two trading blocs, one underwritten by the United States, the other controlled by the Soviet Union. In 1960 Europe was not a meaningful political region, and indeed was a quite dangerous continent in part because it was divided into two blocs.

What causes regional interdependence?

Presumably these are some of the reasons why the World Trade Organization (WTO) encourages regional trade agreements (RTAs) or commitments by states to reduce barriers to trade across entire regions according to mutually agreed timetables. Like other international institutions, RTAs are supposed to sustain productive interactions among states by lowering transaction costs.[88] And RTAs have indeed proliferated since the mid 1990s; as of February 2010 the WTO reported 462 in existence, the vast majority of which are (aspiring) free-trade zones.[89] Why have states come to embrace these regional trade arrangements rather than (or in addition to) bilateral ones, on the one hand, or global (sometimes called multilateral) ones, on the other? Governments have a choice over not only trade liberalization in general, but over which states or groups of states with whom to liberalize. Why do they choose

tratop_e/region_e/scope_rta_e.htm   and   www.wto.org/english/thewto_e/whatis_e/tif_e/bey1_e.htm (accessed April 3, 2010).

[86] Cf. Gowa, *Allies, Adversaries, and International Trade.*

[87] Pervaiz Iqbal Cheema, "Indian Hegemonic Tendencies," *Pakistan Observer* (June 12, 2007), http://ipripak.org/articles/newspapers/hegemonic.shtml (accessed April 3, 2010). As the article points out, Indian troops were in Sri Lanka in the late 1980s and early 1990s to help deal with Tamil separatism; Pakistani fears of Indian hegemony are not groundless.

[88] See Chapter 6 in this volume.

[89] See the WTO's website, www.wto.org/english/tratop_e/region_e/region_e.htm.

states in their own region? The domestic-level and international-level answers outlined above imply answers.

Domestic explanations

Some domestic explanations for regional interdependence look to the configuration of economic interests across states that would benefit from freer regional trade but might lose from freer global trade. Industries at a comparative disadvantage globally might nonetheless enjoy a comparative advantage within their region; their governments would thus encounter less domestic resistance to regional arrangements. Another reason why firms and governments might favor RTAs over global free trade is that the small numbers of states – that is, negotiating parties – in a region mean that RTAs may find it easier than the WTO to exclude certain goods from free trade. This in turn allows a government to buy off uncompetitive producers by exempting their products from regional free trade. It follows that just how much an RTA lowers trade barriers partly depends on the relative political leverage of various industries.[90] Some RTAs, as we shall see, actually do little to increase trade.

Another type of explanation looks to domestic institutions that channel and express those competing domestic interests. For example, in a constitutional democracy an executive that wants to liberalize foreign trade policy might be constrained by law to seek ratification or other approval from a legislature, and the legislature's districting or other rules may allow import-competing producers – for example, farmers – a great deal of sway. Mansfield, Milner, and Pevehouse argue that democracies are more likely than authoritarian states to enter regional trading arrangements, owing to democracies' being more accountable to overall social welfare; but that the number of "veto players," or domestic actors capable of derailing a trade agreement, is also consequential. As the number of veto players rises, so the willingness of a state to enter a regional arrangement decreases. These scholars also find that the depth of integration sought by a state – ranging from trade liberalization to a common external tariff, to deeper ties such as common product regulation and monetary and fiscal policy coordination – increases with democracy and decreases with the number of veto players.[91]

---

[90] Edward D. Mansfield and Helen V. Milner, "The New Wave of Regionalism," *International Organization* 53, no.3 (1999), 602–04.

[91] Edward D. Mansfield, Helen V. Milner, and Jon C. Pevehouse, "Democracy, Veto Players, and the Depth of Regional Integration," *World Economy* (2008), 67–96.

Other scholars argue that, in a given region, states with similar domestic institutions are more likely to become interdependent. Trade liberalization can imply broader policy harmonization, and institutional isomorphism can help. Conversely, states with dissimilar regimes may find coordination more difficult.[92]

International-structural explanations

Other studies look instead to the strategic environment that faces states contemplating regional liberalization. One prominent hypothesis derives from hegemonic stability theory. As American hegemony has waned since the 1970s and the United States itself has acted in a more protectionist fashion, some analysts argue, states have responded by moving toward regional blocs.[93] The prominent institutionalist school of thought, of course, doubts that waning hegemony need necessarily lead to a wave of protectionism.[94]

Mansfield and Reinhardt propose that the WTO itself creates conditions that make economic regionalism more likely. As the WTO increases in size and each individual state finds itself losing relative clout, states have an incentive to form regional blocs so as to restore some of that clout. This is balance-of-power theory applied to international trade. Regionalism is moreover endogenous, as the more RTAs form, the greater the incentive for excluded states to form their own.[95]

Finally, many scholars emphasize the relations of wealth to power in explaining regional integration. Realists argue that states seek relative rather than absolute gains, and hence they must think about the distribution of gains from any economic liberalization within their region. State A will resist free trade that could enrich neighbor B more than itself, because B could convert its income gains to military power. Hence on a regional as well as bilateral level, states are more likely to trade with allies and unlikely to trade with adversaries. It is no accident that trade between Central and Western Europe grew by leaps and bounds following the end of the Cold War.[96]

---

[92] Peter J. Katzenstein, "Introduction: Asian Regionalism in Comparative Perspective," in *Network Power: Japan and Asia*, ed. Peter J. Katzenstein and Takashi Shiraishi (Ithaca, NY: Cornell University Press, 1997), 1–44.

[93] Mansfield and Milner, "New Wave," 608–09.

[94] E.g., Robert O. Keohane, *After Hegemony: Cooperation and Discord in the World Political Economy* (Princeton University Press, 1984).

[95] Edward D. Mansfield and Eric Reinhardt, "Multilateral Determinants of Regionalism: The Effects of GATT/WTO on the Formation of Preferential Trading Agreements," *International Organization* 57, no.4 (2003), 829–62.

[96] Gowa, *Allies, Adversaries*.

A second wealth–power mechanism returns us to hegemonic stability theory. Within a group of trading states, a state less reliant on foreign economic ties will, *ceteris paribus*, have more political leverage than a more reliant state. This logic should apply to regions as well as to any group of states. Thus Prussia blocked Austrian entry into the Zollverein, the intra-German customs union, knowing that the inclusion of Austria would dilute its own disproportionately large political leverage over the union. Knowing this, a smaller state will have good reason to avoid joining an RTA in which it fears tying its fate to the goodwill of a larger, less vulnerable state.[97]

Turning our attention back to South Asia; in 2004 the SAARC formed an RTA, the South Asian Free Trade Area (SAFTA). The original SAFTA agreement required India and Pakistan, the most developed economies, to achieve full implementation by 2012; Sri Lanka, by 2013; and Bangladesh, Bhutan, the Maldives, and Nepal, by 2015.[98] But now we encounter a second problem. It is one thing to form an RTA; it is another to follow through and actually lower trade barriers.[99] It surely does not help that neither India nor Pakistan has yet ratified SAFTA. In a previous section I mentioned that RTAs might be more attractive than global free trade because it is easier to negotiate exceptional goods that can retain tariffs. SAFTA is a case in point, in that each member country has a "sensitive list" of exempted products that "represent between 13 and 25 percent of harmonized tariff lines across SAFTA countries." It is no surprise that these tend to be those products that already have the highest tariffs.[100]

Clearly, if forming an international institution such as SAFTA is insufficient to bring about regional free trade, what other conditions must be met? Scholarly literature on progress and implementation within RTAs is scarce. Concerning South Asia, business leaders, government officials, and academics have offered reasons why the region is integrating economically at such a slow pace. In 1998 India extended Most-Favored Nation (MFN) status to Pakistan, but Pakistan has yet

---

[97] Mansfield and Milner, "New Wave", 611–12.
[98] For more see www.saarc-sec.org/main.php?t=2.1.6.
[99] For an argument that preferential trade agreements do make trade more likely, see David H. Bearce, "Grasping the Commercial Liberal Peace," *International Studies Quarterly* 47, no.3 (September 2003), 347–70.
[100] Antoine Bouët, Simon Mevel, and Marcelle Thomas, "Is SAFTA Trade Creating or Trade Diverting? A Computable General Equilibrium Assessment with a Focus on Sri Lanka," International Food Policy Research Institute, Discussion Paper no. 00950 (January 2010), 1.

to reciprocate.[101] Taneja recommends that India and Pakistan – the two largest SAFTA economies and the two whose bilateral trade is least developed – take a number of steps to increase trade. These include increasing exchanges of information on one another's products and policy environments. They also include decreasing the unusually high transaction costs involved in Indo-Pakistani trade, including more highway and rail links; simplifying border-crossing procedures; a more efficient system for payments; and uninterrupted telecommunication links between the two countries.[102]

These high transaction costs point us to Ripsman's insight in this volume about the top-down nature of regional transformation: as most advocates of commercial liberalism have known well, governments must implement certain policies to bring about international interdependence. In principle, the governments of India and Pakistan could follow Taneja's advice and lower transaction costs. But they do not or cannot. The deeper causes of artificially low Indo-Pakistani trade, and hence of low South Asian interdependence, are whatever conditions inhibit trust among the states. South Asia seems stuck in a vicious cycle of interaction: more trade might well bring more cooperation, but cooperation is needed in order to increase trade. How to break out of that cycle into a virtuous one? Mansfield and Milner note that the same conditions that affect the likelihood of joining an RTA, and the depth of the RTA, should also affect how far RTA members actually liberalize trade.[103] That points us back to the conditions explored above.

One such condition that could move South Asia toward more cooperation is implied by Taliaferro in this volume: hegemony. India is the obvious regional hegemon. But evidence cited above suggests that fear of Indian hegemony is one thing that keeps Pakistan aloof from trade and cooperation with India. Presumably it would take a war victory, or some other heavy coercion, by India to bring Pakistan into line. Inasmuch as both states have nuclear weapons, the price would be high indeed.

So we are left with domestic mechanisms. One, suggested by the capitalist peace thesis, is free-market capitalism. Here the news is not encouraging: India and Pakistan have both been privatizing large

---

[101] Ravinder Singh Robin, "Chidambaram Favours Trade, Commerce with Pakistan," ANI, February 20, 2010, http://in.news.yahoo.com/139/20100220/832/tbs-chidambaram-favours-trade-commerce-w.html (accessed April 3, 2010).

[102] Taneja, "India–Pakistan Trade," 41–43.

[103] Mansfield and Milner, "New Wave", 615–16.

sectors of their economies since the 1990s,[104] but bilateral trade remains negligible. Another mechanism is democracy; this chapter has recounted a great deal of literature that links domestic self-government with interdependence and peace.[105] And indeed, a strong case can be made that the democratization of Pakistan could eventually produce sufficient bilateral trust that Indo-Pakistani cooperation – including trade – could then increase.[106] In fact, Pakistan has oscillated between more and less democratic periods since independence and partition in 1947, and during its more democratic periods – such as the first term of Benazir Bhutto's government from 1988 through 1990 – Indian elites have evinced more trust in Pakistan and bilateral relations improved.[107] More generally, Russett and Oneal argue that interdependence, democracy, and membership in international institutions are a mutually reinforcing "Kantian triangle" or virtuous cycle of interaction.[108]

Of course, sustained democracy in Pakistan, free of the threat of military takeovers, would not guarantee rapid regional integration or enhanced cooperation. Islamism has a following in some segments of Pakistani society. Even the great majority of Pakistanis who are secularists or moderate Islamists tend to favor the independence of Kashmir, a Muslim-majority state (Jammu and Kashmir) in India and flashpoint between the two countries.[109] Doubtless Indians' trust of Pakistan would also need to develop over time. The point, however, is that a stable democratic Pakistan and India would have a better chance of settling the Kashmir issue and hence launching their countries and region on to a path of sustained cooperation and trade.

Would regional interdependence work?

Finally, there remains the question of whether region-wide interdependence, once achieved, has the strong pacifying effects that bilateral

[104] Sunita Kikeri and Aishetu Fatima Kolo, "Privatization: Trends and Recent Developments," World Bank Policy Research Working Paper (November 2005), 12–15.

[105] For another see Helen V. Milner and Keiko Kubota, "Why the Move to Free Trade? Democracy and Trade Policy in the Developing Countries," *International Organization* 59, no.1 (2005), 107–43.

[106] In the Bourdeuian framework used by Vincent Pouliot in this volume, democratization could alter the agents' dispositions, disrupting current practices that mitigate against a South Asian regional identity.

[107] John M. Owen, IV, *Liberal Peace, Liberal War: American Politics and International Security* (Ithaca, NY: Cornell University Press, 1997), 222–27.

[108] Russett and Oneal, *Triangulating Peace*. See also Chapter 7 in this volume.

[109] "Indian and Pakistani Publics Show Flexibility on Kashmir," WorldPublicOpinion. org (July 16, 2008), www.worldpublicopinion.org/pipa/articles/home_page/511.php (accessed April 3, 2010).

interdependence has. Dorussen notes that most empirical work looks at dyads or bilateral relationships rather than larger groups of countries; the research thus leaves us wondering whether interdependence correlates to peace within regions, or whether the effect diminishes when the number of countries increases. His formal model shows that the pacifying effect actually increases with the number of interdependent states, but only if the states can guarantee that any war will permanently end their trade – a condition that, like all commitments, is problematic in an anarchical international system.[110] It could also be the case that, in an interdependent region comprising states A, B, and C, the opportunity costs of war between A and B are lowered if A and B both trade heavily with C. Little empirical work has been done, but Goldsmith reports that the relation of interdependence to peace varies across regions, and that it correlates strongly with peace in Asia (although democracy and international institutions do not).[111] The work of Brooks poses a challenge to the mainstream literature, but opens up a new possible route to regional peace: it is not bilateral trade but rather the internationalization of production – transnational supply chains, intrafirm trade, alliances among multinational corporations – that induces peace. Brooks argues that Mercosur, the South American trade agreement, has helped pacify relations in that region, particularly between Brazil and Argentina.[112]

Conclusion

Can economic interdependence pacify regions? Is it one path to peace in South Asia and the Middle East? Were North Korea well integrated economically with other Northeast Asian states, would the probability of war decrease? We have many theoretically grounded reasons to believe that it would, and the general claim that trade causes peace has much empirical support. In an era of globalization, when states seem to have little choice but to continue reducing their external economic barriers, this scholarly consensus carries significant and hopeful implications.

But questions remain that require harder thinking and more empirical research. Does interdependence work within regions as well as it

---

[110] Han Dorussen, "Balance of Power Revisited: A Multi-Country Model of Trade and Conflict," *Journal of Peace Research* 36, no.4 (1999), 443–62. See also Håvard Hegre, "Trade Decreases Conflict More in Multi-Actor Systems: A Comment on Dorussen," *Journal of Peace Research* 39, no.1 (2002), 109–14; Han Dorussen, "Trade and Conflict in Multi-Country Models: A Rejoinder," *Journal of Peace Research* 39, no. 1 (2002), 115–18.

[111] Benjamin E. Goldsmith, "A Liberal Peace in Asia?," *Journal of Peace Research* 44, no.1 (2007), 5–27.

[112] Brooks, *Producing Security*, especially chapter 5.

does between pairs of states? If it does, how do we get from high trade between a pair of states to high trade in an entire region? The WTO's emphasis on region-wide trade agreements (RTAs) makes sense; but it is clear that simply announcing a new clumsy abbreviation such as SAFTA may do little to increase intraregional trade. Should regional trade be built up stepwise, one dyad at a time? Or might higher Indo-Lankan trade make higher Indo-Pakistani trade less likely? Should we attend more to institutions *within* states? Can democratization make regional integration more likely? If so, how is democracy best promoted? We cannot answer all of these questions. But it is surely significant that, after some decades of dormancy, these are once again pertinent, even vital, questions.

6   Regional organizations *à la carte*: the effects of institutional elasticity

Stephanie C. Hofmann and Frédéric Mérand

Referring to the Kantian tripod, Russett and Oneal famously observed a virtuous circle whereby domestic democratic institutions, economic interdependence, and international organizations encourage peaceful relations among states.[1] As the development of the North American Free Trade Association (NAFTA), Mercado Común del Sur (Mercosur) and the European Union suggests, two of these phenomena – trade and organization – tend to cluster at the regional level. In this volume John Owen looks at economic interdependence while John Oneal addresses both economic interdependence and liberal democracy. In our chapter we borrow the lens of institutionalism to focus on the role of formal international organizations in the creation and maintenance of peaceful regional orders.

Institutionalism has many facets that variably stress different types of agency and stages of institutionalization. We pay particular attention to three of them: neoliberal institutionalism, liberal intergovernmentalism, and neofunctionalism. While we discuss and build on institutionalism, we also propose a somewhat different way of looking at the impact of institutions on regional order. We argue that, although institutionalism has much to contribute to our understanding of the role of formal organizations, there has been a tendency in this literature to look at these organizations in isolation, thus neglecting the specific properties of an *institutional architecture* (i.e., how different regional organizations are assembled together) and the impact that these properties have

The authors would like to thank all the participants at the workshop "When Regions Transform" in Montreal, May 1, 2010 and especially T. V. Paul, Peter Jones, John Oneal, and Steven Lobell for their comments and insights.

[1] These elements are integrally related. "International law and institutions are established in response to the actions of the citizens of democratic states pursuing their interests over a constantly expanding geographical area." Bruce Russett and John Oneal, *Triangulating Peace: Democracy, Interdependence, and International Organizations* (New York: W. W. Norton, 2001), 157. However, Russett and Oneal show that IGOs have an independent direct and indirect effect on peaceful relations (167, 172). See also Chapters 5 and 7 in this volume.

on regional order. Analyzed in isolation, the impact of organizations may thus have been underestimated or not appropriately appreciated. A dense web of international institutions creates differentiated multilateral cooperation, which minimizes the risk of zero-sum politics. Not all states within a region are members of the same institutions and some may have opted out of some policy domains within an institution, but if they are all entangled in a web of institutions (even to varying degrees), this increases the opportunity cost of conflict. While we do not argue that international organizations provide a better explanation of stability and peace than economic interdependence or liberal democracy, our chapter compares the European case with other world regions to illustrate the value added of factoring in the institutional architecture of a region.

Borrowing from the sociology of innovation, we use the term "institutional elasticity" to describe a regional institutional architecture that is simultaneously strong *and* flexible, that is, both stable and able to change peacefully. In plain language, elasticity refers to the tendency of a body to return to its original shape after stretching, stress, or compression – like rubber. An institutional architecture that is weak (e.g., not strongly institutionalized) will not resume its shape after a shock. This is typically the case of informal regional practices in the Persian Gulf or Asia, which break down easily because enforcement of commonly agreed rules is almost impossible. Conversely, an institutional architecture that is rigid (i.e., unable to accommodate differences) will not allow for peaceful change. Here, the case of the African Union or the Organization of American States, which are limited by strict intergovernmental rules among a large number of states, is telling. Our chapter is structured around a simple model whereby institutional strength brings order and stability to a region while institutional flexibility prevents inertia.

Comparing the European institutional architecture with other less successful parts of the world, some of which have tried to emulate specific elements of European regionalism, we argue that institutional elasticity can explain peaceful, stable, and growing interstate relations across a region. Institutional elasticity decreases the likelihood of regional transformation from stability to militarized conflicts because interstate relations are highly codified and rules are enforceable. But elasticity conversely increases the likelihood of regional transformation from simple order to durable peace. Outright bargaining failures become less likely as member states have the flexibility to opt out of certain institutionalized policy domains or they can push for their preferred policy preferences in another institution.[2] As a result, overall regional integration is facilitated. In other words, institutional elasticity produces two important conditions for the creation of a pluralistic security community, namely the possibility for dependable expectations and peaceful change.[3]

The chapter is organized as follows. First we justify our focus on Europe, which has been used as the main reference point in most institutionalist theories, and describe the continent's unique institutional architecture, which serves as a template for our model of institutional elasticity. Second, we review three major strands of institutionalism (neoliberal institutionalism, liberal intergovernmentalism, and neofunctionalism) and assess their causal model for regional formation and transformation. On that basis we argue that institutionalism is well equipped to explain order and stability in Europe, as well as the causes of variable geometry, but not the recursive effects of flexibility on regional integration. In the third section we sketch out the mechanisms of institutional strength and flexibility that have produced a supple and dynamic institutional architecture in Europe. The relative success of the EU in keeping its members at peace with each other – and integrating them further – has meant that it has served as a model for other regional integration attempts, and the EU has been actively exporting its expertise to other parts of the world. Critics bring forth that these templates have been exported without sensitivity to cultural circumstances. In the fourth section we argue that institutional elasticity in particular has not been part of such an export. We end our chapter with a discussion of the limitations of institutionalism in accounting for order and change in regional formation. In particular, we argue that institutionalism requires a better understanding of the social practices through which institutional elasticity is enacted.

Why Europe?

Europe was called a region already in Ancient Greece, not just in mythical but also in geographical terms. Its constitutive units, their attributes as well as the processes and practices linking them, however, have changed significantly over time. No longer organized around feudal or dynastic structures, Europe today consists predominantly of regionally clustered democracies, such as Central and Eastern Europe,

---

[2] The weakly institutionalized post-World War I environment, for example, allowed Germany to hide its intentions.

[3] Emanuel Adler and Michael Barnett, eds., *Security Communities* (Cambridge University Press, 1998).

Western Europe, Mediterranean Europe, and Northern Europe, which are regional subsystems whose boundaries more or less correlate with their respective entry into the EU.[4] While countries such as Norway, Switzerland, and the Ukraine will likely remain outside of the EU in the foreseeable future, Europe is probably the world region with the strongest degree of fit between institutional and geographical boundaries.[5]

Yet while Europe is often understood to be synonymous with the EU, states that qualify as European belong to organizations as diverse as the Organization for Security and Cooperation in Europe (OSCE), the Council of Europe, the European Free Trade Association (EFTA), and the North Atlantic Treaty Organization (NATO).[6] A variety of regional and international association agreements, like the European Neighborhood Policy (ENP) and Partnership for Peace (PfP), make the region densely institutionalized. The majority of these agreements are also highly codified, that is, cooperation among European states takes place through formally established organizations to whom sovereignty has been delegated to guarantee a long-lasting cooperation pattern built on reciprocity (institutional strength). Some of these institutions, like the EU and the Council of Europe, have a court that is judging over the breaches of international legislation. In the case of NATO, a mutual defense clause (Article 5) binds member states together in the most existential sense.

Europe's unusually strong degree of institutional codification and formalization is one factor that makes it the most striking example of peaceful and stable interstate relations.[7] Other regions have known economic integration but, as a growing literature suggests, economic exchanges alone do not necessarily domesticate conflict.[8] An additional

---

[4] They also form UN blocs and groups: the EU 15 and Malta are part of the Western Europe and Other Group (WEOG), the eight CEEC belong to the Eastern Europe Group (EEG), and there is the Nordic Group.

[5] Whether states such as Russia and Turkey belong to Europe, for example, is often contested on geographical and cultural grounds.

[6] As these states are also members of international organizations such as the World Bank, the United Nations, the International Monetary Fund and the World Trade Organization, this region can be considered porous. Peter J. Katzenstein, *A World of Regions: Asia and Europe in the American Imperium* (Ithaca, NY: Cornell University Press, 2005). However, many states of other regions are also members of these international organizations, and their regions develop and change differently. Hence, porosity in and of itself is less likely to explain differences across regions.

[7] Peter J. Katzenstein, "Regionalism in Comparative Perspective," *Cooperation and Conflict* 31, no. 2 (1996), 123–59; Kenneth Abbott and Duncan Snidal, "Hard and Soft Law in International Governance," *International Organization* 54, no. 3 (2000), 421–56.

[8] Owen, Chapter 5 in this volume. Also of importance is the observation that there is no single model of liberal governance.

factor, we argue, that explains Europe's peacefulness and relative stability lies in the fact that its institutional features allow for and even
encourage flexibility (also called "variable geometry" in the European
Union context), both within the European Union and between other
regional organizations. No state of the region feels forced to belong to
the entire club, and hence is more willing to invest in the policy areas
that are close to its interest. In short, while institutionalized policy
domains are highly codified, the EU is very tolerant towards member
states' divergent preferences, which prevents deadlock and lasting conflict. This flexibility, along with the strength of regional institutions, is
a key ingredient in the continuous strengthening of the European institutional architecture.

The EU has received ample attention from scholars working in the
tradition of institutionalism, both in the field of International Relations
and in European Studies. In the next section we look at three related
approaches – neoliberal institutionalism, liberal intergovernmentalism,
and neofunctionalism – to distill variables that fall into the institutionalist creed and to see how they fare in explaining the stability and relative
peacefulness of Europe. We first revisit these theories and their scope in
explaining regional formation, their stability and capacity to transform.
We show that institutionalist approaches have given ample attention
to increased interactions among member states, that is, institutional
strength. Furthermore, they can explain why incremental institutional
changes happen throughout time, while major changes in the institutional set-up require negotiation among member states. However, while
institutionalist approaches are also well equipped to address issues of
interinstitutional flexibility, they have hardly done so. We will see to
this aspect of institutionalism and regional stability and change in the
sections to follow.

Institutionalism and regional formation and maintenance

Institutionalists have in common a focus on the conditions that create
and maintain sustained cooperation among states in the form of international institutions. They share a critique of realism's emphasis on
anarchy's homogenizing effect on member state behavior and argue
that this effect is, at any rate, exaggerated.[9] Instead, states differ, not
only in geopolitical position but also in material interests brought forth

---

[9] For a realist critique of institutions, see John Mearsheimer, "The False Promise of
International Institutions," *International Security* 19, no. 3 (winter 1994/95), 5–49.

by (domestic, transnational, or national) actors. Focusing on agency and not just on (macro)structure, institutionalism is a good starting point in explaining institutional, and hence regional, stability and peace.

This approach offers analytical tools to study the reasons behind and the stability of peaceful interstate relations. Institutions induce order through the formalization of norms and rules, which lead to certainty and predictability.[10] This order facilitates the nonviolent resolution of international conflict as it encourages legal ways to argue over and try to overcome disagreements. Increasing returns to scale and institutional features such as general assets (e.g., a bureaucracy) explain the staying power of regional institutions even after states experience fundamental power shifts.[11] There is no denying that political disagreements persist even in regions where international institutions are deemed successful. And there is no denying that the effectiveness in maintaining peaceful and stable interstate relations varies across international institutions.[12] Disagreements, however, are normally articulated through the (legal and formal) channels established by institutions.

What follows is a discussion of the three main institutionalist theories, many of which have studied Europe almost exclusively. The short-cut of understanding robust and long-lasting institutions as synonymous with regions, while problematic as seen from theoretical perspectives such as constructivism, poses no problem to institutionalism, which attributes behavioral effects to regional institutions whose borders are to a certain extent depoliticized and "deculturalized." Geographically bound institutional forms are intentional creations of states that seek to maximize absolute gains for themselves. Membership in a region is understood in terms of who is sharing mutual interests in Pareto-efficient interactions and cooperation much more than who has cultural affinities with the already existing membership. Regional formations, then, are understood as expressions of the need to enable collective action based on the act of self-constraint, rather than a legacy of history or cultural bonds.

---

[10] Lisa L. Martin, "An Institutionalist View: International Institutions and State Strategies," in *International Order and the Future of World Politics*, ed. T. V. Paul and John A. Hall (Cambridge University Press 1999), 91.

[11] Celeste A. Wallander, "Institutional Assets and Adaptability: NATO after the Cold War," *International Organization* 54, no. 4 (2000), 705–35.

[12] Russett and Oneal argue convincingly that a weak security institution can be less effective in establishing peaceful relations than a strong economic international organization. Russett and Oneal, *Triangulating Peace*, 170, 194.

Neoliberal institutionalism: the state and the institutions it creates

Proponents of neoliberal institutionalism argue that based on increasing interdependence and shared mutual interest, states create mechanisms of credible information exchange and sanctioning through which they try to ensure that institutionalized policy fields are not marked by cheating, or that cheating is kept at a minimum. To minimize risk in uncertain conditions of (economic) interdependence, states promote activities with neighbors most commonly through the creation of stable, formal rules and norms. Based on these norms and rules, institutions facilitate the enforcement of agreement, consultation and coordination, the exchange of information, and the pursuit of a common cause. Once created, institutions increase the return to scale and affect cost-benefit calculations as they shape state strategies, but the fear of exploitation never vanishes. This practice of reciprocity fosters cooperation among members.[13] When these institutions become focal points for organizing cooperation, their robustness fosters longevity and they can be equated with a region preventing militarized violence.[14]

As an almost universal element of institutions, procedural norms of consultation and coordination provide states with information and makes state action predictable. A high density of institutions increases the flow of information, which reduces the benefits of bluffing. While agreement on an issue is not a necessary outcome, the likelihood of foreclosing private information in such a highly institutionalized environment is slim as well, making militarized costly conflicts a very unlikely outcome.[15] Complex interdependencies are created that are costly to break. Disagreements not only within but also across institutions are negotiated and bargained over.

Though institutions make members accountable for their actions and reduce uncertainty, international institutions are not necessarily benign structures that are equally responsive to the interests of all their member

---

[13] Robert O. Keohane, "Neoliberal Institutionalism: A Perspective on World Politics," in *International Institutions and State Power*, ed. Robert O. Keohane (Boulder, CO: Westview Press, 1989), 1–20.

[14] James A. Caporaso, "The European Union and Forms of the State: Westphalian, Regulatory or Post-Modern?," *Journal of Common Market Studies* 34, no. 1 (1996), 29–52. See also John Ikenberry, *After Victory: Institutions, Strategic Restraint, and the Rebuilding of Order after Major Wars* (Princeton University Press, 2001) and J. Joseph Hewitt and Jonathan Wilkenfeld, "Democracy and International Crises," *International Interactions* 22, no. 2 (1996), 123–42.

[15] James D. Fearon, "Rationalist Explanations for War," *International Organization* 49, no. 3 (1995), 379–414.

states. Instead, decisions that have been taken at a particular point in time can sit uneasily with some actors that join the institution at a later point. Hence, though cooperation might be Pareto-efficient, benefits might not be equally distributed.[16] Continued cooperation within one institution depends on member states' interest and the efficient functioning of institutions as each member state remains sovereign.

In this perspective, transformation and change are possible through state agency. Though scholars have not focused much on debilitating disagreements based on this approach, one can argue that dissatisfaction with institutional distributional benefits or additional cooperation and coordination problems can lead to the creation of additional institutions with similar but not identical membership. The costs of creating a new institution are not necessarily high, as uncertainty has been already reduced to a certain degree in previous institutions. Other strategies at hand are exit, exercise veto power, or try to change the institution from the inside.[17] If the institution is set up only around specific assets whose function has disappeared (such as particular military force structures), it most likely will disappear over time. If, however, general assets such as decision-making structures and consultation procedures have been created as well, institutional persistence is very likely.[18] In a deeply institutionalized environment, sunk costs as well as the permanent reduction of uncertainty and transaction costs predispose states to alter the institution rather than exit it completely.

The EU, seen from this perspective, can be explained as the result of shared economic interest among its member states. It provides a forum in which its members share reliable information and negotiate over issue areas in which they would like to reduce transaction costs to make cooperation efficient. Based on mutual reciprocity and increased interdependence, states have come to the realization that they could include further issue areas into the mix and hence even establish a European security institution.[19] Those states that are most interdependent in an issue area will push for the creation of an institutional body within the EU to coordinate their interaction within the policy field. Other states, however, that are less dependent on their neighbors in their formulation of, for example, security, immigration, commercial, or social policy will

---

[16] Martin, "Institutionalist View."
[17] Albert O. Hirschmann, *Exit, Voice and Loyalty: Responses to Decline in Firms and Organizations* (Cambridge University Press, 1970); Wallander, "Institutional Assets."
[18] Wallander, "Institutional Assets."
[19] Helga Haftendorn, Robert O. Keohane, and Celeste Wallander, eds., *Imperfect Unions: Security Institutions over Time and Space* (Oxford University Press, 1999).

either not join such an endeavor or will join it in exchange for a side payment. Interdependence is issue-specific.

This theoretical lens sees the EU as one institution among many, even if its form is highly, but unevenly, institutionalized. It also stresses that, based on issue-specific interdependence felt by all states early on, the economy is the oldest and most robustly institutionalized domain. The EU is perceived as a predominantly economic region. By bringing together their shared interests and resources, European states have created a large single market attractive to foreign trading interests. This again has as a result that EU member states can obtain greater international leverage as part of the EU than they would have by acting individually.

Liberal intergovernmentalism: societal actors, governments, bargaining

Analyzing the state, as neoliberal institutionalists do, as a unitary actor that promotes its exogenously given preferences has been unsatisfying to many scholars. In particular, Andrew Moravcsik marries pluralism with neoliberal institutionalism and bargaining theory to provide a more complex account of institutional formation. Reciprocity and credible commitments are still an important mechanism in this theory. However, to reach these commitments national preferences have to be established first and then bargained for. Before states can bargain on the international stage, their preferences are formed on the domestic level. As in neoliberal institutionalism, Moravcsik assumes rational state behavior but adds a pluralist theory of preference formation to the intergovernmentalist analysis of interstate negotiation. The costs and benefits of economic interdependence remain the primary determinants of national preferences, but they are filtered through domestic actors.

Moravcsik applies his theory to the European Union, stressing that European cooperation can only be explained with reference to general theories of international relations. As Keohane before him, Moravcsik argues that the EU can be analyzed as a successful intergovernmental organization designed to manage economic interdependence through negotiated policy coordination.[20] However, his theory is better set up to explain why some policy areas are institutionalized while others are not, and also why some states belong to the entire EU while others do

---

[20] Andrew Moravcsik, *The Choice for Europe: Social Purpose and State Power from Messina to Maastricht* (Ithaca, NY: Cornell University Press, 1998).

not. In both instances, societal interests explain forms of differentiated integration that can be characterized as institutional flexibility. Different states have different domestic structures and societal interests that are pushing to be heard by the government. Upon domestic pressures, national governments formulate their national preferences. Policies in the area of public goods mobilize little domestic pressure as they have no distributional consequences and hence are not a priority on a state's agenda when bargaining over regional cooperation. In addition, opt-outs exist to placate states where domestic groups are not in favor of certain policies that other states want to bring to the European agenda.

Change and transformation within the European region take place through a shift in state–society relations. Pressure from domestic social groups can vary and shift over time. As intergovernmental institutions are not particularly sticky, member states can reopen the bargain that had been struck by previous governments and attempt to change the institutional set-up.[21] Because institutions tend to adjust to national preferences, institutional set-ups are reversible. Seen from this perspective, the negotiations that led to the Lisbon Treaty and a resurgence of national priorities, instead of deeper integration in the field of European foreign and security policy,[22] should be examined by looking at shifting domestic coalitions in EU member states.

Neofunctionalism: transnational actors and incremental change

While the previous two approaches construe the EU and Europe as one region among many that happens to be the most integrated one in terms of interactions capacity and codification, neofunctionalism (or supranational institutionalism) has come, after more grandiose expectations, to perceive the EU as *sui generis*.[23] This theoretical approach stresses

[21] Andrew Moravcsik and Kalypso Nicolaidis, "Explaining the Treaty of Amsterdam: Interests, Influence, Institutions," *Journal of Common Market Studies* 37, no. 1 (1999), 59–85.

[22] Antonio Missiroli, "The Impact of the Lisbon Treaty on ESDP," policy briefing for the European Parliament, Policy Department External Policy (2008); available at www.statewatch.org/news/2008/feb/ep-esdp-lisbon.pdf.

[23] Ernst Haas, *The Uniting of Europe: Political, Social, and Economic Forces, 1950–1957* (Stanford University Press, 1958). The following institutionalist reconstruction follows the logic of supranationalism as outlined by Wayne Sandholtz and Alec Sweet Stone, *European Integration and Supranational Governance* (Oxford University Press, 1998) and enriched by Neil Fligstein and Alec Stone Sweet, "Constructing Polities and Markets: An Institutionalist Account of European Integration," *American Journal of Sociology* 107, no. 5 (2002), 1373–411. Supranationalism does not argue, as does neofunctionalism, that integration goes necessarily hand in hand with a shift in loyalties to a supranational institution that transcend the national.

a different set of actors pushing for the creation and maintenance of the institution: transnational and supranational actors. As these actors are not state actors but instead formed across national borders, one can speak of unintended consequences seen from a state perspective. Variables such as transnational exchange, supranational organization, and EC rule-making explain the creation and maintenance of the EU through a process of feedback loops.[24] Neofunctionalism attributes great autonomy to transnational and supranational actors, like firms, interest groups, and the European Commission. Variance across different policy domains can only be explained based on the intensity of transnational exchanges. Once the integration process has been launched, it becomes easier for supranational actors to overcome national barriers within a particular functional category.

As in other kinds of institutionalism, actors are more or less rational. The primary players are located above and below the state and the member states are responsive to them. These actors initially push their respective governments to create not only an international but also a supranational institution if and when they perceive supranational mechanisms to be more profitable. Once the institution has been created, it expands incrementally and becomes self-sustaining through the endogenous economic and political dynamic known as "spillover." Through functional (movement from sector to sector) and political (incremental shifting of expectations in response to sectoral integration) spillover, governments find themselves entrapped in unintended consequences based on previous commitments. Continued transformation is expected to happen in incremental stages that favor nominally apolitical issues such as economic problems to more political ones. Regional reinforcement and unidirectional transformation, according to this approach, happens constantly, though in small steps. Burley and Mattli, for example, show how the European Court of Justice has ruled on EC legislation and gradually penetrated into domestic law thereby overcoming national barriers to European integration.[25]

Institutional elasticity: institutional strength and flexibility

Europe is changing and transforming peacefully. Neither its institutional boundaries nor the degree and scope of cooperation between its

---

[24] Anne-Marie Burley and Walter Mattli, "Europe Before the Court: A Political Theory of Legal Integration," *International Organization* 47, no. 1 (1993), 41–76; Sandholtz and Stone Sweet, *European Integration*; Fligstein and Stone Sweet, "Constructing Polities".

[25] Burley and Mattli "Europe Before the Court."

constitutive units are fixed. Peaceful change within the region is made possible through two institutional features: institutional strength and institutional flexibility. As long as regions are able to accommodate national governments' preferences through these two features, we argue that change taking place within the regions will remain peaceful.

Institutional strength and dependable expectations

The three pathways of regional formation and transformation outlined above help to explain how the European Union has evolved over time. They all focus on the creation of formal institutions that guarantee credible commitments. Formal institutions reduce uncertainty not only among national actors but also among transnational and supranational ones. As a result, we observe the creation and development of a robust institution that rests on legal codification.[26] With the help of variants of institutionalism, the broad scope, deep institutionalization, and legal-normative underpinnings of the EU can be contrasted and explained.

All three approaches are also grounded in (more or less bounded) rational choice foundations. Their focus, however, varies with regard to primary actors as well as the structural impact of international institutions once they have been created. Neofunctionalism stresses the impact that nonstate actors can have on pushing for further cooperation in different policy areas.[27] Unintended consequences mean that state actors may be constrained by institutional rules that were designed by their predecessors, limit their choices, and eventually shape their preferences.[28] Neoliberal institutionalism and liberal intergovernmentalism nuance this impact by stressing that member states have most often than not the final say and even if supranational actors, to whom power has been delegated, can act autonomously at times, they hardly do so without previously consulting with some crucial member states first. Hence, regional cooperation evolves, but not as linearly as neofunctionalism would assume. Instead, increased cooperation happens in stops and starts; it is partial and contested. For example, the legal ground rules for a common market were put in place early on. However, the common market then was built in various stages through bargaining and negotiation processes among member states as well as incremental steps pushed by institutional actors.

[26] Katzenstein, "Regionalism in Comparative Perspective."
[27] Ernst Haas, "The 'Uniting of Europe' and the 'Uniting of Latin America,'" *Journal of Common Market Studies* 5, no. 2 (1967), 315–43.
[28] Paul Pierson, "The Path to European Integration: A Historical Institutional Analysis," *Comparative Political Studies* 29, no. 2 (1996), 123–63.

None of the institutionalist theories outlined above argues that regional cooperation unfolds uniformly across policy fields. They all can explain why some policy fields are more integrated than others, stressing either disparate state or societal preferences or the lack of a transnational lobby group. For example, institutionalists show that European governments started with the circulation of goods because they or their firms thought they could benefit from trade and thus they created strong legal provisions at the supranational level to ensure the credibility of their respective commitments. Other sectors, like social policy or security, were not tackled first or with as much energy because key state or nonstate actors could not see how they would benefit.

Institutionalists also can explain why some states are more integrated in the EU than others and why other states are tolerant of this variance. Historically, the UK has been an "awkward partner" because it remained fixated on the Atlantic Ocean rather than the Continent; on the contrary, the Benelux countries, situated at the heart of Europe and thus with strong economic interdependence, were part of every project of integration since the beginning. Based on a quasiconstitutional order, decision rules, functional scope, and the institutional balances it has created, the EU has become very successful at peacefully resolving political tensions, problems, and even conflicts.

In particular, the EU has an elaborate codification system that allows for the accommodation of states' differences by providing them with the possibility for constructive abstention, opt-out, and institutional mechanisms such as enhanced cooperation for those states that want to go further in a certain policy domain or issue area. The EU has meant and continues to mean different things to its member states.[29] The preamble to the treaty and the motto of the EU in general reads, "unity in diversity." Denmark, for example, is not part of the Common Security and Defense Policy (CSDP). Denmark and the European Council agreed in 1992 that "Denmark does not participate in the elaboration and implementation of decisions and actions of the Union which have defense implications."[30] The European Council also accepted Ireland's military neutrality early on. The United Kingdom had initially opted out of the Social Charter in 1992, which did not prevent all the other

---

[29] Jeffrey T. Checkel and Peter J. Katzenstein, eds., *European Identity* (Cambridge: Cambridge Univeristy Press, 2009); Frédéric Mérand, "Social Representations in the European Security and Defence Policy," *Cooperation and Conflict* 41, no. 2 (2006), 131–52; Stephanie C. Hofmann, "Partis politiques et institutions européennes de sécurité," in *Opinions publiques et PESD: acteurs, évolutions, positions*, ed. André Dumoulin and Philippe Manigart (Brussels: Bruylant, 2010).

[30] Danish government, www.euo.dk/emner_en/forbehold/edinburgh/.

member states from moving along. Several EU member states will probably never adopt the Euro even though it is the EU's official currency. State preferences are taken seriously – states feel understood and have ample opportunity to voice their disagreement in the institutional setting that the EU provides. The EU leaves the door open to those governments that are not inclined to join an institutional innovation at first, as for example with the Schengen agreement and the United Kingdom and Ireland. At the same time, some institutional mechanisms allow non-EU member states to join in. Again, the example of Schengen is telling. Switzerland and Iceland, though not members of the EU, have signed up to the Schengen agreement.

In sum, the EU lives up to the realization that specific policies have specific objectives. There is no one overall consistent goal (except for efficiency) and not one European identity upon which European states act.[31] With the help of institutionalism, our attention is being directed towards individual states and transnationally or supranationally organized actors that push for their preferences. Shared preferences can best be realized in a codified international organization. And the more this organization reflects every member state's needs, the more robust it is and its interaction pattern becomes synonymous with a region.

This argument travels across institutions as institutionalists can make more or less the same argument about NATO, which has outlived every expectation by transferring its general assets towards new goals. Like the EU, NATO is a robust institution based on existential solidarity, but is one that has had to accommodate reluctant partners, like France, which long reveled in its semidetached status.[32] Although increasingly empty politically, the Council of Europe has remained a normative force on the European continent through the European Court of Human Rights, one of the strongest international juridical bodies in the world.[33] Compared to these organizations, the OSCE is probably weaker, but it has managed to survive by investing in the fairly intrusive practices of border and election monitoring.[34] In sum, the individual strength of Europe's various international organizations is undoubtedly a major element in the stability of the European institutional architecture.

[31] Sophie Meunier and Kalypso Nicolaïdis, "The European Union as a Conflicted Trade Power," *Journal of European Public Policy* 13, no. 6 (2006), 906–25.

[32] Haftendorn, Keohane, and Wallander, eds., *Imperfect Unions*.

[33] Jeffrey Checkel, "Why Comply? Social Learning and European Identity Change," *International Organization* 55, no. 3 (2001), 553–88.

[34] Emanuel Adler, "Seeds of Peaceful Change: The OSCE's security community-building model," in Adler and Barnett, eds., *Security Communities*, 119–60.

Institutional flexibility and peaceful change

Europe is not only a heavily institutionalized (legalistic and formal) region. Its institutional architecture is also a unique one in that it offers an unusual degree of flexibility. This is the second dimension of institutional elasticity. Although the variable geometry of Europe is well explained by institutionalist theories, it has rarely been studied as a condition for the capacity of the European institutional architecture to generate *peaceful* change, in other words, as an independent rather than a dependent variable.

While institutionalists have devoted their attention to explaining the creation, maintenance, and transformation of international institutions (why, when, and how they matter), they have done so mostly by studying international organizations in isolation from each other. And while the EU is arguably the most robust institution in Europe, it nonetheless coexists with various international and regional organizations that are preoccupied with partially the same policy fields as the EU. For example, NATO, the OSCE, and the EU are all active in crisis management, EFTA and the EU are involved in free trade and the EU and the Council of Europe are both active in the realm of human rights and citizenship laws. In this section we argue that the flexibility of the European institutional architecture helps explain peaceful change. We identify three potentially generalizeable mechanisms of flexibility: the division of labor between regional organizations, institutional embeddedness, and forum shopping.

Division of labor   As long as a division of labor between several international institutions exists, contamination from one policy domain to another is being minimized, allowing each organization to make progress on its own terms. For example, the fact that defense issues are addressed mostly in the context of NATO prevents great powers like Russia or neutral countries like Ireland from blocking developments. Similarly, dealing with human rights in the context of the Council of Europe means that the issue can be sidelined in EU–Russia relations where they would easily hinder progress. Issues can be addressed in various forums. Although this last example may make it sound like a bad thing, division of labor also means that budgetary disputes in the EU – which can be quite harsh – do not affect EU solidarity in the OSCE. Overall, this division of labor, which is often seen as a waste of resources, contributes to preventing deadlock in the European institutional architecture.

When the EU was first conceived, in the form of the European Coal and Steel Community in 1950 and then as the Common Market in 1957, one important policy domain was already institutionalized within another institution: NATO took care of security and defense policy. At a time when security and defense policy was on everyone's mind, it was NATO that provided EU member states with a security umbrella. High politics did not have to be on the European agenda – even though some states, especially France, tried several times to change this.[35] This "outside" institutionalization of security and defense policy allowed European states to take on only a few policy domains at a time, leaving a potentially very controversial policy domain to larger organizations in which the US was very influential.

Seen from an institutionalist perspective, and especially during the Cold War, the relationship between NATO and the EU is characterized by a division of labor. Both institutions were created with different mandates, on which their efficiency would be measured. The division of labor was never formally laid out. But it left states with the option to choose where best to engage with their neighbors and as such increased interactions among states and reinforced a cooperation pattern. In the end, the complex institutional structure in Europe sets the legal parameters within which national actors can play out their preferences.

While strategic uncertainty increased with the end of the Cold War, NATO persisted thanks to its general assets, such as consultation and consensus norms anchored in its security management outlook.[36] There was no material need for the EU to transform in the same direction, though it partially did.[37] Today, the EU focuses on civilian and military crisis management in sub-Saharan Africa and Eastern Europe while NATO focuses on military crisis management in Afghanistan, but both organizations claim a legitimate right as security and defense actors in Europe and abroad.

The same division of labor can be found with the EU's Court of Justice and the Council of Europe's Court of Human Rights. Together, these two courts establish Europe's quasiconstitutional order. While the former is more intrusive in domestic litigation, the latter has allowed for an expansion of European rules beyond the EU on the basis of a binding

---

[35] Suzanne Bodenheimer, *Political Union: A Microcosm of European Politics, 1960–1966* (Leyden: A. W. Sijtoff, 1967); Jolyon Howorth, *Security and Defence Policy in the European Union* (Basingstoke: Palgrave Macmillan, 2007).
[36] Wallander, "Institutional Assets."
[37] Stephanie Hofmann, "Overlapping Institutions in the Realm of International Security: The Case of NATO and ESDP," *Perspectives on Politics* 7, no. 1 (2009), 45–52.

European Convention of Human Rights, signed by forty-seven states. Similarly, the OSCE allows for discussions and confidence-building between democratic EU states and the less savory regimes of Central Asia.

Embedded institutions   Functional specificity is only one dimension of how various international institutions within a region can relate to one another. In certain instances the entire membership of one organization can be completely embedded within another, bigger regional organization. The EU, for example, is nested in the OSCE, that is, all EU member states are also members of the OSCE. But NATO and the EU are "only" overlapping. Based on an institutionalist logic, the flexibility of the institutional architecture reinforces the mitigation of the impact of anarchy. European states are "double-secure" not only because the European Union is such a robust and deep organization but also because European states are embedded in a web of institutions that can mutually reinforce each other. No other region in the world, for example, hosts as many organizational headquarters as Europe.[38] Of course, flexibility is not without its problems. The complexity of the institutional architecture, for example, explains why there is a perceived "lack of direction" within both the EU and NATO.[39]

According to institutionalism, international organizations, and the European Union among them, are created to organize the interactions between actors efficiently. Hence, if a state is a member of various international organizations, it is in their interest to keep these organizations as closely coordinated as possible. Coordination happens especially in international organizations in which the EU is nested.[40] It takes two forms: internal coordination among EU member states and external coordination with other international organizations. The EU and its member states are represented in many international organizations. In policy areas where the European Commission has exclusive competences, it can represent the EU with one voice. Such is the case with most issues handled within the World Trade Organization and the

---

[38] Eight European countries, together with the US, lead the list of states hosting the largest number of international organization headquarters worldwide. And 44.2 percent of all members of international organizations are of European origin. *Yearbook of International Organizations* (New York: Union of International Organizations, 2006), 4 and 84.

[39] Jeffrey T. Checkel and Peter J. Katzenstein, "The Politicization of European Identities," in Checkel and Katzenstein, eds., *European Identity*, 1.

[40] Vinod K. Aggarwal, ed., *Institutional Designs for a Complex World: Bargaining, Linkages, and Nesting* (Ithaca, NY: Cornell University Press, 1998).

Food and Agriculture Organization.[41] With regard to other issue areas, the Commission either shares competences, and hence has to coordinate with member states first, or the member states themselves represent their national interest. Either way, in terms of efficiency, coordination is crucial. In issue areas that are not completely communitarized, such as health policy for example, all EU member states nonetheless coordinate before they enter the negotiation table at the World Health Organization. At the United Nations more generally, with the notable exception of the Security Council, it has become common practice by now to nominate a national representative who will represent the position of the twenty-seven EU member states in multilateral negotiations.

In the regional context the EU is present as a fairly coherent actor within the OSCE. It is not as such in the Council of Europe or NATO, where not all EU member states are embedded in the larger organizations. But Brussels entertains strong historical affinities with the Council of Europe and an institutionalized relationship with NATO. Conversely, a large majority of Allied states belong to the EU, which they have contributed to shape as an unambiguously western organization. What this implies for the regional order is that these different organizations, while competing on turf issues, strengthen each other overall and produce a security community whose robustness hinges on a dense institutional architecture of intersecting relations, loyalties, and constrained rivalries.[42]

Forum shopping Some international institutions more than others have started to occupy partially similar policy spaces, which give member states opportunities to choose among various multilateral forums. This form of flexibility between regional organizations adds an element of regime complexity, or, as it is called in EU studies, "multi-level governance."[43] After all, division of labor and multiple embeddedness are not static. They create a particular dynamic that institutionalism with its focus on state *strategies* is particularly well suited to capture: forum shopping.[44] As most institutionalists argue

[41] Stijn Billiet, "From GATT to the WTO: The Internal Struggle for External Competences in the EU," *Journal of Common Market Studies* 44, no. 5 (2006), 899–919; see also Simon Duke, "Preparing for European Diplomacy?," *Journal of Common Market Studies* 40, no. 5 (2002), 859.

[42] Andrew Cottey, *Security in the New Europe* (Basingstoke: Palgrave Macmillan, 2007).

[43] Liesbet Hooghe and Gary Marks, *Multi-level Governance and European Integration* (Lanham, MD: Rowman & Littlefield, 2001).

[44] Karen Alter and Sophie Meunier, "The Politics of International Regime Complexity Symposium," *Perspectives on Politics* 7, no. 1 (2009), 13–24.

that national divergences among states persist, even though their preferences in the institutionalized policy field might converge, being a member of more than one international institution allows states to pursue their favorite policy in the international or regional institution that suits them best. By providing options for national governments to pick and choose "their Europe" and because the EU is but one international institution that keeps these states together, each European state has managed to concede only the elements of its sovereignty to which it felt least attached.[45] Although states have become entangled, disagreements can be voiced without endangering the institutional architecture as a whole.

Conflict over interests can emerge; but this kind of conflict rarely leaves the boundaries set by legal international structures.[46] Should one international organization not fulfill a state's preferences despite efforts at coordination, that state can chose to pursue it in another. While this might weaken a single institution, its impact on the institutionalized region is more important: it questions the boundaries of the region. Not every international organization has the same membership. Instead, there are various "cores" in Europe depending on the policy domain in question. If some member states start using one institution more than another in pursuing certain policies, the boundary of the region might be reassessed. This is arguably happening in the realm of security policy. While NATO has been taking care of this policy domain for decades, with the creation of CSDP European states chose to use the latter institution more and more in the conduct of crisis management operations. This move away from transatlantic security policy formulation to European security formulation can arguably have an impact upon the regionalization of security policy in the long run.[47]

The main advantage of forum shopping from the point of view of regional formation and transformation is that it makes it less likely that states with status quo preferences (veto players, such as the UK in the EU, France in NATO, or Russia in the OSCE) will be able to grind regional developments to a halt. If the UK is not happy with the euro or Schengen, it can opt out and let the others move forward. Russia's disruptive behavior in the OSCE does not prevent important political and

---

[45] Checkel and Katzenstein, eds., *European Identity*; Anand Menon, *Europe: The State of the Union* (London: Atlantic Books, 2008).

[46] Lloyd Gruber, *Ruling the World: Power Politics and the Rise of Supranational Institutions* (Princeton University Press, 2000).

[47] In addition, Turkey uses its membership in NATO to argue that it also should be part of the EU. Russia wants to redefine the European region with its proposal for the new European security architecture.

Table 6.1 *Regional institutional architectures*

		Institutional flexibility	
		high	*low*
Institutional strength	*high*	(Western) Europe (e.g. EU, NATO, OSCE)	(Sub-Saharan) Africa (e.g. AU, ECOWAS)
	low	(South) East Asia (e.g. ASEAN, SCO)	(South) America (e.g. Mercosur, OAS)

security issues being discussed in the context of NATO or the EU, or even human rights at the Council of Europe, where Russia is a member. In general, forum shopping mitigates the zero-sum logic that characterizes single organizations by making it possible for states that want to cooperate more formally to do so, while accommodating reluctant states.

Elastic Europe in an inelastic world

To sum up so far, we have argued that the creation of a security community in the European region has been greatly helped by two specific features of the European institutional architecture: the strength of each institution, to be sure, but also the flexibility of the overall architecture. The outcome is a regional order that is both very stable in its foundations and able to change peacefully. This is what we have called institutional elasticity. While it is beyond the scope of this chapter to test this argument systematically, it is useful to compare the European case with other world regions. What we find is that although several regions have tried to emulate the EU's model, none of them has replicated the specific features of Europe's institutional architecture as a whole.

The EU remains "the world's most extensive and intensive form of regionalism."[48] Its relative success in fostering peaceful relations and economic stability has spurred regionalism worldwide.[49] In the past two

---

[48] Brigid Laffan, "The European Union: A Distinctive Model of Internationalization," *Journal of European Public Policy* 5, no. 2 (1998), 235.

[49] As others have noted, the EU is not just an exporter of its own regulator norms as part of a market opening or integration package, but also plays a role in rule-setting in other international organizations, such as the WTO. Marisa Cremona, "The Union as a Global Actor: Roles, Models and Identity," *Common Market Law Review* 41, no. 2 (2004), 553–73. See also Michael Reiterer, "Interregionalism as a New Diplomatic Tool: The EU and East Asia," *European Foreign Affairs Review* 11 (2006), 223–43.

decades globalization and the end of the Cold War have resulted in the increasing prominence of regional organizations. A host of "sub-" or "meta-"regional organizations such as the Asia-Pacific Economic Cooperation (APEC), the Association of South East Asian Nations (ASEAN) and the Closer Economic Relations Treaty (ANCERT), Mercosur, NAFTA, the Shanghai Cooperation Organization (SCO), and the Organization of African Unity (OAU, later African Union [AU]) have seen the light of day. These complemented older, more established bodies such as the Organization of American States or the Arab League.

Institutional strength and flexibility vary across these organizations. In institutionalist terms, some such as the AU and Mercosur have been framed along neofunctionalist lines with an emphasis on formal institutions that can facilitate spillover and integration. But other organizations of a more neoliberal institutionalist variety are seen as regional fora that can help member states settle their differences and work on common projects, sometimes under the tutelage of a dominant power such as the OAS or the SCO. Finally, some organizations, like NAFTA, rest on liberal intergovernmentalist foundations, with economic interest groups pushing their governments to strike advantageous bargains for them.

Organizations such as Mercosur and the AU are not only EU-inspired but also benefit from financial and expertise from the EU.[50] The EU perceives regional integration as a tool to manage social and political conflict. More importantly, the EU is fostering regional cooperation abroad in the interests of more liberal trade agreements and open economies. The push for regional integration is just the first step in establishing interregional trade and partnership agreements. Scholars observe the EU engaging in "region-building and region-to-region relationships,"[51] pursuing interregionalism.[52] The EU even has been dubbed "the patron saint of interregionalism in international economic relations."[53] For example, with Mercosur "the EU consistently tries to

---

[50] Karl Kaltenthaler and Frank Mora, "Explaining Latin American Economic Integration: The Case of MERCOSUR," *Review of International Political Economy* 9, no. 1 (2002), 71–97; Jean Grugel, "New Regionalism and Modes of Governance – Comparing US and EU Strategies in Latin America," *European Journal of International Relations* 10, no. 4 (2004), 617; Nicoletta Pirozzi, "EU Support to African Security Architecture: Funding and Training Components," Occasional Paper no. 76, European Institute for Security Studies, 2009, 1–52.

[51] Grugel, "New Regionalism," 604.

[52] Chris Patten, foreword to the EU–LAC Madrid Summit, Madrid, May 17–18, 2002; available at www.europa.eu/int/comm/world/lac.

[53] Vinod Aggarwal and Edward Fogarty, "The Limits of Interregionalism: The EU and North America," *Journal of European Integration* 27, no. 3 (2005), 327.

encourage a shift in Latin America towards balanced growth, social responsibility, and what it sees as good governance through diplomacy and foreign policy, elite interaction, policy advice, political summits and EU-sponsored seminars. The EU seeks to transfer examples of its own best practice to Latin America."[54] In sum, for the same reasons that the EU has been created, it exports its know-how and interest to other parts of the world, becoming a regional integration promoter as a mechanism for economic development and political stability while at the same time also acting according to its economic interest.[55]

The remedy to all conflicts, for institutionalists, is the development of strong institutions. In the words of former European Commission Chris Patten: "By doing this, it will generate democratic development, growing prosperity and respect for human rights. Where prosperity reigns, democracy and human rights can take root. Beyond free trade and greater prosperity, we will have to overcome the problems of poverty, injustice and exclusion."[56] But in most regions, states are not as inclined as in Europe to formalize their relations. Southeast and East Asian cooperation, for instance, remains based on informal practices of consultation and mediation that are a far cry from the EU's primacy of European law. In East Asia as in North America economic interdependence clearly dwarfs political institutionalization.[57] Some regional organizations have borrowed the very legalistic language of the EU. The African Union, for example, has created institutional structures that echo in many ways that of the EU: a Commission, a Court of Justice, a Peace and Security Council, and a pan-African Parliament. But overall, no regional institutional architecture matches the strength of the European one.

Nor can the export of formal institutional structures be automatically equated either with a region or with peace.[58] Flexibility, we argued in this chapter, is also part of the equation. While Africa and the Americas

---

[54] Grugel, "New Regionalism," 612; see also Jean Grugel, "Romancing Civil Society: European NGOs in Latin America," *Journal of Interamerican Studies and World Affairs* 42, no. 2 (2000), 87–108.

[55] Cremona, "Global Actor"; Meunier and Nicolaïdis, "Conflicted Trade Power."

[56] Chris Patten, speech to the EU – Mercosur Biregional Negotiations Committee, Brasilia, November 7, 2000; available at http://europa.eu.int/news/patten/speech 00422htm. See also European Economic and Social Council, *Opinion of the ECS on the EU's Relationship with Latin America* (Brussels: ECS, May 2002).

[57] Katzenstein, "Regionalism in Comparative Perspective"; Katzenstein, *World of Regions.*

[58] Nor does the EU engage in all parts of the world the same way, for example, economic security competition prevents the formalization of an EU–North American link and instead bilateral relationships are fostered. Aggarwal and Fogarty, "Limits of Interregionalism."

display some elements of (admittedly weaker than Europe's) strong institutionalization, their development is hindered by institutional monopolies: in Africa, the AU towers above subregional organizations that do not compete with each other (ECOWAS, SADC, etc.). The same is more or less true of the Americas where under the Organization of American States we find a variety of subregional trade agreements, like NAFTA or Mercosur. In these rigid institutional architectures there is very little room for a division of labor, multiple embeddedness, or forum shopping. As a result, regional organizations can be dominated by a single powerful state (e.g., NAFTA), taken hostage by an unsatisfied one (e.g., AU), or endangered by a local dispute (e.g., the Middle East).

In our analysis only post-World War II Europe has managed to produce an institutional architecture that is both strong and flexible. Europe's institutional architecture is strong because it is based on a set of formal-legal obligations that nation-states have contracted either in the context of the EU (economic law), the Council of Europe (human rights), the OSCE (borders), or NATO (security). And it is flexible because a dense web of international institutions (as opposed to a single regional organization) creates differentiated integration, which minimizes the risk of zero-sum politics.[59] The complex configuration of state membership allows for opt-outs that prevent deadlock and increase the opportunity cost of conflict.

By contrast, the institutional architecture of most regions is both weak and rigid. This is the case of the Middle East, for example, where the Arab League remains an impotent structure that has a poor record at accommodating religious or ideological differences. Some regions, like Southeast and East Asia, have a fairly flexible institutional architecture but it is one that consists of a web of weak institutions. Not surprisingly, this region has developed considerably toward a security community in the past decades; but its varied institutions (ASEAN, ARF, etc.) remain weak compared to Europe.[60] Other regions, like Africa or the Americas, could potentially develop more robust institutions, but they are beset by a lack of flexibility that prevents change and privileges veto players.

Conclusion: the scope of institutionalism

This chapter has offered an institutionalist explanation for Europe's peaceful stability: institutional elasticity. Not just the EU itself but also

---

[59] Russett and Oneal, *Triangulating Peace*, 161.
[60] Amitav Acharya, *Constructing a Security Community in Southeast Asia: ASEAN and the Problem of Regional Order* (London: Routledge, 2001).

the web of international organizations which European states belong to have created a differentiated integration not seen anywhere else on the regional level. Institutional elasticity in Europe has manifested itself in terms of institutional strength and institutional flexibility. These multiple cooperative forms have minimized the risk of zero-sum politics. Through institutional elasticity, credible commitments are easier to guarantee and mutual trust develops, but peaceful change is also made easier.

Despite its dense population in terms of people and states,[61] the core of Europe has been very peaceful since the end of World War II in a context of overall rising military expenditures.[62] Of course, the role of great powers like the US has certainly played a role in the stability of this regional order. But institutional factors are paramount. War has occurred in its periphery and the remedy to overcome it has been *entre autres* to spread the wings of its institutions either through membership options or association agreements, like the ENP or PfP.

Although our perspective in this chapter has concentrated on the contribution of institutionalism in explaining regional peace, the notion of institutional elasticity should lead us to look beyond formal organizations. As Peter Katzenstein points out, regions "have both material and ideational dimensions."[63] While we use the term to describe a formal institutional architecture, institutional elasticity is enacted through the practices of state and nonstate actors.[64] When EU diplomats meet NATO diplomats to discuss, say, Bosnia, the issue is not simply one of finding a Pareto-optimal solution: deeply incorporated practices of European diplomacy also matter.

Institutionalism assumes that every state has incentives to formalize its relations with its neighbors under the condition that they share common interests. However, valuing the formalization of relationships might be contextual. Generic values turn out to be culturally bound. As Robert Keohane reflected, "Institutions whose members share social values and have similar political systems – such as NATO or the European Union – are likely to be stronger than those such as the Organization for Security and Cooperation in Europe or the Association of Southeast Asian Nations, whose more diverse membership does not necessarily

---

[61] For example, Germany borders nine other countries.

[62] Mark Bromley, Paul Holtom, Sam Perlo-Freeman, and Pieter D. Wezeman, "Recent Trends in the Arms Trade," SIPRI Background Paper, 2009; available at http://books.sipri.org/files/misc/SIPRIBP0904a.pdf.

[63] Katzenstein, *World of Regions*, 10. See also Craig Parsons, *A Certain Idea of Europe* (Ithaca, NY: Cornell University Press, 2003), and Acharya's Chapter 8 in this volume.

[64] See Chapter 9 in this volume.

have the same kind of deep common interests."[65] Formalization and institutional flexibility are two values that might be bound to Europe.[66] The deeper foundations of institutional elasticity need to be explored. Most variants of institutionalism are not equipped to do so.

Next to intersubjectivity, institutionalism also does not pay enough attention to time.[67] Time matters in two important ways: first, the timing of institutional creation matters and whether the institution was the first one of its kind. The European Union was created during the Cold War, an era in which the US was preoccupied with security policy and willing to spread its peace-reassuring wings abroad. Furthermore, the EU created a precedent for formalized regional integration. "It was without historical precedent," writes Perry Anderson. "For its origins were very deliberately designed, but they were neither imitative of anything else nor total in scope; while the goals at which it aimed were not proximate but very distant. This was an entirely novel combination: a construction that was highly voluntarist, yet pragmatically piecemeal – and yet vaultingly long-range."[68] As precedent, the EU member states were open to trial and error developments. Secondly, and as the preceding quote already alludes to, not all European member states were hard-pressed to find immediate solutions to coordination problems. Instead, they were willing to see what time brought.

---

[65] Robert O. Keohane, "International Institutions: Can Interdependence Work?," *Foreign Policy* 110 (1998), 91.

[66] See Randall Stone, "The Scope of IMF Conditionality," *International Organization* 62, no. 4 (2008), 589–620 for a discussion on informal governance.

[67] Paul Pierson, *Politics in Time: History, Institutions, and Social Analysis* (Princeton University Press, 2004).

[68] Perry Anderson, "The Europe to Come," *London Review of Books*, January 25, 1996, 17.

7 Transforming regional security through liberal reforms

John R. Oneal

Transforming regions into pluralistic security communities, moving from zones of war to stable zones of peace, has assumed increasing importance as the weapons of war have become more deadly. We have been fortunate thus far. Early predictions regarding the spread of nuclear weapons proved false. Far fewer states have acquired weapons of mass destruction than was feared in the 1960s when the Nuclear Non-Proliferation Treaty was being negotiated, and there were notable cancellations of the nuclear programs of Argentina, Brazil, and South Africa. It cannot be assumed, however, that this good luck will continue, as news regarding Iran and North Korea indicates; and the war centered on the Congo shows that even conventional weaponry can be terribly lethal. It is important, therefore, to identify means of preventing military conflict. The end of the Cold War provides an opportune time to address this issue.

In this chapter I use the liberal-realist model (LRM) of armed interstate conflict to identify the most promising means for transforming regions into zones of peace. The LRM is derived from social scientific research conducted over the past twenty years on the causes of militarized disputes and war. Earlier quantitative investigations proved disappointing. Studies in the 1970s of neorealist claims regarding the effect of the distribution of capabilities among the major powers were contradictory, and research on the greater peacefulness of democratic states was inconclusive. Many despaired of applying scientific methods to the study of international politics. There has been rapid progress in the last two decades, however, in statistical research on the causes of war by examining the behavior of many pairs of states through time. Stuart Bremer's work with the LRM was path-breaking.[1] Here, following Bremer's lead, I analyze time series for over 12,000 pairs of states, 1885–2001, using the same techniques employed by medical

---

[1] Stuart Bremer, "Dangerous Dyads," *Journal of Conflict Resolution* 36, no. 2 (June 1992), 309–41.

epidemiologists. The results confirm that democracy and economic interdependence have important pacific benefits. Major elements of realism are also supported, but they do not provide a path to peace. Finally, I show that alternative explanations of interstate conflict – the clash of civilizations and hegemonic stability theory – are not consistent with systematic analyses of world history over the past one hundred years and more. The best hope for world peace is to continue to encourage liberal reforms: the institution of democracy and nations' participation in the global economy. Fortunately, globalization has rapidly advanced in recent decades, and the prospects for continued expansion look good.

The first section below recounts how research on armed conflict using pairs of states observed through time grew out of earlier efforts to investigate scientifically the causes of war. The liberal-realist model, refined in the course of numerous studies since Bremer's article on "dangerous dyads," is presented in the second section. There the model's variables are defined and the sources of data identified. I present the results of my statistical analyses with the LRM in the third section. Here the practical importance of the liberal prescriptions for peace is shown by estimating the probability of conflict for pairs of states with different, theoretically important characteristics. In the fourth section I address specifically the potential for creating regional security through liberal political and economic reforms and contrast their promise with the bleak prospects for peace based on realist principles. Next, I reconsider the contributions of alternative theories of war and peace that emphasize the importance of culture and regions or the influence of the global system instead of states' bilateral relations or their individual characteristics. These alternatives, too, provide little hope for building a more peaceful world. A concluding section addresses the practical implications of the social science.

Developing a science of interstate conflict

For centuries prior to the First World War international relations was the intellectual realm of philosophers, historians, and legal scholars who worked within the humanistic tradition of belles-lettres. After the carnage of the Great War, idealists presented moralistic arguments that inspired efforts to abolish war by international agreement, an effort that culminated in the League of Nations and the Kellogg-Briand Treaty, which banned war as an instrument of national policy. The failure of these legalistic initiatives led to the realist reaction, most notably in the publication of E. H. Carr's *The Twenty Years' Crisis* in 1939 and the many editions of *Politics Among Nations* by Hans Morgenthau beginning in 1948.[2] The realists dominated the study of international relations for many years in the post-World War II period. Over time, however, it became apparent that they could not agree on fundamentals. Does the uncertainty created by an equal balance of power make violence more or less likely? Is it possible to generalize about the influence of national capabilities on interstate conflict, or even measure the power of nations? The realists were undecided.

During the "behavioral revolution" in political science, efforts were begun to resolve such questions using statistical analyses of systematic-ally collected data rather than detailed historical accounts of individual wars. The adoption of social scientific techniques had succeeded in the 1960s in studies of voting, where data were readily available, and public opinion, where it could be easily created. The revolution began in the United States, due perhaps to the respect for science in academia and the popular culture; but the social scientific approach in international rela-tions eventually spread to Britain, the Nordic countries, and Germany. Research published in the *American Political Science Review*, the leading general-interest journal in the field, provides a useful barometer of the new paradigm's success. In the 1950s approximately 10 percent of the journal's articles featured quantitative tests or formal, mathematically derived theories. By the 1980s three-quarters of the articles were sci-entifically oriented.

The behavioral revolution lagged for many years in international and comparative politics because of the shortage of data. J. David Singer and others of the Correlates of War (COW) project sought to remedy this situation by collecting information about all wars involving the major powers after 1815 and the national capabilities of those states. With these data they could assess the effect of the distribution of power on the likelihood of war. COW researchers were also interested in alli-ances because of their influence on the balance of power and for any direct effect they might have on interstate conflict. In keeping with realist thinking at the time, COW researchers focused on the inter-national system, emphasizing the structural conditions within which states act rather than the characteristics of the individual countries – their domestic political institutions, for example. This was consistent with the neorealist view advanced most famously by Kenneth Waltz

[2] Edward Hallett Carr, *The Twenty Years' Crisis, 1919–1939* (New York: Macmillan, 1939); Hans Morgenthau, *Politics Among Nations: The Struggle for Power and Peace* (New York: Alfred A. Knopf, 1948).

that, in an anarchic world, all nations must act according to the dictates of realpolitik.[3]

The most important early publication of the behavioral revolution in international relations was Singer, Bremer, and John Stuckey's 1972 study correlating the distribution of power among the largest states with the incidence of warfare.[4] Researchers in the Correlates of War project measured national capabilities along three dimensions, with two indicators for each: the *demographic* (total population and the number of people living in cities), *industrial* (energy consumption, in coal-ton equivalents, and iron or steel production), and *military* (total expenditures and the number of armed forces personnel). The demographic and industrial dimensions indicate the potential power of a nation – what it could mobilize if determined – while the third dimension represents immediately available military forces. Lacking theoretical guidance regarding their relative importance, Singer, Bremer, and Stuckey weighted the six measures equally in calculating the COW Composite Index of National Capability (CINC).

While their data were far better than any previously available, the results of this early systematic study of the nineteenth and twentieth centuries were disappointing. A relatively unequal distribution of power among the great powers was associated with more nation months of war in the nineteenth century, but with peace in the twentieth. Moreover, Singer, Bremer, and Stuckey cautioned that, to avoid the ecological fallacy, they could draw no inferences as to which particular nations fought. This was a consequence of their analyzing data at the systemic level of analysis, using measures of power and war in each historical period that were averages for the major powers as a group.

In succeeding years a number of social scientists sought to determine whether democracies are more peaceful than nondemocratic states as the classical liberals predicted. In contrast to research by the Correlates of War project, investigators interested in the influence of national political regimes on the incidence of interstate conflict adopted the individual country as the unit of analysis, not the international system, analyzing statistically the behavior of a large number of countries over time. Again, the results were disappointing. There was no consist-

---

[3] Kenneth N. Waltz, *Man, the State, and War* (New York: Columbia University Press, 1954); Kenneth N. Waltz, *Theory of International Politics* (Reading, MA: Addison-Wesley, 1979).

[4] J. David Singer, Stuart A. Bremer, and John Stuckey, "Capability Distribution, Uncertainty, and Major Power War, 1820–1965," in *Peace, War, and Numbers*, ed. Bruce Russett (Beverly Hills, CA: Sage, 1972), 19–48.

ent relationship between democracy and war.[5] Many concluded that international politics was simply not amenable to quantitative study.

Progress through the analysis of dyadic time series

In recent years, however, there has been rapid progress in the study of war and peace through the analysis of many pairs of states observed through time. Early works by Solomon Polachek (1980) and Bueno de Mesquita (1981) were important, but it was Bremer's research using the liberal-realist model that generated the most new research.[6] In this approach each observation captures the state of relations between two countries in a year, a "dyad year": either there is military conflict in a particular year or not. The explanatory variables, too, are measured annually in order to identify correlates of war, which theory indicates are causally related to the incidence of violence. Dyadic analyses allow researchers to address a question of great interest to scientists and policy makers alike: which states are prone to fight? To answer this question, I use the same statistical technique used in many epidemiological studies of heart attack, stroke, and cancer. Everyone has read that smoking a pack of cigarettes a day increases the risk of lung cancer dramatically. With the same statistical methods, we can estimate the effect on the likelihood of armed interstate conflict of democracy, economic interdependence, the balance of power, and so forth.

One important advantage of the dyadic approach is its flexibility. Statistical analyses of the behavior of pairs of states through time can incorporate as explanatory factors the characteristics of states, dyadic (or bilateral) variables, or the properties of regions or the international system. Research at the state level of analysis, such as early work on the democratic peace, can accommodate national characteristics; but it has great difficulty addressing inherently relational factors – the existence of an alliance or the bilateral balance of power, for example. The dyadic model can accommodate both national and dyadic variables; and when assessing the influence of regional factors or the international system, it avoids the ecological fallacy that plagued early COW studies. In addition

---

[5] Steve Chan, "Mirror, Mirror on the Wall ... Are the Freer Countries More Pacific?," *Journal of Conflict Research* 28, no. 4 (December 1984), 617–48; Erich Weede, "Democracy and War Involvement," *Journal of Conflict Resolution* 28, no. 4 (December 1984), 649–64; William K. Domke, *War and the Changing Global System* (New Haven, CT: Yale University Press, 1989).

[6] Solomon W. Polachek, "Conflict and Trade," *Journal of Conflict Resolution* 24, no. 1 (March 1980), 55–78; Bruce Bueno de Mesquita, *The War Trap* (New Haven, CT: Yale University Press, 1981); Bremer, "Dangerous Dyads."

to its flexibility, the dyadic approach is powerful statistically. There are more than 400,000 observations (dyad years) involving more than 12,000 pairs of states, 1885–2001, over which to generalize. To put so much information in prose would fill several hundred books. Only statistical techniques can possibly be used to summarize such voluminous data.

The liberal-realist model used below includes elements from the two major schools of international relations that are amenable to social-scientific investigation: the liberal or Kantian, in which the character of states' political regimes, their economic relations, and involvement in international organizations are thought to influence international behavior, and the realist school with its emphasis on the absolute and relative power of nations and their alliances. Everyone recognizes that geographic considerations are important. The wide acceptance of the LRM is indicated by the fact that nine of the ten authors most frequently cited in the academic literature on armed interstate conflict, 1996–2006, have used the model extensively.[7]

The LRM is designed to explain (or predict) the state of relations (armed conflict or peace) of two countries in a year. Systematic examination of a large number of cases with the LRM can provide, for example, an estimate of the probability of a conflict between the United States and the Soviet Union or India and Pakistan in particular years. The LRM can also be used, as we will see, to predict the likelihood of interstate violence for hypothetical cases of theoretical interest. In the analyses reported below, I focus on fatal militarized interstate disputes (MIDs), events involving a use of force by one nation against another that results in the death of at least one combatant. Fatal disputes are more numerous than large wars, which increases the precision of the statistical estimates, but are of greater seriousness than militarized disputes that involve just threats or demonstrations of force, which are more apt to involve mere bluffing. Though these characteristics of fatal disputes recommend their use, previous research indicates that results are very similar across the three levels of violence: all militarized disputes, fatal disputes, and wars.[8] The analysis of fatal MIDs also protects against the bias that is likely to come from under-reporting of minor incidents of interstate conflict in remote regions.

In the tests below, liberal theory is represented by measures of the political character of the two states, assessed along the autocracy–democracy

---

[7] Thomson Reuters, "Special Topics: Armed Conflict," (2006); available at http://esi-topics.com/armed-conflict/authors/b1a.html (accessed 02/15/2010).

[8] John R. Oneal and Bruce Russett, "Rule of Three, Let it Be? When More Really is Better," *Conflict Management and Peace Science* 22, no. 4 (September 2005), 293–310.

continuum, and the degree to which the countries are economically interdependent. The latest Polity data provide independent estimates of the political character of national regimes.[9] Including the higher and lower democracy scores in the regression model allows the likelihood of conflict to be estimated for dyads composed of two democracies, two autocracies, and one of each. Interdependence is measured using the economic importance of bilateral trade relative to the countries' gross domestic products (GDP). These data are primarily from the International Monetary Fund and the World Bank.[10] Including the lower trade-to-GDP in the model captures the disincentive for conflict of commerce on the less constrained state.

Jean-Marc Blanchard and Norrin Ripsman have identified ways to refine this trade-based measure of interdependence, but their suggestions are not practical for analyses involving hundreds of thousands of cases.[11] Fortunately, others have shown that financial interdependence, as indicated by foreign direct investments, also reduces the risk of interstate conflict, increasing confidence that the trade-based measure does not produce misleading results.[12] In addition, the independent benefit of dense trade networks involving third parties, over and above the pacific consequences of bilateral commerce, has been confirmed, as Blanchard and Ripsman recommended.[13] Quantitative analyses that consider the composition of trade have not been done because of the scarcity of these data, but there is no reason to believe that an aggregate measure of trade, based largely on prices set by markets, is misleading over the large numbers of cases analyzed below.[14]

Most previous research indicates that democracy and economic interdependence have important, robust pacific benefits. The independent contribution of international organizations (IOs), the third element

[9] Keith Jaggers and Ted Robert Gurr, "Tracking Democracy's Third Wave with the Polity III Data," *Journal of Peace Research* 32, no. 4 (November 1995), 469–82.

[10] Kristian S. Gleditsch, "Expanded Trade and GDP Data," *Journal of Conflict Resolution* 46, no. 5 (October 2002), 712–24. See Bruce Russett and John R. Oneal, *Triangulating Peace: Democracy, Interdependence, and International Organizations* (New York: W. W. Norton, 2001), chapter 4 for the sources of economic data prior to 1950.

[11] Jean-Marc F. Blanchard and Norrin M. Ripsman, "Rethinking Sensitivity Interdependence: Assessing the Trade, Financial, and Monetary Links Between States," *International Interactions* 27, no. 2 (2001), 95–128.

[12] Margit Bussmann, "Foreign Direct Investment and Militarized International Conflict," *Journal of Peace Research* 47, no. 2 (March 2010), 143–53.

[13] Zeev Maoz, "Network Polarization, Network Interdependence, and International Conflict, 1816–2002," *Journal of Peace Research* 43, no. 4 (July 2006), 391–411; Han Dorussen and Hugh Ward, "Trade Networks and the Kantian Peace," *Journal of Peace Research* 47, no. 1 (January 2010), 29–42.

[14] See the review of the literature on the commercial peace by John Owen, Chapter 5 in this volume.

of the Kantian peace, is less certain; but recent work with improved measures of institutional effectiveness provides important evidence for the beneficial role IOs play in managing the process of globalization. Because this research is ongoing, the influence of IOs is not included in the analyses reported below.[15]

In keeping with realist thought, I also incorporate in the LRM model two variables that capture the influence of states' capabilities on the risk of violence: (1) a measure of the balance of power between the two states in each dyad, and (2) an indicator of their ability to project their military capabilities at a distance. Recall that the Correlates of War project measured power along demographic, industrial, and military dimensions. The balance of power is calculated by dividing the larger state's composite index of national capability by the sum of the dyadic members' capability scores. This approximates the probability that the more powerful state would win a military contest.

I incorporate power-projection capabilities into the LRM using COW's annual assessment of the larger state's immediately available and potential military power. It represents the ability of the larger state – the one less constrained – to act at a distance with military force. With the addition of a continuous measure of the capital-to-capital distance separating the countries and a binary indicator of geographic contiguity, essential geographical factors are included.[16] I also consider each dyad's historical experience of violence, measured for each observation by the years of peace since the states' last fatal militarized interstate dispute.[17] Finally, there is a statistical control for the number of states in the international system in each year so that the rapid increase after 1960 does not bias the analyses.[18]

---

[15] Charles Boehmer, Erik Gartzke, and Timothy Nordstrom, "Do Intergovernmental Organizations Promote Peace?," *World Politics* 57, no. 1 (2004), 1–38; Jon Pevehouse and Bruce Russett, "Democratic International Organizations Promote Peace," *Journal of Politics* 60, no. 4 (October 2006), 969–1000; Elizabeth Fausett and Thomas J. Volgy, "Intergovernmental Organizations (IGOs) and Interstate Conflict: Parsing Out IGO Effects for Alternative Dimensions of Conflict in Postcommunist Space," *International Studies Quarterly* 54, no. 1 (March 2010), 79–102. The importance of "variable architecture" in making international organizations effective should also be considered. See Chapter 6 in this volume.
[16] Kenneth E. Boulding, *Conflict and Defense: A General Theory* (New York: Harper & Row, 1962).
[17] Nathaniel Beck, Jonathan N. Katz, and Richard Tucker, "Beyond Ordinary Logic: Taking Time Seriously in Binary-Time-Series-Cross-Section Models," *American Journal of Political Science* 42, no. 4 (October 1998), 1260–288.
[18] Håvard Hegre, "Gravitating Toward War: Preponderance may Pacify but Power Kills," *Journal of Conflict Resolution* 52, no. 4 (August 2008), 566–89. The COW data used are from the most recent version of EUGene. D. Scott Bennett and Allan

Analyses of fatal militarized disputes, 1885–2001

In the first column of Table 7.1 are the estimated coefficients of the standard liberal-realist model for the onset of a fatal militarized inter-state dispute, 1885–2001. The pooled time series of over 12,000 pairs of states are analyzed using logistic regression, the same statistical technique used in medical epidemiology. There are slightly more than 430,000 observations (dyad years).[19] The analysis is limited to countries with populations greater than 500,000. Only the onset of a dispute is considered; subsequent years of a dispute are excluded.[20] The model "predicts" the probability of fatal armed conflict for a pair of states in one year from values for the liberal and realist variables measured in the previous year. Lagging the explanatory variables eliminates the recipro-cal effects of a dispute.

The results reported in column 1 are consistent with the great major-ity of previous research reports where the liberal-realist model has been used: (1) Two democracies are very peaceful, two autocracies less so, and mixed pairs of states fight the most. Wars are less likely when those who pay the price decide whether they will be fought, while ideological differences fuel autocracy-democracy conflicts. The animosity of these political rivals obscured the peacefulness of democratic pairs in many early studies using the state as the unit of analysis. (2) Economic inter-dependence reduces conflict because countries are reluctant to kill the goose laying golden eggs. It permits costly signals to be sent, which reduces uncertainty and helps states avoid military conflict. (3) A pre-ponderance of power increases the prospects for peace, while a bal-ance of capabilities is more dangerous. Privately held information about national capabilities is less important when there is a clear imbalance of power, decreasing the risk of miscalculation and war.[21] (4) But large

---

C. Stam, III, http://eugenesoftware.org (accessed 02/15/2010); Bennett and Stam, "*EUGene*: A Conceptual Manual," *International Interactions* 26 (2000), 179–204. For details regarding the variables and sources of data, see Håvard Hegre, John R. Oneal, and Bruce Russett, "Trade Does Promote Peace: New Simultaneous Estimates of the Reciprocal Effects of Trade and Conflict," *Journal of Peace Research* 47, no. 6 (November 2010), 763–74.

[19] The initiation of conflict, rather than its incidence, is analyzed with directed dyads, i.e., both US–USSR-1950 and USSR–US-1950 would be included in the data. See, for example, John R. Oneal and Jaroslav Tir, "Does the Diversionary Use of Force Threaten the Democratic Peace? Assessing the Effect of Economic Growth on Interstate Conflict, 1921–2001," *International Studies Quarterly* 50, no. 4 (2006), 755–79.

[20] Beck, Katz, and Tucker, "Beyond Ordinary Logic."

[21] James D. Fearon, "Rationalist Explanations for War," *International Organization* 49, no. 3 (summer 1995), 379–414.

Table 7.1 *Estimated coefficients for the liberal-realist model, onset of fatal militarized interstate disputes, 1885–2001*

Lower democracy score$_{ij,t}$	ß	−.097***
	S.E.$_{.ß}$	.018
Higher democracy score$_{ij,t}$		.040***
		.011
Lower trade-to-GDP ratio$_{ij,t}$		−86.6***
		21.4
Allies$_{ij,t}$		−.296
		.191
Larger probability of winning$_{ij,t}$		−2.67***
		.42
Contiguity$_{ij,t}$		1.80***
		.26
Distance$_{ij,t}$ (ln)		−.670***
		.087
Larger CINC$_{ij,t}$		14.1***
		1.2
Constant$_{ij,t}$		1.30
		.75
Wald Chi^2 (df)		1551.15(13)
p of Chi^2		.0001
Pseudo-R^2		.28
N		430,125

* p < .05; ** p < .01; *** p < .001 (two-tailed test). The estimated coefficients of the statistical controls (the years-of-peace and its cubic splines and the logarithm of the number of states in the international system) are not reported to save space; all are statistically significant.

powers are prone to fight *ceteris paribus* because their interests are widespread and their capabilities for defending and promoting them are substantial. I consider the net effect of these two channels through which size and power influence the risk of conflict below. (5) An alliance has only a weak effect in reducing the likelihood of violence. This indicates the importance of liberal, rather than realist, theory: good economic relations provide greater assurance of peace than does an explicit security agreement. (6) Not surprisingly, conflict is much more likely for states that are geographically proximate, especially those that share a border. (7) Countries that have fought recently are likely to fight again. On these seven points, there is widespread scientific agreement.

Table 7.2 *Estimated probability of the onset of a fatal militarized dispute, selected pairs of states: based on the estimated coefficients in Table 7.1*

United States–Soviet Union, 1954	25.7%
United States–Soviet Union, 1965	46.7
United States–Soviet Union, 1991	3.8
United States–Soviet Union, 2000	1.1
United States–Canada, 2000	<0.1%
France–Germany, 1938	8.3%
France–Germany, 1999	<0.1
India–China, 1951	18.8%
India–China, 1999	4.9

Specific historical examples, presented in Table 7.2, illustrate the plausibility of the model's predictions. Based on historical values of the explanatory variables for 1953, the probability of a fatal militarized dispute between the United States and the USSR in 1954 is estimated to have been 26 percent. By 1965 the risk of a serious incident for this pair of states peaked at 47 percent. With the collapse of the Soviet Union and the end of the Warsaw Pact, the probability fell to 4 percent in 1991. By 2000 the prospects for peace had further improved. The LRM estimates that the probability of a fatal MID between the former Cold War adversaries was about 1 percent that year. This represents a dramatic improvement, of course; but as one would expect, the risk of conflict between the US and Russia was still much greater than for the United States and Canada, a mere 0.1 percent in 2000.

The success of reconstruction in Europe after World War II and the development of the European Union is shown in the second set of comparisons, where the estimated risk of conflict between Germany and France is shown to have fallen from 8.3 percent in 1939 to less than 0.1 percent in 2001. This dramatic reduction in the risk of violence between these great powers of historic enmity reflects the democratization of Germany and the growth of European economic integration. The improvement in relations between India and China is also documented in Table 7.2.

These comparisons indicate that the LRM captures important aspects of the causes of war. The estimated values are consistent with common understandings of recent historical developments. The prospects for peace do seem much greater in later years for the US and Russia, and for Germany and France, than earlier. Comparisons

Table 7.3 *Annual probabilities of the onset of a fatal militarized dispute, 1885–2001: based on the estimated coefficients in Table 7.1*

	Probability, in percent	Change from baseline
1. Two large states (90th percentile), one democracy and one autocracy, no trade, contiguous, distance at 10th percentile, not allies, three years of peace	10.5	0
2. Two autocracies	5.0	−52%
3. Two democracies	1.8	−83%
4. Trade-to-GDP ratio at 90th percentile for contiguous pairs	3.8	−63%
5. Two democracies and trade-to-GDP ratio at 90th percentile	0.6	−94%
6. Two small states (10th percentile)	8.1	−22%
7. One large and one small state	3.1	−70%
8. Allies	8.2	−21%

Row 1 is the baseline rate. Rows 2–8 indicate the change in the baseline conditions, *ceteris paribus*.

across dyads are more doubtful, however. Was the probability of superpower conflict during the Cold War really so much greater than the risk for Germany and France in 1939? In addition, none of the predictions of the LRM exceeds 50 percent. Clearly, there is much we do not know about the causes (and especially the timing) of interstate conflict.

If the LRM produces plausible historical estimates, we can use it with confidence to clarify the contributions that various theoretical factors make to the risk of dyadic conflict. The statistical procedures developed by Gary King, Mike Tomz, and Jason Wittenberg are helpful in this regard.[22] In the first line in Table 7.3 I present a baseline estimation of the probability of a fatal MID for two large states, one a democracy and the other an autocracy, with no trade, that share a border, have proximate capitals, and are not allied.[23] The annual risk of a fatal dispute for this especially "dangerous dyad" is 10.5 percent and the

[22] Gary King, Michael Tomz, and Jason Wittenberg, "Making the Most of Statistical Analyses: Improving Interpretation and Presentation," *American Journal of Political Science* 44, no. 2 (April 2000), 347–61.

[23] Specifically, the states are at the 90th percentile of the system-wide CINC scores, at the 10th percentile in capital-to-capital distance, and there were three years since the last fatal MID.

standard error of the estimate is ±1.8 percent. Making both states autocratic reduces the probability to 5.0 percent, but the danger of a fatal MID declines by over eighty percent to 1.8 percent if both states are made democratic. This clearly indicates the significance of the *democratic* peace. The mere similarity of political regimes does not account for the remarkable peacefulness enjoyed by democracies. Economic interdependence, too, has a powerful pacific benefit. The probability of conflict drops from 10.5 percent in the baseline case to 3.8 percent if the referent pair of states has strong trading ties but all other characteristics remain at the values for the dangerous dyad.[24] If the states are both democratic and interdependent, the risk of a fatal MID is only 0.6 percent, *ceteris paribus*, a reduction of 94 percent from the baseline rate. Kant and the other classical liberals were right: the political and economic institutions they recommended have important benefits for world peace. Consequently, the spread of democracy and the growth of the international economy that characterize the contemporary process of globalization are encouraging.

Changes in the power of the dyadic members also materially affect the probability of interstate violence, as shown in lines 6–7 in Table 7.3. Those estimates confirm that a preponderance of power, not a balance, increases the likelihood of peace. The annual probability that the two large states of the dangerous dyad will fight is 10.5 percent. The risk of violence is still 8.1 percent if both states are small (the two countries being at the 10th percentile in terms of national capability rather than the 90th) and the balance of power remains 50–50. It is 3.1 percent if one country is large and the other small. Thus, the net effect of the two realist variables, the balance of power and states' ability to project their capabilities abroad, is that the risk of conflict is greatest for two large countries of equal size, still great for two small nations, and least for a dyad with a small and a large state characterized by a preponderance of power.

It is hardly remarkable that a country's size and military capabilities influence its prospects for peace. It is surprising that the liberal variables are even more influential; and it is nice that states' political regimes and economic relations are amenable to manipulation. No state can increase its size from the 10th to the 90th percentile relative to all others, even over a long period. Certainly, they cannot all do so simultaneously. Consequently, realists can counsel little more than the acceptance of fate; but a state can, in principle, become democratic or

---

[24] To indicate a high level of interdependence, the lower trade-to-GDP ratio was set at the 90th percentile among contiguous dyads.

remove barriers to trade with its neighbors relatively quickly. Liberal reforms are possible even if they are often difficult to accomplish in practice. Similarly, some risk factors associated with heart disease – a diet high in cholesterol or a sedentary lifestyle – are under individuals' control; but others like gender, race, and family medical history are not. Fortunately, nations can take actions that materially affect the prospects for peace. Moreover, most people consider democratization and integration into the world economy inherently desirable. The implication of the LRM analyses is that stable regions of peace can be created by political and economic reform. Recent research on the "capitalist peace" only reinforces the view that liberal institutions offer substantial benefits.[25]

Transforming regional security through liberal reforms

We can estimate the regional benefits of democratization and openness by considering counterfactual cases. Imagine that, contrary to historical fact, all states in a region had been democratic, or autocratic, during the period studied. We can use the results in Table 7.1 to estimate the probability that each pair of states in a region would have been involved in a fatal dispute under these hypothetical circumstances, *all other factors remaining unchanged*. It is a simple matter then to calculate regional averages for the risk of a deadly MID in these counterfactual worlds – all states democratic or all states autocratic – and compare these to the actual, historic values. Similarly, to illustrate the pacific benefits of economic interdependence, we can compare the historical record to a counterfactual world in which all states were open and highly interdependent with other countries in their region. For additional indication of the value of liberal reforms, the pacific benefit of an alliance or other security agreement will also be estimated.

---

[25] Several investigators, echoing the arguments of Joseph Schumpeter, stress the importance of capitalism in creating a more peaceful world. Erik Gartzke, "The Capitalist Peace," *American Journal of Political Science* 51, no. 1 (January 2007), 166–91; Patrick J. McDonald, *The Invisible Hand of Peace: Capitalism, the War Machine, and International Relations Theory* (Cambridge University Press, 2009); Michael Mousseau, "The Social Market Roots of Democratic Peace," *International Security* 33, no. 4 (spring 2009), 52–86. It is often difficult to distinguish between a capitalist and a liberal peace because classical theorists favored democracy at home and capitalism with free markets domestically and internationally. Gerald Schneider and Nils Petter Gleditsch, "The Capitalist Peace: The Origins and Prospects of a Liberal Idea," *International Interactions* 36, no. 2 (2010), 107–14.

In the first column of Table 7.4 are the average annual probabilities of a fatal dispute for each region calculated using the true historical values of the independent variables, 1885–2001. In the second column are the probabilities of a fatal dispute if all the states in each region had been democratic, *ceteris paribus*. There are in all cases dramatic improvements in regional security. The probability of the onset of a MID for the Middle East, the most violence-prone region, drops by 72 percent for example, from an average annual rate of 0.71 percent to 0.20 percent. The benefits of regional interdependence are also substantial. If the lower trade-to-GDP ratio is set at a high level for all dyads in a region (.013), the risk of armed interstate conflict in the Mideast drops by 59 percent, to 0.29 percent. Column four, where the counterfactual condition is that all states were autocratic, confirms that it is not mere political similarity that accounts for the separate peace among democracies.[26] Making all states autocratic reduces violence in only two regions: the Middle East and Asia. There is no "autocratic peace" in Africa, and the risk of a fatal dispute under this counterfactual condition increases for Europe and the Americas, where democracies have been prevalent.[27]

This evidence for the democratic peace is consistent with previous research, but Edward Mansfield and Jack Snyder have warned that newly democratic countries are often unstable and prone to jingoistic violence. Is there a temporary rise in the likelihood of conflict as a result of democratization? Apparently not. No one using scientific methods has corroborated their results.[28] Indeed, six different research groups report that new democracies are *not* more warlike than established

---

[26] Errol A. Henderson, *Democracy and War: The End of an Illusion?* (Boulder, CO: Lynne Rienner, 2002). See also Mark Peceny and Caroline C. Beer, "Peaceful Parties and Puzzling Personalists," *American Political Science Review* 97, no. 2 (May 2003), 339–42.

[27] Errol Henderson and Benjamin Goldsmith suggest that democracy and trade may not have pacific benefits in Africa or Asia. To assess their concerns, I created indicators identifying each of these regions, interacted them with the democracy and trade terms in the LRM, and added these additional variables to the regression analysis. None of the interactive terms involving Africa was statistically significant. Only the interaction with the lower trade-to-GDP ratio was significant for Asia. It indicated that trade has a smaller pacific benefit in that region; the democratic peace was enhanced. Errol Henderson, "Disturbing the Peace: African Warfare, Political Inversion and the Universality of the Democratic Peace Thesis," *British Journal of Political Science* 39, no. 1 (January 2009), 25–58; Benjamin Goldsmith, "A Liberal Peace in Asia?," *Journal of Peace Research* 44, no. 1 (January 2007), 5–27. Goldsmith's analyses are flawed by the inclusion of both trade and the trade-to-GDP ratio in the regression equation.

[28] Edward Mansfield and Jack Snyder, "The Effects of Democratization on War," *International Security* 21, no. 4 (spring 1996), 5–38.

Table 7.4 *Annual probabilities of the onset of a fatal militarized dispute, 1885–2001: historical estimates and counterfactuals, continental averages*

	Historical values	All democracies	High trade	All autocracies	All allies
Middle East	.71%	.20	.29	.57	.60
Europe	.40	.15	.21	.44	.32
Asia	.37	.11	.14	.33	.29
Africa	.28	.09	.10	.28	.22
Americas	.25	.09	.10	.28	.23

Column 1 contains the predicted probabilities, in percent, given the historical values of the variables in the LRM and the estimated coefficients in Table 7.1. The probabilities in column 2 are for the counterfactual case in which all states in a region were democratic; other variables are unchanged. Columns 3–5 indicate the effects of other counterfactual changes in the historical conditions, *ceteris paribus*.

ones.[29] Evidently, the citizens of new democracies, too, are careful about the use of military force.

Finally, the estimates reported in Table 7.4 confirm that realism can make only a limited contribution to transforming regional security. The pacific benefits of an alliance, as shown in column five, are much less than those associated with either democracy or interdependence. More importantly, power, the main factor in realist theories, is simply not

[29] D. Scott Bennett and Allan C. Stam, III, *The Behavioral Origins of War* (Ann Arbor: University of Michigan Press, 2004), 117; David Rousseau, *Democracy and War: Institutions, Norms, and the Evolution of International Conflict* (Stanford University Press, 2005), 300. See also John R. Oneal and Bruce Russett, "The Classical Liberals were Right: Democracy, Interdependence, and Conflict, 1950–1985," *International Studies Quarterly* 41, no. 2 (June 1997), 267–94; Oneal and Jaroslav Tir, "Does the Diversionary use of Force Threaten the Democratic Peace? Assessing the Effect of Economic Growth on Interstate Conflict, 1921–2001," *International Studies Quarterly* 50, no. 4 (December 2006), 755–79; Andrew J. Enterline, "Regime Changes, Geographic Neighborhoods, and Interstate Conflict, 1816–1992," *Journal of Conflict Resolution* 42, no. 6 (December 1998), 804–29; Kristian S. Gleditsch and Michael D. Ward, "Peace and War in Time and Space: The Role of Democratization," *International Studies Quarterly* 44, no. 1 (March 2000), 1–29; William R. Thompson and Richard Tucker, "A Tale of Two Democratic Peace Critiques," *Journal of Conflict Resolution* 41, no. 3 (June 1997), 428–54. Recently Mansfield and Snyder have emphasized the danger of incomplete democratization, but this claim, too, has not been established. Edward D. Mansfield and Jack Snyder, *Electing to Fight: Why Emerging Democracies go to War* (Cambridge, MA: MIT Press, 2005); Bear F. Braumoeller, "Hypothesis Testing and Multiplicative Interaction Terms," *International Organization* 58, no. 4 (autumn 2004), 807–20; Vipin Narang and Rebecca M. Nelson, "Who are these Belligerent Democratizers? Reassessing the Impact of Democratization on War," *International Organization* 63, no. 2 (spring 2009), 357–79.

an effective tool for pacifying regional politics. Not only is it difficult for states to alter materially such a fundamental determinant as population – even industrialization can progress only slowly – no regional distribution of power can bring "perpetual peace," to use the Kantian phrase. A preponderance of power reduces the *dyadic* risk of violence, but there is no formula for regional peace that can be derived from this. Having a region of all large states would be worst, but lots of small states would also be conflict-prone. Some mixture of large and small countries within a region would produce the lowest average probability of conflict, but countries of similar size would still be susceptible to using military force.

Most research with the liberal-realist model indicates that national characteristics and bilateral relations are the primary influences on the likelihood of armed interstate conflict; but in the next section I consider the relevance of two alternative theories, one arguing for the importance of regional cultures and the other emphasizing the influence of the largest state in the international system, the so-called hegemon.

Alternative theories of regional transformation: hegemonic stability theory and the clash of civilizations

Do characteristics of the international system or regional cultures affect the likelihood that two states will become involved in a militarized dispute? In a provocative article James Kurth condemned most research on international relations as banal theorizing conducted "inside the cave," but he singled out for praise hegemonic stability theory – the widespread belief that a powerful state can substitute in part for government at the international level – and Samuel Huntington's theory of the clash of civilizations.[30] In this section I evaluate statistically the importance of these alternative explanations of regional security, assessing first the influence of the leading state and then the effect of regional cultures.

Does a hegemon create stability?

Realists have long been interested in how the major powers influence the incidence of conflict throughout the international system. Recall that the Correlates of War project focused on these especially powerful states in the earliest stage of the behavioral revolution. Many have

[30] James Kurth, "Inside the Cave: The Banality of I.R. Studies," *National Interest* 53 (fall 1998), 29–40.

paid particular attention to the role of the single most powerful state, the so-called hegemon. Hegemonic stability theory holds that this leading state, acting in its own self-interest, will constrain weaker states from resorting to violence.[31] Great Britain after the Napoleonic Wars and the United States after World War II influenced the creation and subsequent operation of the international system, each pursuing its interests directly and through supportive international organizations: the Concert of Europe in the earlier case and the United Nations and Bretton Woods institutions after World War II. If the system operates to the hegemon's advantage as assumed, its satisfaction with the status quo should lead to conservative policies. Wars disrupt the international economy so the leading state has an incentive to maintain the peace. It suppresses wars within its own sphere of influence and deters adversaries from using military force against its allies, trading partners, and others. Thus, the hegemon is thought to act in a limited way as a substitute for world government.

Surely, if we adopt a realist perspective, the ability of the leading state to preserve the peace depends on the magnitude of its power relative to the capabilities of others. A simple measure of a hegemon's ability to suppress conflict would, therefore, be its share of the militarily relevant capabilities of all countries. There is widespread agreement that Great Britain was closer to hegemony than any other country in the late nineteenth and early twentieth centuries, although its power relative to both Germany and the United States declined over time.[32] If any country can be said to have been hegemonic in the post-World War II period, it is, of course, the United States. Consequently, I measure hegemonic power, the ability of the leading state to maintain the peace, using Britain's share of world capabilities, 1885–1939, and America's after 1945.

As when calculating bilateral balances of power and states' power-projection capabilities, I use COW's composite index in my tests of hegemonic stability theory. This captures the influence of fundamental determinants of military capabilities and forces in being. To be explicit, I used the leading state's CINC score – Britain or America's annual share of global demographic, industrial, and military capabilities – to produce a variable (*Hegemony*) that is designed to reveal whether the leading state influences the probability of armed interstate conflict throughout the system.

---

[31] Robert Gilpin, *War and Change in World Politics* (Cambridge University Press, 1981); A. F. K. Organski, *World Politics* (New York: Alfred A. Knopf, 1968).

[32] A. F. K. Organski and Jacek Kugler, *The War Ledger* (University of Chicago, 1980).

To assess the leading's state's ability to maintain the peace, I simply added the variable *Hegemony* to the LRM. The estimated coefficient was far from statistical significance, and the influences of the original liberal and realist variables were little changed. The leading state does not seem to influence the probability of fatal militarized disputes system-wide. Of course, its strength shapes its own bilateral relations: increasing preponderance means the leading state has greater prospects for peace, but apparently it does not generally attempt or is not usually successful in suppressing violence in dyads of which it is not a member. There is no salutary spillover to others of the leading state's strength. Instead, the primary determinants of war and peace are countries' own national characteristics and the state of their bilateral relations. The leading state does not act as a hegemon; nor, as noted below, do regional powers in their smaller spheres of influence.

It is probably just as well that hegemonic stability theory is not true. The power of the United States has declined by half over the post-World War II period. In 1951 the US had 32 percent of the system's militarily relevant capabilities. This had dropped to 15 percent in 2000, a trend that is unlikely to be reversed. Ironically, the world has become substantially more peaceful as US hegemony has declined, the end of the Cold War being only the most obvious example.[33]

Do civilizations clash?

Huntington's central claim is simple: the clash of civilizations is the greatest threat to world peace in the post-Cold War period. The most important distinctions among peoples are now not ideological, political, or economic, but cultural. Huntington's concern is certainly plausible, especially in the aftermath of September 11. At the heart of the argument is the distinction between the in-group and outsiders, a difference that may lead to violence. Fear and hatred of those who are different are all too familiar, but neither is Huntington's thesis obviously true. Nations of one ethnic, religious, or linguistic heritage coexist

---

[33] Ted Robert Gurr, Monty G. Marshall, and Deepa Khosla, *Peace and Conflict 2001: A Global Survey of Armed Conflicts, Self-determination Movements, and Democracy* (College Park, MD: Center for International Development and Conflict Management, 2000); Lotta Harbom and Peter Wallensteen, "Armed Conflict, 1989–2006," *Journal of Peace Research* 44, no. 5 (2007), 623–34; and Nils Petter Gleditsch, "The Liberal Moment Fifteen Years On," *International Studies Quarterly* 52, no. 4 (December 2008), 691–712. For additional reasons to doubt hegemonic stability theory, see Margit Bussmann and John R. Oneal, "Do Hegemons Distribute Private Goods? A Test of Power–Transition Theory," *Journal of Conflict Resolution* 51, no. 1 (February 2007), 88–111.

peacefully with nation-states dominated by another culture in many parts of the world, and many countries are comprised of diverse groups that intermingle peacefully and benefit from diversity. Moreover, in the first half of the twentieth century the most destructive armed conflicts were within the western world. Here I reconsider Huntington's thesis with new quantitative tests using the LRM and data that now include ten years after the end of the East–West ideological confrontation that Huntington believed so distorted international politics.

Huntington's theory is regional at its core. He proposes that culturally connected states will be more peaceful than states split across civilizational boundaries. Usually civilizations are composed of states that are close geographically, as his map in *The Clash of Civilizations* makes clear. States in the same civilization frequently have a common border and proximate capitals. By Huntington's definition, the member states of a civilization share a culture, so they meet both of Paul's criteria for a "region."[34] Thus, Huntington shines a light on the importance of regions and culture in international relations relative to the institutional and material factors emphasized by liberal and realist theories. Huntington identified eight civilizations: the Western, Sinic, Islamic, Hindu, Slavic-Orthodox, Latin American, Buddhist, and African. Culture at this grand level is persistent. A civilization's culture changes, but only slowly over decades or even centuries. Civilizations matter, Huntington tells us, because they are the highest cultural groupings and provide people's broadest sense of identity. He elevates common civilizational beliefs and practices over nationalism or other subregional divides, such as the split between Iran and the Arab states or Sunni versus Shia within Islam.

Do civilizational differences explain conflict better than the factors highlighted by liberalism and realism, or add substantially to the accounts they offer? I conducted several tests using the LRM and the data for 1885–2001. I started with a simple one, creating a variable (*Split*) which indicates whether the two states in a dyad come from different civilizations or not. It is coded 1 if the dyad is culturally heterogeneous; it equals 0 if the two states are from the same civilization.[35] This was added to the basic liberal-realist model in Table 7.1. If Huntington is right regarding the importance of regional cultures based on civilizations, *Split* would be positively associated with interstate violence and explain variation in its distribution over time and space. Including

---

[34] See Chapter 1 in this volume.

[35] The coding for each country is derived primarily from the map provided in Samuel P. Huntington, *The Clash of Civilizations and the Remaking of World Order* (New York: Simon & Schuster, 1998), 26–27; see Russett and Oneal, *Triangulating Peace*, 251–52 for details.

this indicator of civilizational differences might also weaken the influences of the other variables in the LRM. In fact, the estimated coefficient for *Split* was not significantly different from zero, there was little increase in the variance explained, and the influences of the liberal and realist variables were little changed – findings consistent with previous research.[36]

It seemed possible that evidence for the importance of regional cultures was distorted by the Cold War, when disputes over political economy overshadowed civilizational differences. To test this possibility, I allowed *Split* to equal 1 only in years before 1950 or after 1989; but the estimated coefficient was again insignificant. Limiting the influence of civilizations to just the post-Cold War years also failed to provide support for Huntington's theory at conventional levels of statistical significance. Again, the estimated coefficients of the liberal and realist influences were not materially affected.

Finally, I created indicator variables for each of the eight civilizations and added them to the LRM. Two civilizations (Sinic and Islamic) proved more violent than expected, holding the liberal and realist influences constant; two (Western and Hindu) were more peaceful; and the dyads of four civilizations were neither more nor less violent than pairs of states split across civilizational boundaries. This distribution indicates that cultural characteristics associated with Huntington's civilizations do not importantly affect the likelihood of interstate conflict. Nor does the existence of a large country within a region help.[37] Strong regional powers do not suppress violence between smaller countries within their civilizations.[38]

---

[36] Errol Henderson, "Culture or Contiguity? Ethnic Conflict, the Similarity of States, and the Onset of Interstate War, 1829–1989," *Journal of Conflict Resolution* 41, no. 5 (October 1997), 649–68; Ted Robert Gurr, *Peoples versus States: Ethnopolitical Conflict and Accommodation at the End of the 20th Century* (Washington, DC: United States Institute of Peace, 2000); Russett and Oneal, *Triangulating Peace*, chapter 7; Sean Bolks and Richard Stoll, "Examining Conflict Escalation Within the Civilizations Context," *Conflict Management and Peace Science* 20, no. 2 (2003), 85–109; Giacomo Chiozza, "Is there a Clash of Civilizations? Evidence from Patterns of International Conflict Involvement, 1946–97," *Journal of Peace Research* 39, no. 6 (November 2002), 711–34; and Glynn Ellis, "Gauging the Magnitude of Civilization Conflict," *Conflict Management and Peace Science* 27, no. 3 (July 2010), 219–38.

[37] Russett and Oneal, *Triangulating Peace*, 260ff.

[38] Lemke reports only that preponderance reduces violence between the strongest state in a regional hierarchy and powerful rivals. This is consistent with the evidence for preponderance theory reported earlier, but the claim is more limited in scope because Lemke does not consider pairs of contenders or dyads involving noncontenders. Douglas Lemke, *Regions of War and Peace* (Cambridge University Press, 2002), 112f.

Conclusion

Creating stable regions of peace is an important task for humanity in the post-Cold War period. It is all the more pressing because of the danger of the proliferation of weapons of mass destruction, but even conventional wars can be horribly destructive, as World Wars I and II or the "first African World War" in the Congo show. Of course, world peace is threatened not just by the actions of states. Intrastate violence and transnational conflict must also be addressed, but interstate wars can be particularly destructive. Efforts to reduce their incidence must proceed along several tracks at once. First, continuing effort must be made to solve the real problems that serve as the *causi belli*. These often involve disputes over national boundaries.[39] Peace between Israel and the Arab states would, of course, be advanced if the boundaries of a Palestinian state were agreed and the status of Jerusalem resolved. Kashmir, too, is a territorial flashpoint that could again lead to war. But research with the liberal-realist model shows that we need not wait for such very difficult issues to be resolved. We can promote democracy and economic interdependence at the same time. The results reported above show that liberal political and economic reforms can have dramatic pacific benefits. Two democracies are 83 percent less likely to fight than an autocracy and a democracy, and 64 percent less likely than two autocracies. The benefits of economically important trade are almost as great. In addition, freer trade and integration into the international economy also promote economic development, which makes it more likely that a country will adopt and sustain democratic institutions; and developed democracies are especially peaceful.[40]

The potential for advancing regional security through democratization and freer trade is dramatic, as Table 7.4 makes clear. War results from disagreements among nations that they seek to resolve by the use of military force. By giving those who must pay the cost of fighting a war the power to decide whether it will be fought, democracy makes interstate violence less likely. Trade and foreign investment increase the financial incentive for peace. Both the political and economic reforms recommended by the classical liberals contribute to the resolution of disputes by enhancing the process of negotiation and bargaining. International, transnational, and regional organizations also have important roles to play in the nonviolent resolution of international conflict.

---

[39] Paul Senese and John Vasquez, "Assessing the Steps to War," *British Journal of Political Science* 35, no. 4 (October 2005), 607–33.

[40] Mousseau, "Social Market Roots of the Democratic Peace."

Tests with the liberal-realist model do confirm important elements of realist theory, but these findings do not provide an alternative path to regional peace. It is impossible for nations to change the fundamental determinants of power (population and industry) enough to have an effect comparable in magnitude to those associated with liberal reform. Geography, of course, is outside our control. More importantly, there is no regional distribution of power that should bring peace to all states. A preponderance of power – not a balance – reduces the risk of dyadic violence; but it is impossible to "scale up" from this finding. No formula for regional peace can be derived from the results in Table 7.3. Having a number of large states would be worst, but many small states would also be prone to fight. Some mixture of large and small countries would be optimal in a purely mathematical sense, but conflict would still be endemic among the large powers and among the small ones. Hopes that a hegemon can resolve the problem are not borne out in social scientific tests. Large states do not act, or do not act effectively, as hegemons to impose peace throughout the system or within regions.

The relative harmony among the major powers in the post-Cold War era provides a valuable opportunity to advance efforts to establish stable zones of peace on liberal principles. This will not be easy or accomplished quickly, and important steps toward peace can sometimes be taken by authoritarian leaders acting from the top down; but Solons are rare.[41] And if good authoritarian leaders, not being accountable to their publics, have the political freedom to strike unpopular deals, democracies are more likely to abide by the commitments they make.[42] For stable, long-lasting peace, liberalism offers the best hope. Fortunately, the world is becoming more democratic, prosperous, and economically interdependent. These developments not only make peace more likely but are good in themselves. The citizens of democratic countries enjoy greater freedom and are more likely to live in peace. Trade makes war less likely and increases prosperity. These good things go together. We can help transform regions into pluralistic security communities by promoting reforms that most consider desirable in themselves.

---

[41] See Chapter 11 in this volume. On the difficulty of intervening with military force to establish democratic regimes, see Bruce Russett, "Bushwhacking the Democratic Peace," *International Studies Perspectives* 6, no. 4 (November 2005), 395–408; and Andrew Enterline and J. Michael Grieg, "Perfect Storms? Political Instability in Imposed Polities and the Futures of Iraq and Afghanistan," *Journal of Conflict Resolution* 52, no. 6 (December 2008), 880–915.

[42] Brett Ashley Leeds, Michaela Mattes, and Jeremy S. Vogel, "Interests, Institutions, and the Reliability of International Commitments," *American Journal of Political Science* 53, no. 2 (April 2009), 461–76.

Part 4

Constructivist perspectives

8   Ideas, norms, and regional orders

Amitav Acharya

In this chapter I focus on two questions that are central to a social constructivist understanding of regional orders. The first is whether and how "ideas make regions." The second is how to conceptualize the diffusion of ideas and norms (used interchangeably here, mindful that ideas do not necessarily make behavioral claims as norms do) across the regional–global divide, that is, between regions and the global system at large, a process that is crucial to the creation and maintenance of regional orders. Until recently, international relations scholars paid scant attention to these questions. The advent of constructivism as a distinct perspective on international relations has changed that. I will argue, however, that constructivism, despite its claims to be an "ideas first" (as opposed to "ideas only") theory, is yet to fully address these two questions. Constructivism's position on the relationship between ideas and power remains ambiguous at best. And constructivism is especially weak when it comes to exploring the global–regional nexus in the diffusion of ideas and norms, focusing almost exclusively on how universal norms trump local or regional ones.

How do ideas make regional orders? Regions as imagined communities

At the outset an important question needs addressing. What does it take to be an "ideational" view of regions and regional orders? In international relations theories, the use of "ideational" has exploded with the growing popularity of constructivism. But "ideational" can mean a whole range of things, such as values, principles, ideology, culture, and identity, among others. In writings on regions, especially when it comes to defining regionness, it is not uncommon to find references to such variables as sociocultural similarity, shared values, and a common

I am grateful to Michael Lipson, T. V. Paul, and the participants at the Montreal workshop for their valuable comments and suggestions on earlier drafts of this chapter.

identity. And the inclusion of these elements in the literature on regions long predates constructivism.

For example, both regional "integration" and regional "subsystem " (also known as "subordinate international system") theories acknowledged their importance. Even Russett's behavioral study, *International Regions and the International System*, begins by noting the "degree of cultural similarity or at least *compatibility* for the major politically relevant values" as one of the conditions of regional integration, alongside economic interdependence, and the existence of formal institutions with substantial "spillover" or "consensus-building effects" as well as geographic proximity.[1] While he did not think any of these to be a sufficient or even necessary condition for integration, together they could be operationalized and subjected to factor analysis to identify five sets of regions in the world: Afro-Asia, Western Community, Latin America, Semi-Developed Latins, and Eastern Europe. Geographic proximity was the main casualty of this method: it put the Philippines in Latin America, and Argentina, Japan and Israel in the Western Community, attesting perhaps to the importance of culture and values but eliciting much controversy.[2] Karl Deutsch and his associates found that "a compatibility of the main values held by the politically relevant strata of all participating units" was an important characteristic of amalgamated security communities.[3] Louis Cantori and Stephen Spiegel listed four "pattern variables" that determine the "international relations of regions": namely, nature and level of cohesion, nature of communications, level of power, and structure of relations. The first of these, nature and level of cohesion, did include social cohesiveness, including ethnicity, race, language, religion, history, and consciousness of a common heritage. Yet power, defined primarily in material terms – GNP, military strength, scientific and technological developments – merited special attention.[4] And while the authors might be excused for not having foreseen it, the experience of subsequent decades would negate the causal importance of cohesion. The Middle East, which was found to have a "high degree of social cohesion," and Southeast Asia, with its "extremely low degree of social cohesion,"[5] turned out to be

---

[1] Bruce Russett, *International Regions and the International System: A Study in Political Ecology* (Chicago, IL: Rand McNally, 1967), 10.
[2] Oran R.Young, "Professor Russett: Industrious Tailor to a Naked Emperor," *World Politics* 21, no. 3 (April 1969), 486–511.
[3] Karl Deutsch et al., *Political Community in the North Atlantic Area: International Organization in the Light of Historical Experience* (Princeton University Press, 1966 [1957]), 27.
[4] Louis J. Cantori and Stephen Spiegel, eds., *The International Politics of Regions: A Comparative Approach* (Englewood Cliffs, NJ: Prentice Hall, 1970), 1.
[5] Ibid., 342.

at the opposite ends in developing regional institutions and orders, considering the contrasting tales of the League of Arab States and the Association of Southeast Asian Nations (ASEAN). A survey of the work of twenty-two scholars on regions by William Thompson found three clusters of necessary and sufficient attributes of "regional subsystems": general geographic proximity, regularity and intensity of interactions, and shared perceptions of the regional subsystem as a distinctive theatre of operations.[6] Michael Brecher, who adopted the "subordinate international system" perspective, included "common and conflicting ideologies and values" in his descriptive framework of a subordinate system.[7] And Haas referred to "ideological patterns" and "homogeneity" as a background factor conducive to integration.[8]

Yet, these writings did not amount to an ideational perspective. To be regarded as ideational, a theory of region-building must possess two features. First, ideas must be shown to have a significant causal and constitutive influence. This is not to say that ideas must be shown to be the only causal variable, but the theorist, to borrow Wendt's words, should "begin ... theorizing ... with the distribution of ideas ... and then bring in material forces, rather than the other way around."[9] None of the theories of regional integration or regional subsystem took an ideas-first view, not to mention an ideas-only perspective. None gave any significant causality to ideas, ideology, culture, or identity (whether as a cause or effect of regional integration). Moreover, there was no sense that ideas could have a constitutive impact, redefining the interests and identities of actors. Nowhere is there any sense that the prior idea of region or an imagined concept of regioness is what drove integration. Yet, ideational perspectives must demonstrate how a prior set of beliefs or a prior idea of a region acted as a trigger for regional institutions and order. As a constructivist work on Europe argues, a "causal process of the institutionalization of ideas ... is at the heart of the EU story."[10]

---

[6] William R. Thompson, "The Regional Subsystem: A Conceptual Explication and a Propositional Inventory," *International Studies Quarterly* 17, no. 1 (March 1973), 89–117.

[7] Michael Brecher, "International Relations and Asian Studies: The Subordinate System of Southern Asia," *World Politics* 15 (January 1963), 213–35.

[8] Ernst B. Haas, "International Integration: The European and the Universal Process," in *Regional Politics and World Order*, ed. Richard A. Falk and Saul H. Mendlovitz, (San Francisco, CA: Freeman, 1973 [1961]), 405.

[9] Alexander Wendt, *Social Theory of International Politics* (Cambridge University Press, 1999), 370–71.

[10] Craig Parsons, *A Certain Idea of Europe* (Ithaca, NY: Cornell University Press, 2003), 2. I would add that in addition to causality, ideas should also be shown to have a constitutive effect on regional integration processes, actors, and outcomes.

An ideational view of regional orders is also different from studying the normative approaches to regions or regional organizations, like the "regionalist doctrines of peace" that Nye outlined in his classic *Peace in Parts*.[11] Although this work might be considered as an important precursor of normative perspectives on regional order that are the staple of contemporary constructivism, it is unclear whether these doctrines can be said to have independent and prior causal effect or are simply used as analytic devices for identifying and exploring the functions of formal regional organizations. One suspects that the latter was the case; hence the regionalist doctrines by themselves do not amount to taking ideas seriously in the study of regional orders.

Second, and closely related to the above, a nonrationalist epistemology is a key requirement of an ideational perspective on regions. Region-building must not be seen to be purely or mainly the product of instrumental action. But neofunctionalism and transactionalism, the two most influential regional integration theories, fell far short on this score. As Haas summed up, "Neo-functionalism stresses the instrumental motives of actors; ... [it] takes self-interest for granted and relies on it for delineating actor perceptions."[12] Deutsch's transactionalist theory, especially its idea of security communities, which is now appropriated by constructivists, came closer to taking ideational and non-instrumental elements seriously, but mainly as the dependent variable. Its idea of community encompassed such elements as "mutual sympathy and loyalties, of 'we-feeling,' trust, and mutual consideration ... partial identification in terms of self-images and interests ... mutual attention, communication, perception of needs."[13] But insofar as the independent variable was concerned, it was focused too much on measuring material transactions: tourism, mail flows, and so forth – "measure whatever the statistics permits to be measured," to use Haas's mildly sarcastic words.[14] In other words, although the Deutschian concept of "we-feeling" that develops out of transactions might seem to be amenable to social and ideational influence, that feeling emerges out of the growth of material transactions rather than from ideas and norms. It is fair to say that it incorporated perceptual, rather than ideational, elements.

---

[11] Joseph S. Nye, *Peace in Parts: Integration and Conflict in Regional Organization* (Boston, MA: Little, Brown, 1971).

[12] Ernst B. Haas, "The Study of Regional Integration: Reflections on the Joys and Anguish of Pretheorising," in *Regional Politics and World Order*, ed. Richard A. Falk and Saul H. Mendlovitz (San Francisco, CA: Institute of Contemporary Studies, 1972), 117.

[13] Deutsch et al., *Political Community in the North Atlantic Area*, 17.

[14] Haas, "Study of Regional Integration," 118.

Regions are no longer viewed as "natural" or "physical constants." Traditional conceptions of regions focused on relatively fixed variables, such as geographic proximity, shared cultural and linguistic features, and a common heritage. They sought to determine what is common among the peoples and political units that inhabit a given geographic and geopolitical space. In the 1960s there emerged behavioral perspectives on regions. From these perspectives regions were "not to be identified by the traditional geopolitical criteria, but to be discovered by inductive, quantitative methods."[15] Russett's aforementioned study was the most well-known example of this approach. But the behavioral revolution did little to lay to rest the debate over the ambiguities surrounding the regional concept. Indeed, in determining regionness, the early theories of region-building tried but failed to resolve the tensions between the geographic and the perceptual, the fixed and the dynamic, and the rationalistic and the discursive. Constructivism made a virtue out of this failure.

Even in the heyday of the behavioral era, Michael Banks argued that "regions are what politicians and peoples want them to be."[16] But it was the advent of constructivism that gave a much greater space for ideas and identity in defining regionnness. There are vigorous academic debates over what constructivism stands for and whether it is a substantive "theory" (like realism, liberalism, or institutionalism) or a philosophical position and an ontology that does not offer causal arguments that are falsifiable and testable.[17] Moreover, constructivists are hardly a homogenous lot in recognizing the importance of various causal forces: norms, culture, identity, and socialization. There are significant differences between Wendtian constructivism, popular in the US, which tends to be social-scientific, or "softly rational," as Haas put it,[18] and a European variety which stresses argumentative rationality and leans toward reflectivism.[19] There may even be a possible Asian strand distinguished by claims of regional exceptionalism and historical path dependency.[20]

[15] Charles Pentland, "The Regionalization of World Politics: Concepts and Evidence," *International Journal* 30, no. 4 (autumn 1974), 599–630.
[16] Michael Banks, "Systems Analysis and the Study of Regions," *International Studies Quarterly* 13, no. 4 (December 1969), 338.
[17] Andrew Moravcsik, "Constructivism and European Integration: A Critique," in *The Social Construction of Europe*, ed. Thomas Christiansen, Knud Erik Jorgensen, and Antje Wiener (London: Sage, 2001), 176–88, 199–205.
[18] Ernst Haas, "Does Constructivism Subsume Neo-functionalism?," in Christiansen, Jorgensen, and Wiener, eds., *Social Construction of Europe*.
[19] Moravcsik, "Constructivism and European Integration," 179.
[20] See David C. Kang, "Getting Asia Wrong: The Need for New Analytical Frameworks," *International Security* 27, no. 4 (spring 2003), 57–85; Amitav Acharya,

But certain shared elements among constructivist treatments of regions stand out. Regional coherence and identity are not givens, but result primarily from socialization among the leaders and peoples of a region. Adler and Crawford argue that regions are no longer conceptualized "in terms of geographic contiguity, but rather in terms of purposeful social, political, cultural, and economic interaction among states which often (but not always) inhabit the same geographic space."[21] Beyond interactions, regions are built around shared identities.[22] What Adler calls "cognitive regions" are those "whose people imagine that ... borders run, more or less, where shared understandings and common identities end."[23] For Jayasurya "the critical point of difference between" perspectives that hold regions to be "socially constructed" and those who regard them as "natural entities" is that the former "demands greater sensitivity to the contingent nature of regional projects."[24] In the case of the "Asia-Pacific" idea, Dirlik contends that regionness may depend as much on "representation" as on "reality."[25] The work of Benedict Anderson has been particularly inspiring for the constructivist view on regions.[26] As with nation-states, regions may be "imagined," constructed, and defended. Territorial proximity and functional interactions are inadequate to constitute a region in the absence of an "idea of the region," conceived more from inside than imposed from the outside.[27]

Despite some differences and varying points of entry, constructivist international relations scholars studying regions would generally find themselves in agreement with geographer Alexander Murphy's

"How Ideas Spread: Whose Norms Matter? Norm Localization and Institutional Change in Asian Regionalism," *International Organization* 58, no. 2 (spring 2004), 239–75; Amitav Acharya, *Constructing a Security Community in Southeast Asia: ASEAN and the Problem of Regional Order*, 2nd edn. (London: Routledge, 2009).

[21] Emanuel Adler and Beverly Crawford, "Constructing a Mediterranean Region: A Cultural Approach," paper presented at the conference "The Convergence of Civilizations? Constructing a Mediterranean Region," Lisbon, Portugal, June 6–9, 2002, 3.

[22] Ole Wæver, "Culture and Identity in the Baltic Sea Region," in *Cooperation in the Baltic Sea Region*, ed. Pertti Joenniemi (London: Taylor & Francis, 1993), 23–48.

[23] Emanuel Adler, "Imagined (Security) Communities: Cognitive Regions in International Relations," *Millennium: Journal of International Studies* 26, no. 2 (1997), 249–77, 250.

[24] Kanishka Jayasurya, "Singapore: The Politics of Regional Definition," *Pacific Review* 7, no. 4 (1994), 411–20.

[25] Arif Dirlik, "The Asia–Pacific Region: Reality and Representation in the Invention of the Regional Structure," *Journal of World History* 3, no. 1 (1992), 55–79.

[26] Benedict Anderson, *Imagined Communities: Reflections on the Origin and Spread of Nationalism*, rev. edn. (London: Verso, 1991).

[27] Amitav Acharya, *The Quest for Identity: International Relations of Southeast Asia* (Oxford University Press, 2000).

contention that, "As social constructions, regions are necessarily ideological and no explanation of their individuality or character can be complete without explicit consideration of the types of ideas that are developed and sustained in connection with the regionalization process."[28] Regions and regional orders can coalesce around different kinds of ideas: political, security, economic, and sociocultural. Political-security ideas include collective security, common security, cooperative security, human security, democracy, and human rights. Examples of economic ideas for region-building are free trade, neoliberalism, and the so-called (now obsolescent) Washington Consensus. Sociocultural ideas are ethnic group conceptions, or ideologies such as Pan-Africanism, or the more recent notion of Asian values. These ideas do not enjoy fixed meaning and are contested, but they do matter in regional definition and speak to different conceptions of regional orders. I do not argue that ideas make regions, any more than material forces do. But I do think that ideas are a major part of what makes regions, they shape the boundaries and membership of regions, and decide the question of their permanence and transience.

Like the term "region" in general, "regional order" is no longer associated exclusively with material determinants such as economic interdependence or distribution of power. Theories of regional integration, such as neofunctionalism and transactionalism, while not specifically speaking of regional orders, did identify institutional constructs such as political community (Haas) or security community (Deutsch) that can be seen as ideal types of regional orders. Recent perspectives on regional orders have focused on institutions as key elements.[29] Buzan and Wæver's list of regional security complexes, which are in essence descriptions of various possible types of regional orders, include some that are institutionally defined or even institutionally centered.[30] The idea of a regional economic community also has strong institutional elements. Beyond formal institutions, regional orders can be based more or less around shared norms. As Alagappa notes, order can simply mean "rule governed interaction," i.e. "whether interstate interactions conform to accepted rules."[31]

[28] Alexander B. Murphy, "Regions as Social Constructs: The Gap Between Theory and Practice," *Progress in Human Geography* 15, no. 1 (1991), 30.

[29] Peter Katzenstein, *A World of Regions: Asia and Europe in the American Imperium* (Ithaca, NY: Cornell University Press, 2005).

[30] Barry Buzan and Ole Waever, *Regions and Powers: The Structure of International Security* (Cambridge University Press, 2003).

[31] Muthiah Alagappa, "The Study of International Order," in *Asian Security Order: Instrumental and Normative Features*, ed. Muthiah Alagappa (Stanford University Press, 2003), 39.

Traditional perspectives of regions assigned a central causal role to power. Hence, some of the most familiar "names" of the world's regions, such as Middle East, Southeast Asia, or Asia-Pacific, are credited to the political and strategic interests of the leading powers of the past two centuries: Britain or the United States, or both, and their close allies (as with Australia in the case of Asia-Pacific). But ideas and socialization can create regions in the absence of power (the deliberate effort by a hegemonic power to create a region). Southeast Asia, although initially "named" by Allied Command during World War II and given prominence by the US intervention in Vietnam, became viable only through the institution-building efforts of the Association of Southeast Asian Nations. Moreover, while both power and ideas can build regions, when regions are built purely on the basis of material power to reflect or serve the geopolitical needs of great powers, without an ideational core or consensus, they do not last. In other words, power alone does not guarantee regional identity and order. Categories such as Southwest Asia, Near East, Afpak, Middle East (increasingly delegitimized in favor of the "Arab world"), Far East, and Asia-Pacific (giving way to East Asia) are examples not only of the fluidity of regional concepts in general, but also of the fragility of region-naming by great powers *sans* regional normative structure and identity. Ideational regions tend to last longer than regions built our material hegemony.

The claim of some constructivist literature that ideas and norms can spread without the backing of powerful actors is important here. Realists argue that the powerful has an advantage in spreading certain ideas and norms through propaganda, forced emulation, coercive adaptation, coercive socialization, and so on. One can find examples good as well as bad, from the way British military operations were crucial to the antislavery movement, and the way the British forced a lot of ideas on India – some stuck – others did not. Also the religions of the powerful often spread through both coercion and persuasion, for example the Catholic Church in Latin America or Islam in Northern India. In contrast, constructivists argue that ideas can spread without coercive power, for example the spread of the norm against apartheid, chemical weapons, or land mines.[32] Indeed, one of the best illustrations of the "power of ideas" over the "ideas of power" can be seen from the classical regional worlds of the eastern Mediterranean and the eastern Indian Ocean (Southeast Asia). The two powers which shaped the regional world of the Mediterranean were Greece and Rome (Persia was

---

[32] Although constructivism has emphasized the diffusion of good norms, it can and should also explain how "bad" ideas spread.

clearly a third great power, but its role was less enduring), while that of classical Southeast Asia was shaped by India and China. Of these, the influence of Greece and India was mainly ideational, whereas that of Rome and China was mainly geopolitical. There were significant differences. What historians call the Indianization of Southeast Asia during the first millennium AD was different from the Hellenization of the Mediterranean before the advent of full-fledged Roman imperialism in the first century AD. The expansion of Greek ideational influence, although it preceded the military campaigns of Alexander the Great, was nonetheless significantly aided by it. By contrast, military force was not a factor aiding the Indianization of Southeast Asia. A military campaign by South Indian ruler Rajendra Chola in 1025 AD constituted an important exception to this but it did not lead to lasting occupation of the Malay kingdom of Srivijaya. By then, Indianization had been pretty extensive and ironically, the Chola raids helped actually end it by destroying Srivijaya, then the most powerful regional maritime empire which protected the sea lanes. The roles of China in Southeast Asia and Rome in the Mediterranean also differed in the sense that the former only sought suzerainty over parts of Southeast Asia for the sake of tributary trade, while Rome turned the Mediterranean into a Roman lake through direct conquest of its entire littoral.

But three points emerging from a comparison of the flow of ideas in the classical Mediterranean and Southeast Asia are especially noteworthy. First, the fact that India and Greece (before Alexander) could exert such a profound influence on neighboring societies despite not conquering them is significant. In pre-Alexander Greece, and for India more generally, migration rather than conquest was the chief means of the diffusion of ideas, taking the form of Greek settlements around the Mediterranean and Indian settlements in Southeast Asia (sometimes mistakenly called Indian colonization). Second, in one sense at least, the Indianization of Southeast Asia, without the backing of military conquest, had a more profound legacy than the Hellenization of the Eastern Mediterranean and beyond that followed Alexander's conquests. This has to do with the fact that Hellenization weakened after the death of Alexander and the subsequent Roman overthrow of the two Hellenistic empires founded by his generals, the Seleucids in Antioch (in present-day Syria), and the Ptolemies in Alexandria, Egypt. Indian ideas remained influential in Southeast Asia right up to the fifteenth century AD. Third and perhaps most important, in both regional worlds the materially more powerful actor did not turn out to be the most powerful ideational influence. Comparing Greece and Rome in the Mediterranean and India and China in Southeast Asia will underscore this point. In the Mediterranean littoral itself, Greek ideas remained quite influential relative to Roman ideas, even after the total eclipse of Greek authority in the hands of Rome. While Rome ruled over much of the Hellenistic areas, including Athens and the Ptolemaic kingdom of Egypt, Roman emperors (such as Hadrian) and the Roman elite came to rely extensively on Greek ideas and culture to secure their legitimacy. (One might compare this with Alexander's own embracing of Egyptian concepts of universal monarchy, anointing himself as pharaoh in Memphis near Alexandria on November 14, 332 BC, and thus becoming the first universal ruler in western history. Alexander also had no difficulty worshipping the Egyptian deities, such as the Egyptian Amun, whom he regarded as a form of Zeus.) In fact, Rome emerged as the biggest promoter of Greek ideas, far eclipsing the overall ideational resources of the Romans themselves. In Southeast Asia the ideational influence of India, including Hindu-Buddhist political and strategic concepts (including Kautilya's *Arthasastra*) had a profound influence in state-making and intraregional interactions, far eclipsing the ideational influence of China (except in the deltas of Tongking and North Vietnam), the materially and geopolitically more powerful actor. This variance could be attributed to radically different modes of interaction. To quote George Coedès, a major figure in classical Southeast Asian scholarship,

The Chinese proceeded by conquest and annexation; soldiers occupied the country, and officials spread Chinese civilization. Indian penetration or infiltration seems almost always to have been peaceful; nowhere was it accompanied by the destruction that brought dishonor to the Mongol expansion or the Spanish conquest of America. Far from being destroyed by the conquerors, the native peoples of Southeast Asia found in Indian society, transplanted and modified, a framework within which their own society could be integrated and developed.[33]

One might ask: do ideas always precede material factors in all regions? Not necessarily. The sequence may vary from region to region, and be time and context-specific. Some regions are transformed by powerful ideas. This happened in the Middle East in the 1950s and 1960s with Nasserite pan-Arabism. Even though the notion of a Middle East existed earlier on the basis of the British military organization of the world (as did pan-Arabism, but Nasser's idea was more intensely political), the regional order of the Middle East was redefined and much more polarized with Nasser's ideas. Much the same can be said about the impact of Bolivar's pan-Americanism on South America, and Nkrumah's pan-Africanism on African regional order. In other instances, ideational

[33] George Coedès, *The Indianized States of Southeast Asia* (University of Hawaii Press, 1968), 34.

regions may themselves be subjected to new material pressures, examples of which can be found in the way the forces of economic globalization (trade liberalization, financial flows, transnational production, technology, and the information and communications revolution) are affecting changes to preexisting ideational bases of regional orders in Africa, Asia, and Latin America. As Katzenstein sees it, internationalization and globalization make regions more "porous,"[34] thereby facilitating the diffusion of cultural ideas and products from outside and within them (Japanese culture spreading in Asia and beyond on the heels of Japanese investment; a similar dynamic may be occurring with respect to Chinese culture). In most cases, though, ideas and material forces go hand in hand and can be mutually interactive and constitutive. In classical interactions, ideas (including religious worldviews and political ideas) followed trade (as in the Indian Ocean) or conquest (as with Hellenization). In today's world, the information and communication revolution makes it possible for ideas to spread without the help of soldiers and merchants. Today, economic globalization is inseparable from the diffusion of ideas (e.g., democracy and the free market).

There are three ways in which ideas shape regional orders. First, the preexisting ideas (or "cognitive priors") of individuals or societies – whether they are worldviews, causal ideas, or principled ideas – can be the foundation around which regional orders may develop.[35] We have plenty of important examples of this, both from the western and non-western societies. Bolivar, Monnet, Nehru, Nkrumah, all have major influence on regional order in the Americas, West Europe, Asia, and Africa respectively. One of the best examples of constructivist analysis of regional orders, Barnett's work on the postwar Middle East, shows pan-Arabism's crucial, if contested, role in regional order-making in which state sovereignty was initially downgraded in favor of Arab unity and a single Arab state.[36] Although the pan-Arab project ultimately weakened, it did nonetheless have a profound impact on regional order in the Middle East. Interestingly, while the literature on nonwestern regionalism tends to acknowledge the role of ideas held by individual figures, theories of regionalism from the West tend to ignore or downplay them. The heavily Eurocentric theories of region-building, neofunctionalism, transactionalism, and neoliberal institutionalism,

---

[34] Katzenstein, *World of Regions*.

[35] Judith Goldstein and Robert Keohane, "Ideas and Foreign Policy: An Analytical Framework," in *Ideas and Foreign Policy*, ed. Judith Goldstein and Robert Keohane (Ithaca, NY: Cornell University Press, 1993).

[36] Michael N. Barnett, *Dialogues in Arab Politics: Negotiations in Regional Order* (New York: Columbia University Press, 1998).

perhaps for the sake of scientific rigor, made scant references to the ideas of individual visionaries, such as Monnet, Schuman, or Churchill. Neither did they seriously investigate the "idea of Europe," itself a constructed and variable notion with its historical basis on the "culture and civilization" of the "Orient," and which once shared space with chunks of the historical notion of "Asia."[37] But any serious writing on Latin America, Asia, the Middle East, and Africa would not begin without a nod to Bolivar, Nehru, Nasser, or Nkrumah. Similarly, historical and cultural matrixes, such as Christianity or the Roman Empire, played little part in the development of earlier accounts of European institutions, whereas the past (cultural and political) is always present in nonwestern accounts of regionness.

Regional orders emerging from the worldviews and cognitive priors of individuals and societies might be called, using a modified conceptual vocabulary of social psychology, the *first order (or primary) conditioning effect* of ideas. The *second order (or secondary) conditioning effect*, or the second way ideas/norms influence regional orders, is the subsequent redefinition and broadening of initially present and accepted normative structures leading to the development of new norms. Here, ideas that have been made meaningful or consequential for a social group through an initial step of learning are used as the basis for developing and learning about some new ideas, whether indigenous or foreign. The stimulus here is not *preexisting* worldviews endogenous to the region, but ideas resulting of an initial process of socialization and bargaining, and which respond to the changing circumstances and needs of a social group. They may redefine the initial set of ideational elements or create entirely new ones. This causal diffusion of ideas usually occurs through institution-building, where regional institutions provide the crucial site for such normative contestation and selection. Examples of such ideational construction of regional institutions can be found in the contemporary Asia-Pacific region, especially in the diffusion of the norms of ASEAN (the "ASEAN Way") to the wider Asia-Pacific and East Asian regions, leading to constructs such as the Asia-Pacific community or East Asian community.[38] Another example can be found in Africa, where the initial norms of OAU, which included pan-Africanism and nonintervention, gradually morphed into a more complex notion of "responsible sovereignty" that underpins the African Union, which replaced the OAU. Similarly, regional order in Latin America has been

---

[37] Gerard Delanty, *Inventing Europe: Ideas, Identity, Reality* (London: Macmillan, 1995), 16.

[38] Amitav Acharya, "Ideas, Identity, and Institution-Building: From the 'ASEAN Way' to the 'Asia Pacific Way,'" *Pacific Review* 10, no. 2 (1997), 319–46.

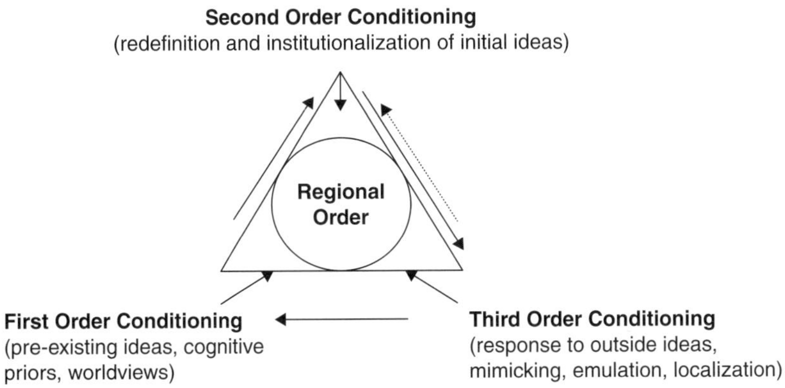

Second Order Conditioning
(redefinition and institutionalization of initial ideas)

First Order Conditioning   **Third Order Conditioning**
(pre-existing ideas, cognitive   (response to outside ideas,
priors, worldviews)   mimicking, emulation, localization)

Figure 8.1 Ideas and regional orders

built around a set of norms that combine the original ideas of pan-Americanism and borrowed norms of Westphalian sovereignty, albeit localized and promoted by agents within the region.

A third way in which ideas shape regional orders, or what might be called the *third order (or tertiary) conditioning effect* of ideas, is through the mimicking and emulation or entirely outside ideas. Here, preexisting or locally created and redefined ideas serve as the receptacle for responding to ideas from other regions or from the international community at large. Examples of such conditioning would be the impact of norms of noninvolvement in military pacts and the keeping out of superpower blocs, which were initially developed in Asia in the 1940s and 1950s, on the Middle East (Nasser) and Africa (Nkrumah).[39] A more recent example is the impact of the "common security" norm developed by the CSCE/OSCE in inspiring regional confidence-building and transparency efforts in other parts of the world, including Asia and Africa. The European Union has also presented itself as a normative model for other regions. In this view, the EU remains the single most important source of ideas and approaches to regionalism and especially of regional transformation, suggesting the possibility of a region moving from anarchy to a security community. But this claim has attracted a considerable amount of attention and controversy. Sceptics argue that the EU is the unique product of historically specific circumstances – a grouping of liberal-democratic states devastated by World War II and disillusioned by the destructive force of nationalism, and facing a common threat

[39] Amitav Acharya, "Norm Subsidiarity and Regional Orders: Sovereignty, Regionalism and Rule-Making in the Third World," *International Studies Quarterly*, forthcoming.

of communism under the US strategic umbrella. These circumstances cannot be replicated in other parts of the world, especially in recently independent countries where nationalism and sovereignty have been the basis of anticolonial struggles. As Haas had correctly noted, the gap between the European and non-European processes of regional integration cannot be easily bridged because of the absence in the latter of some of the key background conditions: "situations controlled by social groupings representing the rational interests of urban-industrial society, groups seeking to maximize their economic benefits and driving along regional homogenous ideological-political lines."[40] The lesson here is not that Europe represents the only pathway to regional integration and order, this is hardly the case (although Haas was more pessimistic about prospects for any genuine regional integration outside of Western Europe), but that the *European model* of regional integration is not easily replicated in other parts of the world, which must therefore develop their own different pathways. Hence the European experience is rarely adopted: it is more likely to be adapted or localized. And the credibility of European ideas cannot be separated from European material assistance and self-promotion. But this has not prevented regional groups in the nonwestern world from borrowing or at least being inspired by certain ideas and institutions of the EU (hence the cliché that the EU is best regarded as an inspiration, not a model). Among contemporary regional groups, the African Union is self-consciously pursuing the EU's ideas and institutions.

Drawing from the above, one might identify different (although interrelated) strands of recent constructivist writings on region-building. In the first are works that examine how ideas and identities create regions and underpin regional institutions. For example, the emergence of Southeast Asia as a distinctive region can be traced to the beliefs and interactions, including a conscious process of identity-building, of the leaders of a group of states emerging from western colonialism and living in the shadows of larger and more powerful neighbours, India and China.[41] Borrowing heavily from the work of historians and historiographical debates about Southeast Asian regional identity, this view challenges the traditionalist argument that Southeast Asia was largely the product of western colonialism, named after a Second World War Allied Command and further developed by western political scientists as a convenient label. Parsons shows how contestation and selection involving two "particular sets of ideas that appeared in Western Europe

---

[40] Haas, "International Integration," 409.
[41] Acharya, *Quest for Identity.*

after the Second World War," namely, the community (supranational) model and the traditional (confederal) model, led its elites "beyond the political framework of the nation-state."[42] Delanty investigates the "invention of Europe" as a regional concept, which emerged from the break-up of the Mediterranean civilization, significantly conditioned as a Christian concept by its competition with Islam, and which "evolved from a mere geographical expression to a cultural idea which had political uses."[43] Europe, particularly the EU, remains the focal point of constructivist perspectives on regional ideas and identity, although other regions are catching up.[44]

A second category of work centers on socialization and norm diffusion. These are more explicitly concerned with regional orders and explore the possibility of their regulation and transformation. A good example can be found in the special issue of *International Organization*, which examines mechanisms, conditions, and outcomes of socialization (featuring norms and microprocesses such as persuasion) through European regional institutions.[45] Although work on norm diffusion in regional orders is heavily Eurocentric, there have been important such perspectives on other regions, including the Middle East,[46] Africa,[47] Asia,[48] and Latin America.[49] It is also important to note that work on regional norms predated the constructivist focus on normative Europe; for example, a conceptually significant body of work on regional norms concerned Africa.[50]

---

[42] Parsons, *Certain Idea of Europe*, 1.

[43] Delanty, *Inventing Europe*, 29.

[44] For an overview of this literature, see Jeffrey T. Checkel and Peter Katzenstein, eds., *European Identity* (Cambridge University Press, 2009).

[45] Jeffrey T. Checkel, "International Institutions and Socialization in Europe," special issue of *International Organization* 59, no. 4 (2005), 801–26.

[46] Michael Barnett, "Nationalism, Sovereignty, and Regional Order in Arab Politics," *International Organization* 49, no. 3 (1995), 479–510; Barnett, *Dialogues in Arab Politics*.

[47] Tore Nyhamar, "How do Norms Work? A Theoretical and Empirical Analysis of African International Relations," *International Journal of Peace Studies* 5, no. 2 (2000).

[48] See Acharya, "Ideas, Identity, and Institution-Building"; Jürgen Haacke, *ASEAN's Diplomatic and Security Culture: Origins, Developments and Prospects* (London: RoutledgeCurzon, 2003); Hiro Katsumata, "Mimetic Adoption and Norm Diffusion: 'Western' Security Cooperation in Southeast Asia?," *Review of International Studies*, forthcoming.

[49] Arie Kacowitz, *The Impact of Norms in International Society: The Latin American Experience, 1881–2001* (Notre Dame University Press, 2005).

[50] See Yassin El-Ayouty and I. William Zartman, eds., *The OAU after Twenty Years* (New York: Praeger, 1984); Francis M. Deng and I. William Zartman, eds., *Conflict Resolution in Africa* (Washington, DC: Brookings Institution, 1991).

Finally, a particularly influential body of constructivist work relates to regional security communities. This literature resurrects the older Deutschian notion, but the latter's fetish for transactions is replaced by a heavy emphasis on social construction.[51] The security community framework has been used to investigate the quality of cooperation in different regions in the world, both individually and comparatively. Usually, the condition of a security community (whether amalgamated or pluralistic) implies a very high degree of cooperation and integration. In such communities actors develop strong mutual interdependence, responsiveness, sensitivity, and empathy; borders are demilitarized; and common institutions for the provision and governance of regional public goods emerge. Not only does war become "unthinkable," but actors also develop a collective identity or "we-feeling." Again, examples of such a terminal condition are rarer to find in the nonwestern world, although the Southern Cone of South America and Southeast Asia may qualify as "nascent" security communities.

Localization and subsidiarity: two pathways to norm diffusion[52]

As argued above, initial theories of regional orders, including regional integration theories, did not develop an adequate understanding of the causal role of ideas or offer a pathway for ideas travelling from the global to the local and vice versa. Constructivism did develop a generic theory of norm diffusion, but it was not clear how much autonomy it gave to ideas relative to power, and whether the diffusion was a one- or two-way process, with regional level interactions influencing global distribution of ideas instead of simply being shaped by it.

Constructivism has offered the most powerful challenge to date to the shared materialism of neorealism and neoliberalism. Norms can be empowering.[53] The constructivist theory of norms focuses on how "discursive, deliberative and persuasive" mechanisms can compensate for the limitations of material power, and how and where "norms ... might enable actors with limited material power to influence outcomes."[54]

---

[51] See Acharya, "Ideas, Identity, and Institution-Building"; Emanuel Adler and Michael Barnett, eds., *Security Communities* (Cambridge University Press, 1998).

[52] This section borrows heavily from my previous work, Acharya, *How Ideas Spread*; and Acharya, *Norm Subsidiarity and Regional Orders*.

[53] Jeffrey T. Checkel, "The Constructivist Turn in International Relations Theory," *World Politics* 50, no. 2 (1998), 324–48; Friedrich Kratochwil, "Contracts and Regimes: Do Issue Specificity and Variations of Formality Matter?," in *Regime Theory and International Relations*, ed. Volker Rittberger (Oxford: Clarendon Press, 1993).

[54] Jane Ford, *A Social Theory of the WTO: Trading Cultures* (Basingstoke: Palgrave Macmillan, 2003), 39.

Yet constructivists have not entirely eschewed the temptations of power. For some, normative change can occur without the explicit backing of powerful actors. Finnemore and Sikkink show that consent of a materially powerful state is not a necessary condition for norm cascades.[55] For example, both Britain and the US were latecomers to the norm of women's suffrage. Their concept of a "critical state" is not necessarily the most materially powerful state; despite US opposition, the norms against landmines cascaded and the treaty was signed.[56] But other constructivists show a surprising degree of deference to power and the importance of hegemonic leadership. Florini points out that norms held by powerful actors "have many more opportunities to reproduce through the greater number of opportunities afforded to powerful states to persuade others of the rightness of their views."[57] Some constructivists merely replace the material power of a hegemon with its ideational influence. While constructivists see ideas and norms as catalysts of change that can counter and overcome material power politics, when power weighs heavily on social interactions they acknowledge the salience of the latter. As Finnemore and Sikkink suggest: "new norms never enter a normative vacuum but instead emerge in a highly contested normative space where they may compete with other norms and *perceptions of power*."[58] Wendt accepts that power relations do play "a crucial role" in the direction and success of social interactions leading to normative change.[59] To be sure, he defines power in noncoercive terms, as the ability of "each side to get the other to see things its way." This is done by rewarding compliant perspective and behavior and punishing deviancy. "Power is the basis of such rewards and punishments." Although power is context-dependent, in general, "where there is an imbalance in relevant material capability social acts will tend to evolve in the direction favored by the more powerful."[60] For Wendt, therefore, while ideas matter in socialization, social processes that produce structural change are "weighted" by considerations of power and dependence.[61]

[55] Martha Finnemore and Kathryn Sikkink, "International Norm Dynamics and Political Change," in *Exploration and Contestation in the Study of World Politics*, ed. Peter J. Katzenstein, Robert O. Keohane, and Stephen D. Krasner (Cambridge, MA: MIT Press, 1998), 247–77, 266.

[56] Ibid., 261.

[57] Ann Florini, "The Evolution of International Norms," *International Studies Quarterly* 40, no. 3 (1996), 363–89, 375.

[58] Finnemore and Sikkink, "International Norm Dynamics and Political Change," 257 (emphasis added).

[59] Wendt, *Social Theory of International Politics*, 331.

[60] Ibid.

[61] Ibid., 341.

The power bias in theoretical explanations of norm diffusion is of course not exclusive to constructivism. Other theories of regional order, structural and eclectic, also show this bias.[62] In their influential (part realist, part constructivist) book, *Regions and Powers*, Buzan and Waever accept that regions can be socially constructed but this is seriously qualified by their emphasis on geopolitics and the distribution of power. Although both accept that regions can be socially constructed, this is seriously qualified in the former by its emphasis on geopolitics and the distribution of power, and in the latter by the central role it assigns to American power in regional construction.[63] Moreover, the power bias in theories of norm diffusion is accentuated by a culture bias (ethnocentrism) and a system bias ("universalism"). In conceptualizing the process through which such ideas spread, constructivists tend to privilege universal (mostly western) moral entrepreneurship at the expense of local agency and feedback. A good deal of constructivist narrative on norms focuses on what Ethan Nadelmann has called the "moral proselytism" of "transnational moral entrepreneurs."[64] Influenced by sociological institutionalism,[65] constructivists have tended to reproduce its assumptions of a "world social structure" that acts as a wellspring of "good" normative ideas and standards. Norms that make a universalistic claim about what is good are seen as more likely to spread than norms that are localized or particularistic.[66] The staple of constructivist writings on norms attests to this; it focuses on the propagation of certain "good" universal norms concerning landmines, the protection of whales, the struggle against racism, intervention against genocide, the promotion of human rights. This strong ethos of "moral cosmopolitanism"[67] predisposes constructivist norm theorists, much like their sociological institutionalist predecessors, against the expansive appeal and feedback potential of regional or localized norms. Yet an understanding of this two-way process of the spread of ideas is important to understanding how ideas shape regional order throughout the world.

---

[62] Buzan and Wæver, *Regions and Powers*.

[63] Amitav Acharya, "The Emerging Regional Architecture of World Politics," *World Politics* 59, no. 4 (2007), 629–52.

[64] Ethan A. Nadelmann, "Global Prohibition Regimes: The Evolution of Norms in International Society," *International Organization* 44, no. 4 (1990), 479–526.

[65] Martha Finnemore, "Norms, Culture and World Politics: Insights from Sociology's Institutionalism," *International Organization* 50, no. 2 (1996), 25–47.

[66] Finnemore and Sikkink, "International Norm Dynamics and Political Change," 257.

[67] Acharya, "How Ideas Spread," 239–75.

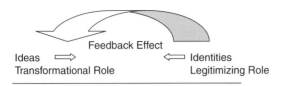

Figure 8.2 Global ideas and regional identities

In short, while constructivist writings on norm diffusion offer plenty of case studies of how universal or global norms espoused by core actors influence and shape regional actors and orders, they scarcely bother themselves with the reverse side of this equation: how locally constructed norms influence global normative structures. Yet, norm diffusion should be understood as a two-way process. While global norms are adopted and adapted by local/regional actors to transform their identities and legitimize their authority, locally constructed norms can feed and infuse into the global level to enrich and empower the global normative structure. In other words, local/regional actors are not only norm-takers, but they are also norm-makers and norm-givers. And when they take outsiders' ideas, they do so not as passive recipients, but as active borrowers, proactively and selectively borrowing foreign norms to legitimize their authority and identity. The two-way relationship can be seen in Figure 8.2.

To understand the importance of the local in norm diffusion and the two-way nexus between regional and global normative structures, I have proposed the concepts of localization and subsidiarity.[68] Localization is "active construction (through discourse, framing, grafting, and cultural selection) of foreign ideas by local actors, which results in the former developing significant congruence with local beliefs and practices."[69] Subsidiarity is a process whereby local actors develop new rules with a view to regulate their relationships and legitimize common global norms that are at risk of neglect, violation, or abuse by powerful and central actors. Both concepts stress the primacy of local agency, but localization is about importing norms created and diffused from outside, whereas subsidiarity is mainly about exporting norms made locally. Whereas localization is *inward-looking* and involves making foreign ideas and norms consistent with a *local* cognitive prior, subsidiarity

[68] Ibid.
[69] Ibid., 245; Oliver Wolters, *History, Culture and Region in Southeast Asian Perspective* (Ithaca, NY: Cornell University Press, Southeast Asian Program, 1999).

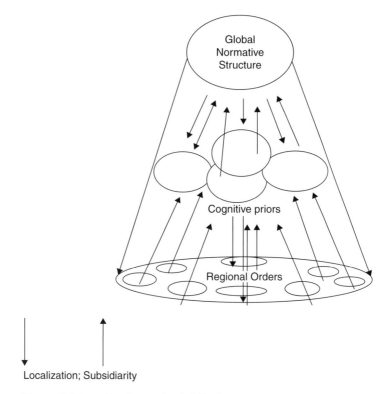

Figure 8.3 Localization and subsidiarity

is *outward-looking*; its main focus is on making local ideas support and strengthen universal norms. The test of localization is that the outcome of the process is a norm which speaks to, supports, and is consistent with the shared local beliefs and identities. The test of subsidiarity is that the outcome of the process must be a norm which speaks to, supports, and is consistent with some higher goals that are shared by the international community at large.

Localization occurs where a group of actors with a developed *sense of uniqueness* of their values and identities seek out new ideas with a view to self-legitimation (by associating with new ideas) and efficiency (to modify existing nonperforming institutions with new ones). Because their sense of identity is well developed, existing ideas are not completely abandoned but enmeshed into a new ideational matrix. Subsidiarity occurs where weaker actors challenge their *exclusion* or marginalization from global norm-making processes and when they are confronted

with great-power *hypocrisy*, that is, when they see the violation of their
cherished global norms by powerful actors and when higher-level institutions tasked with their defense seem unwilling or incapable of preventing their violation. Hence, localization is a tendency that is generic to all
actors, big or small, powerful or weak (even the mighty Roman Empire
accepted the ideas of a much weaker Greek civilization), whereas subsidiarity is applicable mainly to smaller and/or weaker actors, because it
is their representation and autonomy in global norm-making processes
that is more likely to be challenged.

Localization and subsidiarity can be complimentary, however, rather
two sides of the same coin, and can run in tandem. Their motivators
may occasionally overlap. In fact, the creation of a single norm may
involve both processes, whereby a global norm is redefined while a local
norm is infused into a global common. But taken together they offer
a comprehensive framework for understanding and explaining norm
dynamics and diffusion in world politics.

There are many examples of norm localization and subsidiarity
which serve to illustrate the theoretical arguments. Again, classical
regional worlds are useful starting points. Throughout the Roman
regional world, non-Roman local elites adopted Roman political and
legal ideas and institutions to legitimize and enhance their position.
In Roman provinces such as Judaea, there occurred a process of *twin-
ning* whereby "local gods ... were twinned with a Graeco-Roman div-
inity and simply given a double name (Mercurius Dumias)."[70] This has
its parallels in Southeast Asia, where the advent of Indian Buddhist
ideas into Thailand did not lead Thais to abandon the worship of local
spirits. Rather, Thai shrines placed Buddhist deities alongside local
spirits. This transformed the status of both religious practices, resulting in the simultaneous "Parochialization" of Indian Buddhism and
"Universalization" of indigenous and preexisting animism.[71]

Drawing upon these ideas of localization from Southeast Asian
historiography, I have specified the conditions under which localization works as a universal dynamic found in all cultures and societies,
including regional orders and transformations in contemporary Asia,
Africa, and Latin America. In Southeast Asia localization of the key
Westphalian norm of nonintervention led to the delegitimation of
collective defense pacts in the early postwar period, while that of the

---

[70] Robin Lane Fox, *The Classical World: An Epic History of Greece and Rome*
(Harmondsworth: Penguin, 2006), 527.
[71] Thomas C. Kirsch, "Complexity in the Thai Religious System," *Journal of Asian
Studies*, 36, no. 2 (1977), 241–66.

European idea of common security led to the creation of Asia's first multilateral security organization. In Latin America the localization of the democracy promotion norm led to the establishment of the Inter-American Democratic Charter, whereas in Africa the neoliberal norms of New Partnership for Africa's Development failed to diffuse due to the absence of the conditions of localization.[72]

Asia, Latin America, the Middle East, and Africa offer plenty of examples of norm subsidiarity.[73] In each of these regions, local actors have sought to develop subsidiary norms to challenge great power dominance and hypocrisy and secure regional autonomy. In so doing, they also supported existing global norms such as territorial integrity, self-determination, nonintervention, racial equality, and regional autonomy.

In Asia an injunction against participating in superpower-sponsored military pacts, developed at the 1955 Asia–Africa Conference in Bandung, became a key normative foundation for regional order in Southeast Asia. The idea of noninvolvement also morphed into the concept of nonalignment, which influenced the foreign policy of Third World countries across regions, providing a powerful example of how locally developed rule may diffuse globally. Latin American countries, the first to obtain independence from colonial rule, have been "international rule innovators." Among their normative innovations is the doctrine of *uti possidetis juris*, or honoring inherited boundaries, and the principle of nonintervention.[74] The former was developed as a response to imperial collapse (especially of the Spanish Empire) and the consequent inability of European great powers to maintain regional order. Later, under the banner of pan-Americanism, Latin American states developed a regional norm of "absolute nonintervention in the hemispheric community," both as an abstract principle and as a means to challenge US hegemony in the region (embodied in the "Monroe Doctrine") and its perceived hypocrisy in violating the norm of nonintervention.[75] One such rule, the Calvo Doctrine (after Argentine jurist Carlos Calvo) rejected the right of intervention claimed by foreign powers (European and US) in order to protect their citizens

---

[72] Acharya, "How Ideas Spread."

[73] Acharya, "Norm Subsidiarity and Regional Orders."

[74] Jorge I. Dominguez, "International Cooperation in Latin America: The Design of Regional Institutions by Slow Accretion," in *Crafting Cooperation: The Design and Effects of Regional Institutions in Comparative Perspective*, ed. Amitav Acharya and Alastair Iain Johnston (Cambridge University Press, 2007), 126–27.

[75] Thomas Leonard, "The New Pan-Americanism in US–Central American Relations, 1933–1954," in *Beyond the Ideal: Pan-Americanism in International Affairs*, ed. David Sheinin (Westport, CT: Praeger, 2000); David Barton Castle, "Leo Stanton Rowe and the Meaning of Pan-Americanism," in Sheinin, ed., *Beyond the Ideal*, 36.

resident in Latin America. Another rule, the Drago Doctrine, named after Argentine Foreign Minister Luis Drago, challenged the US and European position that they had a right to intervene to force states to honor their sovereign debts. Over US opposition, Latin American congresses recognized revolutionary governments as de jure. Both the Calvo and Drago doctrines constituted subsidiary norms of state sovereignty in Latin America's regional order. The Latin American advocacy led the US to abandon the Monroe Doctrine in 1933 and accept nonintervention as a basic principle in its relations with the region.

In the Middle East norm subsidiarity can be discerned from what Barnett calls the "norms of Arabism," whose principal elements were "quest for independence, the cause of Palestine, and the search for [Arab] unity," as well as nonalignment.[76] These may be regarded as the subsidiary norms of the Arab states system. The Arab Middle East under Nasser's leadership also adopted the anticollective defense norm similar to that prevailing in Asia. This was evident in the Egyptian-led opposition to the Baghdad Pact, which was seen by its critics as an instrument of US and British intervention and hegemony (the tyranny of great power management) and an affront to regional aspirations and arrangements for peace and security. Nasser viewed the Baghdad Pact as severely undermining the scheme for an indigenous Arab Collective Security System, which had been mooted by Egypt. Nasser would sign an arms deal with Czechoslovakia and nationalize the Suez Canal, thereby setting the path for a major confrontation with the US and the West in 1956.

In Africa, Kwame Nkrumah of Ghana, the first sub-Saharan African country to gain independence, led the formulation of the subsidiary norms of an African regional order, which would feature a demand for nonintervention by outside powers in African affairs and the abstention of Africans in superpower-led collective defense pacts.[77] In April 1958 Nkrumah hosted the first Conference of Independent African States. In so doing, he was deeply influenced by the Bandung Conference three years earlier, to which he had been prevented from attended by the British, who still controlled Ghana's foreign policy. The holding of the CIAS suggests imitation and learning as a pathway for norm diffusion (albeit this was a South–South mimicking, rather than a North–South one, which is

[76] Barnett, *Dialogues in Arab Politics*, 56, 106.
[77] Colin Legum, *Bandung, Cairo and Accra: Report on the First Conference of Independent African States* (London: Africa Bureau, 1958); Kwame Nkrumah, *Africa Must Unite* (New York: Praeger, 1963), 136; Bala Mohammed, *Africa and Nonalignment: A Study in the Foreign Relations of New Nations* (Kano, Nigeria: Triumph Publishing Co., 1978).

stressed in western scholarship). The African conference was geared not only to discussing ways to secure independence from colonial rule, but also to developing norms of foreign policy conduct aimed at addressing "the central problem of how to secure peace" (similar to the Bandung agenda of World Peace and Cooperation). Among the principles agreed to at the African conference was Bandung's "abstention from the use of arrangements of collective defense to serve the particular interests of any of the great powers."[78] The normative result of the Conference was "a signal departure from established custom, a jar to the arrogant assumption of non-African nations that Africa affairs were solely the concern of states outside our continent."[79] This marked the beginning of the African subsidiary norms of regional self-reliance in regional security and economic development. Even after Nkrumah's eclipse, the African normative order would continue to reject superpower intervention, espouse regional autonomy, and develop regional institutions geared to achieving African cooperation if not outright political unity.[80]

As noted, regional orders can be built around both types of normative dynamic occurring simultaneously. The Asian regionalist response to the Cold War superpower rivalry involved the localization of universal norms of sovereignty while at the same time creating new norms concerning great power dominance and military alliances for export and universalization. Subsidiary norms need not be entirely original or locally invented. Rather, they can be region-specific applications of global norms or norms borrowed from other regions. The African states borrowed the doctrine of honoring inherited boundaries originally developed in Latin America to create a relatively successful boundary maintenance regime. The originally European idea of sovereignty and nonintervention formed the basis of subsidiary norms in Latin America, Asia, and Africa.

Norm subsidiarity may involve international and transregional feedback and extensions of locally developed rules. Asian norm subsidiarity clearly had a discernible effect on other postcolonial regions. The Non-Aligned Movement, which attracted considerable membership in Latin America, Africa, and the Middle East, was a direct offshoot of the Bandung Conference.[81] A meeting of foreign ministers in 1961 limited

---

[78] John Woronoff, *Organizing African Unity* (Metuchen, NJ: Scarecrow Press, 1970),39.
[79] Nkrumah, *Africa Must Unite*, 136.
[80] Robert H. Jackson and Carl G. Roseberg, "Why Africa's Weak States Persist: The Empirical and the Juridical in Statehood," *World Politics* 35, no. 1 (1982), 259–82; Jeffrey Herbst, "Crafting Regional Co-operation in Africa," in Acharya and Johnston, eds., *Crafting Cooperation*.
[81] George H. Jansen, *Afro-Asia and Non-alignment* (London: Faber & Faber, 1966).

membership in NAM to states that were not members of "a multilateral alliance concluded in the context of Great Power conflicts."[82] This remained a core principle of NAM.

Another implication of the theories of localization and subsidiarity is that despite the borrowing and imitation that is implied by both processes, the resulting norms need not and frequently do not have exactly the same meaning in different regions. Region specificity is a hallmark of norm diffusion. Latin Americans borrowed the European doctrine of nonintervention but turned it into a more *absolute* doctrine (in European practice, intervention could still be justified for the sake of maintaining balance of power). Asians, too, zealously adopted nonintervention, but introduced another significant local variation: abstention from superpower-led military pacts.[83] Although subsidiary norms may travel from one region to another due to snowballing, learning, and emulation, and thereby retain a certain basic meaning across regions, the process of diffusion can also cause new variations in their understanding and application. Hence while all postcolonial regions, including Latin America, Asia, the Middle East, and Africa developed subsidiary norms linked to nonintervention, this took on different meanings and even different institutional forms. In Asia, as the SEATO experience suggests, it produced a total opposition to collective security or defense pacts, but Latin Americans used it as a precondition for participating in a regional collective security system with the US as long as Washington pledged not to interfere in their internal affairs. The Arabs and Africans rejected superpower-led defense pacts much like the Asians, but they were prepared at least to try indigenous schemes for collective security and defense cooperation to an extent not found in Asia. Regional context, need, and discourses determine how subsidiary norms develop in different regions.

Finally, it is important to take note of how ideational regions and regional norm dynamics, including localization and subsidiarity, might produce change, and what kind of change. Here much more empirical work needs to be done to demonstrate the causal and constitutive effects of norms, but some indications are already available. I have argued elsewhere that localization produces gradual, or "every-day," forms of normative change.[84] Subsidiarity is no different. Yet since

---

[82] Mohammed Ayoob, *The Third World Security Predicament: State-Making, Regional Order, and the International System* (Boulder, CO: Lynne Rienner, 1995), 104.

[83] For a fuller discussion on how the interaction of global and local norms produces change in non-European regional settings, see Amitav Acharya, *Whose Ideas Matter? Agency and Power in Asian Regionalism* (Ithaca, NY: Cornell University Press, 2009).

[84] Acharya, *How Ideas Spread*.

both processes are largely voluntary and driven by local initiative, the effects of change could be lasting, although not necessarily permanent (as indicated in the diffusion of classical Indian ideas into Southeast Asia). An important indicator of the impact of norm diffusion is institutional change, or changes to existing structures and processes of regional institutions that are exposed to new norms. The experience of Europe shows that the impact of norm diffusion might lead to significant changes to hitherto balance-of-power orders, as happened with its internal relationships (the shift from nationalism and sovereignty to supranationalist integration) after the formation of the European Coal and Steel Community (ECSC) and later (from the mid 1970s) with the common security norm (which calls for inclusiveness, transparency, and dialogue) that redefined the East–West Cold War relationships in Europe. Also evident now in Europe is the European Union's "normative power," comprising "rule of law, good governance, democracy, human rights, order, and justice."[85] These norms are promoted not only to other parts of Europe, including the new member states of EU, but also internationally to other regions of the world.

In Asia the localization of the cooperative security norm (similar to common security but without the latter's emphasis on legalistic and formal mechanisms of compliance and verification) had a similar, although less deep-rooted impact on the highly polarized balance-of-power system of the Cold War period. Hence the ASEAN Regional Forum, established in 1994 after a great deal of normative debate, has embraced inclusiveness in its membership; embracing Cold War dyads such as the US and China, India and Pakistan, and North and South Korea, and undertaking a limited number of confidence-building measures among its members. Notably, it is playing a significant role in the socialization of China. ASEAN as a subregional grouping itself promptly accepted Vietnam, its main adversary during the Cold War years. The Middle East is perhaps the only major region where the common/cooperative security norm has had little institutional effect, and this may be explained in terms of the conditions that explain successful norm localization identified in the literature (including but not limited to the strength of preexisting beliefs such as pan-Arabism, and the absence of credible insider proponents of new norms). In Africa, the most relevant norm is not common-cooperative security but the norm of humanitarian

---

[85] Michelle Pace, "The Construction of EU Normative Power," *Journal of Common Market Studies* 45, no. 5 (December 2007), 1045; Thomas Diez, "Constructing the Self and Changing Others: Reconsidering 'Normative Power Europe,'" *Millennium: Journal of International Studies* 33, no. 3 (2005), 613–36.

intervention whose localization has led the African Union (formerly the Organization of African Unity) to develop modalities and mechanisms for intervention in domestic conflicts which were previously outside of the mandate of the regional body. In Latin America the members of the Organization of American States have developed a mechanism, the Inter-American Democratic Charter, as a result of the localization of the democracy promotion norm. Although it is too early to conclude that these changes are irreversible, and the role of nonideational factors in effecting these changes deserves notice, there is little indication that these changes to regional order are the result of changing balance-of-power dynamics (in the sense of being shaped by the shifting distribution of power) or are merely short-term tactical adaptations on the part of the norm-takers. Ideas and norms have shaped regional orders, rather than being shaped by material power structures.

9   Regional security practices and Russian–Atlantic relations

Vincent Pouliot

In this chapter I argue that regions in world politics are constituted by sets of specific ways of doing things – practices – that create more or less ordered spaces and narratives of regional interaction. Because they are socially meaningful and organized patterns of action, practices have structuring effects on politics.[1] At the regional level of analysis, security practices such as war, deterrence, diplomacy, arms control, and military exchanges generate configured fields of interaction with variable degrees of order. Security communities, for example, are constituted by the self-evident practice of diplomacy.[2] Likewise, regional nuclear deterrence is made possible by a limited set of patterned gestures – weapons deployment, summit diplomacy, rhetorical formulas, disarmament talks, and so forth – that organize the security game in mutually intelligible terms.

As the case of post-Cold War Russian–Atlantic relations makes clear, however, regional security practices do not always form coherent and well-ordered wholes. Quite often, regional configurations are comprised of competing ways of doing things. This practice clash may lead to unstable security dynamics in which the meanings of interaction are contested or at least not mutually recognized. The case of NATO–Russia politics is particularly evocative here. In the early 1990s both former enemies appeared to be seeking to transform regional security practices from Cold War realpolitik to a new game of cooperative security and democratic peace. But the practices that each side enacted to that end were generally encountered by the other as a continuation of the past instead of a call for change. NATO's enlargement, to take the most prominent example, was linked back to containment practices in Moscow. Reciprocally, Russia's reactions to expansion, particularly

[1] Emanuel Adler and Vincent Pouliot, "International Practices: Introduction and Framework," in *International Practices*, ed. Emanuel Adler and Vincent Pouliot (Cambridge University Press, 2011).
[2] Vincent Pouliot, "The Logic of Practicality: A Theory of Practice of Security Communities," *International Organization* 62, no. 2 (2008), 257–88.

during the negotiations of the 1997 Founding Act with the Alliance, were construed as outdated superpower diplomacy in Brussels. As a result, respective security practices partly failed to constitute a new pattern of regional order. Although some change occurred, as evidenced by new practices of seminar diplomacy or joint military exercises, twenty years after the end of the Cold War Russian–Atlantic relations remain structured by a combination of competing practices that do not always sit easily with each other.[3]

The chapter contains two sections. First, I explore what "regionness" consists of in and through practice. I review existing literatures on regions in world politics and identify two main conceptualizations: regions as geographical versus cognitive entities. I assess the merits and limits of each approach and then propose a practice approach that seeks to move beyond the "idea versus matter" scheme. By beginning with practices, I look into how spaces and narratives of regionness are constituted, as well as how their ordering and transformative dynamics often clash. In many regions the meanings of key practices are contested and mutually unintelligible, creating unstable regional security games. In the second section of the chapter, I illustrate this argument with the case of post-Cold War Russian–Atlantic relations. I focus on one significant episode of diplomatic interaction, running from NATO's decision to enlarge, taken in late 1994, to the signing of the Founding Act in May 1997. I show that what each side was apparently trying to do at the time – establishing new terms of security interaction different from Cold War realpolitik – was consistently encountered by the other in terms of past dynamics. Instead of a democratic peace initiative, as NATO apparently intended it, Moscow appraised enlargement as a new form of containment. Reversely, for Brussels Russia's quest for a negotiated settlement to manage the consequences of expansion was tantamount to old superpower diplomacy. As a result, Russian–Atlantic regional security dynamics changed at the margins, but not as fundamentally as both parties seemed intent on at the end of the Cold War.[4]

A quick note about how this chapter's case study fits in this edited volume is in order. Historically, Russian–Atlantic security relations

---

[3] For a more detailed analysis see Vincent Pouliot, *International Security in Practice: The Politics of NATO–Russia Diplomacy* (Cambridge University Press, 2010), and Vincent Pouliot, "The Materials of Practice: Nuclear Warheads, Rhetorical Commonplaces and Committee Meetings in Russian-Atlantic Relations," *Cooperation and Conflict* 45, no. 3 (2010), 294–311.

[4] See Vincent Pouliot, "Pacification Without Collective Identification: Russia and the Transatlantic Security Community in the Post-Cold War Era," *Journal of Peace Research* 44, no. 5 (2007), 603–20.

have been structured along rather clear regional lines. For one thing, geographical interdependence, in particular on the European theatre, has long been a defining feature of the relationship. Indeed, Buzan and Wæver group together the European and post-Soviet security complexes as part of one "supercomplex."[5] In addition, throughout past decades a variety of identity narratives, whether conflicting or friendly, have structured Russian–Atlantic relations – from the "Iron Curtain" to the "joint fight on terror" through the "Common European home." As I will develop below, however, geography and identity do not tell the whole story. What looms behind regional order and disorder, or transformation and stability, is a limited and evolving set of security practices that create patterns of interaction that are more or less mutually intelligible. As such, and precisely because in this chapter I start from practices, I do not assume Russian–Atlantic regionness, but treat it as an open, empirical question. My main conclusion, to give away the punch line, is that contemporary security practices have limited constitutive effects when it comes to organizing an orderly domain of regional interaction between past Cold War enemies – peaceful or otherwise. Put differently, joint practices do generate Russian–Atlantic regional dynamics, but these are much more erratic than in many other cases.

Beyond "geography versus identity": regionness in practice

What makes a region a region? In other words, what constitutes "regionness" in world politics?[6] In the IR literature there are typically two main answers to this question. While realists and liberals define regions as geographical entities characterized by higher levels of interdependence, constructivists conceive of regions as cognitive entities that coalesce around a collective identity. In this book the editor strikes a middle ground when defining a region as "a cluster of states that are proximate

---

[5] Barry Buzan and Ole Wæver, *Regions and Powers: The Structure of International Security* (Cambridge University Press, 2004).
[6] "Regionness" is Hettne's term; see for example Björn Hettne, "Beyond the 'New Regionalism,'" *New Political Economy* 10, no. 4 (2005), 543–71. On definitional matters see: Rick Fawn, "'Regions' and their Study: Wherefrom, What For and Whereto?," *Review of International Studies* 35, special issue (2009), 5–34; Louise Fawcett, "Exploring Regional Domains: A Comparative History of Regionalism," *International Affairs* 80, no. 3 (2004), 429–46; Raimo Väyrynen, "Regionalism: Old and New," *International Studies Review* 5, no. 1 (2003), 25–51; and Andrew Hurrell, "One World? Many Worlds? The Place of Regions in the Study of International Society," *International Affairs* 83, no. 1 (2007), 127–46.

to each other and are interconnected in spatial, cultural, and ideational terms in a significant and distinguishable manner."[7]

First, as geographical entities, regions are primarily defined by significant levels of interdependence and proximity.[8] This dominant approach in IR, particularly popular in realist and liberal circles, places the emphasis on the spatial dimension of regions. In security terms, this is primarily because, as Buzan puts it, "threats operate more potently over short distances."[9] A related argument based on proximity is that states that inhabit the same geographic area typically need to deal with one another's "externalities."[10] The boundaries of regions, from this perspective, fall where the effects of interdependence end, whether it is in the economic, environmental, societal, or other domain. For example, the notion of "regional security complex" seeks to capture this dimension: "In order to qualify [as a regional security complex], a group of states or other entities must possess a degree of security interdependence sufficient both to establish them as a linked set and to differentiate them from surrounding security regions."[11] For realists, liberals, and a number of other IR scholars, geographical proximity generates interdependence and, by implication, regionness.

Second, as cognitive entities regions are defined by shared norms and identities. This line of argument is particularly evident in constructivist scholarship. The essence of a security community, to take a classic example, is collective identity or "we-ness."[12] Mutual identification

[7] Chapter 1 in this volume.
[8] Joseph Nye, *International Regionalism* (Boston, MA: Little, Brown, 1968); William R. Thompson, "The Regional Subsystem: A Conceptual Explication and a Propositional Inventory," *International Studies Quarterly* 17, no. 1 (1973), 99–117.
[9] Barry Buzan, *People, States and Fear: An Agenda for International Security Studies in the Post-Cold War Era* (Boulder, CO: Lynne Rienner, 1991), 191.
[10] David A. Lake and Patrick M. Morgan, *Regional Orders: Building Security in a New World* (University Park: Pennsylvania State University Press, 1997).
[11] Buzan and Wæver, *Regions and Powers*, 47–48.
[12] Karl Deutsch et al., *Political Community and the North Atlantic Area: International Organization in the Light of Historical Experience* (Princeton University Press, 1957); Emanuel Adler and Michael Barnett, eds., *Security Communities* (Cambridge University Press, 1998). For a variety of views on the security community concept see: Thomas Risse-Kappen, "Collective Identity in a Democratic Community: The Case of NATO," in *The Culture of National Security: Norms and Identity in World Politics*, ed. Peter J. Katzenstein (New York: Columbia University Press, 1996), 357–99; Janice Bially Mattern, "The Power Politics of Identity," *European Journal of International Relations* 7, no. 3 (2001), 349–97; Michael C. Williams, "The Discipline of the Democratic Peace: Kant, Liberalism, and the Social Construction of Security Communities," *European Journal of International Relations* 7, no. 4 (2001), 525–53; Vincent Pouliot and Niels Lachmann, "Les Communautés de sécurité, vecteurs d'ordre régional et international," *Revue Internationale et Stratégique* 54 (2004), 131–40; Stéphane Roussel, *The North American Democratic Peace: Absence of War and Security Institution-building in Canada–US Relations, 1867–1958* (Montreal and

plays a constitutive role by redefining states' interests and instilling a pacific disposition. We-ness, the cement of security community, becomes part of states' self-understandings and practices, thus making peaceful change dependably expectable. In response to the rationalist view that it is common interests – driven by geographical externalities, for example – that foster cooperation, constructivists argue that shared preferences are never simply "read off" international structures of material capabilities. Instead, common interests are socially constructed through interaction and the social construction of identities.[13] In the case of a security community, thanks to collective identification (i.e. the blurring of Self and Other), a state's interests come to merge with the collective interests of the community. For example, Acharya explains security community development in Southeast Asia through the development of a set of interstate norms dubbed the "ASEAN way."[14] Because they rest on socially constructed norms and identities, for constructivists regions are fundamentally cognitive: they comprise states "whose people imagine that, with respect to their own security and economic well-being, borders run, more or less, where shared understandings and common identities end."[15] In this understanding, we-ness constitutes regionness.

Despite some limitations to which I shall turn below, the cognitive/constructivist understanding of regions improves upon the geographical one in three important ways. First, it adds a temporal dimension to regions by showing how a region's present and future are carved out of the past. States within a region do not just happen to bump into

Kingston: McGill-Queen's University Press, 2004); Vincent Pouliot, "The Alive and Well Transatlantic Security Community: A Theoretical Reply to Michael Cox," *European Journal of International Relations* 12, no. 1 (2006), 119–27; Alex J. Bellamy, *Security Communities and their Neighbors: Regional Fortresses or Global Integrators?* (Basingstoke: Palgrave Macmillan, 2004); Corneliu Bjola and Markus Kornprobst, "Security Communities and the Habitus of Restraint: Germany and the United States on Iraq," *Review of International Studies* 33, no. 2 (2007), 285–305; Pouliot, "Logic of Practicality"; Veronica Kitchen, "Argument and Identity Change in the Atlantic Security Community," *Security Dialogue* 40, no. 1 (2009), 95–114; and Charles A. Kupchan, *How Enemies Become Friends: The Sources of Stable Peace* (Princeton University Press, 2010).

[13] Alexander Wendt, *Social Theory of International Politics* (Cambridge University Press, 1999).

[14] Amitav Acharya, *Constructing a Security Community in Southeast Asia: ASEAN and the Problem of Regional Order* (New York: Routledge, 2001). See also Amitav Acharya, "How Ideas Spread: Whose Norms Matter? Norm Localization and Institutional Change in Asian Regionalism," *International Organization* 58, no. 2 (2004), 239–75; and Chapter 8 in this volume.

[15] Emanuel Adler, "Imagined (Security) Communities: Cognitive Regions in International Relations," *Millennium: Journal of International Studies* 26, no. 2 (1997), 250.

one another all of a sudden; they usually have a long history of more or less conflictual interactions, which leave traces in the form of more or less entrenched norms and identities.[16] Such intersubjective structures typically take the form of narratives (or "stories") that construct similarity and difference – that is, regionness – over time. In the form of a narrative, identity is not only relational (meaning that defining "us" necessarily relates to defining "them") but also historical: it is a particular way to frame one's current existence in terms of one's past. To paraphrase Neumann, "if the [region's] reality in space is testified to by its territory, its reality in time is a question of getting itself a history … This is done by identifying, and thus making relevant to the identity of the human collective in question, a host of political ties, cultural similarities, economic transactional patterns, and so on."[17] In effect, any narrative of identity, regional or otherwise, tends to emphasize certain markers of similarity and difference while leaving others aside. This eminently arbitrary process, it should be underscored, does not necessarily follow geographical lines. Take, for instance, the Mediterranean basin: despite the rare combination of, firstly, an obvious geographical proximity and coherence, secondly, long episodes of political interaction in the past (starting with the Roman empire), and thirdly, in recent years a very active promotion by NATO, the European Union as well as a number of coastal states, the notion of a Mediterranean region has yet to triumph over other markers of identity and difference in order for it to gain political momentum in the twenty-first century.

Second, the cognitive take on regionness usefully brings social agency back into the picture. After all, if the boundaries of a region are determined by the fact that "national securities cannot realistically be considered apart from another," to use Buzan's words,[18] then it logically follows that human beings must be involved at some point in order to make the "realistic considerations" in question. Apart, perhaps, from a few impassable mountains, oceans or deserts, geographic features rarely speak for themselves in bounding regions – and decreasingly so given human technological prowess. Look at the political map of Europe, for example: the fact that certain rivers demarcate international frontiers while others (sometimes even larger ones!) play no political function whatsoever is a useful reminder that, as Hemmer and Katzenstein paraphrase Simmel, a border is not a geographical fact that

---

[16] See also Chapter 2 in this volume.
[17] Iver B. Neumann, *Uses of the Other: "The East" in European Identity Formation* (Minneapolis: University of Minnesota Press, 1999), 114.
[18] Barry Buzan, *People, States and Fear: The National Security Problem in International Relations* (Chapel Hill: University of North Carolina Press, 1983), 106.

has sociological consequences, but a sociological fact that takes a geo-graphical form.[19] Put differently, the transmission belt of regionness is not proximity as captured from some sort of god's eye, but polit-ical agency under a variety of constraints and possibilities – including geography. In this spirit, Buzan's observation that threats travel more easily over short distances tells us only one part of the story: in order for a threat to take hold and mobilize, it has to be framed as part a Self and Other relationship that turns proximity into a source of otherness. After all, many neighboring countries – Canada and the United States being the archetype – do not threaten each other despite considerable territorial vicinity. As constructivists point out, the intimate connec-tion between identity and threat means that menaces are never entirely endogenous to geographical proximity. This point, it should be noted, is taken on board by Buzan's addition of securitization theory to the concept of regional security complex.[20]

Third and related, the cognitive definition addresses the important question of who gets to define regions. After all, drawing the boundar-ies of a political entity, including those of a region, can never be reduced to a simple analytical move. This is because the very essence of politics consists of defining groups and policing their borders. In response to the first view that regionness is a material fact given by geography and technology, Hemmer and Katzenstein argue that "[e]ven regions that seem most natural and inalterable are products of political construc-tion and subject to reconstruction attempts."[21] As political projects, regions are not "objective facts" but categories of practice. Regionness, then, is an intersubjective process of political construction in which many agents fight over the precise contours of space and belonging. By implication, the goal is not to "discover" regions out there by various measurements, but rather to understand the processes by which cer-tain borders get fixated and not others: "One should not ask 'How can this region be defined?' but 'Why do certain people, at a certain point in history, within a certain political context, try to build a region?'"[22] The task of filling regionness with content – that is, of defining markers of similarity and difference – is better left with practitioners and pol-itical agents themselves. After all, as Neumann concludes: "Cultural

---

[19] Christopher Hemmer and Peter J. Katzenstein, "Why is there no NATO in Asia? Collective Identity, Regionalism, and the Origins of Multilateralism," *International Organization* 56, no. 3 (2003), 587.

[20] Buzan and Wæver, *Regions and Powers*.

[21] Hemmer and Katzenstein, " Why is there no NATO in Asia?," 575.

[22] Neumann, *Uses of the Other*, 146. See also Amitav Acharya, "The Emerging Regional Architecture of World Politics," *World Politics* 59, no. 4 (2007), 629–52.

differences are *made* relevant by political actors, to serve some political cause, and their activation is therefore *itself* a political act."[23]

Because it equates regionness with narrative, however, the cognitive/constructivist approach also runs up against two main difficulties. First, while at the level of action regions are, indeed, social artifacts that depend on people narrating them into existence, there are nonetheless conceptual gains to be made from inserting, at the level of observation, a regional level of analysis in between the state and international ones. For IR students, the regional level of analysis helps isolate a realm of political and social interaction that reaches beyond national communities without becoming global.[24] Historically, many crucial international dynamics have tended to revolve at that level. While acknowledging that regions are first and foremost social artifacts, then, in this chapter I use the term "regional" to heuristically delimit a realm of social analysis located above the state but below the system.

A second and more problematic limitation of the cognitive/constructivist approach is that, ultimately, reducing regionness to narrative fails to explain why some narratives of regionness fly while others do not. To return to the Mediterranean example, why did the active promotion by several powerful actors of a regional narrative not lead, so far at least, to significant feelings of regionness? Both geography and narrative are present in this case, yet regionness refuses to follow. I contend that what would best serve IR scholars is an understanding of regionness that can simultaneously account for *both* the spatial/interdependence *and* temporal/narrative dimensions of regions – not as two separate determinants of regional dynamics, but as part of one single process of practice.

Starting from this premise, I argue that *what constitutes regionness is a set of specific ways of doing things – practices – that create a coherent space and narrative of regional interaction.* This approach requires turning conventional wisdom on its head: instead of positing the region (either as a geographical or as a cognitive entity) as the cause of state behaviors, *I begin with practices* in order to understand how they generate socially meaningful and organized patterns of action at the regional level. Traditionally, IR scholars focus on how interdependence and/or identity create regions, which in turn produce specific dynamics at the substate level. Starting from the opposite end, I look into how regional practices constitute spaces and narratives of regionness. This reversed perspective illuminates often overlooked aspects of regional dynamics.

---

[23] Neumann, *Uses of the Other*, 139–40.   [24] Buzan, *People, States, and Fear.*

From this angle, for instance, European regionness owes as much, if not more, to repeated warring and diplomatic practices over the centuries than to geographical features or identity narratives – both of which happen to be eminently contested in the case of Europe. In effect, the contours of today's Europe fall pretty much where the geographical reach of certain dominant ways of doing things political – war, diplomacy, governance mores, and so forth – have historically extended. Interdependence and identity certainly played a role as well in lending coherence to the European region, but they were largely the result of centuries of political interaction structured by recurring patterns of mutually recognizable actions.[25]

Practices are "socially meaningful patterns of action which, in being performed more or less competently, simultaneously embody, act out and possibly reify background knowledge and discourse in and on the material world."[26] Practices are distinct from both behavior and action. The notion of behavior captures the material aspect of doing; the concept of action adds on a layer of meaningfulness, at both the subjective (intentions, beliefs) and intersubjective (norms, identities) levels. Practices, however, are not only behavioral and meaningful, but also organized and patterned. Because they are regular forms of action within a given social context, practices tend to become mutually recognizable for their communities of practitioners. As Cook and Brown illustrate: "In the simplest case, if Vance's knee jerks, that is behavior. When Vance raps his knee with a physician's hammer to check his reflexes, it is behavior that has meaning, and thus is what we call action. If his physician raps his knee as part of an exam, it is practice. This is because the meaning of her action comes from the organized contexts of her training and ongoing work in medicine (where it can draw on, contribute to, and be evaluated in the work of others in her field)."[27] In the end, anything that people do in a contextually typical way counts as a practice. In international politics, for example, diplomacy is one of the oldest and most central practices.[28]

---

[25] On contemporary Europe as a community of practice, see Emanuel Adler, "Europe as a Civilizational Community of Practice," in *Civilizations in World Politics: Plural and Pluralist Perspectives*, ed. Peter J. Katzenstein (New York: Rouledge, 2010), 66–90.

[26] Adler and Pouliot, "International Practices," 6.

[27] Scott D. N. Cook and John Seely Brown, "Bridging Epistemologies: The Generative Dance Between Organizational Knowledge and Organizational Knowing," *Organization Science* 10, no. 4 (1999), 387.

[28] See among others Iver B. Neumann, "To be a Diplomat," *International Studies Perspectives* 6, no. 1 (2005), 72–93; and Adam Watson, *Diplomacy: The Dialogue Between States* (New York: Routledge, 1991).

The patterned nature of practices matters a great deal in making sense of politics. To put it in a nutshell, *practices structure social interaction*.[29] Because they are meaningful, organized, and repeated, practices generally convey a degree of mutual intelligibility that allows people to develop social relations over time. After all, in order to count as such, a practice of X-ing needs to be recognizable and recognized as such by an audience of fellow practitioners. As a result, social groupings tend to coalesce around the collective accomplishment of shared practices.[30] In the field of international security, for example, the practice of deterrence is premised on a limited number of gestures, signals, and linguistic devices that are meant, as Schelling puts it, to "getting the right signal across."[31] Because it aspires to mutual intelligibility, the regular enactment of these deeds within a particular political context of state-to-state relations organizes social interactions along more or less shared lines. The patterned ways of doing deterrence, in other words, is what makes it possible for actors to mutually recognize the meaningfulness of their respective actions. Crucially, it is also the patterned nature of practices that structures both the space and discourse of interaction. For instance, outside established and reiterated practices of conventional and nuclear deterrence, the Cold War regional dynamics between the East and the West would have lacked a social structure. Of course, NATO and the Warsaw Pact countries also shared a geographical space (the northern hemisphere, the European continent) and a prominent narrative (the capitalist versus communist ideological clash). Yet in the end what organized East–West security dynamics – what lent order to regional political relations – was, first and foremost, a limited set of more or less confrontational practices that were reiterated over time in a mutually intelligible way. Think, for example, of arms control, summit diplomacy, confidence-building measures, nuclear deterrence, sphere-of-influence interventions, and so on.[32]

By putting the practice horse ahead of the region cart, this chapter joins a growing number of studies arguing that "[b]eyond the traditional geographical/geopolitical notion of regional boundaries and the social or cognitive notion of boundaries defined with reference to identity, [we should also conceive] of a 'practical' notion of boundaries according to which regions' boundaries are determined by the practices that

---

[29] Adler and Pouliot, "International Practices."
[30] Etienne Wenger, *Communities of Practice: Learning, Meaning, and Identity* (Cambridge University Press, 1998).
[31] Thomas Schelling, *Arms and Influence* (New Haven, CT: Yale University Press, 1966).
[32] Adler and Pouliot, "International Practices."

constitute regions."[33] *What constitutes regionness, in other words, is the joint enactment of certain established practices.*[34] For example, Adler documents the specific practices of cooperative security that the OSCE promotes in the northern hemisphere.[35] He similarly theorizes NATO's post-Cold War expansion in terms of diffusing practices of self-restraint.[36] Elsewhere, I conceive of security communities as constituted by the self-evident practice of diplomacy or nonviolent settlement of disputes[37] and make the wager that it is not only who we are that drives what we do – but also what we do that determines who we are.[38] In a similar vein, balancing practices form a distinct repertoire of action whose prevalence distinguishes a number of regional settings from others.[39] Even warring practices, as conflicting and destructive as they may be, produce structuring effects that hold a number of regions together by organizing pretty much every dimension of state-to-state relations. Whatever the nature of its political dynamics, a region is delimited by the joint and regular enactment of a set of practices. Interdependence and narrative surely play a role as well, but at the constitutive level the boundaries and processes of a region are, ultimately, a very practical matter – based on what a subgroup of states do together.

However, because social life and politics are so complex, multifaceted, and even messy, the structuring effects of practices are often considerably curbed. When practices clash with one another, their meanings become contested and as a result social order cannot obtain.[40] For that reason there is nothing automatic between an actor doing something

[33] Emanuel Adler and Patricia Greve, "When Security Community Meets Balance of Power: Overlapping Regional Mechanisms of Security Governance," *Review of International Studies* 35, no. 1 (2009), 59. Katzenstein has also taken a similar direction recently by conceiving of regions as institutionally patterned interactions between states (instead of purely geographic objects or cognitive constructs): Peter J. Katzenstein, *A World of Regions: Asia and Europe in the American Imperium* (Ithaca, NY: Cornell University Press, 2005).

[34] This is not to say, though, that the practices constitutive of a given region need to be performed as part of the region-building project, as in regionalism. Region-structuring practices may, or may not, be part of an intentional policy.

[35] Emanuel Adler, "Seeds of Peaceful Change: The OSCE's Security Community-building Model," in *Security Communities*, ed. Emanuel Adler and Michael Barnett (Cambridge University Press, 1998), 119–160.

[36] Emanuel Adler, "The Spread of Security Communities: Communities of Practice, Self-restraint, and NATO's Post-Cold War Transformation," *European Journal of International Relations* 14, no. 2 (2008), 195–230. See also Alexandra Gheciu, "Security Institutions as Agents of Socialization? NATO and the 'New Europe,'" *International Organization* 59, no. 4 (2005), 973–1012.

[37] Pouliot, "Logic of Practicality."

[38] Pouliot, *International Security in Practice*, 5.

[39] Adler and Greve, "When Security Community Meets Balance of Power."

[40] Pouliot, *International Security in Practice*, 46–50.

in a contextually typical way, on the one hand, and that performance being recognized as such by the audience, on the other. In fact, a defining characteristic of international politics is that, even more so than in other social realms, one's practices always risk being encountered by others in ways that do not align with the intended signal. The (largely failed) deterrence game between Iran and the western powers over the nuclear issue is a case in point.[41] Each side is trying to gesture into being an interaction framework that is incompatible with the other's; the fight over the meanings of respective practices is generally inconclusive. In such cases mismatched practices fail, to a variable extent, to organize or structure political interaction. For the agents involved, the significance of patterns of action is so contested that they are not mutually recognizable. As a result, the structuring effects of practices are held in check, and regional order, or transformation, becomes erratic.

To sum up, IR scholars typically argue that regions, whether as geographical entities or cognitive forms, explain practices. I contend that the reverse is also true, though seldom noticed. *By beginning with practices, I explain how doing certain things in socially organized and meaningful ways comes to constitute fields of international interaction called regions.* The coherence or "boundedness" of regions stems from the fact that practices produce interactional domains that are both spatially and cognitively situated, with interdependence and narrative effects. That said, in many regions of the world security practices are contested, rendering mutually intelligible patterns of interaction difficult to establish. This is precisely what the following case study about post-Cold War Russian–Atlantic security dynamics tends to demonstrate.

Contentious patterns of security practices in the Russian–Atlantic region

In the post-Cold War era, NATO and Russia partly failed to transform regional terms of interaction due to the contentious patterns that many of their respective security practices have expressed. In theoretical terms, the structuring effects of practices were considerably curbed by the fact that, more often than not, each side's gestures ended up not "sending the right signal across" to the other party. Instead of organizing a new, mutually recognizable game of regional security, respective

---

[41] For example, Janice Stein, "Rational Deterrence against 'Irrational' Adversaries? No Common Knowledge," in *Complex Deterrence: Strategy in the Global Age*, ed. T. V. Paul, Patrick M. Morgan, and James J. Wirtz (University of Chicago Press, 2009), 58–82.

performances were often linked back, albeit in a significantly attenuated fashion, to the previous social structure of the Cold War. In order to substantiate this claim, I focus on a short but crucial episode of Russian–Atlantic diplomatic interaction in the post-Cold War era: the negotiation of the Founding Act, signed in May 1997, in response to NATO's decision to enlarge to include Eastern European countries.[42] The practices that Russia and the Alliance enacted over this issue illustrate particularly well how difficult it can be for states to transform regional dynamics in and through practice. On the one hand, NATO's enlargement practices, which were devised as part of a new security game of democratic peace, were encountered in Moscow as a form of Cold War-like containment. On the other, Brussels associated the reactive gestures that Russia performed with an outdated superpower game. In consequence, the regional security order partly failed to transform, combining past patterns of interaction with hybrid forms of post-Cold War practices.

In launching its enlargement process in the mid 1990s, NATO was largely implementing its new vision of regional security premised on the notion of democratic peace.[43] Instead of power balancing, nuclear deterrence, and other realpolitik practices, the Alliance was determined to use new, softer security tools centered on liberal domestic institutions, ranging from the civilian control of the military to human rights protection through election monitoring and so forth. Most of these practices were in fact inherited from the Conference on Security and Cooperation in Europe (CSCE)'s "third basket." However, contrary to the CSCE, which combined innovative practices with a rather conservative understanding of territorial sovereignty, in the early 1990s NATO's intended shift was a radical one, breaking with the "outdated" security practices of the Cold War such as superpower spheres of influence, for instance. A series of bold initiatives, ranging from the Partnership for Peace (PfP) to postconflict reconstruction in the Balkans, were meant to implement, in and through practice, the new NATO order of regional security. In a similar vein, enlargement to new members was framed as the natural extension of a community of values – a democratic process that would foster security in the whole region. In a 1995

---

[42] For a more detailed analysis of post-Cold War NATO–Russia diplomacy, see Pouliot, *International Security in Practice*, and Vincent Pouliot, "The Year NATO Lost Russia," in *European Security since the Fall of the Berlin Wall*, ed. Frédéric Mérand, Martial Foucault, and Bastien Irondelle (University of Toronto Press, 2010), 239–59.

[43] Alexandra Gheciu, *NATO in the "New Europe": The Politics of International Socialization after the Cold War* (Stanford University Press, 2005); Michael C. Williams, *Culture and Security: Symbolic Power and the Politics of International Security* (New York: Routledge, 2007); Adler, "Spread of Security Communities."

study, for example, NATO envisioned that the first "contribution" of enlargement would be in "encouraging and supporting democratic reforms, including civilian and democratic control over the military."[44] For Brussels, enlargement was part and parcel of a set of new practices meant to transform the terms of regional security dynamics with other players in the region, including Moscow.

However, Moscow did not encounter NATO's enlargement practices in the way that Brussels had apparently intended them. Contrary to other initiatives like the PfP, which was lauded in Russia as an inclusive and cooperative new framework for regional security, enlargement was linked back to former practices of "containment," to use Foreign Minister Andrei Kozyrev's words.[45] As his successor similarly put it in 1996: "We don't need to be convinced that NATO is not preparing to attack us. We do not intend to attack the United States, either. But let us suppose, purely hypothetically, that we were to conclude a military alliance with Mexico, Venezuela and Cuba. Surely that would elicit a negative reaction from the United States."[46] Appraised from Moscow, the Alliance gradually swallowing countries up to the Russian border was reminiscent not of the new, NATO-proposed democratic peace, but of Cold War zero-sum games. Despite all the Alliance talk to the contrary, for Moscow the December 1994 decision to enlarge breached the three basic CSCE principles that had been so fundamental in putting an end to the Cold War: that security is indivisible, mutual, and cooperative.

To begin with, from a Russian perspective expanding NATO would create new dividing lines in the European security system. NATO's claim that an enlarged alliance would not create demarcations in Europe made little sense for Moscow: one is either inside or outside the tent. So long as Russia remained on the margins of a tightly knit alliance that arrogated to itself the central role in European security, it could not but lead to its exclusion. The Russians felt they were unfairly pushed away from a place they thought they belonged to. Furthermore, expansion seriously undermined the chances of developing a pan-European security institution with teeth in which Russia could exert influence. To counter this view, many Atlantic officials insisted that the door would always remain open for Russia to eventually join

---

[44] NATO, *Study on NATO Enlargement* (1995), 3; available at www.nato.int/docu/ basictxt/enl-9502.htm (accessed 26 March 2006).

[45] Andrei Kozyrev, "Partnership or Cold Peace?," *Foreign Policy* 99 (1995), 13.

[46] Yevgeny Primakov quoted in Stanislav Kondrashov, "The Diplomatic Gospel According to Yevgeny on the Eve of the Second Coronation of Boris," *Izvestia*, August 9, 1996, translated in *Current Digest of the Post-Soviet Press* 48, no. 32 (1996).

NATO. Clinton repeatedly told president Boris Yeltsin, for example, that enlargement could, in theory, also embrace Russia. In actuality, however, Brussels turned down each of Moscow's declarations of interest in 1992, 1996, and 2002. In September 1994 the German Defense Minister expressed what was already the dominant view in the Atlantic world: "Russia cannot be integrated, neither into the European Union nor in NATO ... if Russia were to become a member of NATO it would blow NATO apart ... It would be like the United Nations of Europe – it wouldn't work."[47] Acutely aware of this discourse, security practitioners in Moscow construed geographical enlargement as a contravention to the principle of indivisible security.

Instead of sending the "democratic peace" signal intended by Brussels, the enlargement policy sparked new security dilemmas reminiscent of past regional dynamics. Relegated to the regional periphery, Moscow feared that in gaining even more strength, NATO would become able to force any and all policies on Russia. In Defense Minister Igor Rodionov's words: "I do not think that NATO is expanding to start a war, but it is becoming a military alliance whose power cannot be matched by anybody. We fear that as it gains strength and moves closer to Russian borders, NATO will try to impose on us its conditions – political, economic and others."[48] Such a regional dynamic would defeat the principle of mutual security, which implies that one's security cannot be enhanced at the expense of others'. What is particularly interesting in Moscow's reaction is how rooted in the security dilemma it is. At issue were not intentions but the fact that increasing one side's forces necessarily has consequences for the other.

Finally, in Russian eyes NATO expansion contradicted the principle of cooperative security by which international order must be achieved through negotiated settlement. Russian officials felt that the decision to enlarge was imposed on them regardless of their country's legitimate security interests. In his memoirs, Yevgeny Primakov recounts a one-on-one conversation with Warren Christopher in early 1996: "My discussion with Christopher left no doubt that our opinion would be ignored during the expansion of NATO. It was not the process of expansion that would have to take Russia's position into account but Russia that would have to adapt to the process."[49] Contrary to the spirit

---

[47] Volker Rühe quoted in David Yost, "The New NATO and Collective Security," *Survival* 40, no. 2 (1998), 139.

[48] Quoted in Ian Black, "Albright to Offer Arms Cuts as Russia Digs in on NATO," *Guardian*, February 20, 1997.

[49] Yevgeny Primakov, *Russian Crossroads: Toward the New Millennium* (New Haven, CT: Yale University Press, 2004), 135.

of cooperative security, any substantive compromise with Russia to accommodate its concerns was excluded from the outset. The net result was that throughout the enlargement process Russia basically faced the facts as NATO laid them out. Resentment was palpable among Russian elites: Andranik Migranyan, a Yeltsin advisor, regretted that "Russia's reward for destroying the totalitarian Soviet empire is not a return to civilization as a respected and equal partner, but the isolation and serious weakening of the country."[50] Far from opening a new era of regional cooperative security, NATO appeared to be exploiting Russia's difficulties in order to secure cheap gains. As Russian elites came to construe NATO's discourse of democracy and cooperative security as a cover-up for collecting "geopolitical trophies," the transformation of regional security became increasingly contentious.

In a kind of self-reinforcing spiral, the practices that Russia enacted in reaction to expansion further narrowed the possibilities for change in the region. The diplomatic negotiations that led to the NATO–Russia "Founding Act on Mutual Relations, Cooperation and Security between NATO and the Russian Federation," signed in May 1997, illustrate particularly well how Moscow's practices failed to organize new terms of security between the former enemies. The key bone of contention was that Moscow's principle, in institutionalizing security relations with the Alliance, was never to be a normal partner, as Brussels wanted it, but rather to maintain its Cold War status as "first among equals, with the only possible exception of the United States."[51] From the NATO point of view, however, this quest belonged to a bygone era of superpower competition. Times had changed, and the Alliance, as the main standard-bearer of democracy and liberalism, now occupied the driver's seat of regional security. As a result, the gestures that Russia performed in reaction to enlargement were systematically construed in Brussels and other NATO capitals as a return to the Cold War past. Russian practices can be grouped in four categories: counterproposals, hindrance, soft balancing, and veiled threats.

First, throughout the negotiation process the Russians made a number of counterproposals so as to keep the initiative and obtain concessions from NATO. From the NATO point of view, however, these tactics

[50] Andranik Migranyan, "Russia's Foreign Policy: Disastrous Results of Three Years," *Nezavisimaya Gazeta*, December 10, 1994, translated in *Current Digest of the Post-Soviet Press* 46, no. 50 (1994).

[51] Dmitri Trenin, "Russia's Security Integration with America and Europe," in *Russia's Engagement with the West: Transformation and Integration in the Twenty-first Century*, ed. Alexander J. Motyl, Blair A. Ruble, and Lilia Shevtsova (Armonk, NY: M. E. Sharpe, 2005), 282.

belonged to old regional security logics of superpower condominium. For example, in March 1996 Primakov proposed to Poland that NATO give it security guarantees that would stop short of full-fledged membership. In April the Kremlin suggested the establishment of a Baltic–Black Sea nuclear-free zone, to be codified legally and comprised of the Baltic states, the Visegrad four, Belarus, Ukraine, Moldova, Romania, and Bulgaria. Shortly thereafter Yeltsin put forward a "French scenario" providing for the admission of new members only to the bloc's political structures without joining military structures. Primakov even visited Norway and Denmark to demonstrate how some established NATO member states had never allowed bases or troops deployments on their territories. In July 1996 Yeltsin wrote a letter to Clinton consenting to NATO enlarging to Poland on the condition that Baltic states would be excluded from any future enlargement. Several months later, in his summit with Clinton in Helsinki, the Russian President tried that line again as part of a gentlemen's agreement. From the Alliance point of view, such practices were not legitimate in the new democratic peace era of regional security.

The second strategy that Russia followed was one of hindrance, at times bordering on obstruction. In January 1996, for instance, the Duma delayed ratification of the second Strategic Arms Reduction Treaty (START), invoking the problem of NATO expansion. In September 1996, at the very last minute, Russia refused to participate in PfP Black Sea exercises with Bulgaria, Romania, and Turkey. In October 1996 the Duma adopted one of several resolutions against NATO expansion, warning that an enlarged NATO would undermine the validity of the Conventional Forces in Europe (CFE) treaty. Thirdly, Russia took a number of foreign policy initiatives akin to "soft balancing" – limited and indirect balancing strategies of coalition-building and diplomatic bargaining within international institutions, short of formal alliances.[52] In April 1996, during a Sino-Russian summit in Beijing, the parties adopted a declaration premised on the notion of strategic partnership. A year later Moscow and Beijing agreed on a "Joint Russian-Chinese Declaration about a Multipolar World and the Formation of a New World Order." In March 1997, together with Belarus, Russia declared its unwillingness to accept NATO's plans to advance eastward, and the two countries even took steps to plan joint military exercises. Again, from the NATO point of view Russia was playing a balancing game that had no bearing in the new regional security dynamics.

---

[52] T. V. Paul, "Soft Balancing in the Age of US Primacy," *International Security* 30, no. 1 (2005), 46–71.

Fourth and finally, Russian officials also issued a handful of veiled threats. Even before the negotiations over the Founding Act formally opened, the Russian government listed five countermeasures that it was prepared to implement should enlargement proceed: (1) revision of the military doctrine; (2) creation of a defensive alliance, within and beyond the CIS framework; (3) significant build-up of the southern, western and northwestern groups of force, the CFE treaty notwithstanding; (4) build-up of new tactical nuclear weapons and retargeting against new NATO members; (5) withdrawal from START I and II.[53] Later on, Primakov threatened to cut off all relations with NATO if any country from the former Soviet Union was invited to join. In the end these practices proved unsuccessful in deterring NATO from proceeding with enlargement, largely because they belonged to a security logic that had little to do with the Alliance's transformative agenda of democratic peace.

The negotiation of the Founding Act is but one instance of post-Cold War NATO–Russia diplomacy in which mismatched practices prevent the establishment of mutually intelligible terms of interaction. One could have also examined political interaction over the Bosnian and Kosovo crises, for example, as other cases of mutually unintelligible patterns of action.[54] Taken together, these various episodes help us to understand why transforming regional security practices often runs into complications. Creating international patterns of action is not easily done. For example, signaling deterrence, as students of international security know quite well, can be quite hard to do, particularly in the absence of preexisting frameworks of interaction. Changing the nature and structure of a regional security game is even more complicated. Moving from one practice to another (e.g., from warring practices to deterrence, or from deterrence to disarmament) is an eminently difficult transformative process – even when all players aspire for change. In the Russian–Atlantic case, both sides appeared intent to move away from Cold War practices; yet in the end their respective gestures often failed to meet along a new, mutually intelligible pattern of interaction. NATO's enlargement smacked of Cold War containment; while Russia's reaction resembled outdated superpower politics. As a result, since the

---

[53] Igor Rodionov, "What Sort of Defense Does Russia Need?," *Nazavisimoye Voyennoye Obozreniye*, November 28, 1996, translated in *Current Digest of the Post-Soviet Press* 48, no. 50 (1996).

[54] Pouliot, *International Security in Practice*. For an historical analysis that looks much further into the past, see Iver B. Neumann and Vincent Pouliot, "Untimely Russia: Hysteresis in Russian-Western Relations over the Past Millennium," *Security Studies* 20, no. 1 (May 2010).

Cold War days regional dynamics have evolved, but only at the margins. Today's Russian–Atlantic security relationship is comprised of hybrid practices ranging from nuclear deterrence to military exchanges, through rhetorical escalation and everyday seminar diplomacy.[55]

Interestingly, the partial failure to constitute a new social structure of regional security regularly comes out in the open, typically through forms of political oddity or social discomfort. Recently, this happened again with NATO's cold reaction to president Dmitri Medvedev's proposed European Security Treaty. As with so many similar initiatives in the region, what the Russians envision as a way to transform outdated, exclusive security practices in the region, Alliance capitals construe as an attempt to return to a concert form of security governance that does not belong to this era. Even one full generation after the end of the Cold War, transforming security practices in the Russian–Atlantic region remains a particularly daunting task.

Conclusion

In this chapter I argued that in order to make sense of regional order and transformation in world politics, scholars should begin with what it is that state representatives do, at the regional level of analysis, that brings them together in the joint enactment of a specific set of practices. Neighboring countries at war, for instance, enact a number of daily routines and performances that create the conflicting and violent structure of their political interaction. From these practices follow the oft-noted constitutive features of regionness: interdependence, which mainstream IR theories prioritize, and narrative – the constructivist main focus. By beginning with practices, it becomes possible to understand not only why but also how patterns of meaningful actions obtain in a given region, while in another, security performances create disorganized and often incoherent structures of interaction. In the case of post-Cold War Russian–Atlantic relations, a mutual willingness to move beyond realpolitik practices was ultimately insufficient for bringing about significant regional change. As one side tried to gesture into being a new pattern of security politics, the other encountered those practices as reminiscent of the past. As a result, regional transformation, while real, stays limited; and regional order, though present, remains contested and fragile.

I have focused here on the structuring effects of security practices on regional patterns of interaction. Because of space constraints, I have

---

[55] Pouliot, "Materials of Practice."

not sought to explain how such political orders set in at the level of agency. Suffice it to say that any social order obtains when interacting agents "naturally" come to do things in ways that resonate with one another. This is what I called elsewhere the "logic of practicality."[56] At the micro-level order rests on practices that have become axiomatic inside a human collective. Where it exists, this practical sense feeds on the intersection of dispositions (ingrained and mostly inarticulate pro-clivities and tendencies accumulated through personal and collective history) and positions in a field (defined by the distribution of valued resources). Essentially, practices become established – or, put differ-ently, a pattern of social order settles in – when there exists a match or "homology" between positions and dispositions. Under such cir-cumstances, the practical sense becomes a self-regulating mechanism whereby inclinations are in perfect tune with the structure of positions and the rules of the game. Under conditions of homology, necessity makes virtue: the (objectively) impossible is (subjectively) unthinkable and the (objectively) plausible is (subjectively) inevitable.[57] It is this "orchestra without a conductor," as Bourdieu called it, that lies at the root of social order – regional or otherwise.

[56] Pouliot, "Logic of Practicality." See Pierre Bourdieu, *The Logic of Practice* (Stanford University Press, 1990).
[57] Pierre Bourdieu, *Méditations pascaliennes* (Paris: Seuil, 2003), 332–33.

Part 5

Eclectic perspectives

10   The transformation of modern Europe: banalities of success

John A. Hall

No region in the history of the world has created more insecurity – more wars, more deaths, in its heartland and throughout the world – than has Europe, especially in its dark and vicious twentieth century. The realization that the core of Europe has become a zone of peace and prosperity can only make one weep with joy. What needs to be explained is – precisely – a transformation, that is, not just a return to the stability that had marked most of the nineteenth century but the creation of a new world, in large part populated by states of a different character. It can be said immediately that sophisticated accounts of this transformation have already been offered, perhaps the best of them within international relations theory being that of Norrin Ripsman, whose general viewpoint is presented in this volume.[1] I am largely in agreement with his eclectic view, stressing as it does the importance of realist considerations in the creation of a zone of peace and of liberal factors that then solidified this achievement in such a way as to create the transformation in question. However, there are differences at the margins: I will stress the continuing role of geopolitics, both American and European; emphasize tensions within the transatlantic community; show skepticism toward the extent of European liberalism; add elements of sociological class analysis; and thicken the analysis at all points.

The nature of the argument to be made can usefully be highlighted in a different way. The fact that such a significant transition has taken place has often led (as is the case now) to ecstatic commentaries

---

[1] Norrin M. Ripsman, "Two Stages of Transition from a Region of War to a Region of Peace: Realist Transition and Liberal Endurance," *International Studies Quarterly*, 49, no. 4 (December 2005), 669–93. Cf. James J. Sheehan, *Where Have All the Soldiers Gone? The Transformation of Modern Europe* (Boston, MA: Houghton Mifflin, 2008); Peter Katzenstein, *A World of Regions: Asia and Europe in the American Imperium* (Ithaca, NY: Cornell University Press, 2005); Benjamin Miller, *States, Nations and the Great Powers: The Sources of Regional War and Peace* (Cambridge University Press, 2007). I differ from these excellent accounts at the margins – stressing the continuing role of geopolitics, both European and American, noting tensions within the transatlantic community, and stressing certain limits to liberal achievements.

suggesting that Europe may "run" this century, given that its "vision of the future" has more to offer than "the American Dream."[2] Hold on! An equally familiar set of commentaries are issued from time to time about the failings of Europe – the "democratic deficit" seen in the way in which the main elements of the failed constitution were foisted on its peoples, its inability to seize the day in the choice of its first president. This oscillation between extremes rests on a failure to understand the nature of European institutions. I will argue that these are successful but less grandiose than is often imagined. Perhaps the most crucial way in which this is so concerns the lack of autonomy of this particular region. Europe has been changed as much by external forces as it has by internal forces: bluntly, this region lives within the American sphere of influence.[3] Hence as important for this chapter as the social theory of regions that this volume seeks to develop must be the classic treatment of political community offered by a team led by Karl Deutsch.[4] Alliances, essentially *ad hoc* and often temporary, were compared, let us remember, with security communities, both amalgamated and pluralistic. Emphasis was placed on the necessity for a leading power to help construct a security community, habitually in the midst of a shared sense of threat. The maintenance of community depended, however, upon some sense of shared value and a firm commitment to talk and bargain rather than to polarize and fight. Pluralism necessarily meant the presence of greater levels of conflict, but this could be seen as a safety valve: the flexibility of pluralism was to be preferred, in circumstances of difference, to the brittleness likely to result from amalgamation.[5] The subtlety of this position has been abandoned in recent years, replaced by an oscillation between extremes as violent as that already noted concerning European internal affairs. Powerful voices suggest that the levels of conflict between the United States and Europe are

---

[2] Mark Leonard, *Why Europe Will Run the 21st Century* (London: Fourth Estate, 2005); Jeremy Rifkin, *The European Dream: How Europe's Vision of the Future is Quietly Eclipsing the American Dream* (Cambridge: Polity Press, 2004).

[3] Katzenstein, *World of Regions*.

[4] Karl W. Deutsch et al., *Political Community in the North Atlantic Area: International Organization in the Light of Historical Experience* (Princeton University Press, 1957). Cf. Emanuel Adler and Michael Barnett, eds., *Security Communities* (Cambridge University Press, 1998).

[5] Robert Kagan, *Of Paradise and Power: America and Europe in the New World Order* (New York: Alfred A. Knopf, 2003); Elizabeth Pond, *Friendly Fire: The Near-Death of the Transatlantic Alliance* (Washington, DC: Brookings Institution Press, 2004); Thomas Mowle, *Allies at Odds: The United States and the European Union* (Basingstoke: Palgrave Macmillan, 2004); David M. Andrews, ed., *The Atlantic Alliance under Stress: US-European Relations after Iraq* (Cambridge University Press, 2005); Nikos Kotzias and Petros Liacouras, eds., *EU–US Relations: Repairing the Transatlantic Drift* (Basingstoke: Palgrave Macmillan, 2006).

now so great that divorce is on the cards. Descriptively this position has been advanced by Charles Kupchan, who is convinced that the elites and peoples of Europe have the capacity and determination to become masters of their own fate.[6] Jurgen Habermas could be cited by Kupchan as evidence for his position. For the German philosopher recently urged Europe to stand apart from the United States, suggesting that the invasion of Iraq could serve as a rallying call for the united federal Europe for which he so longs.[7] In contrast, equally powerful voices expect or long for – here too authors can be either prescriptive or descriptive – a return to a unified voice for the West.[8] An understanding of the transatlantic relationship will show that this opposition, between divorce and absolute love, is as false now as it has been since 1945. My general theme can be stressed again: here too is success, but the banalities that hold it together need to be remembered.

The chapter begins by stressing the eclectic elements that went into the making of the European region at the end of the Second World War, before turning to changes and continuities both within Europe and in its relationship with the United States. One complexity needs to be borne in mind at all times. The nature of "Europe" was, is, and always will be "essentially contested." Russia is part of the same landmass, with some Russians and more Europeans hoping that arrangements can eventually be found to draw it within the core European sphere, thus replicating the marvelous success of European policy in integrating Central European and Baltic states. Of more immediate concern is the fact that some countries in the European Union are not part of NATO, while a key member of NATO, Turkey, is not a member of the Union – to the irritation of the United States. As important is the presence of different political economies within the Union itself, most obviously Social Democracy, Christian Democracy, and the neoliberal model present in Great Britain. The full list of omissions and overlaps could fill a large volume with some ease.

Present at the creation

The central feature that differentiated Europe a century ago from its contemporary variant was the presence of world states possessing

---

[6] Charles Kupchan, *The End of the American Era: US Foreign Policy and the Geopolitics of the Twenty-first Century* (New York: Vintage, 2002).
[7] Jürgen Habermas, *Time of Transitions* (Cambridge: Polity Press, 2005).
[8] Timothy Garton Ash, *Free World: America, Europe and the Surprising Future of the West* (New York: Random House, 2004); John Ikenberry, *After Victory: Institutions, Strategic Restraint, and the Rebuilding of Order after Major Wars* (Princeton University Press, 2002).

multinational empires and engaged in fierce geopolitical struggle.[9] These authoritarian regimes were faced with the challenge of modernity – that is, with the complex intertwining of nationalism, democratization, and industrialization. They attempted a special combination of nationalism with imperialism with industrialism, at the expense of democratization. The exclusion of the people, as workers and nations, created radical political mobilizations that destroyed the Habsburg and Ottoman regimes at the end of the First World War – and the restoration of the Russian Empire under new management. But the imperial moment was far from over. The huge increase in the size and salience of French and British Empires did much to make Hitler feel that he too needed secure sources of supply together with *Lebensraum* for his people. It was this general belief – echoed of course in the Far East – that led to the huge interimperial war that changed the course of the twentieth century. The tectonic shift caused by the ending of imperial rule and the consequent creation of nation-states in the European heartland occasioned vicious practices of ethnic cleansing, population transfer, and genocide, all carried out in the midst of the fog of world wars. Accordingly, it is entirely appropriate to call twentieth-century Europe "the dark continent."[10]

This is the shameful background which lay behind and did much to initiate the varied initiatives of European integration. It is impossible to stress enough the importance of social constructivism as a background condition to European developments. The memory of the 100 million killed created visceral desire to beget a new world. This is the sea within which three more familiar institutional changes swam.

The first element to be considered is the contribution made by European states. The most high-powered history of the European Union, and of its precursors, is that of Alan Milward. His first general treatment made a powerful case for the importance of the European contribution to economic recovery, thereby downplaying that of the Marshall Plan. He further demonstrated how important participation in advanced markets was for European economies, noting that Britain's continued membership in imperial markets did a great deal to damage its chances for economic growth.[11] Much was made in that book of the

---

[9] Dominic Lieven, *Empire: The Russian Empire and its Rivals* (London: John Murray, 2000).

[10] Mark Mazower, *Dark Continent: Europe's Twentieth Century* (London: Allen Lane, 1998).

[11] Alan Milward, *The Reconstruction of Western Europe, 1945–51* (Berkeley: University of California Press, 1984). There is a touch of unjustified anti-Americanism in this book. It may well be that capital formation was more European than American,

historical class compromise, of the impact both of social democracy and Christian democracy in creating the social cement that allowed for greater utilization of the market principle. Of course this is one example of the attempt to understand the past, the insistence here being that social liberalism would ensure peace and prosperity.

Milward's second intervention has greater importance. He recognized that European states had sought, between 1870 and 1945, to be complete power containers, nationally homogenous and in possession of secure sources of supply and markets which they could control.[12] The fact that this led to complete disaster produced humility, a becoming sense of modesty. But this is *not* to say for a moment that state power somehow lost its salience. The crucial calculation, that of Robert Schuman the French foreign minister, was clearly realist. If Germany could not be beaten militarily, an alternative strategy might be possible: a permanent embrace of mutual cooperation could neutralize aggression. The origin of what is now the European Union came from the 1950 decision by the two leading powers to give up their geopolitical autonomy by establishing genuine interdependence in coal and steel, thereby giving up the capacity to make their own weapons. The condominium between these two powers has structured the European Union throughout its history. And the negative realist calculation blended into something positive, endorsed by many more countries. States discovered that giving up the desire to control everything in fact gave them more: interdependence within a larger security frame allowed for prosperity and the spread of citizenship rights. Differently put, breaking the link between nationalism and imperialism enhanced rather than undermined state power.

If these calculations were fundamental, they did not dictate the political form that resulted. The group around Jean Monnet had drafted the agreement around coal and steel, and they were as involved in drawing up the plans for the European Economic Community, formed in 1957. Their dream – and dream it was, making this a clear example of the importance of social construction – was federalist, seen above all in the creation of a commission, a parliament and a court. Monnet was highly cosmopolitan, a high-flying representative of international finance. Accordingly, the plans he developed differed in character from those described by Milward: they privileged economic liberalism – something which then came to dominate European integration thereafter.

but it remains the case that the establishment of security was a precondition for investment.

[12] Alan Milward, *The European Rescue of the Nation-State* (Berkeley: University of California Press, 1992).

But how was it that a group of French bureaucrats, albeit in league with colleagues in other countries, came to have sufficient power to change Europe's constitutional structure? One element was certainly geopolitical, namely the discovery by France at the time of Suez that British power was exhausted, and that a measure of autonomy could only be guaranteed through cooperation with Germany. But another factor was at work, itself part of the third general force that allowed for the creation of a new Europe after 1945.

Europe's security dilemma at last found a solution in the years following the close of the Second World War. One element of this was the creation of an "empire by invitation."[13] The formulation of Lord Ismay – that the purpose of NATO was to keep the Russians out, the Americans in, and the Germans divided – bears repetition. The Russian threat was real, and it was felt as acutely by those on the front line as it was in Washington. Accordingly, the Americans took active steps to remove the extreme left of European politics in the years immediately after 1945 – taking particular care, for instance, to support Christian Democracy in Italy against its Communist rivals.[14] Of course, Europeans appreciated the American presence for an entirely different reason. They had fought endlessly, and to the point of absolute exhaustion. The United States was to act as an umpire, or court of last appeal. When distrust is very high there is a great deal to be said for a mediator – and one in this case possessed of powerful means of coercion and persuasion. The decision to keep Germany divided exemplifies the difference between the way the First and Second World Wars ended: power mattered in 1945, not least since obeisance before the principle of national self-determination in 1919 was considered to have contributed to geopolitical disaster. Geopolitical stability is a precondition for investment and economic growth. Just as interdependence was undermined by geopolitical competition in the interwar period, so too was it made possible within Europe after 1945 because a stable international order had been put in place. The ability to become traders rather than heroes rested on secure geopolitical foundations. And it is at this point that we can complete the explanation for the impact of federalism within Europe. At key points in his career, Monnet drew on his influence within the United States to push European integration forward.[15] The desire to

---

[13] Geir Lundestad, "Empire by Invitation? The United States and Western Europe, 1945–1952," *Journal of Peace Research* 23, no. 3 (September 1986), 263–77.

[14] Charles Maier, "The Two Postwar Eras and the Conditions for Stability in Twentieth-century Western Europe," *American Historical Review* 86, no. 2 (April 1981), 327–52.

[15] Perry Anderson, *The New Old Europe* (London: Verso, 2009), chapter 1.

create a new Europe was as present in the hegemon as in its allies, albeit in the American case overwhelmingly for geopolitical reasons, and the construction would not have taken place without its pressure – and its forbearance, seen above all in the acceptance of a European model of "embedded liberalism" which it did not itself favor.[16]

Change and continuity within Europe

The frame created by stability allowed for processes of integration to get underway. Such integration had had a long and complex history; and it is multifaceted. Two particular contributions must be noted. The first is that of a social force of transnational character, operating below the level of states – albeit, its impact eventually transformed key European states. Christian Democracy in the period after 1945 finally divorced itself from radical right politics, thereby changing Germany and Italy, and eventually much of Southern Europe as well. The great historian and analyst of this world, Wolfram Kaiser, makes it clear that this was a marvelous piece of pure social construction, driven by an idea whose consequences were very great.[17] The second is perhaps better known. Integration in Europe has fundamentally concerned the extension of capitalist relations, as is clear with regard to the huge proportion of legislation in the Union. More than 20 percent of European GDP is traded internally, a figure which amounts to half of all world trade; crucially, new members from the East have abandoned their external markets, and are as closely tied to Union markets as were earlier members.[18] This is effectively a single economy within which the capitalist class moves with ease.

A particularly notable character of that history has been its curiously stop–go character: just when stalemate seemed in place, a sudden lurch forward took place. The passing of the Single European Act (1987) and ratification of the Maastricht Treaty (1991) exemplify this pattern. This unpredictability deserves emphasis as it makes one realize that the future of Europe is by no means closed. Who, after all, would have predicted twenty years ago that the end of Communism would allow so many new states to enter the heartland of Europe, most in NATO and

[16] John G. Ruggie, "International Regimes, Transactions and Change: Embedded Liberalism in the Postwar Economic Order," *International Organization* 36, no. 2 (1982), 379–415.

[17] Wolfram Kaiser, *Christian Democracy and the Making of European Union* (Cambridge University Press, 2007).

[18] Neil Fligstein, *Euroclash: The EU, European Identity, and the Future of Europe* (Oxford University Press, 2008).

the Union, with such astonishing success? But what is Europe now? Will it become as enthusiasts suggest a federalist area equivalent to the United States? Arguments over the level of integration within Europe often boil down to interpretations as to whether a glass is half full or half empty. There is no intention here to deny the importance of the integrative developments that have taken place, certainly in the economic realm and to a lesser extent in the legal sphere. Nonetheless, the argument here is of the half-empty variety.[19] The justification for this is simple: there are clear constraints on further integration. The purpose of this section is to specify four home truths that should be borne in mind by those imagining that transnationalism is likely to increase within the European Union.

The first point is implicit in the account given of the origins of the European project. The calculation of states created the European Union and its precursors, and those calculations remain in force today. Consider some powerful but banal examples. First, the collapse of Communism famously led Margaret Thatcher to get in touch with President Mitterand in order to ask, "What should be done with the Germans?" Thatcher's views about Germany reflected prejudice rather than reality, but the analytic point about state calculation should still be retained. For geopolitical calculation was quite as much at work in France's response to this huge change. If one element was the insistence that Germany be tied to Europe by means of the euro, still more striking was France's return to the NATO command structure – a decision that had at its heart the desire to keep Americans in Europe so as to balance reunified Germany. Secondly, consider the bargaining at the December 2002 Nice summit on enlargement, some details of which were provided thanks to leaks published in the *Economist*. This was a forum at which Bismarck would have felt at home: "if you give me this, then I'll give in on that issue" was the characteristic tone of the meeting, especially insofar as voting rights for new states was concerned. Similar points can be made about the new institutional arrangements ratified in 2009: state interests have been protected, with the role of the Commission falling ever lower in comparison to that of the key intergovernmental institution, the Council of Ministers. Thirdly, skepticism needs to be shown to the claim, far too frequently made, that the Franco-German condominium is losing its salience within Europe: it was these powers that played the decisive role in choosing the first

[19] This is also the viewpoint of the best single treatment of the European project, Andrew Moravcsik, *The Choice for Europe: Social Purpose and State Power from Messina to Maastricht* (Ithaca, NY: Cornell University Press, 1998).

European president. Finally, attention should be given to empirical work probing behind the ideology of integration so as to examine its realities. Francesco Duina's work is exemplary in this regard. His first book took two directives, those on equal pay and on air pollution, and then examined the extent to which different countries actually implemented rules suggested to them. Analysis of three countries per directive produced a picture of very considerable variety. Implementation was likely to succeed when it fitted with previous policy choices and had the support of national pressure groups; when the history and group organization of a nation-state pointed in a direction opposed to the directive, implementation was likely be fudged, delayed or ignored.[20] A similar story is told in a more recent study over tobacco control: both the initial blocking and eventual acceptance of the directive on advertising for tobacco depended upon the particular constellation of national interests in place at the time.[21]

The second point is that it is crucial to remember that the European Union is in a fundamental sense weak; it is not the Leviathan made much of by most Eurosceptics. The European Union is able to fiscally extract only about 1 percent of the national product of the member states, that is, far less than the proportion – characteristically between 40 and 50 percent – that the various nation-states take from their societies. "The existing budget ceiling," the European enthusiast Loukas Tsoukalis notes, "is simply unrealistic and inconsistent with officially stated objectives."[22] Further, plans to allow for direct taxation have been dropped. It remains the case that the Union by and large has only one policy on which it spends large amounts of money, indeed most of its own budget, namely the Common Agricultural Policy.

Remembering this basic fact gives a sense of perspective about the key question of identity, the third area in which skepticism is needed. The fiscal considerations noted suggest that it is very unlikely there will be very many significant European political movements in the near future. For one of the most firmly established generalizations of comparative historical sociology is that social movements gain force when state demands are placed upon civil society. Perhaps the key social process creating identity has traditionally been that of citizenship struggles over taxation. As the Union makes few fiscal demands,

---

[20] Francesco Duina, *Harmonizing Europe: Nation-States within the Common Market* (Albany: State University of New York Press, 1999).
[21] Francesco Duina and Paulette Kurzer, "Smoke in Your Eyes: The Struggle Over Tobacco Control in the European Union," *Journal of European Policy* 11, no. 1 (2004), 57–77.
[22] Loukas Tsoukalis, *What Kind of Europe?* (Oxford University Press, 2003), 136.

a sense of European identity is unlikely to be created through popular struggles. European identity is at present very limited indeed. All opinion polls show that national identities trump those of Europe in every single country of the Union. Of course, there are very great differences between countries, with loyalty to the European project characteristically being higher in countries that suffered badly in the war compared to those that did not – between, for example, Holland and Belgium. In any case, identities are not simple, with many having multiple, overlapping, and changing identities. But national loyalty remains the most important. In general, what is noticeable is that attitudes to Europe are path-dependent: they follow the characteristic histories of the nation-states involved.[23] Crucially, opinion polls also make it quite clear that the European Union is essentially an elite affair, with strong support throughout Europe habitually being related to high socioeconomic status. In this connection, it is worth considering language. David Laitin has suggested with characteristic brilliance that the linguistic repertoire that Europeans will need in the future is a two plus or minus one language regime.[24] One necessary language would be English, the world language used most often in Union affairs, with the second being that of one's nation-state. The minus in his formula refers to Great Britain, with the plus being the need to speak a minority language when one's nation-state has a different tongue. Laitin's claim is that such a repertoire will help to solve European problems. I am not so sure. Europeans are good at learning languages. But to be really sophisticated, to be able to perform at a high level in other languages, is difficult.

Brilliant recent work by Fligstein makes one realize still more that European identity is limited.[25] Less than 3 percent of Europeans live outside their own countries, with the number of students spending significant time abroad being scarcely higher. Europe seems to have three core populations: a small number (13%) think of themselves as Europeans, an additional number (43%) sometimes think of themselves as Europeans, while the largest number (44%) has no European identity. "Given the right circumstances, 56 per cent of people in Europe think of themselves as Europeans (13% + 43%). But under other social conditions, 87 per cent might think of themselves as mostly having a

[23] On this matter, see the brilliant empirical investigation by Juan Diez Medrano, *Framing Europe: Attitudes to European Integration in Germany, Spain and the United Kingdom* (Princeton University Press, 2003).
[24] David Laitin, "The Cultural Identities of a European State," *Politics and Society*, 25, no. 3 (1997), 277–302.
[25] Fligstein, *Euroclash*, chapters 5 and 6.

national identity (43% + 44%)."[26] At a minimum, this suggests that there will be a limit to popular enthusiasm for the Union – as seems apparent from the decline in numbers of those voting at European elections. At a maximum, one might expect something worse. The mood of nationalism may be about to change once again. Nationalism was once an elite project, an element of forced development planning designed to help to compete with the leading edge of power. In Europe it now seems that elites wish to be part of the action within a territorial frame larger than that of a single nation-state, albeit they doubtless feel that this is the best strategy for their countries. The rise of varied social movements opposed to further integration suggests that those who are left behind, caged within national borders, resent the creation of a world that disadvantages them. Nationalism may yet gain new force as a reactionary nativist project. The title of Fligstein's volume, *Euroclash*, underlines his fear for the future of Europe.

Finally, skepticism needs to be shown to Europe's liberal achievements. Economic integration is secure, albeit the large states breach rules as to budget limits with impunity. Minority rights are equally secure, at least in comparison with the historical record. States wishing to join the Union must change their societies to gain admission, a force entirely for the good. Still, self-satisfaction is most certainly not in order. Geopolitical peace makes possible liberal consociational arrangements of all sorts largely because the "unitariness" of the state is less important when there is no immediate prospect of war. To that extent liberalism has contributed, for example, to the consolidation of multinational Spain. But the brute fact about nationalism remains that ethnic cleansing has taken place within Europe in the last century, most recently of course during the last Balkan war. So liberalism's capacity to mollify and compromise came into full force only when none of the great problems of the first half of the twentieth century remained. One might further note the intent of Europe to prevent immigration from the South and the East, that is, its desire to remain white and Christian. Finally, the role played by European states since September 11 in aiding and abetting the rendition of prisoners suspected of terrorism, at times to centers within Europe at which torture was used, places very serious questions about Europe's supposed liberalism.[27]

It is worth concluding this section by repeating what was said at its start. The fact that the limits to integration have been stressed here should not be taken as a claim that integration has no significance. In

---

[26] Fligstein, *Euroclash*, 4.   [27] Anderson, *New Old Europe*, chapter 2.

this matter, the work of Duina is exemplary.[28] For all his stress on the varied ways in which different nation-states react to directives of the Commission, he nonetheless recognizes the novelty of a situation in which a single agenda is placed before so many states at the same time. He certainly does not rule out the possibility that this may in the longer run diminish the range of variation between nation-states within the European Union. Still, on the other side of the equation remains the fact that the Constitution was rejected, albeit most of its (weak) proposals came into force in any case, without popular endorsement. In this context attention can usefully be drawn to Brendan O'Leary's powerful demonstration that successful federalism has always depended upon the presence of a *Staatsvolk*.[29] In the absence of a dominating people, federalism can only work when it is combined with consociational arrangements designed to reassure minorities – as was historically the case in Canada, where care was taken to alternate between anglophone and francophone prime ministers. Given that there are not enough Germans to form a *Staatsvolk* in Europe, stability may well depend upon allowing the blocking powers of small states to remain in place.

A neuralgic Europe trails petulantly in America's wake

This subtitle – given to a recent piece in the *Financial Times* assessing the state of transatlantic relations – usefully returns us to the lack of real autonomy of the European Union.[30] A first task must be that of showing that this political community was never amalgamated; a second must be that of demonstrating that divorce within the community is extremely unlikely. But the bulk of attention needs to be phenomenological in character. How do the tensions of a pluralistic community feel, and how have those feelings changed over time?

Genuine attempts were made to amalgamate the transatlantic relationship, to create a situation of absolute love in which both sides of the Atlantic would see the world in exactly the same way. This was especially true at the elite level.[31] All those CIA-funded Congresses for

---

[28] Duina, *Harmonizing Europe*.

[29] Brendan O'Leary, "An Iron Law of Nationalism and Federation? A (Neo-Diceyan) Theory of the Necessity of a Federal *Staatsvolk*, and of Consociational Rescue," *Nations and Nationalism* 7, no. 3 (2001), 273–96.

[30] Philip Stephens, "A Neuralgic Europe Trails Petulantly in America's Wake," *Financial Times*, January 22, 2010, 13.

[31] Thomas Schaeper and Kathleen Schaeper, *Cowboys and Gentlemen: Rhodes Scholars, Oxford and the Creation of an American Elite* (New York: Berghahn Books, 1998); Kees van der Pijl, *The Making of an Atlantic Ruling Class* (London: New Left Books,

Cultural Freedom sought to cement a shared identity, an enterprise in a sense personified in the vigorous figure of Edward Shils – whose career was split between the University of Chicago and the University of Cambridge. Still, how extensive and deep was transatlantic identity in practice? It is worth keeping at the center of one's mind that identities habitually involve some sort of mix between interest and affect. If we now revert to continental European cases, the air of calculation rather than of shared identity comes to the fore. As an intellectual, Raymond Aron, despite his fabulous intelligence and carefully nurtured American relationships, was first and foremost French. He is the perfect exemplar of what the community was in practice – a community, for sure, but one that was based on bargaining, calculation, and a combination of shared and dissimilar values. Calculation seems stronger still in Harold Macmillan's celebrated words to Richard Crossman while attached to Eisenhower's headquarters in Algiers in 1942: "[We] are the Greeks in this American Empire. You will find the Americans much as the Greeks found the Romans – great big, bustling people, more vigorous than we are and also more idle, with more unspoiled virtues but also more corrupt. We must run [this HQ] as the Greek slaves ran the operations of the Emperor Claudius."[32] The same note was struck by Keynes, when commenting to his staff before beginning meetings about the British loan: "they may have all the money, but we've got all the brains."[33] And the experiences of Keynes at this time point to fundamental limits to the Special Relationship. Bluntly, the hopes that Britain has rested upon the relationship have tended to be illusory, as was so dramatically apparent when Mrs. Thatcher was told of the bombing of Libya only when American planes were airborne. America has always tended to listen only on occasions when it suited its own interest so to do. Key transatlantic institutions were dominated in the last resort by the leading power. This was obviously true of NATO, whose commanding officer was, is, and always will be an American.

In order to discover the true character of the pluralism of the transatlantic community there is much to be said for noting the variety of positions that stand between love and divorce. Inequality in gender relations can mean that women are unhappily caged within a relationship, bereft of opportunities for exit, forced to stay but filled with resentments. Complexities lurk here. On the one hand, there are those who

1984); Volker Berghahn, *America and the Intellectual Cold Wars in Europe* (Princeton University Press, 2001).
[32] Alastair Horne, *Harold MacMillan*, vol. I, *1894–1956* (New York: Viking, 1988), 160.
[33] This story was told to me in 1983 by the late James Meade, who worked closely with Keynes.

would escape if they could but are prevented from so doing because of the presence of children and the knowledge that divorced men all too often refuse to pay for the support of their children. On the other hand stands the psychology dramatized in *Who's Afraid of Virginia Woolf?* The mental state so well portrayed in that play fully justifies the technical term "codependency." This is a world in which resentments are nourished and maintained, a situation of endless complaint bereft of any real determination to change, let alone to leave. Divorce is indeed the opposite of absolute love. But matters are far from simple at this end of the scale. There can be trial separations, continued life within the same house, separations that do not lead to divorce – and of course both messy and amicable divorces. On top of all this, one needs to remember that it is not always the case that people occupy one place along the scale in a consistent manner. Resentment is in itself unstable, at once filled with complaint yet stalled in terms of action. Much more importantly, human beings suffer from what Marcel Proust termed "the intermittences of the heart." It is well known, for instance, that the breakdown of a marriage tends to be easier to deal with than the death of a spouse. In the latter case, memories remain intact, and so does one's sense of self; the former situation raises doubts, habitually insoluble, and tends to mandate reconstruction of identity. And this is but an extreme example of something much more common. How often we wobble back and forth, trying again and again, to give another example, to bargain before finally slipping into resentment.

A whole series of suggestive if staccato points about the nature of transatlantic relations rise to the surface immediately. First, different countries occupy very different places in such relations.[34] The Polish situation is close to one of pure love, given the feeling that America helped end the Cold War and assure the freedom of the nation – a feeling of course massively reinforced by links to Polish-Americans. France is complicated. This great republican rival to the United States, now bereft of its empire, has always longed for some way to sustain grandeur – often assuaged by doing much to design the European Union but prone on that very ground to call for separation from the United States.[35] Second, the affections of states are often as inconstant as those within marriage. France is a classic example. De Gaulle's withdrawal from the NATO command structure stands as a supremely complex move – in the end, a separation without consequence rather than a

---

[34] Andrews, *Atlantic Alliance under Stress* is particularly useful in identifying differences within Europe.

[35] Robert Jackson, "Non, merci," *Times Literary Supplement*, June 3, 2005.

genuine divorce. German reunification ended French withdrawal, as noted, for the strengthening of NATO was instantly seen as a way of maintaining the American presence and thereby of limiting the potential of German power. Perhaps this shows the realist calculation of the national interest. But France is not immune from the intermittences of the heart, reacting emotionally to the invasion of Iraq before retreating from a moment of romanticism.

There are equal complexities within the United States. Historically, there has been considerable change in the attitudes of Americans towards particular countries. Admiration for Germany before the First World War was extensive, reflecting, of course, massive immigration from Central Europe. Two world wars changed admiration to distaste. In contrast, the visceral dislike of Great Britain – at the popular level sustained in part by Irish-Americans, at the elite level driven by a desire to take over as hegemon – has now been all but forgotten, astonishingly so given its importance in American foreign policy for such an extended period. Particularly noticeable in the most recent years, of course, has been the ascendancy, perhaps now terminated, of a group of intellectuals, driven by romantic ideals far more than by any traditional sense of national interest.[36] But what matters most here is the fact that the United States has an ever-present choice within the Atlantic Community. On the one hand stands the demand, articulated by elite and popular forces, that Europe stand up for itself. The continuing presence of American troops in Europe was certainly not planned, and there is much to be said for the view that this presence is historically idiosyncratic – making the occasional call for burden-sharing, at times insistent, entirely comprehensible. On the other hand stands the pleasure and benefit of being number one. Pleasure derives from the ability to set the agenda of world politics, and thereby to establish a predictable environment. Benefit has derived from the extraction of seigniorage, seen most clearly in the past in European financing of the twin deficits and always present in varied ways for a country which provides the world's top currency. In a nutshell, the United States in this matter is prone to its own intermittence of the heart, that is, to wobble between asking for European independence and not liking for a moment what it sees when such a process seems to be underway.

---

[36] There is a vast literature here. An early contribution from the outside was made by Michael Mann, *Incoherent Empire* (London: Verso, 2004). Francis Fukuyama's *America at the Crossroads: Democracy, Power and the Neoconservative Legacy* (New Haven, CT: Yale University Press, 2006) is an auto-critique from the inside, written after the difficulties of the Iraqi situation had become generally apparent.

It is well known that passions can run amok, thereby making rational calculation impossible. But if this is true of the moments of oscillation noted above, quite as important are those moments when sober second thoughts return. Such thoughts arise fundamentally because attention returns to structural constraints that cannot be avoided. In this matter there is a measure of difference between the United States and Europe.

It would be quite possible for the United States to turn its back on Europe. This would certainly be unusual historically given the desire of great powers for a predictable political environment – it being probable that retreat from a leading role would lead to a more complex multipolar world. There might be economic risks attached to such a move. Further, a multipolar world might well diminish the privileges of seigniorage that the United States enjoys, it being noticeable in this regard that Europe still holds a vast amount of dollars.

In contrast, Europeans face severe constraints that have to this point curtailed momentary thoughts of greater autonomy. The most obvious historical constraint has been that of geopolitical fear, that is, awareness of the fact that defense has in the last analysis been guaranteed by the United States – with American soldiers being less important as a fighting force than as hostages guaranteeing that the United States would come to Europe's defense if need arose. Geopolitical fears have now diminished greatly, although it is vital to note that the historical experience of Central European countries gives them a continuing appreciation of America's geopolitical role – an appreciation vastly enhanced by Putin's threats to cut off supplies of natural gas first to Ukraine and then to Belarus. But appreciation of objective facts needs to be complemented by awareness of the subjective situation. The presence of the United States in NATO has been of immense importance to Europeans for the simplest of reasons: two world wars have made it clear that Europeans do not trust each other, and so consider themselves best served by having an external power able to enforce decent rules of behavior. The presence of competing visions within Europe remains a contemporary fact, as was seen both at the time of the last wars of the Balkans and in the rather generalized desire to maintain American troops in Europe so as to limit the power of reunified Germany. These considerations are supported by a further brute fact. A greater measure of European autonomy would necessitate increasing military capacity. There is every reason to believe that any sustained move in this direction will be massively unpopular.[37] European states have changed: they have lost their

---

[37] Sheehan, *Where Have All the Soldiers Gone?*, 217 and chapter 9 passim.

bellicose character, concentrating instead on civilian affairs.[38] By and large the majority of Europeans – more or less consciously at elite levels, somewhat unconsciously at the level of popular forces – have come to live with an odd, slightly schizophrenic mixture of complaint at American power in combination with a lack of will to change the situation.

Still there has been a significant change in feelings, perhaps from the late 1960s and early 1970s. The benign exercise of American hegemony did allow for a rather consensual atmosphere within the Atlantic community in the quarter of a century after the end of the Second World War, but that atmosphere has not existed, for most of Europe for most of the time, for a further quarter of a century. The events of the last years make it very unlikely that any taken-for-granted cordiality and civility will be restored. Once trust has gone, it is very hard to restore it. We live somehow in the middle: the increase in American power leads to less consultation, and so to greater European resentment – with neither side really being prepared to change the rules of the game. Many Europeans – even the British – were deeply opposed to American actions in Vietnam. In a sense this was the business of the United States alone. This was not true of the consequences of American actions. Lyndon Johnson famously could not decide between guns and butter; rather than paying for massively increased spending, the United States used its hegemonic powers in a predatory manner. Seigniorage became a serious matter. This was seen under Johnson in the extraction of loans from Germany at below market rates.[39] Nixon's closing of the gold window in 1971 was felt acutely, less for the change it brought than for the unilateralism so much enjoyed by John Connally. What mattered most of all was that the printing of money to finance the American deficit set off the great inflation of the postwar period.[40] A striking symbol of the change at an intellectual level was the fact that the thinker most loyal to the United States, perhaps the leading intellect of the postwar community, Raymond Aron, wrote a powerful treatise on the *Imperial Republic*.[41] Of course, the great French thinker did not suggest turning away from the United States, but a tone of irritation, perhaps even of resentment, was present in his elegant treatise. The less sophisticated were more emotional. But what was established in general was

[38] Ibid., chapter 8.

[39] Gregory F. Treverton, *The Dollar Drain and American Forces in Germany: Managing the Political Economics of Alliances* (Columbus: Ohio University Press, 1978).

[40] Michael Smith, *Power, Norms and Inflation: A Skeptical Treatment* (New York: Aldine de Gruyter, 1992).

[41] Raymond Aron, *The Imperial Republic: The United States and the World 1945–1973* (London: Weidenfeld & Nicolson, 1979).

the stability of oscillation, between resentment suggesting action and the reversion to sullen compliance once realization set in that the costs of change were too great. Europeans had learnt to whine while remaining supine. One remembers the moment when William Perry, President Clinton's last secretary of defense, suggested at a NATO meeting that the United States might withdraw its troops for Europe. There was shocked silence, followed by an immediate plea to stay. The title of this section is all too accurate.

Academics should resist being clearer than the truth. Given that predicting the past is hard, it is mere foolishness to offer certainty about the future. Some structural conditions of the Atlantic Community have changed, but it is clear that particular personalities have lent a flavor to transatlantic relations. Many European countries loathed George W. Bush, not least when faced with Donald Rumsfeld's attempt to divide so as better to rule Europe; in contrast, the reception for Barack Obama has been ecstatic, a huge sigh of relief indicating that autonomy need not be sought after all![42] But if caution is called for, so too is there need for recognizing the types of variables that might matter. Let us begin with the forces of change, seen from both sides of the Atlantic, before considering other factors that suggest continuity.

Steve Walt has insisted that the end of the Cold War has removed the glue for a community in which diverging interests – in geopolitical vision, value orientation, styles of political economy, and in matters of trade – had anyway been increasing in range and depth.[43] Walt predicted the emergence of a multipolar world in which the euro would eventually challenge the continuing supremacy of the dollar. Divergences have certainly increased in recent years. Most striking in European eyes was the character of nationalism within the United States, revived and exacerbated by the terrorist attacks on New York and Washington. Anatol Lieven is surely correct when arguing that the behavior of the United States has been idiosyncratic in historical terms.[44] The United States had the possibility of cooperating with its allies, of behaving as a conservative, satisfied power. This most certainly has not happened. The radicalism of intellectuals driven by geopolitical dreams marked American policy, to which can be added both a popular politics that favors a particular attitude toward Israel and the extreme confidence

---

[42] This is a careful formulation. As noted, much of Central Europe stood close to Bush – and now stands at some distance from Obama.

[43] Stephen M. Walt, *Taming American Power: The Global Response to US Primacy* (New York: W. W. Norton, 2005).

[44] Anatol Lieven, *America Right or Wrong: An Anatomy of American Nationalism* (Oxford University Press, 2004).

resulting from military success. Perhaps as important – at least, should it continue – is the lessening of the economic salience of Europe for the United States. The twin deficits are no longer financed by Europeans – and no longer by petro-dollars as well. East Asia has provided formal and informal financing, that is, the purchase of Treasury bonds and stocks, which have kept the dollar strong and the market on which they depend open. The United States is less constrained by Europe than was once the case.

The European situation represents the other side of the coin. European anti-Americanism has always existed, but it has gained new intensity in recent years, especially given revelations of torture by British and American troops in Iraq.[45] There is noticeable irritation over American pressure on Europe to allow Turkey to enter the Union – a matter on which this author cannot restrain himself from wholly endorsing the American position. While arguments have existed before, near daily perusal of American and European newspapers in recent years sometimes reveals nothing less than different mentalities, at least in the perceptions of the problems of the Middle East. At the extreme have been very interesting calls for a completely novel and wholly European policy. The absence of an external threat, so the argument goes, should lessen dependence on the United States, with confidence resulting from the realization that the exercise of soft European power – above all, in the post-Communist world – has been exceptionally effective. Surely the Union can now act: in 2009 its GNP was $18 trillion dollars and its population 470 million, placing it above the $14 trillion and 330 million of the United States.

Despite the cogency of these points, the weight of evidence still points, in my view, to the likelihood of continuity. What was noticeable in response to the ending of the Cold War was, as noted, the desire to maintain the American presence so as to balance Germany. The emotional exuberance of very recent years has now been contained on both sides of the Atlantic; reasons have again dictated stepping back from the unknown abysses of a new world. German leadership within Europe currently seeks to repair transatlantic relations, as does that of Sarkozy, who is closer to the United States than any French president in the postwar period. More important than the to-and-from of events, however, are structural conditions. Does anybody really think it likely

---

[45] Jean-François Revel, *L'Obsession anti-americaine: son fonctionnement, ses causes, ses inconsequences* (Paris: Plon, 2002); Philippe Roger, *The American Enemy: A Story of French Anti-Americanism* (Chicago University Press, 2005); Andrei S. Markovits, *Uncouth Nation: Why Europe Dislikes America* (Princeton University Press, 2007).

that Europe's status as economic giant and military worm will change? A huge shock was administered to Europe by its failure to act cohesively in the face of ethnic cleansing in the Balkans during the last years of the Clinton administration. The promises to produce greater unity at that time have borne no fruit. Despite the changes of 2009, who really speaks for Europe in foreign policy matters? The European Rapid Reaction Force has so far been a disappointment, not least perhaps as it is effectively in conflict with NATO's Response Force. Divisions between France and Britain remain great in military matters. America has increased its defense spending; European countries are doing exactly the opposite, in the teeth of their public proclamations. There is not the remotest sign that Europe imagines its weapons systems working in an autonomous manner: differently put, the sunk capital of shared technologies really does look to create a dependent path. Further, most macroeconomic matters remain in the hands of national governments. "These governments will not voluntarily give up their over-representation in the G8 or the IMF in favor of a common EU stance."[46] Is it really likely that the euro can triumph over the dollar when the United States remains the provider of geopolitical security – vitally necessary still in the eyes of the new member states of Central Europe? The interpenetration of American and European economies is very great, with perhaps fully 50 percent of American foreign direct investment being in Europe: this matters more than trade, since it gives direct access of each others' markets. Many other considerations reinforce skepticism. Beneath the surface there remains a good deal of commonality in value, as was evident in the initial European response to the terrorist attacks – and which is ever more reinforced by the expansion of vibrant American consumer culture.[47] Further, against the crisis over Iraq should be set the successful cooperation of France and the United States in getting Syria out of Lebanon, the very fact of the NATO role in Afghanistan, and somewhat greater coordination of policy towards Iran. A final general point can be made: getting divorced requires real decisiveness, staying together has the force of habit and inertia on its side.

Concluding with Montesquieu

Two points can be made by way of conclusion. To begin with it is as well to admit that this chapter is written by a mildly disillusioned European,

[46] Charlemagne, "The Puny Economic Powerhouse," *Economist*, December 8, 2005.
[47] Victoria de Grazia, *Irresistible Empire: America's Advance through Twentieth-century Europe* (Cambridge, MA: Harvard University Press, 2005).

by someone who had hoped for more from the European project. There are dangers here, present in Perry Anderson's brilliant but far more disillusioned account of Europe.[48] Europe is seen in that account as so loyal to the United States that it is all but impossible to imagine anything better. One can hope for a little more. Both Katzenstein and Walt hope that the United States might move to a more multilateral position in which legitimacy might be in part restored.[49] Certainly, greater cohesion within the Atlantic community, derived from agreement, might even have made Saddam Hussein aware of the futility of his divide-and-rule tactics. This is not to contradict what has been said immediately above: neither absolute love nor the straightforward and cordial bargaining of the immediate postwar period can be restored. What might work is something completely different, the character of which can be highlighted by reflecting on the nature of civil society. That popular concept is often seen in terms of difference. But what really matters is the *agreement* to differ. The Atlantic Community would now be best served by a measure of separation in some areas so as to allow for greater harmony in others. Doubtless this would require some restraint both within the United States and within Europe, but that may well already be on the cards. It would also require sophistication. For there are new challenges to order within international society, and liberal societies need to think, very hard, as to how to manage them. At times this might require the transatlantic community to act forcefully outside its own area; on other occasions, however, there may be much to be said for a division of labor.[50] It is as well to remember that successful marriages survive both through the division of labor and through the application of intelligence.

The more general conclusion concerns Montesquieu's insistence that laws must fit the customs of different countries. The institutions of one country or region may not suit another, making it unwise to seek or to expect any automatic transfer. Awareness of this fact lies at the heart of Duina's superb recent work on the spread of regional trade authorities. Everyone wants one, but everyone picks and chooses those details that suit their particular circumstances best.[51] What is striking about

---

[48] Anderson, *New Old Europe*.
[49] Katzenstein, *World of Regions*; Walt, *Taming American Power*.
[50] For American desire for an expansion of NATO's role, see "How to go global," *Economist*, March 25, 2006; for a cautionary word from Europe, see François Heisbourg, "Why NATO needs to be less ambitious," *Financial Times*, November 22, 2006.
[51] Francesco Duina, "Frames, Scripts, and the Making of Regional Trade Areas," in *Constructing the International Economy*, ed. Rawi Abdelal, Mark Blyth, and Craig Parsons (Ithaca, NY: Cornell University Press, 2010).

NAFTA and Mercosur, the most developed authorities, is the extent to which they differ from the European model they claimed to have copied.[52] It is of course necessary to remember, as John Owen notes in Chapter 5 of this volume, that regional agreements do not work – that is, trade does not expand as hoped – unless peace has broken out. This is most obviously true of the agreement reached between India and Pakistan. At a more general level one must surely be skeptical that the conditions behind European integration are likely to be matched elsewhere. For one thing, peace came to Europe once the nationalities question had been solved in the most vicious manner. That question haunts most of the regions of the world that are so much marked now by civil rather than interstate war. The thought of such regions following the European route to national homogenization is dreadful, making investigation of other means to solve the national question of crucial import. For another, it is very unlikely that the United States, freed from the pressure of a genuine global rival, will act toward other regions in the benign way that it did towards Europe in the years after 1945. In a nutshell, Europe's route was unique, at once horrible and lucky, and as such gives few lessons to the rest of the world.

[52] Francesco Duina, *The Social Construction of Free Trade: The EU, NAFTA, and Mercosur* (Princeton University Press, 2006).

11 Top-down peacemaking: why peace begins with states and not societies

Norrin M. Ripsman

The common assumption that runs through most contemporary western approaches to fostering peace and stability between combatants in war-torn regions is that peace is a bottom-up process. The impetus for peace, they assume, is not from states but from their societies. Peace is achieved, therefore, by creating common interests and identities between the populations and key societal interest groups in the combatant societies, and then forging political institutions that allow society to restrain aggressive leaders.[1] In other words, the path to peace consists of creating cooperative international institutions, fostering economic interdependence, and encouraging democratization.

In this regard, the western approach to peacemaking fits squarely in the liberal and constructivist traditions of international relations theory and, in particular, the traditions of institutionalism, commercial liberalism, and democratic peace theory. It also is based on the analogy of peacemaking in Western Europe after World War II, which many interpret to be the result of the creation of a pluralistic security community based on common democratic regimes, extensive economic interdependence, and cooperative European institutions.[2] Consequently,

I would like to thank Amitav Acharya, John Hall, Michael Lipson, T. V. Paul, and Vincent Pouliot for their helpful comments, and Shaun Cavaliere, Nadine Hajjar, and Sandra Helayel for their research assistance.

[1] For arguments that international institutions can be utilized to change the mindsets of peoples and states, thereby fostering cooperation, see Bilson Kurus, "Understanding ASEAN: Benefits and *raison d'être*," *Asian Survey* 33, no. 8 (August 1993), 819–31. For arguments that economic benefits can drive a peace process between states and societies, see Shimon Peres with Arye Naor, *The New Middle East* (New York: Henry Holt, 1993). Finally, authors who argue that democratic political institutions are the key to peacemaking include Benjamin Netanyahu, *A Durable Peace* (New York: Warner Books, 2000), 259–70.

[2] See, for example, Ole Wæver, "Insecurity, Security, and Asecurity in the West European Non-war Community," in *Security Communities*, ed. Emanuel Adler and Michael Barnett (Cambridge University Press, 1998), 69–118; Bruce Russett and John R. Oneal, *Triangulating Peace: Democracy, Interdependence, and International Organizations* (New York: W. W. Norton, 2001); and John MacMillan, *On Liberal Peace: Democracy, War and International Order* (New York: Tauris, 1998).

255

they recommend that the way to spread peace and stability to troubled regions, such as the Middle East and South Asia, is to promote democratization, economic interdependence, and liberal regional institutions to create a similar community in those regions.

As I argue elsewhere, however, the postwar European settlement did not begin as a Kantian peace and was not driven by a bottom-up logic. Western European security cooperation was initially driven by a realist logic (principally a common fear of the Soviet Union and active American pressure), which was more consistent with realist balance-of-power theory and hegemonic stability theory. This led governments – particularly the French government – to agree to cooperate with Germany in the security theater by 1954, long before French society changed its attitudes toward the former enemy. It took years after security affairs were resolved for societal attitudes to change, ultimately entrenching regional cooperation.[3] Western European peacemaking, therefore, began as a top-down process rather than a bottom-up one. Bottom-up mechanisms were useful only after the top-down transition, as a means of socializing or entrenching the settlement. Consequently, the transformation of Western European security cooperation after 1954 from a fragile, great-power-driven process to a stable cooperative partnership occurred due to the success of bottom-up mechanisms such as democratization, economic interdependence, and participation in international institutions.

In this chapter I will overview the dynamics of the Western European settlement and then examine two other notable peace settlements between regional rivals – the 1979 peace treaty between Egypt and Israel and the 1994 agreement between Israel and Jordan – to explore whether bottom-up or top-down strategies and mechanisms brought them about.[4] These settlements – the only two successful Middle Eastern (Arab–Israeli) peacemaking initiatives to date – are appropriate to study, since they, too, involve peace settlements between regional antagonists with territorial disputes and a history of hot wars. In each case I investigate whether the settlement was top-down or bottom-up by identifying (1) the impetus for peacemaking, (2) societal attitudes

---

[3] Norrin M. Ripsman, "Two Stages of Transition from a Region of War to a Region of Peace: Realist Transition and Liberal Endurance," *International Studies Quarterly* 49, no. 4 (December 2005), 669–93.

[4] For other attempts to derive generalizable propositions from these regions, see Galia Press Barnathan, *The Political Economy of Transitions to Peace: A Comparative Perspective* (University of Pittsburgh Press, 2009), and Benjamin Miller, "Contrasting Explanations for Peace: Realism vs. Liberalism in Europe and the Middle East," *Contemporary Security Policy* 31, no. 1 (April 2010), 134–64.

toward an agreement, and (3) governmental attitudes toward an agreement. In addition, I explore the role of third-party actions to facilitate the agreement, with an emphasis on the target of third-party intervention (i.e., whether the third party seeks to influence the governments or societal actors of the belligerent states) and on the time frame of their efforts (i.e., whether the third party seeks to drive the peacemaking process, facilitate an ongoing process by overcoming obstacles, or simply assist in selling the agreement after the fact to disaffected groups).

My conclusion is that all three settlements began as top-down settlements undertaken by governments that faced strong societal opposition to peacemaking efforts. The governments involved willingly decided to conclude peace agreements with their enemies on the basis of calculations of strategic and state interests; they were not compelled by domestic pressures to do so. Third party efforts, namely those of the United States, were initially strategic efforts to persuade belligerent governments to reach an agreement, followed by postagreement economic rewards designed largely to help the governments sell a deal domestically. Therefore, I argue that regional peacemaking should be started at the governmental level rather than at the societal level. During the initial phase societal efforts are likely to be unsuccessful and perhaps even counterproductive. I further conclude that the European settlement was able to transform itself into a stable partnership, whereas the Middle Eastern settlements have not been entrenched societally, because of the widespread European application of postagreement liberal, bottom-up mechanisms, whereas such measures were actively resisted in the Middle Eastern cases. This suggests that the proper time for bottom-up mechanisms is after the agreement has been reached, as a means of socializing or entrenching the agreement. In this regard, my approach is multiparadigmatic or eclectic, relying on realist and statist mechanisms in the first stage and liberal, constructivist, and societal mechanisms in the second stage, as part of a comprehensive approach to regional peacemaking.[5]

This chapter consists of four sections. The section that follows discusses the theories underlying both the bottom-up peace perspective and the top-down approach, and identifies their prescriptions for ending protracted conflict. The second section will overview my research on the Western European settlement to illustrate how top-down

[5] On eclectic theories, see John A. Hall and T. V. Paul, "Preconditions for Prudence: A Sociological Synthesis of Realism and Liberalism," in *International Order and the Future of World Politics*, ed. T. V. Paul and John A. Hall (Cambridge University Press, 1999), 67–77; and Rudra Sil and Peter J. Katzenstein, *Beyond Paradigms: Analytic Eclecticism in the Study of World Politics* (Basingstoke: Palgrave Macmillan, 2010).

mechanisms drove the transition to security cooperation while bottom-up mechanisms subsequently socialized the settlement. The third section investigates how top-down versus bottom-up prescriptions fared in the two successful Middle Eastern peacemaking episodes that I am examining. The final section will present hypotheses and recommendations for achieving peace settlements between former enemies.

Contending theoretical approaches to regional peacemaking

Bottom-up theories (liberal and constructivist)

Bottom-up approaches to peacemaking seek to make the societies of the belligerent states the engine of conflict resolution, in the conviction that they can rein in their governments and restrain conflict if they so desire. Consequently, they consist of strategies to create vested interests in favor of compromise and conflict resolution, to foster societal norms that eschew conflict, and to promote political institutions that facilitate societal control over government. In this regard they are inspired by liberal theories of cooperation emphasizing interests and institutions, and by constructivist theories emphasizing the role of societal norms.

1. *Democratic institutions and norms.* According to the democratic peace theory democratic states are not likely to wage war with each other for two reasons. First, since the public bears the costs of war it is more peaceful than its leaders. When democratic political institutions allow the public some say over foreign policy matters, they will restrain their leaders and favor peace, particularly with other democratic states.[6] Second, since democratic societies share political norms that reject coercion as a means of securing consent from other free peoples, these values will constrain leaders from waging war against other democracies.[7] Democratic peace theory suggests that the way to bring about peace in troubled regions would be to spread democracy throughout the region, making war less likely between regional participants.

---

[6] See, for example, Bruce M. Russett, *Grasping the Democratic Peace: Principles for a Post-Cold War World* (Princeton University Press, 1993), 38–40.
[7] Zeev Maoz and Bruce Russett, "Normative and Structural Causes of Democratic Peace, 1946–1986," *American Political Science Review* 87, no. 3 (September 1993), 624–38; William J. Dixon, "Democracy and the Peaceful Settlement of International Conflict," *American Political Science Review* 88, no. 1 (March 1994), 14–32; John M. Owen, "How Liberalism Produces Democratic Peace," *International Security* 19, no. 2 (fall 1994), 87–125.

2. *Creating economic interests in peace.* Commercial liberals argue that high levels of economic interdependence between states foster peace for two reasons.[8] First, when interdependence is high, states face considerable opportunity costs of the use of force in terms of trade and investment forgone. Second, when trade and investment flow freely across national borders, trade becomes a more efficient means of securing resources from territory than conquest. These losses would accrue to business interests in interdependent countries who are most vulnerable to the economic costs of war, which, in turn, makes them pressure their governments for restraint.[9] Therefore, it stands to reason that extending economic relations between military rivals can create a vested transnational interest group that will pressure both sides to resolve their conflicts peacefully.

3. *Cooperative institutions.* Constructivists would argue that societies are shaped by the ideas and institutions that help forge their identities. To the extent that states and societies become embedded in cooperative international institutions, they begin to view conflict differently.[10] Indeed, conflictual behavior becomes anathema to society and the leaders they select. Therefore, creating powerful international institutions with adversarial states as members can stabilize conflict between them.[11] This is most effective if the three mechanisms discussed work together: that is, if regional institutions, together with democratization and the generation of economic interdependence, create a pluralistic security community that ties national identity to membership in the group, making conflict unthinkable.[12]

---

[8] See, for example, Chapter 7 in this volume.

[9] See Michael W. Doyle, *Ways of War and Peace: Realism, Liberalism, and Socialism* (New York: W. W. Norton, 1997), 230–50; Robert O. Keohane, "International Liberalism Revisited," in *The Economic Limits to Modern Politics*, ed. John Dunn (Cambridge University Press, 1990), 186–87; Erik Gartzke, "The Capitalist Peace," *American Journal of Political Science* 51, no. 1 (January 2007), 166–91; and John Mueller, "Capitalism, Peace, and the Historical Movement of Ideas," *International Interactions* 36, no. 2 (June 2010), 169–84.

[10] See Alexander Wendt, *Social Theory of International Politics* (Cambridge University Press, 1999), particularly 297–308; and Audie Klotz, *Norms in International Relations: The Struggle Against Apartheid* (Ithaca, NY: Cornell University Press, 1995), 25–27.

[11] Technically, this might be considered a top-down mechanism rather than a bottom-up one, as institutions and elites act on societal interests from without the state. See, for example, Vincent Pouliot, *International Security in Practice: The Politics of NATO–Russia Diplomacy* (Cambridge University Press, 2010). I thank Michael Lipson and Vincent Pouliot for bringing this to my attention. Nonetheless, as the dominant source of change in this causal path is societal attitudes, which then compel state restraint, rather than state-level decisions despite societal attitudes, it too is truly a bottom-up mechanism.

[12] See Emanuel Adler and Michael Barnett, "Security Communities in Theoretical Perspective," in Adler and Barnett, eds., *Security Communities*, 3–28; and Russett and

Each of these bottom-up approaches to peacemaking assumes that peace occurs as a result of societal pressure on the state due to either economic, self-preservation, or moral motives. They work best, therefore, with states that allow societal input into the foreign policy process, or with less-autonomous states.[13]

Top-down theories (realist and statist)

In contrast, top-down approaches view the state, rather than society, as the engine of peacemaking. Indeed, in much the same way that classical realists, such as Walter Lippmann and Reinhold Niebuhr, believed that the public was more resentful of the enemy than the state – which is too pragmatic to hold grudges – realists believe that the state is the most likely to bury the hatchet if its interests required it, often over societal objections.[14] It may do so for several reasons. In accordance with realist theory, it may be compelled to do so by the great powers or by the need to balance against a more threatening adversary. Alternatively, state leaders might feel compelled to compromise with regional rivals if they believe that continuing conflict could undermine their hold on power domestically.

1. *Balancing.* Realists argue that in the anarchic realm of international politics, where the slightest misstep can have disastrous consequences for national security, states cannot afford the luxury of either permanent alliances or permanent enmities. Therefore, they must be prepared to put aside their differences with former enemies when a greater international power threatens them both. Neither balance-of-power theory nor balance-of-threat theory suggest any strategy for peacemaking, but they do suggest that the time should be ripe for regional peacemaking when enemy states face a common external threat.[15]

Oneal, *Triangulating Peace.* In the case of ASEAN states, Amitav Acharya suggests a security community might be possible without democratization being necessary. Amitav Acharya, *Constructing a Security Community in Southeast Asia: ASEAN and the Problem of Regional Order* (London: Routledge, 2001).

[13] On the impact of state autonomy on foreign security policy, see Norrin M. Ripsman, *Peacemaking by Democracies: The Effect of State Autonomy on the Post-World-War Settlements* (University Park: Pennsylvania State University Press, 2002).

[14] Walter Lippmann, *Essays in the Public Philosophy* (Boston: Little, Brown, 1955), 18–21; Reinhold Niebuhr, *The Structure of Nations and Empires* (New York: Scribner's, 1959), 197.

[15] On balance-of-power theory, see Hans J. Morgenthau, *Politics Among Nations: The Struggle for Power and Peace*, 6th edn. (New York: McGraw-Hill, 1985); Kenneth N. Waltz, *Theory of International Politics* (Reading, MA: Addison-Wesley, 1979); Edward Vose Gulick, *Europe's Classical Balance of Power* (New York: W. W. Norton, 1967), and T. V. Paul, James Wirtz, and Michel Fortmann, eds., *The Balance of Power: Theory and Practice in the 21st Century* (Stanford University Press, 2004). For the logic of

2. *Hegemonic influence.* Hegemonic stability theory assumes that order and peace derive from an international concentration of power. When one state possesses considerably more economic, military, and political power resources than the other states in a system of states, it can use that power to coerce the other states or provide them with selective incentives in order to induce cooperation. In this manner the dominant state, or hegemon, increases the costs of defection and decreases the risks of cooperation, thereby making peace and stability possible.[16] In order to promote regional peacemaking, therefore, a hegemon can motivate states to bury the hatchet by providing pressure on regional governments, issuing security guarantees, providing economic and other incentives, and, where appropriate, making threats.

3. *State motives.* A third statist explanation of regional peacemaking, more consistent with neoclassical realism than with structural realism, would explain peacemaking in terms of other, nonsecurity-related, governmental motives.[17] Thus, the fear of losing power might encourage leaders to make peace with former enemies in much the same way that the diversionary war theory expects them to wage war to secure their position.[18] In particular, if a protracted, costly state of conflict has

---

balance-of-threat theory, see Stephen M. Walt, *The Origins of Alliances* (Ithaca, NY: Cornell University Press, 1987), 21–28.

[16] The best statement of this argument is Robert Gilpin, *War and Change in World Politics* (Cambridge University Press, 1981). See also Stephen D. Krasner, "State Power and the Structure of International Trade," *World Politics* 28, no. 3 (April 1976), 317–47; A. F. K. Organski and Jacek Kugler, *The War Ledger* (University of Chicago Press, 1980); William C. Wohlforth, "The Stability of a Unipolar World," *International Security* 24, no. 1 (summer 1999), 5–41; and Stephen G. Brooks and William C. Wohlforth, *World out of Balance: International Relations and the Challenge of American Primacy* (Princeton University Press, 2008).

[17] Neoclassical realists contend that domestic political circumstances affect the way in which states respond to the international environment. See Gideon Rose, "Neoclassical Realism and Theories of Foreign Policy," *World Politics* 51, no. 1 (October 1998), 144–72; Jeffrey W. Taliaferro, Steven E. Lobell, and Norrin M. Ripsman, "Introduction: Neoclassical Realism, the State, and Foreign Policy," in *Neoclassical Realism, the State, and Foreign Policy*, ed. Steven E. Lobell, Norrin M. Ripsman, and Jeffrey W. Taliaferro (Cambridge University Press, 2009), 1–41. As I argue elsewhere, the likelihood of domestic pressures determining foreign policy increases dramatically when the leadership believes its hold on power is slipping. Norrin M. Ripsman, "Neoclassical Realism and Domestic Interest Groups," in Lobell, Ripsman, and Taliaferro, eds., *Neoclassical Realism, the State, and Foreign Policy*, 170–93.

[18] See Jack S. Levy, "The Diversionary Theory of War," in *The Handbook of War Studies*, ed. Manus I. Midlarsky (Boston, MA: Unwin Hyman, 1989), 259–88; Alastair Smith, "Diversionary Foreign Policy in Democratic Systems," *International Studies Quarterly* 40, no. 1 (1996), 133–53; Sara McLaughlin Mitchell and Brandon C. Prins, "Rivalry and Diversionary Uses of Force," *Journal of Conflict Resolution* 48, no. 6 (December 2004), 937–61.

262   Eclectic perspectives

undermined the economy of a belligerent to the point that the government risks losing power in an election, revolution, or coup, that government could be willing to terminate the conflict to ameliorate domestic
conditions (even if society favors continuing the conflict). This would
suggest that third parties (states and international institutions) could
promote peacemaking by imposing costly economic sanctions on
regional rivals.

All these top-down approaches share the common assumption, which
I advance elsewhere, that more autonomous states are more conducive
to peacemaking, as they allow governments – which are more susceptible than societies to realist and statist incentives for peacemaking –
to make the unpopular compromises that are frequently necessary to
achieve stable settlements.[19]

Overview of the Western European case

My initial test of these competing theoretical approaches to regional
peacemaking was a case study of the transition of Western Europe from
a region of persistent insecurity and war to a region of stable security cooperation after World War II.[20] The heart of this transition was
the stabilization of the contentious Franco-German rivalry, which had
erupted in war three times in seventy-five years. I determined that
there were two distinct phases of regional peacemaking: (1) the transition phase, from 1945 to 1954, when a regional settlement for Western
Europe was agreed upon; and (2) the entrenchment phase, 1955–1990,
when peaceful cooperation became routinized and changed the character of regional relations.

In the first phase there was little evidence that the transition to
security cooperation was driven by liberal or constructivist mechanisms. Although the Federal Republic of Germany (FRG) was established as a democratic state in 1949, neither French leaders nor the
French public viewed that fact by 1954 as a sufficient guarantee against
future German aggression, which explains why they would not agree
to German rearmament and German participation in NATO without substantial American and British security guarantees.[21] Nor could

---

[19] Ripsman, *Peacemaking by Democracies.*
[20] This section draws heavily upon Ripsman, "Two Stages of Transition."
[21] In July 1954, for example, a public opinion poll conducted by L'Institut Français
d'Opinion Publique revealed that 66 percent of decided French respondents believed
that German rearmament was a danger in any form, while 28 percent believed it could
be benign only if adequate safeguards were in place. Jean Stoetzel, "The Evolution
of French Opinion," in *France Defeats EDC*, ed. Daniel Lerner and Raymond Aron
(New York: Praeger, 1957), 84.

cooperation be attributed to commercial liberal mechanisms, as extensive economic interdependence between France and Germany did not materialize until after the 1957 Treaty of Rome, three years after the political and security arrangements agreed upon as part of the Paris Accord of 1954. Finally, institutionalist approaches that explain peacemaking in terms of attitudinal change and the creation of a sense of we-ness between regional participants also are unable to explain the Western European transition, as both French leaders and the public at large remained distrustful of the Germans and retained a strong antipathy toward them at the time that they signed up to the 1954 security framework.[22] Nor, for that matter, were the central institutions that were to constitute the region of Western Europe, principally the European Economic Community and its successors, established until well after the security framework was in place.

Instead, the transition phase was driven primarily by top-down, realist mechanisms.[23] The catalyst for peacemaking was the common Soviet threat experienced by all regional states. Faced with the recognition that the Soviet Union represented a far greater threat in the short to medium term than a defeated and occupied Germany, and that, with US troops returning home, a German military contribution was essential to provide an effective defense of Western Europe, even French military and political leaders began to accept the need to cooperate with the FRG. Yet the Soviet threat was insufficient to compel cooperation. The other necessary condition for the transition was active US hegemonic involvement to guarantee French security against a possible future recrudescence of German militarism.

In contrast, the entrenchment of Western European cooperation had little to do with top-down mechanisms. From 1955 to 1990, although the Soviet threat waxed, waned, and even collapsed, and although US hegemonic participation in continental security affairs was scaled back somewhat, the level of cooperation and regional trust actually increased exponentially. As I demonstrate elsewhere, this was due primarily to the effect of the democratization of regional states, especially the FRG, and to their integration within cooperative regional security institutions,

---

[22] In a 1950 Gallup poll a majority (55%) of decided French voters opposed even "cordial relations" with Germany. George H. Gallup, *The Gallup International Public Opinion Polls: France, 1939, 1944–1975* (New York: Random House, 1976), vol. I, 141. While attitudes might have improved somewhat by 1954, the overwhelming fear of Germany indicated in note 21 is difficult to square with a sense of common identity and "we feeling."

[23] In this regard, my conclusions are similar to John Hall's chapter in this volume, although our conclusions about the utility of bottom-up mechanisms in the second phase differ.

such as NATO and the EEC (and its successors). Increasing economic integration between the former rivals also helped. These bottom-up mechanisms helped socialize the settlement initially achieved through top-down mechanisms so that, by October 1989, the vast majority of the French population (80%) did not fear German reunification in the context of European institutions.[24]

Middle Eastern case studies

To determine whether the Western European experience is unique or whether peacemaking in other troubled regions also fits this pattern, I examined two successful peace settlements between former regional rivals in a contemporary region of perpetual conflict, the Middle East: the 1979 peace treaty between Egypt and Israel and the 1994 treaty between Israel and Jordan. Both of these settlements involved bitter enemies who were involved in repeated wars over several decades. Therefore, we can assume that the strategies that were able to terminate these conflicts could also help resolve less intense rivalries.

Once again I assume that the mechanisms causing the transition to peace are not necessarily the same as those that help entrench the settlement afterwards. Therefore I am interested in two distinct phases of these peace agreements. In the first instance I am interested in the factors that caused the transition to peace in each of these cases. But I am also interested in the post-agreement period to determine the degree to which the agreement was entrenched in constructive bilateral relations and the factors which affected their quality. I will begin with a discussion of each of these settlements and then evaluate whether and how liberal/constructivist and realist/statist elements contributed to the agreement and to postagreement stability.

Case overviews

1. *The Camp David Accord*. Egypt and Israel were bitter rivals since the establishment of the Jewish state in 1948.[25] Since the Arab states rejected what they considered to be an alien, European presence in lands they considered Arab, they met Israeli leader David Ben-Gurion's declaration of independence with a declaration of war. Although the

---

[24] Eric Dupin, "Les Français voient l'est en rose," *Liberation*, October 4, 1989, 7.
[25] The roots of the Arab-Israeli conflict are discussed in Ian J. Bickerton and Carla Klausner, *A Concise History of the Arab-Israeli Conflict*, 4th edn. (New York: Prentice Hall, 2002); and Walter Laqueur and Barry Rubin, eds., *The Israeli-Arab Reader: A Documentary History of the Middle East Conflict* (Harmondsworth: Penguin, 1995).

Arab coalition of Egypt, Syria, Jordan, Iraq, Lebanon, and Saudi Arabia (with a small Yemeni contingent) was defeated by the nascent Israeli Defense Forces (IDF), the postwar armistices failed to resolve the underlying conflict.

Under Gamal Abdel Nasser's revolutionary leadership, Egypt continued to put pressure on Israel by intercepting Israeli shipping through the Suez Canal and allowing cross-border raids on Israeli territory by *fedayeen*. This led to two more Egyptian–Israeli wars: the Sinai War of 1956 and the Six-Day War of 1967. In the 1967 war – in which Israel struck Egypt and Syria preemptively in response to the Egyptian military build-up, its blockade of the Straits of Tiran, and its request to the UN Secretary-General to remove UN peacekeepers in the Sinai – Israel captured the Gaza Strip and the strategically significant Sinai peninsula from Egypt. This effectively transformed the stakes of the conflict for Egypt. Up until 1967 it sought to eject the Jewish state from the region. After 1967 it sought to regain core Egyptian territory.[26]

Following Nasser's death, new Egyptian president Anwar Sadat faced a number of interrelated challenges. First, after three unsuccessful wars with Israel the Egyptian economy was in desperate shape, with stagnant growth, a shortage of foreign currency, and heavy foreign debt. More seriously, Egyptian inflation ranged between 30 to 50 percent per annum in the mid 1970s, which led to widespread protests as the cost of food skyrocketed. And defense spending continued to account for over half the government's national budget. In this context, Sadat's economic liberalization program (the *infitah*) failed to ignite the Egyptian economy and led only to greater social unrest.[27] Second, Egyptian society was humiliated by the loss of the Sinai and expected the government to get it back. Finally, Sadat came to believe that his Soviet benefactors were blocking Egyptian strategic objectives by dragging their feet on providing Egypt with state-of-the-art equipment, and by attempting to stabilize the Arab–Israeli conflict as part of the détente strategy.[28]

---

[26] See Michael B. Oren, *Six Days of War: June 1967 and the Making of the Modern Middle East* (Oxford University Press, 2002); and William B. Quandt, *Peace Process: American Diplomacy and the Arab-Israeli Conflict since 1967* (Washington, DC and Berkeley: Brookings Institution/University of California Press, 2001).

[27] Kirk J. Beattie, *Egypt During the Sadat Years* (Basingstoke: Palgrave Macmillan, 2000), 137–217; Raymond Hinnebusch, Jr., *Egyptian Politics under Sadat: The Post-Populist Development of an Authoritarian-Modernizing State* (Boulder, CO: Lynne Rienner, 1988), 57–63; and Thomas W. Lippman, *Egypt after Nasser: Sadat, Peace and the Mirage of Prosperity* (New York: Paragon House, 1989), 83–116.

[28] See Alvin Z. Rubinstein, *Red Star on the Nile: The Soviet-Egyptian Influence Relationship since the June War* (Princeton University Press, 1977), chapters 5–6.

These problems led him to rethink the Arab–Israeli conflict and take steps that would lead to an Egyptian-Israeli peace treaty.

Sadat concluded that reliance on the Soviet Union and Soviet equipment had failed to secure Egyptian interests in the past and that they were unlikely to do so in the future. Therefore, the Arabs were unlikely to eliminate the state of Israel, or even regain the territory lost in 1967, with Soviet support while Israel enjoyed military superiority and American support. Attempting to do so would only further impoverish Egypt, thereby putting the regime in jeopardy as domestic conditions continued to deteriorate, without providing any likely material gain. In contrast, if Egypt could improve its relationship with the United States, it could hope to achieve both American pressure on Israel to return the Sinai and American economic assistance to bail out the flailing Egyptian economy. In 1971 this rationale led Sadat to endorse a report by UN envoy Gunnar Jarring, indicating that Egypt would agree to a peace treaty with Israel if Israel were to withdraw from all territory occupied as a result of the 1967 war. The following year he expelled Soviet military advisors from Egypt, in part to facilitate improved relations with Washington and in part to allow him to prepare a secret attack against Israel together with Syria, aimed at making Israeli leaders feel vulnerable and in order to force them to the bargaining table.[29]

The consequent 1973 Yom Kippur War turned out to be a disastrous military defeat for Egypt, but early losses in the Golan Heights and, to a lesser degree, the Sinai did highlight to Israel that it was still vulnerable to an Arab attack and that a peace treaty that took one or more Arab states out of the conflict would be worth making limited concessions for. From Sadat's perspective, the war actually increased his domestic difficulties by accelerating Egypt's economic woes. Indeed, as Sadat attempted to set Egypt's economic house in order through deregulation and the elimination of price controls, the impoverished masses responded in 1977 with bread riots that threatened to topple the regime. Consequently, Sadat was all the more desperate for a peace dividend and American economic assistance, especially since the Arab League states were not forthcoming with a sufficient aid package for Egypt.

Sadat's strategy was to forge a united Arab front to negotiate a comprehensive peace treaty with Israel on the basis of UN Security Council Resolution 242, requiring Israeli withdrawal from territory occupied in the 1967 war. When it became clear both that Israel was reluctant to reach a comprehensive settlement and that Syrian leader Hafez

---

[29] See ibid. and Quandt, *Peace Process*.

al-Assad was unwilling to reach a deal, Sadat refused to allow Syria a veto over Egyptian interests and proceeded to negotiate a separate deal for Egypt.

The deal negotiated at Camp David involved the complete return of the Sinai to Egypt – something about which Sadat was adamant – in exchange for peace. Key provisions of the treaty provided for the dismantling of Israeli settlements in Sinai, the provision of oil to Israel from Sinai wells, security arrangements, and about fifty-five to sixty normalization agreements covering everything from economic cooperation to cultural exchanges and tourism.[30] After Sadat's assassination in October 1981, the successor government of Hozni Mubarak failed to implement these normalization agreements, but the essential elements of the security component of the treaty have been observed by both sides.

2. *The Israeli–Jordanian Treaty.* The Israeli-Jordanian relationship was qualitatively different from the Egyptian-Israeli rivalry. To begin with, Jordanian leaders were not always implacably hostile to the existence of a Jewish presence in the Middle East. Alone among Arab countries, Transjordan (after 1949, the Hashemite Kingdom of Jordan) had a history of bilateral relations with the Jewish settlement in mandated Palestine dating back to 1921.[31] Although King Abdullah of Transjordan played a leading role in the Arab coalition against the nascent state of Israel in 1948, after the war he entered into secret negotiations with Israel to replace the postwar armistice with a comprehensive peace treaty. For these "secret dealings with the Jews," Abdullah was assassinated.[32]

In 1967 King Abdullah's grandson and immediate successor, King Hussein, fought alongside Egypt and Syria in the Six-Day War and lost control of the West Bank, which Abdullah had annexed to Jordan in 1950. Yet in the years after the war Hussein had a series of secret meetings with Israeli leaders to coordinate on matters of mutual interest. During the civil war in Jordan in 1970, when Syria threatened to intervene on behalf of the Palestinians in Jordan, the Israeli government mobilized the IDF along the border to deter Syrian leader Hafez

---

[30] For the text of the treaty, see "Peace Treaty Between Israel and Egypt," March 26, 1979, available at www.mfa.gov.il/MFA/Peace%20Process/Guide%20to%20the%20 Peace%20Process/Israel-Egypt%20Peace%20Treaty (accessed October 6, 2010).

[31] Yehuda Lukacs, *Israel, Jordan, and the Peace Process* (Syracuse University Press, 1997), chapter 1; Avi Shlaim, *Collusion Across the Jordan: King Abdullah, the Zionist Movement, and the Partition of Palestine* (New York: Columbia University Press, 1988).

[32] Dennis Ross, *The Missing Peace: The Inside Story of the Fight for Middle East Peace* (New York: Farrar, Straus & Giroux, 2004), 165; Lukacs, *Israel, Jordan, and the Peace Process.*

al-Assad and preserve the Hashemite regime. In return, in September 1973 King Hussein warned Israeli Prime Minister Golda Meir that the Syrian army was preparing a surprise attack against Israel.[33]

Despite this unusual cooperation between the two states, Israel and Jordan remained enemies from 1948 until 1994, with Jordan contributing forces to three Arab wars against Israel, in 1948, 1967, and 1973. In the years after these wars Jordan remained the staunchest opponent of Israel's policies in the West Bank. This bizarre relationship has thus been characterized as an "adversarial partnership," with elements of remarkable cooperation within the context of an enduring rivalry.[34]

The basis of this cooperation between adversaries stemmed from several mutual interests. To begin with both Israel and Jordan had an overriding interest in defusing and containing Palestinian nationalism and the Palestinian Liberation Organization (PLO), which threatened the very existence of a Jewish state and Israel's control over the West Bank and Gaza on the one hand, and the Jordanian state on the other. After all, the majority of the Jordanian population consists of Palestinian refugees from 1948 and 1967. These Palestinians have been opponents of the Jordanian monarchy and, in the 1970 civil war, almost overthrew it. In addition, both Israel and Jordan had an interest in the survival and territorial integrity of the Hashemite regime in Jordan. For the King of Jordan, this interest is obvious. For Israel, the monarchy's would be disastrous, as it would replace a relatively moderate Arab government with either a hostile Palestinian governing coalition, radical Islamists, or perhaps Syrian agents, as happened in Lebanon. Moreover, it would remove a stable buffer between Israel and Iraq, which was implacably hostile to Israel. The two states also had a mutual interest in stability along their border – the longest border for each country – and to prevent the infiltration of hostile elements from one country to another, especially, from Jordan's point of view, the influx of additional Palestinian refugees. Finally, they depended on each other for access to, and the safety of, their water supply in the arid Middle East.[35]

In this context, after King Hussein's 1988 disavowal of Jordanian claims to the West Bank, at the official level the relationship between

---

[33] The king's warning went unheeded. Consequently, the Israelis were surprised in early October when Syria and Egypt jointly attacked on Yom Kippur. Lukacs, *Israel, Jordan, and the Peace Process*, 1–4.

[34] Ian Lustick, "Israel and Jordan: The Implications of an Adversarial Partnership," *Policy Papers in International Affairs*, no. 6 (Berkeley: Institute of International Studies, University of California Press, 1978).

[35] For a detailed discussion of Israeli and Jordanian mutual interests, see Lukacs *Israel, Jordan, and the Peace Process*.

Jordan and Israel would always remain hostile as long as Israel did not reach an agreement with its Palestinian population that would satisfy Palestinians in the kingdom. After all, the king risked another civil war if he appeared too soft on Israel. Once Israel and the PLO concluded the 1993 Oslo Agreement, however, a strategic window opened up that not only enabled but actually compelled a peace treaty between Amman and Jerusalem. For, if Israel and the Palestinians were to make decisions on security in the West Bank without Jordanian participation, Jordanian security interests would be jeopardized.[36] Furthermore, after alienating the United States with its neutrality in the 1991 Gulf War, the king was eager to take the opportunity to mend fences with Washington by reaching a peace treaty with Israel now that the Palestinian issue appeared to be on the verge of resolution.[37]

Consequently, a little over a year after the Oslo signing ceremony, the two parties concluded a treaty of peace, delimiting the western border of Jordan, restoring some West Bank land to Jordan, allocating a significant share of water from the Jordan and Yarmouk rivers to Jordan, and laying the groundwork for cooperation in a host of economic fields, including trade, transportation, tourism, communications, energy, navigation, health, and agriculture.[38] Unlike the Egyptian-Israeli peace, the peace treaty between Israel and Jordan has been more successful in economic terms, especially under the auspices of the American-sponsored Qualified Industrial Zone (QIZ), which offered preferential access to the US market for goods produced in the zone with joint Israeli-Jordanian input.[39] Nonetheless, since its signature events such as the 1998 Israeli assassination attempt on Hamas leader Khaled Mashal in Jordan and the outbreak of the al-Aqsa intifada in 2000 have bolstered opponents of "normalization" of relations with Israel, which has inhibited the development of a warm peace.[40]

---

[36] Interview with former United States Envoy to the Middle East, Dennis Ross, February 14, 2008.

[37] Interview with Jordanian Ambassador to the United Nations, Mohammed al-Allaf, November 5, 2007; Interview with Hamid Walid, Deputy Chief of Mission, Jordanian Embassy in Washington, February 20, 2008.

[38] The text of the treaty is reproduced at www.kinghussein.gov.jo/peacetreaty.html (accessed August 19, 2008).

[39] Howard Rosen, "Free Trade Agreements as Foreign Policy Tools: The US–Israel and US–Jordan FTAs," in *Free Trade Agreements: US Strategies and Priorities*, ed. Jeffrey J. Schott (Washington, DC: Institute for International Economics, 2004), 60; Steven E. Lobell, "The Second Face of American Security: The US–Jordan Free Trade Agreement as Security Policy," *Comparative Strategy* 27, no. 1 (2008), 1–13.

[40] Interview with Ambassador al-Allaf; Interview with Shimon Shamir, Israeli Ambassador to Amman, 1995–97.

Analysis: international relations theory and the origins of the peace treaties

Bottom-up approaches

1. *Democratic peace theory.* The two Arab–Israeli settlements cannot be attributed to democratic institutions or processes, for several reasons. First and foremost, neither Egypt nor the Kingdom of Jordan are democracies. While Egypt is a presidential republic which holds presidential elections, they are generally viewed as dominated by the president and the National Democratic Party, with significant restrictions on political and electoral participation. In Jordan, the legislature is also dominated by the king and political participation has similarly been constricted. For these reasons, neither Egypt in the late 1970s nor Jordan in 1994 is classified by the POLITY IV dataset as democratic.

Second, until after the agreement with Egypt was reached, public opinion in Israel opposed the extent of the concessions made to Egypt (e.g., giving back all of the Sinai, including the oilfields and strategic positions, and evacuating settlements), suggesting that the government was ahead of the public. Significantly, a confidential 1977 report on the state of Israeli public opinion commissioned by the Carter administration revealed that "[b]y 78–15% a big majority oppose 'returning the entire Sinai Desert to Egypt."[41] On the Egyptian side, the treaty was remarkably unpopular, as evidenced by Sadat's assassination and the fact that, after his death, his successor, Mubarak, felt unable to follow through with all the economic, social, and cultural protocols to the agreement that were negotiated. Indeed, in July 1977 Sadat reportedly told Carter that, "if we resurrected Jesus Christ and Prophet Mohammed together, they would not be able to persuade Moslem or Christian Arabs to open the borders with Israel after 29 years of hatred, four wars, rivers of blood and massacres."[42]

While the Israeli public broadly supported the Israeli-Jordanian treaty, the same cannot be said of Jordan.[43] In Jordan the treaty with Israel is immensely unpopular and always was. Palestinians comprise

---

[41] "An In-depth Study of the Voting Public in Israel, July 1977," attachment to Jim Fallows to Zbigniew Brzezinski and Carter, July 18, 1977, Jimmy Carter Presidential Library, National Security Affairs (NSA) File, Brzezinski Material, Country File, Israel, Box 35, Israel, 7/77.

[42] Morris B. Abram to Carter, July 5, 1977, Jimmy Carter Presidential Library, National Security Affairs (NSA) File, Brzezinski Material, Country File, Israel, Box 35, Israel, 7/77.

[43] Avi Shlaim, for example, observes that "Regarded in Jordan as 'the king's peace,' the treaty enjoyed wide popular support in Israel and elevated Rabin's prestige to

over 50 percent of the Jordanian population. As a group, they reject the existence of the State of Israel, which they accuse of usurping their land.[44] Consequently, support for the treaty was largely confined to a small circle around the king.[45] In response to the treaty, numerous groups protested, prompting a governmental ban on demonstrations in the aftermath of the treaty.[46] Indeed, according to the British Broadcasting Corporation (BBC), the protest movement included "the secretaries-general of the Jordanian opposition parties, trade unions, popular organizations, women and youth groups and a number of House of Representatives members."[47] Moreover, Jordanian labor unions banned all Jordanian workers from working on Israeli projects. In addition, the Jordanian professional bar, which certified most of the country's professionals, banned their members from working with Israelis.[48] That these organizations could oppose the king so openly indicated the degree to which the treaty was unpopular, which made the government unwilling to crack down on the opposition.[49] It is clear, then, that the Jordanian government was more conciliatory than its public was.

In neither of these agreements, then, did democracy and public opinion seem to have been the engine driving peacemaking. Instead, the treaties were signed despite public opinion. Democratic peace theory would thus appear to be a poor guide for explaining these settlements.

2. *Commercial liberalism.* Economic interdependence and pressures from business communities that had vested interests at stake also

---

new heights." "Israeli Politics and Middle East Peacemaking," *Journal of Palestinian Studies* 24, no. 4 (summer 1995), 20–31.

[44] Laura Zittrain Eisenberg and Neil Caplan, "The Israel–Jordan Peace Treaty: Patterns of Negotiation, Problems of Implementation," *Israel Affairs* 9, no. 3 (spring 2003), 87–110, 100.

[45] Ibid., p. 87; Paul L. Scham and Russell E. Lucas, "'Normalization' and 'Anti-Normalization' in Jordan: The Public Debate," *Middle East Review of International Affairs* 5, no. 3 (September 2001), http://meria.idc.ac.il/journal/2001/issue3/jv5n3a5.html (accessed September 12, 2010).

[46] "Jordanian Police Stage Security Crackdown after Large Moslem Demo," *Jerusalem Post*, October 27, 1994 (accessed through LexisNexis, September 27, 2010); "Opposition Protests in Amman against Peace Treaty," *BBC News*, October 27, 1994 (accessed through LexisNexis, September 27, 2010). On other forms of protest, see Scham and Lucas, "'Normalization' and 'Anti-Normalization' in Jordan."

[47] "Opposition Statement Rejects Peace Treaty; Massive protests Planned," *BBC News Summary of World Broadcasts*, October 27, 1994 (accessed through LexisNexis, September 27, 2010).

[48] Interview with Eynat Shlein-Michael, Second Secretary for Political Affairs and Acting Commercial Attaché at the Israeli Embassy in Amman from 1995 to 1997, February 14, 2008; Interview with Professor Asher Susser, Tel Aviv University, May 7, 2008.

[49] Interview with Tuvia Israeli Director, Jordan Department, Israeli Foreign Ministry, June 18, 2008.

cannot explain the two Middle Eastern settlements. Indeed, the Arab boycott of Israel meant that there was very little economic exchange between Israel and Egypt and Israel and Jordan prior to the peace treaties.[50] Thus, there were no significant vested economic interests to drive the peace process.

It is possible that groups that expected to gain from new-found economic ties may have supported peacemaking, but that would constitute a different theoretical dynamic. Besides, there is no evidence that economic interest groups drove decision-making in either settlement. Indeed, the Egyptian business community was rather cool to the idea of a peace treaty with Israel, which accounts for the economic provisions of the treaty never being implemented.[51] And, although the 1994 treaty has developed a more significant economic relationship between Israel and Jordan, the level of cooperation is significantly below the level the countries had envisioned, in large part because of the opposition of key economic interests, including professional organizations. Thus commercial liberalism is not a useful guide for explaining these settlements.

3. *Institutionalism.* It would be difficult to explain the Middle East peace settlements as the product of cooperative international institutions. Prior to the treaties there were no regional institutions that included both Arab states and Israel as members. Even after the treaties were signed that remains largely true. While the Arab states are part of the Arab League (a rather weak institution) and the Arab Monetary Fund, the lack of Israeli membership makes it impossible to create a sense of common identity or we-ness that could inspire reconciliation.

We can conclude, therefore, that neither of these settlements can be properly described as having originated in a bottom-up manner. It remains possible that democratization, the generation of extensive economic interdependence, and the creation of meaningful security-providing institutions in the Middle East might help solidify the peace agreements reached there, as they did in Western Europe. But peace was not brought about through bottom-up mechanisms.

Top-down approaches

1. *Balancing.* Balance-of-power considerations appear to have played an important role in the Israeli-Jordanian peace settlement. The 1990 Iraqi

---

[50] On the Arab boycott, see Gil Feiler, *From Boycott to Economic Cooperation: The Arab Boycott of Israel* (London: Taylor & Francis, 1998).

[51] Interview with Alan Baker, Legal Advisor to the Israeli Foreign Ministry, June 21, 2004.

invasion of Kuwait and the threat Iraq posed to Saudi Arabia made moderates in the Arab world (and even less moderate states, such as Syria) fear Saddam Hussein more than they feared Israel, which they felt was the only regional power capable of containing Iraq. Although Jordan had hedged its bets by staying neutral in the Gulf War and maintaining good ties with a sanctioned Iraq, the Jordanian leadership, too, feared Iraq more than it did Israel.[52] This is especially true since, having come to King Hussein's assistance in 1970, when Syria threatened to invade Jordan in support of the PLO, the Israelis had persuaded the Kingdom that they viewed an independent, secure Jordan as an essential Israeli national security requirement. Resolving the destructive conflict with Israel within the context of the Israeli-Palestinian peace process that was underway following the 1993 Oslo Agreement would help to assure American goodwill, which would also help to secure Jordan from Iraq and other regional threats.

The Egyptian-Israeli settlement, however, cannot be explained by balance-of-power or balance-of-threat theory, as Egypt was not responding to the existence of a greater common threat. Although Egypt had a rivalry with neighboring Libya and Sadat told Carter that "further conflict with Libya is in the cards," Egypt was still the dominant Arab state in the late 1970s, with no apparent challengers yet.[53] As we shall see, the threats that Sadat confronted were internal rather than external, making a balance-of-power approach focusing on more pressing external threats inappropriate.

2. *Hegemonic stability theory.* American hegemonic leadership played a central role in both Middle Eastern peace treaties. Having realized after the 1973 war that Soviet arms and influence were unable to secure the return of the Sinai peninsula, Sadat concluded that the US was the only actor with the power and influence over Israel to help him. When Secretary of State Henry Kissinger and then President Jimmy Carter proved willing to broker a deal provided that it included a formal recognition of Israel and a peace treaty as the price for the Sinai, Sadat was willing to acquiesce to gain US leverage.

Moreover, the US prodded Sadat along during the process by promising him food aid, military assistance, and equipment as part of a peace treaty with Israel. The Carter administration also provided Sadat with "one of the largest aid programs in [US] history" prior to the treaty

---

[52] See, for example, Eisenberg and Caplan, "Israel–Jordan Peace Treaty," 99.
[53] National Security Council (NSC) Office Director for Middle Eastern Affairs William Quandt to Deputy National Security Advisor David Aaron, August 16, 1977, Jimmy Carter Presidential Library, NSA File, Brzezinski Material, Country File, Egypt, Box 18.

in the hope of reducing the domestic friction Sadat faced as he made peace.[54] Following the treaty's signature, Carter sent a supplemental appropriations request to Congress, requesting a two-part aid package for Egypt totaling $1.8 billion to supplement existing aid facilities to the country. The first part consisted of $1.5 billion in military sales credit financing. The second consisted of $300 million of special economic aid loans for development projects and to "help satisfy the expectations of the Egyptian people for a better life."[55] It is noteworthy that, after receiving $1 billion in economic assistance from the US in 1979, the year of the treaty, Egypt had become "the single largest recipient of US economic assistance in the world."[56]

The US also put quite a bit of pressure on Israel to make territorial concessions to Egypt and accommodate Egyptian demands for concessions to the Palestinians, which, indeed, soured the relationship between Begin and Carter.[57] There are suggestions that the Carter administration was stalling on new arms and military financing requests from Israel prior to and during the negotiations to pressure Begin into concessions on the West Bank.[58]

Washington also softened the blow of Israeli concessions by providing military assistance, and hardware, and by covering the costs of airport and base relocations from the Sinai to the Negev desert. Consequently, Carter requested a larger aid package for Israel than for Egypt after the treaty, mainly consisting of $800 million in grants to cover the airport and base relocations and $2.2 billion in foreign military sales credits to "finance other Israeli relocation costs and some upgrading of force structure consistent with the new territorial arrangements."[59]

Under Bill Clinton's leadership the US also pressured Jordan to make a formal peace with Israel or risk being kept out of the new Middle East taking shape in the wake of the Oslo Agreement. In return, Clinton

[54] Chief Presidential Speechwriter James Fallows to Carter, March 31, 1977, Jimmy Carter Presidential Library, WHCF, Subject File, Countries, Box CO-23, CO 45 1/20/77–3/31/77.
[55] Carter to Church, April 2, 1979, Jimmy Carter Presidential Library, WHCF, Subject File, Countries, Box CO-24, CO 45 1/1/79–6/30/79.
[56] "Foreign Assistance and Related Programs Appropriation Bill, 1980," June 11, 1979, Jimmy Carter Presidential Library, NSA File, Brzezinski Material, Country File, Egypt, Box 18, 45.
[57] See, for example, Foreign Ministry to Washington, "Letter from President Carter to the Prime Minister regarding the Thickening of Settlements," October 26, 1978, Israel State Archives, Foreign Ministry Files, Cairo File, het tsadi-6824/7.
[58] See, for example, Quandt to Brzezinski, June 28, 1978, Jimmy Carter Presidential Library, NSA File, Brzezinski Material, Country File, Israel, Box 35, Israel, 5–6/78.
[59] Carter to Church, April 2, 1979, Jimmy Carter Presidential Library, WHCF, Subject File, Countries, Box CO-24, CO 45 1/1/79–6/30/79.

promised to cancel all Jordanian debts to the US (which amounted to a one-time grant of about $1 billion) upon signature, and committed to making an appeal to the Paris Club countries to forgive Jordanian debts to them (about $4.3 billion) as well.[60] Finally, Clinton promised to recommend that Congress pass a large foreign aid package to Jordan if it were to sign a peace treaty.[61]

A peace treaty with Israel allowed King Hussein to solidify his status as a moderate, pro-western Arab leader, which secured American support in the event of war with Iraq, American military assistance and advanced hardware (such as F-16s), and American economic support. Moreover, it would help get Jordan back in the American good book after being the only Arab state not to support the Gulf War coalition. Thus, active American encouragement of both peace settlements were instrumental in bringing them about.

3. *State motives.* The two Arab–Israeli settlements were undertaken in large part due to the personal/group interests of the Egyptian and Jordanian leaderships. Sadat faced an economic shambles at home and growing unrest at the *infitah* market reforms that were impoverishing the masses. Indeed, the January 1977 food riots, in which thousands of protesters around the country burned police stations and attacked government property, led Sadat to seek a way to stabilize his power position and cushion the blows of his reforms.[62] Although the public and most of the Arab world opposed recognition of Israel and were horrified by his 1977 visit to Jerusalem, he calculated that the economic benefits of regaining the Sinai (including its oil wells) and demobilization on the Egyptian-Israeli front, together with US food aid, would pay both short-term and long-term dividends that would strengthen his hold on power.[63]

---

[60] This appeal was not terribly successful. Interview with Deputy Chief of Mission Walid; and Asher Susser, "Jordan: Al-Mamlaka al-Urdunniyya al-Hashimiyya," in *Middle East Contemporary Survey 1993*, vol. XVII, ed. Ami Ayalon (Boulder, CO: Westview Press, 1995), 449–89, 473.

[61] Ross, *Missing Peace*, 171–75.

[62] On the riots, see Tamara Gutner, "The Political Economy of Food Subsidy Reform: The Case of Egypt," *Food Policy* 27, no. 5/6 (October–December 2002), 455–76; Thomas W. Lippman, "Thousands in Egypt Protest Price Rise," *Washington Post*, January 18, 1977 (accessed through LexisNexis, September 12, 2010).

[63] Interview with William Quandt, NSC Office Director for Middle Eastern Affairs, 1977–79, February 19, 2008. At least overtly, Egyptians thronged the streets to greet Sadat as a hero on his return from Jerusalem. In reality, however, this result was manufactured by a mixture of repression (preventing protests) and incentives (providing a paid day off work, food, and transportation to those who attended the welcome gathering). Judith Tucker, "While Sadat Shuffles: Economic Decay, Political Ferment in Egypt," *MERIP Reports* no. 65 (March 1978), 3–9. Moreover, there was significant opposition among the political elite, particularly the National Progressive

In the Israeli-Jordanian treaty the personality and history of King Hussein loomed large. Hussein had been much closer to Israel than were the other Arab leaders, especially since the 1970 Black September uprising, when Israel supported him against the PLO and Syria. Hussein realized at this point that, as a moderate Arab leader, he could count on Israeli support to secure himself from potentially aggressive Arab neighbors and a radical Palestinian majority. Furthermore, according to Dennis Ross, the king had been influenced by his grandfather's strategic vision, and wished to fulfill King Abdullah's destiny by reaching a strategic agreement with Israel.[64] Given the Palestinian majority in Jordan and Jordan's relative weakness in the Arab world, however, an open treaty was never possible until the Oslo Accord gave him diplomatic cover. Clearly, then, the king's delicate power position and his sense of historic mission favored friendlier relations with Israel.

Analysis: international relations theory and the entrenchment of the peace treaties

Neither of these Middle Eastern peace settlements has yielded the degree of warm relations between former regional combatants that materialized as a result of the Western European settlement.[65] Although the Camp David treaty has kept the peace between Israel and Egypt for the last thirty years, the peace has remained a cold one, without extensive economic, cultural, or social ties between the two nations. Since Egypt faced severe external pressure from the Arab world and domestic pressure from opposition groups over the peace treaty, especially as its provisions for resolving the Palestinian issue were not implemented, the Mubarak government had little interest in pursuing either a deepening of peace with Israel or the socialization of peace within Egyptian society.[66] Instead, Egyptian-Israeli

Unionist Party – many of whose members were arrested due to their anticipated opposition – and even within Sadat's inner circle itself. Notably, Foreign Minister Ismail Fahmi resigned over the trip, as he believed it played into Israeli hands and demonstrated naïve overreliance on the US. Kirk J. Beattie, *Egypt During the Sadat Years* (Basingstoke: Palgrave Macmillan, 2000), 231–32; Hinnebusch, *Egyptian Politics under Sadat*, 72–73.

[64] Ross, *Missing Peace*, 165–66; interview with Dennis Ross.

[65] The language of "cold" and "warm" peace used here is drawn from Benjamin Miller, *States, Nations and the Great Powers: The Sources of Regional War and Peace* (Cambridge University Press, 2007).

[66] See, for example, Herbert C. Kelman, "Overcoming the Psychological Barrier: An Analysis of the Egyptian-Israeli Peace Process," *Negotiation Journal* 1, no. 3 (July 1985), 224–25; Stanley F. Reed, "Shaken Pillar," *Foreign Policy* no. 45 (winter 1981/82), 175–85.

relations have been dominated by mutual recriminations and only limited cooperation. Moreover, the specter of war has not completely disappeared from the relationship. Indeed, Hillel Frisch observes that "Almost all of Egypt's capabilities, equipment, and deployment of forces are concentrated on one front, to engage one opponent only: the Israel Defense Force. The Egyptians have made this explicit since the Badr-96 exercises in 1996, in which they specifically named Israel as the training target."[67]

The Israeli-Jordanian treaty has not fared much better. Certainly, the security components of the treaty have held and war between the two states is quite unlikely. Furthermore, there has been some economic cooperation between the two countries within the context of the US-sponsored QIZ.[68] Nonetheless, the opposition of the Jordanian professional bar and widespread opposition within Jordanian society to normalization made a warm peace unlikely right from the beginning. Furthermore, the Israeli security climate, which requires careful monitoring of trans-border movement and careful vetting of applicants for visas, has further discouraged Jordanians who might have been interested in economic, educational, or cultural exchanges.[69] Finally, frustration over stalled progress in Israeli-Palestinian negotiations and renewed violence after the Camp David summit of 2000 made the treaty very unpopular in Jordan and strained relations between the two countries, undermining the warmth of the peace.[70]

These peace agreements have not, therefore, been entrenched. They remain in place largely due to the realist and statist factors that inspired them. Compared to the Western European settlement, they lack the socializing effects of the bottom-up liberal mechanisms of economic interdependence, democratic regimes, or cooperative international institutions. As indicated, neither Egypt nor Jordan developed meaningful economic relations with Israel. Needless to say, neither Arab regime has made the transition to full democracy. Nor have regional institutions been established that include Israel together with their former rivals. Consequently, the peace settlements have failed to become entrenched and remain eternally fragile. The social movement shaking Egypt and elsewhere in the Middle East in 2011, therefore, could lead to regime

[67] Hillel Frisch, "Guns and Butter in the Egyptian Army," in *Armed Forces in the Middle East: Politics and Strategy*, ed. Barry Rubin and Thomas A. Keaney (London: Frank Cass, 2002), 102.

[68] See above note 67.

[69] I thank Assaf David for bringing this to my attention.

[70] Interview with Jordanian Ambassador to the United Nations, Mohammed al-Allaf, November 5, 2007.

change that could effectively dissolve the statist peace between Egypt and Israel.

Conclusion

Each of these three settlements was achieved due to the efforts of the governments involved, statist goals, and international imperatives, rather than societal pressures. They were top-down settlements rather than bottom-up ones. As these have been amongst the most successful and most dramatic peacemaking approaches (even if they vary in the depth of the peace agreement, or in Benjamin Miller's terms, the warmth of the peace), it leads us to believe that top-down approaches can be very successful.[71] In contrast, bottom-up dynamics did not bring about any of these settlements. Indeed, in the case of the Middle Eastern settlements, none of the requisite bottom-up mechanisms were in place prior to the agreement. In the Western European case, they did not generate sufficient trust by the time of the settlement and clearly did not drive peacemaking. Nonetheless, after the Western European peace settlement was concluded, societal mechanisms helped socialize the settlement and ensure its survival beyond the founding realist and statist conditions.[72] In contrast, the Arab–Israeli settlements failed to entrench themselves by bringing society on board. The limited economic contacts between Israel and Jordan after the treaty have helped keep the peace a somewhat warmer and potentially more durable peace than the Camp David Accord, but Jordanian societal efforts to resist "normalization" have prevented the kind of socialization of peace that characterizes the post-World War II Western European settlement.

The implication is that the key to stabilizing conflict-prone regions and dyads is to generate both incentives and pressure for hostile governments to cooperate and create conditions that encourage governments to negotiate and compromise with former enemies, even if such a course is domestically unpopular. To achieve this, belligerent governments should be encouraged to negotiate secretly to prevent the content

---

[71] See Benjamin Miller, "Explaining Variations in Regional Peace: Three Strategies for Peace-making," *Cooperation and Conflict* 35, no. 2 (June 2000), 155–91; Miller, *States, Nations, and the Great Powers.*

[72] For related arguments, see Miller, *States, Nations and the Great Powers*; Benjamin Miller, "When and How Regions Become Peaceful: Potential Theoretical Pathways to Peace," *International Studies Review* 7, no. 2 (2005), 229–67; Jonathan Rynhold, "The German Question in Central and Eastern Europe and the Long Peace in Europe after 1945: An Integrated Theoretical Explanation," *Review of International Studies* 37, no. 1 (2011), 249–75; and Charles Kupchan, *How Enemies Become Friends: The Sources of Stable Peace* (Princeton University Press, 2010).

of agreements from becoming public and possibly tying leaders' hands. Third parties should use economic and other incentives as carrots to facilitate the process, but should also employ coercive pressure to keep the heat on belligerent governments.

Nonetheless, these peace treaties suggest that third parties should also distinguish between opportune and inopportune moments to press for top-down peace agreements. The case studies presented in this chapter suggest several hypotheses about the particular circumstances that facilitate peacemaking: (1) when the adversaries face common threats that are more immediate and more threatening, they are more likely to bury the hatchet as a means of focusing on the greater threat; (2) when belligerent states are led by moderate leaders, they are more likely to achieve peace agreements, as they are more likely to contemplate peacemaking and their commitments are more credible to adversaries and third parties; (3) highly autonomous states, whose domestic political institutions, decision-making procedures, and procedural norms limit the societal influence over foreign policy, are also more likely to achieve successful peace agreements, as they will be better able to escape domestic hostility toward the adversary if their leaders believe a peace agreement is in the national interest (or in their own personal interest); (4) when belligerent states face domestic political or economic crises due to the costs of conflict, they will be more receptive to peace overtures.

In addition, it is possible that attempting bottom-up peacemaking, particularly where nondemocracies are involved, can be counterproductive, as it could interfere with the top-down efforts that are more likely to bring about successful agreements. In principle, if they are to succeed, bottom-up strategies require a considerable amount of time to change societal attitudes. This means that in pinning our hopes on spreading peace through economic interdependence, democracy, or international institutions, we are abdicating any chance of success in the short run. Of course, bottom-up and top-down strategies can be pursued simultaneously, as they were in Western Europe after World War II, but that entails certain risks. First, if the third parties have limited resources to devote to peacemaking, diverting some to societal efforts from the more promising state-oriented trajectory could be unwise. Second, and more importantly, bottom-up strategies can undermine the governmental goodwill that is necessary. After all, the leader of a nondemocratic state (such as a Sadat or a King Hussein) will view an attempt to democratize states in the region as an attempt to undermine his/her hold on power. He/she may then identify cooperation with the outside power and with the peacemaking process as counter to his/her

interests. Finally, if the leaders of the belligerent states are more willing to compromise than their societies, efforts to strengthen domestic
actors either economically or politically may undermine the leader's
ability to commit to a peace of compromise.

It would appear, then, that top-down peacemaking approaches offer
a more promising avenue to stabilize conflicts, leaving bottom-up strategies for the post-agreement phase as a means to socialize the societies
over time and, thereby, stabilize agreements reached by the respective
states.

Part 6

Conclusions

12 Strategies and mechanisms of regional change

Stéfanie von Hlatky

The goal of this volume is to broaden the scholarship on regions and regional change. We seek to move away from the "war of paradigms," to address regional transformation through an intra- and inter-paradigmatic exchange.[1] Each International Relations (IR) theoretical paradigm, whether from the realist, liberal, or constructivist tradition, can only partially account for patterns of regional conflict and cooperation. A natural division of labor has emerged in the study of regional security, where realists tend to focus on the likelihood of war and stability, liberals on the conditions leading to peace, and constructivists on the foundations of long-lasting or deep peace and the emergence of pluralistic security communities. Together, these theoretical traditions unevenly cover the broad empirical spectrum of regional transformation. Instead of opting for a division-of-labor approach, based on each theory's comparative advantage, the contributors to this volume were tasked with answering a common set of questions and encouraged to relax their theoretical assumptions so as to offer middle-range eclectic approaches. The objective was to bring the authors outside of their comfort zone and engage each other in an effort to provide a richer analysis of regional change.

The research questions that focused the analyses were stated in the introduction in general terms. What are the prerequisites for a stable regional order? How can we make sense of transitions from war to peace, peace to war, or from peace to enduring peace? IR theories propose different causal mechanisms to explain change in the international system, but can these theories be adapted to make sense of regional-level change? The authors in this volume think so. This chapter is organized in four sections: the first section presents the concepts that are central to the book; the second discusses new theoretical guidelines to study

[1] The expression "war of paradigms" was coined by Harry Eckstein but was applied to the field of comparative politics, see Harry Eckstein, "Unfinished Business: Reflections on the Scope of Comparative Politics," *Comparative Political Studies* 31, no. 4 (1998), 505–34.

regional order; the third provides an overview of the main arguments advanced in this book; while the final section discusses a research agenda for greater understanding of regional order and peace.

Key concepts: regions, regionalism, regionalization

What are regions? For our cross-theoretical dialogue, the contributors to this volume worked from a common general definition of regions, identifying proximity and the intensity of interstate interactions as the most crucial components, but not to the exclusion of cultural or ideational factors. In Barry Buzan's chapter the emphasis is placed on this interaction capacity.[2] Buzan explores the different pathways to the formation of regions, an exercise that is key to understanding the patterns of regional transformation that necessarily follow. For example, he singles out the European experience as an instance of unbroken creation, characterized by regional competition and a leadership position in the world economy. In contrast, he describes a distinct pathway in the experience of colonization and decolonization, which would result in unmistakably different patterns of regional transformation. To compare regions, Buzan combines regional security complex theory (RSCT) with an international society perspective at the regional level, which yields four ideal-types: the first, power political, is characterized by intense regional competition; the second and third types, coexistence and cooperation, involve an incremental increase in the level of regulated regional interactions; and finally there is an international society type characterized by a convergence of values – leading to the most stable and peaceful configuration.[3]

As there are many paths to regional formation, as detailed by Buzan, there is considerable variation with regard to how regional dynamics evolve over time. The contributors identified and referred to a broad range of outcomes: war, conflict, stability, peace, enduring peace, while rejecting a linear view of regional transformation. As mentioned before, it seems there is a natural division of labor among IR theories, where realist, liberal, and constructivist explanations tend to focus on different segments of the spectrum of regional transformation. The chapters show that the transitions from one phase to another are crucial, not only to understand the phenomenon of regional transformation, but

---

[2] This term is developed in Barry Buzan and Richard Little, *International Systems in World History: Remaking the Study of International Relations* (Oxford University Press, 2000).

[3] For a full account of RSCT, see Barry Buzan and Ole Wæver, *Regions and Powers: The Structure of International Security* (Cambridge University Press, 2003).

also for interparadigmatic engagement. The empirical realm for the study of regional change is equally vast. A classification of contemporary regions according to this range of outcomes can be useful as a heuristic device, where North America and Western Europe are presented as security communities, while Southeast Asia and Latin America are partial security communities. These regions are characterized by peaceful interactions; some more entrenched, belonging to the realm of enduring peace. The Middle East and South Asia, for their part, are characterized by enduring rivalries. Finally, East Asia presents features of both stability and limited conflict.[4]

Regional orders also vary in terms of the level of political or economic integration, which may impact upon the level of stability within a region and the ability of states to resolve disputes without resorting to war. The authors discuss several examples of regional integration. An important distinction can be found in comparing the concepts of regionalism and regionalization.[5] The term "regionalism," for example, refers to cooperation between regional partners through the creation of multilateral regional institutions. It refers to institutionalized regional integration. The term "regionalization," in contrast, is the product of bottom-up sociopolitical processes and is tied to notions of identity.[6] Regions can also be differentiated by whether states interact cooperatively or competitively within the subsystem. The European Union (EU) has been the point of reference for both regionalism and regionalization, a seemingly successful model of regional transformation since the end of World War II. Is regional integration a prerequisite for regional peace and security?

Because of its success, many aspects of the EU model have been borrowed and adapted to other regional contexts. Is the European model really replicable? While studying Europe has lead to insightful theorizing about regional and international cooperation, the extent to which these theories can be generalized is an open question. Some scholars have

---

[4] Africa is difficult to place within the prevailing IR frameworks as it comprises a vast number of weak states with several subregions such as Southern Africa, where the mainstream IR variables may apply. However, it is difficult to apply any single or combination of paradigms to Africa. An alternative to study regional order in Africa may be postcolonial approaches focusing on state capacity and state formation. Work in this vein is still limited.

[5] Andrew Hurrell, "Explaining the Resurgence of Regionalism in World Politics," *Review of International Studies* 21, no. 3 (1995), 331–58; and Richard Higgott, "De Facto and De Jure Regionalism: The Double Discourse of Regionalism in the Pacific," *Global Society* 11, no. 2 (1997), 165–83.

[6] Hurrell, "Explaining the Resurgence of Regionalism in World Politics," and Higgott, "De Facto and De Jure Regionalism."

openly criticized the lack of nonwestern international relations theory, arguing that the discipline has developed supposedly universal explanations of world politics that are essentially rooted in the western experience, a point I will address separately in the next section.[7] Thinking back on the European experience, it is clear that American involvement in the region allowed enough stability for economic exchanges to take hold. The level of American investment in Europe after the Second World War was unique in history and would be hard to find today. American security guarantees were also offered and were institutionalized through NATO in 1949, which contributed, over time, to the development of a pluralistic security community. What distinguished the European experience from the North American experience, both examples of security communities, is the level of political integration.[8] In the European model, states were willing to give up a fraction of their sovereignty for the EU project. In the North American model, economic integration has evolved through NAFTA, but political interactions are better characterized by *dual bilateralism*, where the United States prefers to deal with Canada and Mexico separately.[9] In sum, the EU model is an extremely demanding one and its replicability should be questioned. However, as the chapters in this volume make clear, we can certainly theorize about particular features of the EU experience, such as interdependence, institutionalization, and the development of trust in interstate relations, which may be amenable to other contexts.

Strategies for theoretical innovation

In our effort to move away from opposing IR theoretical camps, we see two strategies to promote a fruitful exchange on regional transformation. The first strategy, analytical eclecticism, has been gaining more attention on the grounds that "the complex links between power, interests, and norms defy analytical capture by any one paradigm."[10]

---

[7] Amitav Acharya and Barry Buzan, "Why is there no Non-western International Relations Theory? An Introduction," *International Relations of the Asia-Pacific* 7, no. 3 (2007), 287–312.

[8] Ann Capling and Kim Richard Nossal, "The Contradictions of Regionalism in North America," *Review of International Studies* 35, no. 1 (2009), 147–67.

[9] Chris Demchak and Stéfanie von Hlatky, "North American Regionalism in Defence," in *Comparative Regional Security Governance*, ed. Shaun Breslin and Stuart Croft (London: Routledge, 2011); Stéfanie von Hlatky and Jessica N. Trisko, "Sharing the Burden of the Border: Layered Security Cooperation and the Canada–US Frontier," *Canadian Journal of Political Science* (forthcoming).

[10] Peter J. Katzenstein and Nobuo Okawara, "Japan, Asian-Pacific Security, and the Case for Analytical Eclecticism," *International Security* 26, no. 3 (winter 2001/02), 154.

Therefore, the proponents of an eclectic approach argue that more variables should be considered in the analysis of empirical puzzles, rather than striving for a parsimonious and often incomplete explanation. At the root of the problem are "irreconcilable, unverifiable assumptions" that make interparadigmatic exchanges difficult.[11] Analytic eclecticism has been defined has "an intellectual stance that supports efforts to complement, engage, and selectively utilize theoretical constructs embedded in contending research traditions to build complex arguments that bear on substantive problems of interest to both scholars and practitioners."[12] An eclectic framework also helps the researcher in considering a broader range of alternative explanations by casting a wider theoretical net.

The second strategy calls for new analytical frameworks, tailored to different regional contexts. What we label the context-specific approach to theorizing argues that IR paradigms are the product of inductive theorizing based on the European experience.[13] This reality makes our theories ill-fitted to address transformation in other regions and suggests we should develop more context-dependent frameworks. What we need instead are new theoretical tools to study other regions, without necessarily sacrificing the quest for parsimonious explanations. David C. Kang, for example, contends that "the same social-scientific standards – falsifiability, generalizability, and clear causal logic – should apply in the study of Asian international relations as has been applied to the study of Europe."[14] The basic idea is to encourage a more rigorous dialogue between theory and evidence, by unencumbering our analyses of weighty theoretical baggage. For both approaches, however, the key is to develop a framework to address an empirical puzzle. This book is a call for problem-driven research applied to regional transformation.

This need is especially pressing when considering the uneven record of western scholarship on East Asian security. There is a growing sense that mainstream IR theories have failed to properly explain and predict

[11] Rudra Sil, "The Foundations of Eclecticism: The Epistemological Status of Agency, Culture, and Structure in Social Theory," *Journal of Theoretical Politics* 12, no. 3 (2000), 354.
[12] Rudra Sil and Peter J. Katzenstein, "Analytical Eclecticism in the Study of World Politics: Reconfiguring Problems and Mechanisms Across Research Traditions," *Perspectives on Politics* 8, no. 2 (June 2010), 411. See also Rudra Sil and Peter J. Katzenstein, *Beyond Paradigms: Analytical Eclecticism in the Study of World Politics* (Basingstoke: Palgrave Macmillan, 2010).
[13] Acharya and Buzan, "Why is there no Non-western International Relations Theory?"
[14] David C. Kang, "Getting Asia Wrong: The Need for New Analytical Frameworks," *International Security* 27, no. 4 (spring 2003), 59.

regional transformation in Asia, especially in the context of China's rise. Drawing on the approaches mentioned above, some scholars argue that security relations in Asia may be more flexible and adaptable than previously assumed in the literature.[15] Indeed, an overreliance on traditional IR theories, and their rigid assumptions, has led to important oversights and a misunderstanding of Asian cooperation. In fact, most pessimistic predictions about the rise of China have not materialized; on the contrary, in order to defend its interests in the region it has engaged and invested in rule-making through regional and international organizations.[16] In their view, we should not expect, as realists do, that Asian states such as Japan will attempt to balance China. Instead, they view the region's future as more optimistic, pointing to nascent multilateral ties and deeper engagement on the part of the major regional players. A more forceful role by the United States, based on its bilateral alliances in the region, could therefore endanger the future of Asian cooperation and stability, especially if it gets enmeshed in territorial disputes between Japan and China.[17]

This section has proposed two approaches to revitalize research on regional transformation: analytical eclecticism and context-specific theoretical frameworks. While both strategies differ with regard to the theory-building process, they are motivated by the same realization: that interparadigm debates have grown stale and that their theoretical shortcomings are especially noticeable when applied to other regional contexts. The next section presents the main contributions of the volume, where some authors have attempted to adapt IR theories to regional-level problems while other authors have developed eclectic approaches to explain regional change, based on the framework outlined above.

Mechanisms of regional change

The discussion so far has focused on the need for renewed approaches to study the processes and outcomes of regional change. By updating

---

[15] Katzenstein and Okawara, "Japan, Asian-Pacific Security"; Kang, "Getting Asia Wrong."
[16] Kang, "Getting Asia Wrong," 69. See also Steve Chan, "An Odd Thing Happened on the Way to Balancing: East Asian States' Reactions to China's Rise," *International Studies Review* 12, no. 3 (September 2010), 387–412; T. V. Paul, "China's Rise: Engagement, Hedging, Soft Balancing and the Alliance System in East Asia," paper presented at the conference "The Rise of China and Alliance in East Asia: Implications for Diplomatic Truce," Institute of International Relations, National Chengchi University, Taipei, December 9–10, 2010.
[17] Mark Lander, "US Works to Ease China–Japan Conflict," *New York Times*, October 30, 2010.

and adapting realism, liberalism and constructivism, the contributors to this volume propose novel causal mechanisms tailored to different regional contexts. Furthermore, some authors have embraced the eclectic approach and have devised frameworks by drawing on several theories. We will first discuss the chapters that deal respectively with realism, liberalism, and constructivism, and will then highlight the eclectic analyses.

For realism, the focus has traditionally been on great powers and their ability to impose international order and stability. Realists disagree on which configuration of power at the international level is more likely to lead to a peaceful order; but one can question if these stabilizing influences trickle down at the regional level. For example, the bipolar system during the Cold War and the post-Cold War unipolar system impacted upon regional dynamics in different ways. During the Cold War, regions were theaters where superpower rivalries would clash in a contained way, keeping relative stability at the international level, but fuelling regional conflict. Since the 1990s, countries that were strategic in the East–West competition are no longer seen as important to the US, which mostly maintains a presence in Europe, East Asia, and the Middle East through power projection.

While an American presence can contribute to regional stability, we need to look at regional dynamics in isolation to fully explain the patterns of conflict and cooperation. Jeffrey Taliaferro and Dale C. Copeland each offer a realist analysis that assesses the likelihood of conflict and the conditions for regional stability. Realists generally do not expect meaningful cooperation to develop between states under anarchy as the relative-gains problem acts as an impediment to cooperation.[18] Nevertheless, realist predictions are faced with some baffling trends: the relative absence of major interstate wars, the avoidance of intense balance-of-power politics, declining military expenditures, and the rise of transnational actors in the security arena. Taliaferro's chapter investigates how state strategies can influence the likelihood of war in a given region. By drawing on illustrative examples from Western Europe and East Asia, he explains why the likelihood of conflict is so low in these regions, even if there are systemic incentives to engage in regional war. By focusing on loss aversion, as experienced by political elites, and state power, the goal is to explain variations in grand strategies, which can ultimately influence the likelihood of conflict. In his neoclassical realist model, two types of actors are predominant: extra-regional hegemons,

---

[18] Joseph M. Grieco, *Cooperation among Nations. Europe, America, and Non-tariff Barriers to Trade* (Ithaca, NY: Cornell University Press, 1990).

great powers that can influence regional dynamics, and pivotal states, defined as dominant states within a region. Pivotal states must be attuned to changes in the distribution of power at both the regional and systemic levels when contemplating war. The role of American alliances is prominent in both case studies, Japan and Germany, but is complemented by an understanding of constraints operating at the domestic level for both pivotal powers.

Copeland's chapter first presents classical, structural, and offensive variants of realism and their perspectives on regional order. He then adapts his own previously published dynamic differential theory (DDT) to the regional context and argues that similar mechanisms should operate: war will continue to be the lesser of two evils in the face of deep decline.[19] By focusing on how power distribution affects the likelihood of war, he makes a counterintuitive policy prescription, namely that in the short term, at least, we can prevent conflict through great-power intervention, which should be easier than domestic changes imposed on regional powers. By restoring the balance of power in the face of deep decline, regional stability may be preserved.

Copeland's argument leads to drastically different implications than the argument put forth by John R. Oneal, who presents a liberal perspective on regional peace. Liberals view cooperation as possible and as a product of instrumental trust generated by three pillars – democracy, regional institutions, and economic interdependence – that provide powerful incentives for cooperation.[20] In his chapter, Oneal contends that democratization is the most reliable path leading to a peaceful regional order. Based on his analysis, he finds optimism in the fact that regimes can be changed and economic relations altered. Indeed peaceful regions can be created through domestic reform. He points to the pacifying influences of democracy and interdependence by estimating the probability of conflict between state dyads through statistical analysis, discounting alternative explanations such as hegemonic stability theory and Samuel Huntington's clash-of-civilizations argument. He also finds no evidence to support Snyder and Mansfield's claim that democratizing states are more conflict-prone.[21] Oneal's approach is

---

[19] For the original version of DDT, see Dale C. Copeland, *The Origins of Major War* (Ithaca, NY: Cornell University Press, 2000).

[20] Bruce M. Russett, John R. Oneal, and David Davis, "The Third Leg of the Kantian Tripod for Peace: International Organizations and Militarized Disputes, 1950–85," *International Organization* 52, no. 3 (1998), 441–67; John R. Oneal and Bruce M. Russett, "Assessing the Liberal Peace with Alternative Specifications: Trade Still Reduces Conflict," *Journal of Peace Research* 36, no. 4 (1999), 423–42.

[21] Edward Mansfield and Jack Snyder, "The Effects of Democratization on War," *International Security* 21, no. 4 (spring 1996), 5–38.

firmly rooted in the liberal tradition, with its focus on the conditions leading to a peaceful regional order, through three mechanisms, namely democracy, economic interdependence, and institutions.

John Owen's argument is in line with Oneal's but focuses on the commercial-liberal thesis, namely that economic interdependence can contribute to peace. This mechanism is pretty straightforward when observing bilateral relationships, but studying interactions involving three or more states is more complex. In fact, Owen notes that hegemonic involvement, or the presence of a democracy within a region, could be required for economic interdependence to yield those pacifying benefits. Certain conflict-prone regions, such as South Asia, must increase their level of intraregional cooperation and trust before dense trade networks can take root. The lack of trust in the region, he argues, could only be redressed through South Asia's dominant power, India, the spread of free-market capitalism, or further democratization. As Owen notes, "a stable democratic Pakistan and India would have a better chance of settling the Kashmir issue and launching greater cooperation." The dyadic effect of economic interdependence appears robust, but more empirical evidence is needed to tell whether this dynamic can be reproduced at the regional level.[22] There is some cause for optimism, however, that the benefits of economic interdependence could help pacify troubled regions.[23]

The chapter by Stephanie Hofmann and Frédéric Mérand focuses on the third feature of the liberal peace argument, the role of international institutions for regional peace. They argue that formal international organizations (IOs) contribute to the establishment of stable regional orders. Hofmann and Mérand expand the analysis beyond the role of single IOs, focusing instead on the broader institutional architecture within regions. How regional organizations coexist and sometimes overlap creates multiple channels for peaceful interstate relations. For this dynamic to take hold, the institutional architecture must be fairly elastic, meaning that it must be strong enough to bind states into credible commitments but flexible enough to adapt and prevent organizations from falling apart when disagreements occur. In the authors' own words, institutional strength brings stability while flexibility prevents inertia. They draw on the European experience to demonstrate how unique its dense institutional architecture is, showing why transferring

---

[22] Håvard Hegre, John R. Oneal, and Bruce Russett, "Trade does Promote Peace: New Simultaneous Estimates of the Reciprocal Effects of Trade and Conflict," *Journal of Peace Research* 47, no. 6 (November 2010), 763–74.

[23] For more on this point, see Chapter 7 in this volume.

the lessons of the European experience to other regions proves challenging. Nevertheless, the mechanisms they propose to explain how IOs can promote peaceful interactions certainly have generalizable implications. They also encourage broadening the analysis to include an appraisal of intersubjective dynamics within regional institutions, an observation that ties in to constructivist analyses in this volume.

Constructivism focuses on norms, ideas, and practices to explain regional dynamics. Constructivists see cooperation as the result of common identities and intersubjective norms that foster trust.[24] In his chapter Amitav Acharya is concerned with the causal and constitutive influence of ideas on regions. Without denying the influence of other factors, such as material forces, he does point to the pervasiveness and permanence of the ideational realm, even in the absence of coercive power. Acharya presents three mechanisms by which regions are shaped by ideas: the first one identifies foundational ideas that act as cognitive priors within regions; the second one looks to the broadening of existing norms or the integration of new norms through a process of socialization and bargaining; and finally, the third mechanism draws on conditioning and emulation where regions can borrow foreign models, adapting and localizing them in the process. Acharya also notes that norm diffusion is a two-way process where local or regional actors are both norm takers and norm givers. In this process where norms are exchanged, meanings evolve and take on distinct regional interpretations. This variation could be a potential source of conflict between regions.

This point is reiterated in Vincent Pouliot's chapter. He draws on the example of post-Cold War Russian-Atlantic relations to show how key practices can be interpreted in divergent ways by participating actors, which can lead to mismatched practices and translate into diplomatic tensions. In the context of Russian-Atlantic relations, even when all the players were keen on change, there were some disconnects in how the regional security game was played. The end result was that only superficial change occurred because of this gap in interpreting the new rules of the game in the post-Cold War environment. For true transformation to occur, actors have to agree on the terms of change and engage in diplomatic practices that are rooted in compatible meanings. The nature of security practices thus structures regional patterns of interaction.

---

[24] Emanuel Adler and Michael Barnett, eds., *Security Communities* (Cambridge University Press, 1998); Alexander Wendt, *Social Theory of International Politics* (Cambridge University Press, 1999).

The previous contributors chose to adapt existing theories – realism, liberalism, and constructivism – to the regional context. The other challenge lies in combining theories to offer a more complete account of regional transformation. Two authors in this volume took to this task by writing from an "eclectic perspective." John Hall's chapter asks whether the European model is replicable. The short answer is no. Explanations of regional transformation need to account for geopolitics and particular historical contexts, but beyond that, Hall is sympathetic to the idea of an eclectic approach. To be sure, a certain level of geopolitical stability is a precondition for prosperity, as the European experience shows. However, these preconditions were ensured through American involvement and investments in the region. To that end, perhaps we should not expect further integration in Europe. State sovereignty is still quite robust and European identity is still trumped by national identities. By outlining the limits of integration, Hall draws from different research traditions. Whether or not the United States disengages from the European continent, which may then impact upon the EU's autonomy in regional and world politics, what is important is the agreement to differ. The European experience shows that mechanisms are solidly in place to accommodate a diversity of positions without undermining the EU project, a point that is also stressed in Hofmann and Mérand's chapter. Hall's account reminds us that there were clear strategic imperatives, driven by the US, which ensured the level of regional stability to temper regional competition, allowing the EU project to take hold. Institutionalization and practice has ensured the viability of the European model, regardless of whether further integration will be forthcoming.

Similarly, Norrin Ripsman's chapter targets regional transformation by simultaneously drawing on the three main research traditions in IR. By focusing on cycles rather than any single outcome to explain regional change, he draws on those theories by referring to two stages in the regional peacemaking process. Drawing broadly from his previous work on stages of regional order, Ripsman argues that, contrary to what is argued by democratic peace theorists, peace is not a bottom-up process.[25] Rather, realist conditions have to be present for regional cooperation to emerge. Once peace settlements are achieved, liberal and constructivist explanations are insightful to explain the endurance of those arrangements. He draws on three case studies, Western Europe after World War II, the 1979 peace treaty between Egypt and

---

[25] For his earlier work on this, see Norrin M. Ripsman, "Two Stages of Transition From a Region of War to a Region of Peace: Realist Transition and Liberal Endurance," *International Studies Quarterly* 49, no. 4 (December 2005), 669–93.

Israel, and the 1994 treaty between Israel and Jordan, to show that the state acts as the primary engine of peacemaking, referring to realist mechanisms of balancing, hegemonic influence, and state motives. In doing so, he amalgamates different realist contributions, such as neo-realism, hegemonic stability theory, and neoclassical realism. Ripsman contends that, in all three cases, states enacted a peace settlement in spite of, not because of, strong societal pressures. The realist explanation can best explain cooperative outcomes that are the product of adversarial partnerships. Postagreement stability, on the other hand, is best explained by the socialization process which occurs with the creation of institutions and norms, following the transition phase. By referring to two stages, the transition to peace and postagreement stability, Ripsman combines different IR theories and provides an eclectic analysis of regional transformation.

Even if writing from different theoretical perspectives, the contributors grappled with similar methodological challenges, chief among which was separating the systemic and regional levels of analyses. Indeed, the role of the United States is recurrent in most accounts of regional transformation after World War II. How can we isolate the role of external powers from regional analyses without negating their influence? We examine this question in the next section.

Great powers and regional stability

At the heart of this book is the recognition that adapting IR theories to the regional context is a desirable and worthwhile endeavor. How can we transfer system-level theories to the regional level? How can we adapt our theoretical tools to new contexts without diluting their explanatory power? To undertake this, certain qualifications are needed, especially when it comes to the involvement of external powers in regional dynamics. A point which elicited some discussion concerned the exclusion of great-power influence from our definition of regions. Although great powers can exert a lot of pressure on regional players and often play a large part in maintaining regional stability, it is useful to separate great powers conceptually from our operational definition of regions. As mentioned in T. V. Paul's chapter, great powers are part of regional subsystems or regional security complexes, a wider grouping which accounts for interactions between the main regional players and external powers that are deeply involved in the region.[26]

---

[26] David A. Lake, "Regional Security Complexes: A Systems Approach," in *Regional Orders: Building Security in a New World*, ed. David A. Lake and Patrick M. Morgan

In his chapter, for example, Buzan notes that social structures present at the global level can be identified at the regional level. In this sense, he argues that the English School's insights can be applied to the study of regions. Buzan notes that outside great powers do not determine regional security patterns, but that we should turn to dominant states in the region to tune into regional dynamics. Furthermore, he contends that the demise of superpower interactions and the decline of the United States will make regional structures more salient and more important in the study of world politics. Copeland similarly argues for the transfer of systemic-level theories to the regional level, but from the realist perspective. He suggests that this can be achieved by isolating the role of the external power at first, bringing it in at a later stage of the analysis. Regardless of the method used, authors agree that American involvement in different regions (and for that matter Soviet involvement during the Cold War and an emerging China's involvement in the future) must be factored in, without blurring our understanding of regional-level processes. This difficulty is also underscored in Taliaferro's chapter, where he notes that Japan and Germany possess a number of characteristics that would make them war-prone according to realists: favorable systemic incentives, advantageous relative military and economic capabilities, as well as sufficient extractive and mobilization capacities. Determining the relative causal weight of each of these factors is tricky, considering the importance of the American presence in both countries, which includes forward-deployed troops.

Since the end of the Cold War, the United States has been unrivalled as a provider of security guarantees. If states can now exercise more autonomy in foreign policy than they did during the Cold War, most US allies are not willing to forgo American security assurances. For example, European states have not abandoned the North Atlantic Treaty Organization (NATO), as they build a common security policy.[27] Their alliance with the United States is still central to their defense. Being partner to an alliance allows states to spend fewer resources on their military but makes them more reliant on their dominant alliance partner. Through global security and economic arrangements, American involvement plays a role in stabilizing regions. As David Lake notes, "higher average levels of United States security and economic hierarchy

(University Park: Pennsylvania State University Press, 1997), 45–67; Barry Buzan, "A Framework for Regional Security Analysis," in *South Asian Insecurity and the Great Powers*, ed. Barry Buzan and Gowher Rizvi (Basingstoke: Macmillan, 1986), 8; Buzan and Wæver, *Regions and Powers*.

[27] Scott Siegel, "Bearing their Share of the Burden: Europe in Afghanistan," *European Security* 18, no. 4 (December 2009), 461–82.

are associated with 'higher' or more peaceful regional orders less prone to actual or threatened violence."[28] However, the nature and scope of American involvement in other regions varies substantially. It seems that arrangements that are designed to foster regional multilateral cooperation are more conducive to peaceful change than arrangements based on bilateral exchanges.[29] Let us turn to military alliances specifically, a topic that has been sidelined from the discussion thus far.

The United States is embedded in a web of defense pacts in Latin America, Europe, and Asia. In certain cases, American military alliances are constructed using a multilateral framework; while in other cases, bilateral ties dominate. A US-led multilateral framework is well established in America and Europe. In Latin America, the United States is part of the InterAmerican Treaty of Reciprocal Assistance; in Europe, there is the North Atlantic Treaty, which of course also includes Canada; in the South Pacific, there is ANZUS, although New Zealand was formally expelled in 1986. In Asia, on the other hand, there is a predominance of bilateral military alliances rather than multilateral security arrangements with the United States. In Asia, the United States is bound by defense pacts with the Philippines and Japan individually. South Korea only shares an entente with the United States, although there are still 30,000 American troops in the country. Finally, the US signed a defense pact with Taiwan in 1954 but these security guarantees were lifted in 1979. So in the case of Taiwan there is no formal security guarantee, although this is more ambiguous in practice, to say the least.[30] Could these bilateral alliances led by the United States be hampering deeper multilateral cooperation in the Asian theater? Will the American presence stifle emerging multilateralism in both the economic and security realms? The development of burgeoning multilateral initiatives, such as the Northeast Asia Cooperation Dialogue, the Council for Security Cooperation in the Asia-Pacific, and the ASEAN Regional Forum, will be telling.

Conclusion

The chapters in this volume offer different pointers toward a future research agenda on regions. From these analyses, it is clear that decades of research on regions has yielded much progress and our understanding

---

[28] David A. Lake, "Escape from the State of Nature: Authority and Hierarchy in World Politics," *International Security* 32, no. 1 (summer 2007), 26.

[29] Kang, "Getting Asia Wrong"; See also Chapter 5 in this volume.

[30] For the full catalogue of military alliances since 1648, see Douglas M. Gibler, *International Military Alliances, 1648–2008* (Washington, DC: CQ Press, 2008).

is improved with the evolution of a pluralistic security community in Europe and partial security communities in Southeast Asia and Latin America. The research agenda needs new emphasis on what else is required to make stable orders in regions. We need to know why regions take on different characteristics and if the presence or absence of a given variable in each IR theory may cause or contribute to the creation and persistence of a conflictual or cooperative regional order. This kind of research also may encourage scholars to dig deep to see if the inclusion of variables beyond their paradigms can provide a better framework for theory and policy on regional order. Theoretical innovation ought to have major policy applications as regions mired in deep enduring rivalries and protracted conflicts need new ideas to break the vicious cycle of violence and transform into peaceful regions.

While we recognize that each IR theory has a comparative advantage in explaining regional transformation, this book attempts to go beyond this realization. Through each chapter in this volume, we attempt to draw bridges between realism, liberalism, and constructivism rather than opting for a division-of-labor approach. Research questions often hide a theoretical bias and the paradigmatic enterprise is clouded by narrow, unverifiable assumptions, leading to the atomization of the major theories in IR. We should judge the merits of different theoretical perspectives based on their ability to explain regional change, rather than on their ability to score points in the inter-paradigmatic debates. Doing so requires the necessary discipline to design theoretically neutral questions based on the range of potential outcomes and processes we have previously identified: conflict, peace, and enduring peace, as well as the transitions between each phase. We also stress the importance of context specificity when comparing regions, as well as the need to relax some of the basic assumptions which are normally taken for granted in IR. By paying more attention to these guidelines, we believe that each theoretical perspective can speak to regional change, whether that change is cooperative or conflictual in nature.

We should also note that certain aspects of regional transformation, to date, are not well explained by any of the main theories. A prominent theme that cuts across all chapters is the time dimension. Here again, IR theories are vague about the timing of regional transformation. For realists, stable orders have an expiration date; for liberals, it is unclear how long it takes for democratic transitions to mature or IOs to take root; while for constructivists there is no clear timeframe for the development of intersubjective understanding. Accounting for time remains a challenge even when IR theories are adapted to regional contexts. There is much room for future research along this dimension and for more exchanges between and within theoretical perspectives, including research traditions that have not been included in this volume.

Finally, some authors have offered prescriptions for change based on their theoretical analysis. Whether change is best implemented domestically, from the top down or bottom up, or whether change should be driven by a powerful external power remains an open question. What is clear is that the lessons learned from one region need not be fully transferable to another. Whatever the theoretical challenges we have outlined here, we are confident that closer interactions between different theoretical traditions can only improve our understanding of regional transformation.

Index

Page numbers followed by n indicate footnotes.